A Letter Does Not Blush

By the same author

Dipped in Vitriol

A Letter Does Not Blush

A COLLECTION OF THE MOST MOVING, ENTERTAINING AND REMARKABLE LETTERS IN HISTORY

Nicholas Parsons

Buchan & Enright, Publishers
London

For my parents

First published in 1984 by
Buchan & Enright, Publishers, Limited
53 Fleet Street, London EC4Y 1BE

British Library Cataloguing in Publication Data
A Letter does not blush.
1. Letters
I. Parsons, Nicholas
808.86   PN6131

ISBN 0 907675 21 5

Printed and bound in Great Britain by
Biddles Ltd, Guildford and King's Lynn

Contents

Author's Acknowledgements

I would particularly like to thank the Lillington family, Ken, Steve and Elizabeth, for supplying much interesting material, and for numerous intelligent suggestions and always sensible ideas. In addition, the staff of the London Library have been as courteous and efficient as so many writers have now come to expect, and patient far beyond the call of duty. The conditions in which the book was put together were made more agreeable to me both by the generosity of my parents and the kindness and hospitality of Karen Elder. An enormous manuscript was expertly typed by Diana Balfour, Leo Clark, Kate Fleming, Peta Murray and Helen Swansbourne. To my wife Ilona I am indebted for unfailing moral support while the book was taking shape, but more especially for numerous sensible criticisms and original insights.

I am greatly indebted to the many holders of copyright material who have allowed me to quote from it. A complete list of sources appears at the back of the book.

Introduction

Natural inquisitiveness lends a fascination to other people's correspondence, an inquisitiveness that this anthology aims to satisfy. It is drawn from the letters of all sorts of people at all times and in all, or nearly all, places. I have unrepentantly selected letters for their human interest, their capacity to arouse respect or pity, their wit and (occasionally) their outrageousness. Mere exercises in stylistics are not to be found here, nor have I included very brief and banal notes from famous people, items that are so beloved of academic moles and deferential editors. Such communications can be left to those who need them as research fodder, or to collectors who will doubtless pay too much for them. In a year when Orwelliana threatened to engulf us all, *Private Eye* printed in its 'Pseud's Corner' column the following cautionary item:

> 124. ORWELL, GEORGE, Typed letter, 14.11.46, as follows: *'Dear Sir,* I have only just received your letter dated October 11, which had to be forwarded to me. Since you ask for a copy of my signature here it is. Yours truly, Geo. Orwell.' *With original mailing envelope, on the rear of which the recipient has written (in pencil) 'author famous George Orwell London 1946'. Excellent condition. The letter, though terse to the point of self-extinction, seems to me characteristically Orwellian.*
>
> £275
>
> BOOKSELLER'S CATALOGUE

Correspondents to *Private Eye* are also warned in the Editor's characteristically crisp phrase that 'long boring letters will be cut', and I have followed the same policy, believing with Dorothy Osborne that the reader wishes to be entertained, informed, or moved, but not impressed. ''Tis an admirable thing,' she writes to Sir William Temple, 'to see how some people will labour to find out terms that may obscure a plain sense. Like a gentleman I knew, who would never say "the weather grew cold", but that "the winter began to salute us".' And again, writing of an incorrigibly pompous correspondent: 'I never had, I think, but one letter from Sir Justinian, but 'twas worth twenty of anybody's else to make me sport. It was the most sublime nonsense that in my life I ever read; and yet, I believe, he descended as low as he could to come near to my weak understanding . . .'

Dorothy Osborne's sensible prescription that letters should be 'free and easy as one's discourse' has most evidently been followed by female letter writers—herself, Lady Mary Wortley Montagu, Madame de Sévigné, Virginia Woolf, to name but a few of the greatest. Apart from their gift for anecdote and acute observation, they can turn a communication that is little more than phatic into something delightful and fresh. Male writers tend to struggle when faced simultaneously with the necessity to write and a poverty of inspiration. Even William Cowper, one of the most consistently amusing of correspondents, found himself in difficulty and wrote disconsolately to William Unwin: 'My dear Friend—I wrote my last letter merely to inform you that I had nothing to say, in answer to which you have said nothing . . .'

Of course, not all female letter writers have the gifts of a de Sévigné or an Osborne, nor the capacity to mingle delicacy with a sometimes brutal candour that makes the former so irresistible to read. Horace Walpole refers us to one lady whose attractions as a correspondent he was apparently able to resist:

> The Italians are as proud of a person of the same sex: Lucretia Gonzaga was so celebrated for the eloquence of her letters and the purity of their style, that her very notes to her servants were collected and published. I have never read the collection: one or two billets that I have met with, have not entirely all the delicacy of madame de Sévigné. In one to her footman the signora Gonzaga reprehends him for not readily obeying dame Lucy her housekeeper; and in another, addressed to the same Mrs. Lucy, she says, 'If Livia will not be obedient, turn up her coats and whip her till her flesh be black and blew, and the blood run down to her heels.' To be sure this sounds a little oddly to English ears, but may be very elegant, when modulated by the harmony of Italian liquids.

Lucretia Gonzaga's letters, having been collected by some industrious hack or courtier of the time, at least met no worse a fate than to be torn to shreds by Walpole. But we are unable to judge the love letters that Gide wrote because his wife burned them; and we cannot know what felicities are lost to us in the letters of Marvell to William Skinner, as the latter gave them to his pastry maid to put under pie bottoms.

Of letters that *have* survived there are more than enough to make several anthologies. Inevitably in selecting for one collection from so vast a field one has to follow personal preference— and that means leaving out this or that pet author of an individual reader. Those who think that an anthology of this kind should be like a literary Honours List, a procession of great and familiar names that somehow seem to have secured revolving credit with the bestowers of awards and appraisers of merit, will perhaps be disappointed; but I hasten to add that no one has been left out simply because they are among the greats. Dr Johnson is represented as is his arch-enemy Lord Chesterfield. Horace Walpole and Lady Mary Wortley Montagu, Madame de Sévigné, Michelangelo, Mozart—all are justly famed for their letters, and all are to be found here and there in the anthology. But so also are anonymous sailors with Nelson's fleet, and anonymous correspondents writing from situations of unbearable squalor and distress to Marie Stopes. Wit is provided by, amongst others, Groucho Marx, Sydney Smith, Bertrand Russell, Mark Twain, James Thurber and E.B. White. There are lunatics, lovers, poets; the great and the good; the bad and the ugly; families and other animals; politicians, perverts, queens and kings. In a word, as a well-known newspaper proudly and untruthfully claims, 'all human life is here.'

It is life viewed from the inside, the raw material of biography and history. '*As keys do open chests/So letters open breasts*', wrote James Howell in the seventeenth century, and he is more or less right. But it does depend on the letter writer and the recipient. James Joyce is coarse and vivid to his wife; but to his male correspondents he tends to be, in Richard Ellmann's phrase, 'bespectacled and walking-sticked'. In contrast, sentimental Laurence Sterne, writing his saccharine epistles to Eliza, displayed a cynicism of which Joyce was incapable, altering the draft of a letter that he had composed some years before for another woman, and sending on the polished-up version to his 'Bramine'. And Pope, before publishing *his* letters, set about doctoring them, altering dates and names of recipients.

Those who are at such pains to cover their tracks know that a great deal of the pleasure derived from reading the letters of others is the same as that to be got from eavesdropping. 'In a man's letters, you know, madam, his soul lies naked. His letters are only the mirror of his heart,' writes Dr Johnson in a letter to Mrs Thrale where his emotional vulnerability is painfully evident. It is the little asides that often tell the whole story: the disappointment and frustration at the heart of an apparently successful and celebrated career, as in this remark by Bernard Berenson in a letter to a cousin: '. . . I myself regret having wasted my talents in sowing and tending a field which has reaped nothing but weeds and thorns and brambles;' or the sharp remark that slips out from behind a mask of urbanity and wisdom—like this one from Jane Austen writing to Cassandra where the gratuitous nastiness just outbalances the wit: 'Mrs Hall of Sherborne was brought to bed yesterday of a dead child, some weeks before she expected, owing to a fright. I suppose she happened unawares to look at her husband.'

Public letters are not self-revelatory in the same way as private ones, though they may reveal more than their authors intend. In the preface to his collection of letters to *The Times*, Kenneth Gregory describes drily how he applied to one man for permission to reprint his dissertation on (let us say) roast pig, only to be met with the response: 'Sir, I did not write it. Only an idiot could write on such a topic.' On being shown a copy with his signature he relented graciously: 'My dear Sir, You must permit me to say this is admirable both in style and content. I have a hazy recollection I wrote it after an excellent lunch at my club.' It is, as we all know, extremely dangerous to dash off a letter after consuming a bottle of claret and being convinced by one's own rhetoric. In any case, it is usually only loonies and exhibitionists who write to the papers—the loonies in green ink which, according to Bernard Levin, is an infallible sign. It was probably in green ink that a man wrote to Lawrence Durrell inviting him to 'walk in a wheat field and throw [his] excrement at the stars while [the sender] put a freshly killed lamb at the rectory'. But caution is required in answering the most eccentric letters. An MP recently responded to a tiresomely foolish letter from a constituent with the acid witticism: 'I think you should know that some lunatic has been writing to me and using your name'—only to find that this was perfectly true. A problem as trying as eccentric matter in a letter is eccentric handwriting. Many people do not seem to care if a hand is legible or not, candidly admitting that they cannot read their own; and perhaps in most cases this complacency is justified since there is nothing of interest in the letter anyway. Illegibility may even have certain advantages—as Thomas Bailey Aldrich wrote to Edward Morse: 'It was very pleasant to me to get a letter from you the other day. Perhaps I should have found it pleasanter if I had been able to decipher it. I don't think that I mastered anything beyond the date (which I knew) and the signature (which I guessed at). There's a singular and perpetual charm in a letter of yours; it never grows old, it never loses its novelty . . . other letters are read and thrown away and forgotten, but yours are kept forever—unread. One of them will last a reasonable man a lifetime.' This is all very well, but what if one is illegibly asked to dinner or offered an enormous bribe? Then, clear handwriting comes into its own. George Lyttelton had some amusing things to say on the subject in a letter to Rupert Hart-Davis—one supposes in a beautiful round hand:

. . . In a world where nearly all is dark, as Bishop Gore used to say, two things are luminously clear: viz that your letters are of first-class interest and quality, and that your handwriting is perfectly legible, and, in fact, very pleasant to look on. And the second is very important. Did you ever get a letter from Monty James? I once had a note from him inviting me to dinner—we *guessed* that the time was 8 and not 3, as it appeared to be, but all we could tell about the day was that it was not Wednesday. The late Bishop Brook of Ipswich maintained that all great men—Shakespeare, Napoleon, Brook, etc.—had illegible hands, and conveniently forgot, or more likely didn't know, that Michael Angelo, Henry VIII, Elizabeth (when she chose), Lord Palmerston, all had conspicuously fine hands. But, though I hate to admit it, there is something in what he said—explained by some pundit, apropos, I think, of Napoleon's monstrous script, that where a brain is *very* quick, the hand just cannot keep up. An odd corollary to this is the undeniable fact that in a C or D division the stupidest boys did the best maps, the Collegers always the worst. I wonder why. 'Sir, you *may* wonder.' . . .

Hart-Davis responded to this with some learned remarks on the handwriting of the great, and added that Lady Colefax was famous for sending the most illegible invitations of all time. 'The only hope of deciphering *her* invitations was to pin them up on the wall and *run* past them.'

Lord Chesterfield had difficulty in understanding his son's handwriting and did his best to correct the young man's sloppiness with his usual luminous and circumstantial advice:

> . . . For instance, if you were to write in such a character to the Secretary's office, your letter would immediately be sent to the decipherer, as containing matters of the utmost secrecy, not fit to be trusted to the common character. If you were to write to an antiquarian, he (knowing you to be a man of learning) would certainly try it by the Runic, Celtic, or Sclavonian alphabet; never suspecting it to be a modern character. And, if you were to send a *poulet* to a fine woman, in such a hand, she would think that it really came from the *poulaillier*, which, by the bye, is the etymology of the word, *poulet*; for Henry the fourth of France used to send *billets-doux* to his mistresses, by his *poulaillier*, under pretence of sending them chickens; which gave the name of *poulets* to those short, but expressive manuscripts . . .

'Short but expressive' letters, in Chesterfield's phrase, constitute a genre in themselves, and I have included a number of them in the anthology. The best manage to suggest many more insults than they actually state, like the famous communication from Sir W. S. Gilbert to the station master at Baker Street:

> *Sir,*
> Saturday morning, although recurring at regular and well-foreseen intervals, always seems to take this railway by surprise.

Perhaps the shortest ever letter was from Victor Hugo to his publishers wanting to know if they liked his *Les Misérables*. He wrote simply '?' and his publishers responded with '!'. Mr Robert Hendrickson, author of *The Literary Life and other Curiosities*, to whom I am indebted for the above information, has also discovered the longest letter ever written. It is not wholly surprising to find that the American 'beat' poets have carried off this record: Jack Kerouac claimed that his friend Neal Cassady wrote (and poet Allen Ginsburg lost) a 40,000-word letter to him that was so great a piece of writing it would have made 'Melville, Twain, Dreiser, Wolfe, I dunno who, spin in their graves.' Readers will doubtless be disappointed that this masterpiece was too long to be included in this collection.

Beginnings and endings for letters such as Cassady's are of course mere formalities, unnoticed interruptions in the staunchless flux. But it is just as well to get titles and nomenclatures right especially if you want something from your correspondent. An eleventh-century epistolary manual for university students not only gave correct forms of address, but set out twenty-two different ways of approaching an archdeacon for a loan; other models suggested suitably delicate phrasing for extracting money from tight-fisted fathers or tender-hearted married sisters. In our own century Bertrand Russell was badgered with requests for advice and assistance which he dealt with serenely—on the whole. Those from America were often addressed to 'Sir Bertrand' or even 'Sir Russell', 'Earl' evidently being regarded as a Christian name. And the Bishop of Swansea and Brecon, writing to *The Times* in 1931, said he had just received a letter from the Chief Inspector of Taxes addressed to 'Messrs Swansea and Brecon'. They sound rather like a comedy duo.

Ending letters is even more of a problem than beginning them. Old-fashioned forms of subscription seem unbearably pompous. Groucho Marx complains that 'I beg to remain' is usually at once cringing and threatening—what Max Beerbohm described as the habit of English tailors of 'crawling on their knees and shaking their fists in your face'. Better, however, than 'Your humble and obedient servant', with which Dr Johnson ended his letter to Lord Chesterfield, having just dealt the Earl the verbal equivalent of a series of karate chops. Franz Kafka is at least honest when he reminds Felice Bauer that whatever she might think after receiving a few thousand words of neurotic egotism from her putative admirer, she has really only been allotted a walk-on part in the great drama going on inside Franz's head: 'Did I think of signing myself *Dein*? No, nothing could be more false. No, I am forever fettered to myself, that's what I am, and that's what I must try to live with.' However, these heartwarming sentiments did not release Felice from the obligation to write to *him*—preferably every day.

So even endings, even beginnings, reveal a personality and let a cat or two out of the bag. Therein lies the fascination of letters. It is hoped that the present selection will cater for most tastes, and entertain as well as inform. There may be some surprises in store; Nietzsche regarded the postman as simply 'the intermediary of impolite surprises'. 'Every week,' he said, 'we ought to have one hour for receiving letters and then go and take a bath.' I don't recommend that this anthology be followed by constant bathing—it is too long for one thing—but that it should itself be dipped into and luxuriated in like a bath. The reason that this anthology is long is because there are so many wonderful letters written by more or less wonderful people. The letters constitute fragments of autobiography which are often more revealing than a considered utterance. They can preserve a living personality almost intact. 'I have preferred,' says Dr Johnson, that, like the great chemist, 'the . . . episodes of my life should make a clear solution in the fluid menstruum of time, rather than that they should be precipitated in the opaque sediment of history.' Here are a few items from the 'opaque sediment'.

NICHOLAS PARSONS
London 1984

THE PRIME OF LIFE

1

Invited Everywhere . . .

For those embarking on a social career a number of skills are a prerequisite, not least that of knowing how to please. Lord Chesterfield endeavoured to impart the appropriate wisdom in his famous series of letters to his natural son. As pieces of advice, they do not seem to have been the success his lordship had hoped, since the young man apparently remained ill-favoured and not much sought after; but as literature they were a huge success and have been in print ever since their first appearance in the mid-eighteenth century. Dr Johnson's view of them was that they taught 'the morals of a whore and the manners of a dancing-master'. Of Chesterfield himself, to whom he wrote his celebrated letter indignantly refusing patronage, he remarked that having thought him a 'Lord among wits' he found him on acquaintance to be but a 'wit among Lords'. Here is Lord Chesterfield on how to appeal to people's vanity (the Walpole referred to is the Whig politician and first Prime Minister of Britain):

. . . You will easily discover every man's prevailing vanity by observing his favourite topic of conversation; for every man talks most of what he has most a mind to be thought to excel in. The late Sir Robert Walpole (who was certainly an able man) was little open to flattery upon that head, for he was in no doubt himself about it; but his prevailing weakness was, to be thought to have a polite and happy turn to gallantry—of which he had undoubtedly less than any man living. It was his favourite and frequent subject of conversation, which proved to those who had any penetration that it was his prevailing weakness, and they applied to it with success.

Women have, in general, but one object, which is their beauty; upon which, scarce any flattery is too gross for them to follow. Nature has hardly formed a woman ugly enough to be insensible to flattery upon her person; if her face is so shocking that she must, in some degree, be conscious of it, her figure and air, she trusts, make ample amends for it. If her figure is deformed, her face, she thinks, counterbalances it. If they are both bad, she comforts herself that she has graces; a certain manner; a *je ne sçais quoi* still more engaging than beauty. This truth is evident, from the studied and elaborate dress of the ugliest woman in the world. An undoubted, uncontested, conscious beauty is, of all women, the least sensible of flattery upon that head; she knows it is her due, and is therefore obliged to nobody for giving it her. She must be flattered upon her understanding, which, though she may possibly not doubt of herself, yet she suspects that men may distrust.

Do not mistake me, and think that I mean to recommend to you abject and criminal flattery: no; flatter nobody's vices or crimes: on the contrary, abhor and discourage them. But there is no living in the world without a complaisant indulgence for people's weaknesses, and innocent, though ridiculous vanities. If a man has a mind to be thought wiser, and a woman handsomer, than they really are, their error is a comfortable one to themselves, and an innocent one with regard to other people; and I would rather make them my friends by indulging them in it, than my enemies by endeavouring (and that to no purpose) to undeceive them.

What doctors delicately call personal hygiene was as important as social graces:

The cleanliness of your person, which by the way will conduce greatly to your health, I refer from time to time to the bagnio. My mentioning these particulars arises (I freely own) from some suspicion that the hints are not unnecessary; for when you were a schoolboy, you were slovenly and dirty above your fellows. I must add another caution, which is, that upon no account whatever you put your fingers, as too many people are apt to do, in your nose or ears. It is the most shocking, nasty, vulgar rudeness that can be offered to company; it disgusts one, it turns one's stomach; and, for my own part, I would much rather know that a man's fingers were actually in his breech, than see them in his nose. Wash your ears well every morning, and blow your nose in your handkerchief whenever you have occasion; but, by the way, without looking at it afterwards.

And don't be a bore:

. . . There is . . . species of learned men, who, though less dogmatical and supercilious, are not less impertinent. These are the communicative and shining pedants, who adorn their conversation, even with women, by happy quotations of Greek and Latin; and who have contracted such a familiarity with the Greek and Roman authors, that they call them by certain names or epithets denoting intimacy. As *old* Homer; that *sly rogue* Horace; *Maro* instead of Virgil; and *Naso*, instead of Ovid. These are often imitated by coxcombs, who have no learning at all, but who have got some names and some scraps of ancient authors by heart, which they improperly and impertinently retail in all companies, in hopes of passing for scholars. If, therefore, you would avoid the accusation of pedantry on one hand, or the suspicion of ignorance on the other, abstain from learned ostentation. Speak the language of the company that you are in; speak it purely, and unlarded with any other. Never seem wiser, nor more learned, than the people you are with. Wear your learning, like your watch, in a private pocket; and do not merely pull it out and strike it merely to show you have one. If you are asked what o'clock it is, tell it; but do not proclaim it hourly and unasked like the watchman.

On the other hand, on no account should one be diffident, for 'How many people does one meet with everywhere, who with very moderate parts, and very little knowledge, push themselves pretty far, singly by being sanguine, enterprising and persevering?'

Of course lack of diffidence can be taken too far. In the seventeenth century, James Howell in one of his gossipy letters wrote to Sir Thomas Hawk complaining of just such a vice. His remarks will strike a chord in many readers' hearts:

I was invited yesternight to a solemn supper by B.I. [Ben Jonson] where you were deeply remembered; there was good company, excellent cheer, choice wines, and jovial welcome; one thing intervened which almost spoiled the relish of the rest, that B. began to engross all the discourse, to vapour extremely of himself, and by vilifying others to magnify his own muse. T.C. [Thomas Carew the poet] buz'd me in the ear, that though Ben had barrelled up a great deal of knowledge, yet it seemed he had not read the Ethics, which among other precepts of morality forbid self-commendation, declaring it to be an ill-favoured solecism in good manners. It made me think upon the Lady (not very young) who having a good while given her guests neat entertainment, a capon being brought upon the table, instead of a spoon she took a mouthful of claret and spouted it into the poop of the hollow bird. Such an accident happened in this entertainment you know.

The 'Lady's' performance with the claret may possibly have excited mirth, the exhibition of which Lord Chesterfield strongly disapproved: 'A man's going to sit down, in the supposition that he had a chair behind him, and falling down upon his breech for want of one, sets a whole company a-laughing, when all the wit in the world would not do it; a plain proof, in my mind, how low and unbecoming a thing laughter is. Not to mention the disagreeable noise that it makes, and the shocking distortion of the face that it occasions.'

Trying to be a good guest according to Chesterfield's precepts would certainly involve a lot of initial preparation; one might almost say a lifetime's observation of fellow humanity would be required before the system worked ideally. The object of all this was to be able to live a harmonious life on good terms with oneself and the world—and to be asked everywhere. Some guests, however, have an ulterior motive for making themselves agreeable; such are the frustrated anecdote collectors described in a letter from George Lyttelton to Rupert Hart-Davis:

   . . . How maddening these people are who have had experiences of great interest and remember nothing about them . . . Old Ram [an Eton master] had an uncle (I think) who wanted to write about Hazlitt and heard of some old chap who had known him well. He went to see this veteran, all agog with excitement. And the old man merely went off into deep, tantalising chuckles at his memories and produced nothing but 'Aha, yes, Wully Hazlitt! He was a queeer, queeer fellow!' and followed up this repeated remark with longer and deeper chuckles. Did you ever read Alfred Austin's conversations with Tennyson? He always addressed him as 'Immortal Bard' but got very little but grunts out of him.

Being a difficult host is of course one form of ill manners, though one sympathizes with the old boy described above who perhaps had nothing further to say about Hazlitt. Being a difficult guest is also bad manners, though if you were Lady Holland it seems you could get away with murder. Thomas Creevey to Miss Ord in 1833:

. . . I met Lady Holland again on Thursday at Lord Sefton's. She began by complaining of the slipperiness of the courtyard, and of the danger of her horses falling; to which Sefton replied that it should be gravelled the next time she did him the honour of dining there. She then began to sniff, and turning her eyes to various pots filled with beautiful roses and all kinds of flowers, she said: 'Lord Sefton, I must beg you to have those flowers taken out of the room, they are much too powerful for me.' Sefton and his valet Paoli actually carried the table and all its contents out of the room. Then the poor dear little Ly. Sefton, who has always a posy as large as life at her breast when she is dressed, took it out in the humblest manner, and said: 'Perhaps, Lady Holland, this nosegay may be too much for you.' But the other was pleased to allow her to keep it, tho' by no means in a very gracious manner. Then when candles were lighted at the close of dinner, she would have three of them put out, as being too much and too near her. Was there ever?

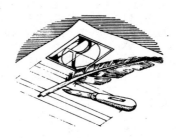

2

Upstairs, Downstairs

One of the first problems to be overcome for anyone rich enough to acquire a servant is to get a passably truthful reference from the candidate's former employer. This is what Lady Seymour is trying to do by applying to Lady Shuckburgh in the following exchange, the original motive of which becomes lost in a flurry of ruffled feathers. Lady Seymour was the granddaughter of the dramatist Sheridan, to whose family slighting reference is made by Lady Shuckburgh.

Lady Seymour presents her compliments to Lady Shuck-burgh, and would be obliged to her for the character of Mary Steadman, who states that she has lived twelve months, and still is in Lady Shuckburgh's establishment. Can Mary Stead-man cook plain dishes well, and make bread, and is she honest, sober, willing, cleanly and good tempered? Lady Seymour will also like to know the reason she leaves Lady Shuckburgh's house. Direct under care to Lord Seymour, Meridan Bradley, Wiltshire.

Lady Shuckburgh presents her compliments to Lady Seymour; her ladyship's letter, dated October 28th, only reached her yesterday, November 3rd. Lady Shuckburgh was unacquainted with the name of the kitchen-maid until mentioned by Lady Seymour, as it is her custom neither to apply for, nor give, characters to any of the under servants, this being always done by the housekeeper, Mrs Couch, and this was well known to the young woman. Therefore Lady Shuck-burgh is surprised at her referring any lady to her for a character. Lady Shuckburgh, keeping a professed cook, as well as a housekeeper, in her establishment, it is not very probable she herself should know anything of the abilities or merits of the under servants, she is therefore unable to reply to Lady Seymour's note. Lady Shuckburgh cannot imagine Mary Steadman to be capable of cooking anything, except for the servants' hall table.

> *Madam,*—Lady Seymour presents her compliments to Lady Shuckburgh, and begs she will order her housekeeper, Mrs Couch, to send the girl's character, otherwise another young woman will be sought for elsewhere, as Lady Seymour's children cannot remain without their dinners because Lady Shuckburgh, keeping a professed cook and housekeeper, thinks a knowledge of the details of her establishment beneath her notice. Lady Seymour understands from Steadman that, in addition to her other talents, she was actually capable of cooking food for the little Shuckburghs to partake of when hungry.

> *Madam,*—Lady Shuckburgh has directed me to acquaint you that she declines answering your note, the vulgarity of which she thinks beneath her contempt, and although it may be characteristic of the Sheridans to be vulgar, coarse, and witty, it is not that of a lady, unless she chances to have been *born in a garret and bred in a kitchen.* Mary Steadman informs me that your ladyship does not keep either a cook or housekeeper, and that you only require a girl who can cook a mutton chop; if so, I apprehend that Mary Steadman, or any *other scullion,* will be found fully equal to the establishment of the Queen of Beauty.—I am, Madam, your Ladyship's etc. etc.,
>
> ELIZABETH COUCH

There seems to have been nothing wrong with the qualifications of the unfortunate Steadman, but there was clearly quite a lot to complain about in the behaviour of Luther's servant Rosina von Truchses. He fulminates about her in a letter to John Goritz at Leipzig in 1544:

> [I] can only think she was sent me by the papists as an archwhore, desperate character, and sack of lies, who did all sorts of harm to my cellar, kitchen and rooms . . . Who knows what else she planned to do, for I took her into my own house with my own children. She had lovers and became pregnant and asked one of my maids to jump on her body and kill the unborn child. She escaped through the compassion of my

Katie [Luther's wife]; otherwise she would have deceived no more men unless the Elbe ran dry.

Luther's biographer charitably attributes the virulence of this outburst to the fact that Luther was suffering from a kidney stone at the time.

Fanny Kemble divorced her Southern planter husband in 1848 and later returned to England to set up house, where she found the attitudes of domestics much changed since her departure, and not for the better. One should bear in mind that 1848 was the year of uprisings in Europe, but in 1877—the date of this letter—Miss Kemble's problem was more one of overmanning than of rebellion:

My small troubles are swelled by the addition of poor F——'s, and hers are complicated with my own incessant and unsuccessful efforts to obtain two out of the four servants I require. I feel quite addled with a sort of cook, kitchen, and housemaid idiotcy, and as if I should address my friends and visitors with, 'What wages do you expect?' or, 'Why did you leave your last situation?' I do not quite understand who does the work in English houses now. I hire a cook, and she demands a kitchen-maid under her. I look for a kitchen-maid, and she asks for a scullery-maid under her; and I suppose the least the latter functionary would expect would be a turnspit dog *under her*. Used this to be all so, or do I dream that it was otherwise? And how did my father and mother and four children contrive to exist upon their small income? and six servants—which we never had; a cook, a housemaid, and a footman forming our modest establishment. But to be sure that was a long time ago, for I was young then!

The manners and general demeanour, too, of the lady domestics are very novel and surprising to me, They stand close up to one, with their hands thrust into their jacket pockets, and before you can ask them a single question, enquire if your house is large or small, how many servants you keep, if you keep a man-servant; until I quite expect that the next thing I shall hear will be, and 'how many back teeth have you left?'

Certainly things and people have greatly changed since I had anything to do with housekeeping in England. Not pleasantly, I think, for the employers. I hope the employed find it more agreeable . . .

Of course actors themselves can be troublesome employees, as we learn in an exchange between David Garrick and his factotum W. Stone. The latter was having difficulty in finding suitable extras:

> *Stone*,—You are the best fellow in the world—bring the Cupids to the Theatre to-morrow; if they are under six, and well made, you shall have a guinea a-piece for them. Mr. Lacy will pay you himself for the Bishop . . . if you can get me two murderers, I will pay you handsomely, particularly the spouting fellow who keeps the applestand on Tower-hill; the cut in his face is just the thing. Pick me up an alderman or two for Richard, if you can; and I have no objection to treat with you for a comely Mayor. The Barber will not do for Brutus . . .
>
> D.G.

> *Sir*,—The Bishop of Winchester is getting drunk at the *Bear*—and swears he will not play to-night.—I am yours,
>
> W. STONE

The recalcitrant attitude of Garrick's Bishop of Winchester is also a constant hazard for domestic employers. Servants are not all like the well-drilled deferential team portrayed in *Upstairs, Downstairs*, as Creevey points out in a letter to his wife in 1828. He had been staying at the Egremonts', and it sounds only marginally more attractive than staying with Count Dracula.

> . . . The dinner was of the first order, turtle, venison, moor game, &c. without stint. The servants, too, very numerous tho' most of them very advanced in years and tottered, and comical in their looks. The wax candles too were sufficiently numerous to light us all up well tho' we were at one end of a room sixty feet long, the wainscoat of which was Gibbons' carving in wood . . . However, all went off extremely well . . . By half past ten the Ladies of the house were all gone to bed, leaving those of this house to follow their own inventions, nor was this the only proof of the early habits of the whole house, for observing a footman bring in a glass of wine and water to the Chaplain, Sefton said to me, 'You'd better take this

opportunity of getting some too, or you'll be done,' so I went and asked him to bring me a glass likewise, and the self same footman returned in a very few minutes saying the Butler *was gone to bed*. I thought Sefton would have burst at this, as being much too good a thing to have ever happened . . . Mr. King's account of the servants was, that there were more of them in that house of both sexes, and in all departments, than in any house in England, that they were all very good in their way, but that they could not stand being put out of it, and were never interfered with, that they were all bred upon the spot, and all related to each other . . .

Edward Lear, recovering his health at a private hotel in Walton-on-Thames in 1860 describes similar difficulties of ensuring that one gets enough to eat. In this case the waiter can hardly be blamed, as the stinginess and avarice of the proprietor were at fault and the waiter had to put the best face he could on things. The whole description reads like an episode from *Fawlty Towers*, not excluding the representation of fellow guests:

The only other person who has gone is a large old lady, who the first night (Thursday) I was here, came slowly across the large reading-room, steadily looking at me. When she had advanced within 3 feet of my chair, I could bear it no longer, for I knew she would do one of two things, either embrace me, or charge me with a religious tract—so I rose up in terror. On which she said in a loud voice, 'Sit down, Sir! I only came across the room to see if you was anyone I knew.'—To return to the Dining table, there is a young Hussar who has been in French service—& later all through the Indian Mutiny: rather a nice fellow, Irish, & knows the 'Bellews': A very well informed & clever man, I conclude a physician: his wife wears spectacles & seems literary.—A grand dark man, who says Hay?—if ever I speak to him, (so I have left off doing so):—& various other characters. The head waiter is a praiseworthy individual, & his efforts to make a goose go round 18 diners were remarkable yesterday, as well as his placid firmness when there was only one bit left—& 4 persons yet unserved. 'Who's this for?' said an agitated buttony boy,—foreseeing the invidiousness of the task set him. 'HENNYBODDY!' said the waiter in a decided

tone,—& then coming to the three gooseless persons, of
whom I was one,
 (Three were in such fortune cast—
 Of whom myself was left the last),
he said in a conscientious & pained under-voice—'Gentlemen
—I am really sorry this has happened!—but I declare to you
that there shall be another goose to-morrow!' . . .

The Basil Fawltys of the world are notoriously poor at man-
management. So was Ludwig van Beethoven, who seems to
have conducted a running battle with his servants throughout
his life. Poor tortured Beethoven, how much happier he would
have been with a wife to manage him and his affairs! His own
domestic arrangements were generally a misery; and even when
he stayed with his brother Johann at Gneixendorf in 1826, he
was treated with surliness and refused a fire in his room. His
succession of servants all seem to have been unsatisfactory,
though one can see why they didn't stay long.

 Beethoven to Mme Streicher, 1817(?)
 . . . Thank you for taking an interest in me—meanwhile,
today, I have had a great deal to put up with from that girl
N.—but I threw half a dozen books at her head by way of
New Year's greeting . . .

 Beethoven to Mme Streicher, 1817
 . . . Miss N. is a changed woman since I threw those half-
dozen books at her head. Something in them must have
penetrated by chance into her brain or her evil heart—at least
we have a bosomy deceiver in her . . . Yesterday morning she
began her devilry again; I made short shrift of it and hurled
my heavy armchair at B.—the one that stands beside my bed;
after that I had peace for the whole day . . .

Up until modern times musicians were themselves treated like
servants; this didn't necessarily imply bad treatment, if they
worked for a generous patron, but must certainly have meant
insecurity and sometimes the patient endurance of philistinism
and ignorance. The only people wealthy enough to employ
composers were great noblemen and monarchs, but one at least
of these took a dim view of such expenses. When the Archduke
Ferdinand of Austria wrote to his mother, the formidable

Empress Maria Theresa, asking her advice about taking the sixteen-year-old Wolfgang Amadeus Mozart into his household, he got the following tart reply:

> . . . You ask my opinion about taking the young Salzburg musician into your service. I do not know where you can place him, since I feel that you do not require a composer, or other useless people. But if it would give you pleasure, I have no wish to prevent you. What I say here is only meant to persuade you not to load yourself down with people who are useless, and to urge you not to give such people the right to represent themselves as being in your service. It gives one's service a bad name when such types run about like beggars; besides, he has a large family . . .

If composers have their problems, artists and sculptors are by no means immune. They have servants and apprentices to control, and for sculptors there is the further aggravation of unscrupulous suppliers of materials. Michelangelo writes from Seravezza in 1519 to Pietro Urbano about an incident that could have cost him his life.

> *Pietro*: Things have gone very badly, and what has happened is that Saturday morning I started out to have a column hoisted very neatly, and nothing was missing, and after I had hoisted it a hundred feet, one link of the chain that was on the column broke and it went into the river in a hundred pieces. This link Donato had had made by his friend Lazzero the blacksmith, and as far as bearing a load goes, it would have held four columns if it had been sound, and to look at from the outside it seemed past all doubt. After it broke we saw the fraud, for it was not solid inside, and there was no more thickness of iron to hold it than a knife handle, so I am amazed it held as far as it did. All of us who were around were in great danger of life and a wonderful stone was spoiled . . .
>
> MICHELANGELO
> *in Seravezza*

Michelangelo's personal relationship with his loyal servant Urbino was a warm and happy one. Indeed, Urbino was one of his closest friends in his old age, and when the man died in 1555, Michelangelo was grief-stricken. He wrote to the painter and biographer Giorgio Vasari expressing his affection for his dead companion:

23 February 1556

Messer Giorgio, dear friend,

It is hard for me to write, but I will make some answer to yours. You know Urbino is dead; his death was to me an infinite grace of God, but grave loss and boundless sorrow withal. The grace came in that, having kept me alive during his life, by his death he taught me how to die, not with reluctance, but with desire for death. I kept him with me for six and twenty years, and found him most loyal and faithful; and now, when I had made him rich and looked to him to be the staff and repose of my old age, he is gone from me; and my only hope is to see him again in paradise.

Of this God gave me a sign, by his most happy death; which grieved him far less than the leaving me to live on in this treacherous world, amid so great suffering; though indeed the most of me is gone with him, leaving naught behind but infinite wretchedness . . .

Your MICHELAGNIOLO BUONARROTI
in Rome

3

Hot Gossip

Use of the telephone has sadly diminished the flow of epistolary gossip, but there seems to have been no time when letters were not a medium for scandal and unflattering anecdote. Like the diary column of a newspaper, these passages in letters are the ones towards which readers hasten over the barren acres of improving advice, descriptions of ailments and requests for money. M. Caelius Rufus writing to Cicero in 50 B.C. is resigned to this:

> There is absolutely no news, unless you want me (and I'm sure you do) to write to you about this kind of thing: Young Cornificius has promised marriage to Orsetilla's daughter. Paulla Valeria, Triarius's sister, got a divorce, without giving a reason, the very day her husband was to return home from his province. She is to marry D. Brutus. She has sent back all her ornaments.
>
> A lot of incredible things like this have happened in your absence. Servius Ocella would never have persuaded any one that he was an adulterer if he hadn't been caught at it twice in three days. Where, you will ask? Where I should least have wished, by Hercules! I leave you something to find out from others.

The erratic and frequently scandalous behaviour of expatriates is a rich source of gossip, much of which is happily available to us from contemporary letters. Edward Lear writes to Chichester Fortescue from Corfu in 1858, where the English colony was disporting itself in an eccentric manner:

> It is but right you should know the important life concerns of the Island, and therefore I shall not hesitate to insert the following facts before I conclude this morning's scribble. . . .

Lady H. (with an aide de camp) has been 'doing' the sights of Corfu & among others the churches. At the Greek Cathedral a beggar came and importuned the glittering Marchioness, who at the moment was indulging in the natural & pleasant act of sucking an orange. Lady H. after a time paused & said or implied 'silver & gold have I none', but such as she had (being the half sucked orange) she politely gave the beggar-woman, who (oranges being any number for a half-penny) threw the fruit in her Ladyship's face, and rushed frantically out of the desecrated edifice.

Horace Walpole was an incurable gossip, and some of his letters read like an eighteenth-century equivalent of *Private Eye*'s 'Grovel' column. But he is not always malicious, and his naturally accurate observation of character prevents him from painting his subjects in monotonal colours. Here he is recovering from a drama in the winter of 1755:

I am at present confined with a cold, which I caught by going to a fire in the middle of the night, and in the middle of the snow, two days ago. About five in the morning Harry waked me with a candle in his hand, and cried, 'Pray, your honour, don't be frightened!'—'No, Harry, I am not: but what is it that I am not to be frightened at?'—'There is a great fire here in St James's Street.'—I rose, and indeed thought all St James's Street was on fire, but it proved in Bury Street. However, you know I can't resist going to a fire; for it is certainly the only horrid sight that is fine. I slipped on my slippers, and an embroidered suit that hung on the chair, and ran to Bury Street, and stepped into a pipe that was broken up for water.—It would have made a picture—the horror of the flames, the snow, the day breaking with difficulty through so foul a night, and my figure, party per *pale*, mud and gold. It put me in mind of Lady Margaret Herbert's providence, who asked somebody for a *pretty* pattern for a nightcap. 'Lord!' said they, 'what signifies the pattern of a nightcap?'—'Oh! child,' said she, 'but you know, in case of fire.'

Walpole wasn't always so kind in his sartorial comments:

Lady Mary Wortley is arrived; I have seen her; I think her avarice, her dirt, and her vivacity are all increased. Her dress, like her languages, is a galimatias of several countries; the groundwork, rags; and the embroidery, nastiness. . . .

No one can catch a whole personality in a phrase better than Walpole: but Thomas Creevey is also seldom dull and has a good eye for farce. In the following extract from one of his letters he is reporting to Mrs Creevey on the social life with the Devonshires, and the difficulty (considerable) of managing the Duke successfully:

I saw Copley today in Doncaster and heard from him that Lord Charles Fitzroy is going to be married to Miss Cavendish. They are but a dry couple. Ld. George gives his Daughter £40,000. I asked Copley how he managed with his deaf Duke during the Race Week, and he said he was perfectly sure the said Duke never heard one word he said during the whole time. He mentions one trait of his friend that was not amiss. There is a Mrs Lumley in this neighbourhood, a little, pretty, flirting, Irish woman, that all the men make up to, so the Duke to be in the fashion desired to be introduced to her, and the next time she saw him she presumed to *nod* at him, a liberty which he instantly resented by declaiming her to be very vulgar woman, and that he never sh'd take any further notice of her . . .

Snobbery is an essential ingredient of gossip, together with adverse comment on other people's appearance, age and habits. Here is a Lady Campbell in full cry, writing from Argyll House on a Monday morning, and using techniques of punctuation and spelling to ram home her points in a way that reminds one of Queen Victoria's style, though certainly *not* her tone:

Well, you See, The Opera went off pleasantly, & so did I Home to Bed, & was in time for King Street chapel yesterday Morning, where we Had a Good Sermon tho' I thought too Political. At Night I went to An Assembly (not a *Belle Assemblée*) at Ly Cecilia's. There was Lady Betty Mackenzie shaking Her Head, & t'other old Female Sister Mandarin shaking *Her Head* also, The Maiden House keeper Miss Jennings, with Sundry other Antique Maids, widows, Wifes, & *what Not* too tedious to Mention . . . Mrs Johnstone looks very well, tho' not so fat as she was ye last time I saw Her. Mrs C: is in High Beauty. Mrs Anderson's Face is Plumpd up & looks well; Her Figure is Broken down & looks Disjointed, with Slatternly Petticoats Hanging *upon Nothing*. Lady Cecilia enquired kindly for you, so did Ly Ailesbury, who is really a good Natured Worthy Woman when they let Her alone. Lady Frederick was not there; she said Yesterday Morning she was surprised, she wonder'd you did not prefer being at Edinr to remaining *alone at Roseneath*. I replied that every one judged these Matters best for their own Taste & feelings, & tho' Perhaps I might Not Have prefer'd a total retirement at My Age, that were I no longer *so* Young My choice Might very likely coincide with Yours, & Her wonders ceased for that Time. Ld F: looks ill & thin, particularly His Legs.

Jane Austen, playing very much the same game in a letter to her sister Cassandra in 1800, is considerably more feline, and the net effect, especially in the closing sentence, is somehow more devastating than Lady Campbell's uninhibited rudeness:

There were very few beauties, and such as there were were not very handsome. Miss Iremonger did not look well, and Mrs Blount was the only one much admired. She appeared exactly as she did in September, with the same broad face, diamond bandeau, white shoes, pink husband, and fat neck. The two Miss Coxes were there: I traced in one the remains of the vulgar, broad-featured girl who danced at Enham eight years ago; the other is refined into a nice, composed-looking girl, like Catherine Bigg. I looked at Sir Thomas Champneys and thought of poor Rosalie; I looked at his daughter, and thought her a queer animal with a white neck. Mrs Warren, I was constrained to think, a very fine young woman, which I must regret. She danced away with great activity. Her husband is ugly enough, uglier even than his cousin John; but he does not look so *very* old. The Miss Maitlands are both prettyish, very like Anne, with brown skins, large dark eyes, and a good deal of nose. The General has got the gout, and Mrs Maitland the jaundice. Miss Debary, Susan, and Sally, all in black, but without any stature, made their appearance, and I was as civil to them as circumstances would allow me.

Three years later Harriet Cavendish was writing to *her* sister,

Georgiana, of a tedious evening unredeemed by the presence of
the Prince of Wales:

> And now for my sufferings and misfortunes. I have been to
> the Priory and live to tell you of it. It was formidable,
> disagreeable, uncomfortable and *royal*, for to complete the
> misery, the Prince was there. We arrived to dinner there on
> Friday, an hour too soon, as we waited for the Westmorlands,
> who, after all, dined in their own rooms. Lady W. is really as
> mad as it is possible to be. Her clear and connected reasons for
> not dining with us were—'We lost our way dreadfully; that is,
> we came quite right, but I fancied we should, which was as
> bad. I then *spilt* a *cup* of *milk* and so it was quite impossible!'
> Lady Sarah looked as well as she could with a very swelled
> face which she got by a fall at Apthorpe. Lady Augusta is not
> altered, her face looked beautiful, but her figure bad and very
> high shouldered.
> . . . Lady Asgill was present and more ridiculous than ever.
> I sat next to her during the performance, and in the Epilogue
> there was, *à l'ordinaire*, a compliment to the Ladies of the
> House. Lady Asgill, of course, took it to herself, and covering
> her face with her shawl, sunk upon the arm of my chair, quite
> overcome with modesty.

Sydney Smith's correspondence is replete with good gossip,
and lacks the extreme bitchiness of the previous letter. Even his
malice is redeemed by a continuous vein of self-mockery in his
anecdotes, as in this one:

> As I know you love a bit of London scandal learn that Lady
> Caroline Lamb stabbed herself at Lady Ilchester's Ball for the
> love of Lord Byron, as it is supposed. What a charming thing
> to be a Poet. I preached for many years in London and was
> rather popular, but never heard of a Lady doing herself the
> smallest mischief on my account.

Nevertheless, he can be brutal if he wishes.

> You will be amused with John Murray's marriage. It was
> concocted at Mr Philips under the auspices of Mrs Sydney and
> myself. The lady has £60,000, is a considerable Greek Scholar,
> a Senior Wrangler in Mathematics and the most perfect
> Instrumental Musician I ever heard. Ten days finished the

matter; indeed she has no time to lose since she is 39. I never saw two longer fatter Lovers, for she is as big as Murray. They looked enormous as they were making love in the plantations. She is so fond of Murray that she pretends to love porridge, cold weather and metaphysics. Seriously speaking it is a very good marriage, and acting under the direction of medical men, with perseverance and the use of stimulating diet there may be an heir to the house of Henderland.

Walpole, Creevey, and Sydney Smith are the most irresistible gossipers; of recent letter-writers few handle an anecdote with comparable deftness. Evelyn Waugh is one of those who do, and his best letters in this respect contain all the cardinal ingredients of gossip. They consist of a hilarious mixture of farce, snobbery, malice and arcane social information delivered with a terrible relish. The Yorke referred to in the following letter to Lord Kinross is the novelist Henry Green:

31 December 1958

Dear Patrick
I hope you have a rollicking Hogmanay.
The major humiliations suffered by Yorke after your luncheon do not directly involve Dame Rose [Macaulay]. She, you may remember, was without water at her flat. Yorke claimed intimate acquaintance with a dignitary called 'Stop Cock' or 'Turn Cock' whom we pursued through a number of fire stations at each of which Yorke's efforts to pass himself off as a proletarian met ludicrous rebuffs. Yorke then reverted from fireman to engineer & said he would mend Dame Rose's cistern himself. (He had been telling some pretty tall stories of his intrepidity on roofs during the 'blitz'.) When we got to Dame Rose's flat we found the cistern was on the roof approached by a rather steep iron ladder. Dame R. shinned up it like a monkey. Yorke trembled below. Only my taunts made him climb. He got to the top, panting & groaning, clung to the tank for a few moments and then came down. He had some sort of spasm, seizure or collapse at the foot.

Yours ever
EVELYN

Evelyn Waugh spent a lot of time in Whites, that terrifying London bastion of reaction and snobbery. Clubs of course are the best place outside Whitehall and Westminister to pick up gossip about the famous and infamous. And naturally there is a complicated snobbery that revolves around which club you belong to; the sort of thing that Rupert Hart-Davis described in a letter to George Lyttelton.

I've always understood that it was *Frank Harris* who, on being taken to the Saville Club at a time when the conversation and the cellar were famous, said: 'The worst thing about this club of faded prigs is that you can't get a decent glass of wine.' ('faded' is better than 'seedy', don't you think?) I expect you know that the S.C.'s present premises in Brook Street were formerly the home of 'Lulu' Harcourt. When Max was asked how he would describe the *décor*, he said: '*Lulu Quinze*'. And I'm certain I've already told you of J. B. Priestley's superb remark, 'The *Savage* Club is the place where dirty stories go when they die.'

4

A Misunderstanding Between Friends

'Reason is, and ought only to be, the slave of the passions' was the much-quoted opinion of the philosopher David Hume. Considerable demands were made on his reason, and no doubt much stimulation given to his passions, when he rashly offered Jean-Jacques Rousseau asylum in England. The Swiss philosopher had been forced to flee Luxembourg under the protection of Frederick the Great after the publication of his novel *Emile*, the contents of which had succeeded in enraging Protestants and Catholics alike. Rousseau, an unpleasant man greatly admired by the French, had had a chequered career before becoming a celebrity in 1752. He is regarded as the precursor of romanticism and wrote didactically at length about the beauty and innocence of childhood, while consigning his own five illegitimate children by Thérèse Le Vasseur to the foundling hospital. Towards the end of his life he became increasingly unstable and was showing signs of paranoia by the time he arrived in England. Unfortunately Horace Walpole played a cruel practical joke on him by publishing a forged letter purporting to be a rebuke to Rousseau written by Frederick the Great, and Rousseau became convinced that the British Government was planning to assassinate him, and that its agent in this plot was Hume. All of this was fantasy. In the following letter poor Hume complains to Dr Blair of his protégé's behaviour:

July 15, 1766

Dear Doctor,—I go in a few hours to Woburn; so can only give you the outline of my history. Through many difficulties I obtained a pension for Rousseau. The application was made with his own consent and knowledge. I write him that all is happily completed, and he need only draw for the money. He answers me that I am a rogue and a rascal; and have brought him into England merely to dishonour him. I demand the reason of this strange language, and Mr. Davenport, the gentleman with whom he lives, tells him that he must necessarily satisfy me. To-day I received a letter from him, which is perfect frenzy. It would make a good eighteen-penny pamphlet; and I fancy he intends to publish it. He there tells me, that D'Alembert, Horace Walpole, and I, had from the first entered into a combination to ruin him, and had ruined him. That the first suspicion of my treachery arose in him while we lay together in the same room of an inn in France. I there spoke in my sleep, and betrayed my intention of ruining him. That young Tronchin lodged in the same house with me at London; and Annie Elliot looked very coldly at him as he went by her in the passage. That I am also in a close confederacy with Lord Lyttelton, who, he hears, is his mortal enemy. That the English nation were very fond of him on his first arrival; but that Horace Walpole and I had totally alienated them from him. He owns, however, that his belief of my treachery went no higher than suspicion while he was in London; but it rose to certainty after he arrived in the country; for that there were several publications in the papers against him, which could have proceeded from nobody but me or my confederate Horace Walpole. The rest is all of a like strain, intermixed with many lies and much malice. I own that I was very anxious about this affair, but this letter has totally relieved me. I write in a hurry, merely to satisfy your curiosity. I hope soon to see you, and am &c.

There are other ways of testing friendship to destruction than merely biting the hand that feeds you. A more usual burden on long-suffering friends is simply the demanding of far too much, materially and emotionally, and for far too long. Charles Lamb, in a letter of 1801 to John Richman, describes a visit from his old friend George Dyer, who, though he tended to over-dramatize his ailments, eventually did become blind from the stress of a lifetime of grinding hack work. Lamb was a loyal ally and actually held him in great affection. All the same, Dyer could be a bit of a trial:

A letter from G. Dyer will probably accompany this. I wish I could convey to you any notion of the whimsical scenes I have been witness to in this fortnight past. 'Twas on Tuesday week the poor heathen scrambled up to my door about breakfast time. He came thro' a violent rain with no neckcloth on, and a *beard* that made him a spectacle to men and angels, and tapped at the door. Mary opened it, and he stood stark still and held a paper in his hand importing that he had been ill with a fever. He either wouldn't or couldn't speak except by signs. When you went to comfort him he put his hand upon his heart and shook his head and told us his complaint lay where no medicines could reach it. I was dispatch'd for Dr Dale, Mr Phillips of St Paul's Churchyard, and Mr Frend, who is to be his executor. George solemnly delivered into Mr Frend's hands and mine an old burnt preface that had been in the fire, with injunctions which we solemnly vow'd to obey that it should be printed after his death with his last corrections and that some account should be given to the world why he had not fulfill'd his engagement with subscribers. Having done this and borrow'd two guineas of his bookseller (to whom he imparted in confidence that he should leave a great many loose papers behind him which would only want methodizing and arranging to prove very lucrative after his death), he laid himself down on my bed in a mood of complacent resignation. By the aid of meat and drink put into him (for I all along suspected a vacuum) he was enabled to sit up in the evening, but he had not got the better of his intolerable fear of dying . . . He is got quite well again by nursing, and chirps of odes and lyric poetry the day long—he is to go out of town on Monday, and with him goes the dirty train of his papers and books which follow'd him to our house. I shall not be sorry when he takes his nipt carcase out of my bed, which it has occupied, and vanishes with all his Lyric lumber, but I will endeavour to bring him in future into a method of dining at least once a day. . . .

Some friendships turn sour that had begun in mutual admiration. Not a few of these ruptures may be attributed to an imbalance that existed at the beginning of the relationship, but which has been ignored because the victim of it was receiving enough succour and stimulation not to give voice to an underground feeling of grievance, or even of suppressed hatred. Where both characters are fairly strong, it is likely that there will eventually be an explosion as there was finally between Carl Jung and Sigmund Freud. Jung's attitude towards Freud had once been nearly idolatrous, but as his own work developed and inevitably began to lead away from Freud's theories, tension steadily grew. The final break, which is recorded in the following exchange of letters, had a deep emotional impact on both men; but more visibly on Jung who in 1913 began to feel 'menaced by psychosis'. His letter to Freud interestingly reveals the moment when long-suppressed mistrust finally bursts its bonds. Jung's coldly critical remarks about Freud fail to break down the latter's Olympian stance, and the Freudian counter-attack uses the now familiar ploy of treating Jung's aggression merely as a symptom of his neurosis. The actual bone of contention between them was Jung's increasing reservations about Freud's exclusively sexual definition of libido.

Vienna, 16 December 1912

Dear Dr Jung

I shall submit your suggestion for changing the name of the *Zeitschrift* both to the society and to the two editors, and report to you on the outcome.

The habit of taking objective statements personally is not only a (regressive) human trait, but also a very specific Viennese failing. I shall be very glad if such claims are not made on you. But are you 'objective' enough to consider the following slip without anger?

'Even Adler's cronies do not regard me as one of *yours*.'
Yours nevertheless, FREUD

Kusnacht-Zürich, 18 December 1912

Dear Professor Freud,

May I say a few words to you in earnest? I admit the ambivalence of my feelings towards you, but am inclined to take an honest and absolutely straightforward view of the situation. If you doubt my word, so much the worse for you. I would, however, point out that your technique of treating your pupils like patients is a *blunder*. In that way you produce either slavish sons or impudent puppies (Adler-Stekel and the whole insolent gang now throwing their weight about in Vienna). I am objective enough to see through your little trick. You go around sniffing out all the symptomatic actions in your vicinity, thus reducing everyone to the level of sons and daughters who blushingly admit the existence of their faults. Meanwhile you remain on top as the father, sitting pretty. For sheer obsequiousness nobody dares to pluck the prophet by the beard and inquire for once what you would say to a patient with a tendency to analyse the analyst instead of himself. You would certainly ask him: 'Who's got the neurosis?'

You see, my dear Professor, so long as you hand out this stuff I don't give a damn for my symptomatic actions; they shrink to nothing in comparison with the formidable beam in my brother Freud's eye. I am not in the least neurotic—touch wood! I have submitted *lege artis et tout humblement* to analysis and am much the better for it. You know, of course, how far a patient gets with self-analysis: *not* out of his neurosis—just like you. If ever you should rid yourself entirely of your complexes and stop playing the father to your sons, and instead of aiming continually at their weak spots took a good look at your own for a change, then I will mend my ways and at one stroke uproot the vice of being in two minds about you. Do you *love neurotics* enough to be always at one with yourself? But perhaps you *hate* neurotics. In that case how can you expect your efforts to treat your patients leniently and lovingly *not* to be accompanied by somewhat mixed feelings? Adler and Stekel were taken in by your little tricks and reacted with childish insolence. I shall continue to stand by you publicly while maintaining my own views, but privately shall start telling you in my letters what I really think of you. I consider this procedure only decent.

No doubt you will be outraged by this peculiar token of friendship, but it may do you good all the same.

With best regards,
Most sincerely, yours, JUNG

Vienna, 3 January 1913

Dear Doctor,

. . . I can answer only one point in your previous letter in any detail. Your allegation that I treat my followers like patients is demonstrably untrue. In Vienna I am reproached for the exact opposite. I am held responsible for the misconduct of Stekel and Adler; in reality I have not said one word to Stekel about his analysis since it was concluded some ten years ago, nor have I made any use of analysis with Adler, who was never my patient. Any analytical remarks I have made about them were addressed to others and for the most part at a time when we had ceased to associate with one another . . .

Otherwise your letter cannot be answered. It creates a situation that would be difficult to deal with in a personal talk and totally impossible in correspondence. It is a convention among us analysts that none of us need feel ashamed of his own bit of neurosis. But one who while behaving abnormally keeps shouting that he is normal gives ground for the suspicion that he lacks insight into his illness. Accordingly, I propose that we abandon our personal relations entirely. I shall lose nothing by it, for my only emotional tie with you has long been a thin thread—the lingering effect of past disappointments—and you have everything to gain, in view of the remark you recently made in Munich, to the effect that an intimate relationship with a man inhibited your scientific freedom. I therefore say, take your full freedom and spare me your supposed 'tokens of friendship'. We are agreed that a man should subordinate his personal feelings to the general interests of his branch of endeavour. You will never have reason to complain of any lack of correctness on my part where our common undertaking and the pursuit of scientific aims are concerned; I may say, no more reason in the future than in the past. On the other hand, I am entitled to expect the same from you.

> Regards,
> Yours sincerely, Freud

A spectacular interruption in a friendship is recorded in the correspondence between André Gide and Paul Claudel when the latter, very belatedly, realized that his friend was homosexual. Claudel was a fiercely proselytizing Catholic and his long correspondence with Gide affords the amusing spectacle of the latter's ironic scepticism emerging totally unscathed from Claudel's continuous evangelical bombardment.

> *Hamburg, 2nd March 1914*
> In the name of heaven, Gide, how could you write the passage which I find on page 478 of the last issue of the *N.R.F.*? Don't you know that after *Saül* and *L'Immoraliste* you cannot commit any further imprudence? Must I quite make up my mind, as I have wished to do, that you are yourself a participant in these hideous practices? Answer me. You owe me an answer. If you remain silent, or if you don't make yourself absolutely clear, I shall know where I stand. If you

are not a pederast, why have you so strange a predilection for
this sort of subject? And if you are one, cure yourself, you
unhappy man, and do not make a show of these abomina-
tions. Consult Madame Gide; consult the better part of your
own heart. Don't you see that you will be lost—you yourself
and all those who are nearest to you? Don't you realize the
effect which your books may have upon some unfortunate
young people? It pains me to say these things, but I feel
obliged to do so.

Your distressed friend,
P. CLAUDEL

Florence, 7th March 1914

What right have you to issue this summons? In what name
do you put these questions? If it is in the name of friendship,
can you suppose for an instant that I should evade them?

It pains me very much that there should be any misap-
prehension between us; but your letter has already done
much to create a new one—for, no matter how I take it, and
whether I answer or whether I don't, I foresee that you are
going to misjudge me. I therefore beg you to consider this
only: that I love my wife more than life itself, and I could not
forgive any word or action on your part which might endan-
ger her happiness. Now that has been said, I can tell you that
for months, for years, I have longed to talk to you—although
the tone of your letter makes me despair of receiving any
advice from you to-day.

I am speaking now to a friend, as I should speak to a priest,
whose binding duty it is to keep my secret before God. I have
never felt any desire in the presence of a woman; and the
great sadness of my life is that the most constant, the most
enduring, and the keenest of my loves has never been
accompanied by any of the things which normally precede
love. It seemed, on the contrary, that in my case love
prevented me from desiring . . .

As for the evil which, you say, is done by my books, I can't
believe in it, for I know how many others are stifled, as I am,
by lying conventions. And do not infer from this that I
commend any particular habits, or even any particular
desires; but I loathe hypocrisy, and I know that some hypocri-
sies are mortal. I cannot believe that religion leaves on one
side all those who are like myself. By what cowardice, since

God calls me to speak, should I evade this question in my
books? I did not choose to be so. I can fight against my
desires; I can triumph over them, but I can neither choose the
object of those desires, nor can I invent other objects, either to
order or in imitation. . . .

A. GIDE

Claudel replied with some heavy mortar-fire that included a
recital of Catholic dogma and a swipe at Protestantism. But he
did not break with Gide, although he used the occasion to break
numerous confidences and display the least agreeable facets of a
Christian in a fit of self-righteousness:

No, you know quite well that the habits of which you tell
me are neither permitted, nor excusable, nor avowable. You
will have against you both *Revelation* and the natural order of
things.
Common logic and decency tell you that man is not an end
in himself; still less so are his pleasures and private delights. If
sexual attraction does not lead to its natural conclusion—that
is to say, reproduction—it is irregular and evil. That is the
only firm principle. Without it, you abandon yourself to
private fantasies. Where will you draw the line? If one person
claims to justify sodomy, another will justify onanism, vam-
pirism, the rape of minors, anthropophagy, etc. There's no
reason to stop anywhere.
. . . You claim to be the victim of a physiological idiosyn-
crasy. That would be an attenuating circumstance, but it
would not constitute a permit or a licence. You are the victim
of two things above all: your Protestant heredity, which has
accustomed you to look only to yourself for your rules of
conduct, and the fascination of aesthetics which lends lustre
and interest to the least excusable of actions. In spite of all the
doctors I absolutely refuse to believe in physiological deter-
minism. If you have abnormal instincts, the natural upright-
ness of your nature, allied to your reason, your education and
the fear of God, should have given you the means of resistance. Medicine is meant to cure, not to excuse.

Happily, not all breaches of friendship need be permanent. It is
pleasant to read Beethoven making up with his friend Johann
Hummel after a misunderstanding entirely of Beethoven's

making. One letter followed the other within the space of twenty-four hours:

Don't come to me any more! You are a false dog, and may the hangman do away with all false dogs.

BEETHOVEN

Dear Little Ignaz of My Heart!

You are an honest fellow and I now realize that you were right. So come to me this afternoon. You will find Schuppanzigh here too and we shall both blow you up, cudgel you and shake you so that you will have a thoroughly good time. Kisses from your Beethoven, also called dumpling.

5

Lovers

In 1887 the following letter was picked up on a beach at Sidmouth. Its force of expression makes it a more moving document that many more highly sophisticated and polished love letters:

> *Dear Marey*, dear Marey, I hant got no partcler news to tell ye at present but my sister that marryd have got such a nice littel babey, and I wish how as that we had got such a little dear too. Dearest Mary, I shall not be happy until then. Dearest Mary pure and holy meek and loly lovely Rose of Sharon. Sometimes I do begin to despare as I am afraid our knot will never be tied, but my Master have promised I how as that when I git ye he will put ye in the Dairy yard to feed the Piggs and give ye atin pense a week. . . . I be coming over tomorrow to buy the ring and you must come to the stashun to meet me and bring a pese of string with you the size of your finger. . . . Father is going to give us a bedstead and Granny a 5 lb note to buy such as washing stand fire irons mousetrap and Sope, and we must wayte till we can to buy carpeting and glass, crockery-ware and chiny. . . . And Father is going to get us a Rooseter for our Weding Breakfast. Dearest Marey pure and holey meek and loly lovely Rose of Sharon. So no more at present from your future husband WILLIAM TAYLOR.

Plain language is again employed in the following extracts of a letter from Thomas Betson to his thirteen-year-old sweetheart Katherine Ryche written on 1 June 1476. Betson was involved in the wool trade, which would have taken him to Calais. There was, of course, opposition to the match, as young persons in the fifteenth century were not supposed to go around marrying whomsoever they wished; but the outcome was a happy one.

. . . I understand right well that ye be in good health of body and merry at heart. And I pray God heartily to His pleasure to continue the same; for it is to me very great comfort that ye so be, so help me Jesu. And if ye would be a good eater of your meat alway, that ye might wax and grow fast to be a woman, ye should make me the gladest man of the world, by my troth; for when I remember your favour and your sad loving dealing to me wards, forsooth ye make me even very glad and joyous in my heart: and on the other side again when I remember your young youth, and seeth well that you be none eater of your meat, the which should help you greatly in waxing, forsooth then ye make me very heavy again. And therefore I pray you, mine own sweet Cousin, even as you love me, to be merry and eat your meat like a woman.

. . . I pray you greet well my horse, and pray him to give you four of his years to help you withall: and I will at my coming home give him four of my years and four horse loaves till amends. . . .

I pray you, gentle Cousin, commend me to the Clock, and pray him to amend his unthrifty manners, for he strikes ever in undue time, and he will be ever afore, and that is a shrewd condition. Tell him without he amend his condition he will cause strangers to avoid and come no more there. I trust to you that he shall amend against mine coming, the which shall be shortly with all hands and all feet with God's grace.

. . . At great Calais on this side of the sea, the first day of June, when every man was gone to his dinner, and the clock smote nine, and all our household cried after me and bade me come down, come down to dinner at once! and what answer I gave them ye know it of old.

By your faithful cousin and lover
THOMAS BETSON

I send you this ring for a token.

An interesting contrast with the love affairs of the young is provided by this tender description in 1886 by Mark Twain of his mother's youthful passion for a bashful young man, which unexpectedly resurfaced when she had reached the ripe age of eighty-two.

. . . Here's a secret. A most curious and pathetic romance, which has just come to light. Read these things but don't mention them. Last fall my old mother, then 82, took a notion to attend a convention of old settlers of the Mississippi Valley in an Iowa town. My brother's wife was astonished and represented to her the hardships and fatigue of such a trip and said my mother might possibly not even survive them, and said there could be no possible interest for her in such a meeting and such a crowd. But my mother insisted and persisted and finally gained her point.

They started, and all the way my mother was young again with excitement, interest, eagerness, anticipation.

They reached the town and the hotel. My mother strode with the same eagerness in her eye and her step, to the counter, and said:

'Is Dr Barrett of St Louis here?'

'No. He was here but he returned to St Louis this morning.'

'Will he come again?'

'No.'

My mother turned away, the fire all gone from her, and said, 'Let us go home.'

They went straight back to Keokuk.

My mother sat silent and thinking for many days, a thing which had never happened before. Then one day she said:

'I will tell you a secret. When I was eighteen a young medical student named Barrett lived in Columbia (Ky.) eighteen miles away and he used to ride over to see me. This continued for some time; I loved him with my whole heart and I knew that he felt the same toward me, though no words had been spoken. He was too bashful to speak, he could not do it. Everybody supposed we were engaged, took it for granted we were, but we were not. By and by there was to be a party in a neighboring town, and he wrote my uncle telling him his feelings and asking him to drive me over in his buggy and let him (Barrett) drive me back, so that he might have that opportunity to propose. My uncle should have done as he was asked, without explaining anything to me, but instead he read me the letter and then, of course, I could not go, and did not. He (Barrett) left the country presently and I, to stop the clacking tongues and to show him that I did not care, *married* in a pet. In all these sixty-four years I have not seen him since. I saw in a paper that he was going to attend that Old Settlers'

Convention. Only three hours before we reached that hotel, he had been standing there!'

Since then her memory is wholly faded out and gone and now she writes letters to the schoolmates who have been dead forty years, and wonders why they neglect her and do not answer.

Think of her carrying that pathetic burden in her old heart sixty-four years, and no human being every suspecting it!

Yrs ever,
MARK

The melancholy tale of Twain's mother is in stark contrast to the cheerful shamelessness of Pietro Aretino. In the following letter the old rogue reminisces about love-affairs of his youth to Signora Girolama Fontanella:

. . . At that moment I seemed to be carried back to the time when my beard was the colour of ebony and not ivory, and I boasted feathered wings rather than leaden feet, and I sped like lightning through that ancient and noble city on my pony which was whiter than the snow and faster than the wind; and then, so as to keep up with the passionate love of my so easy-going, so hard-to-please Giovanni de' Medici, I fell deliriously in love with Laura.

. . . In truth, my eyes fill with tears when I remember how lovingly in the street or in church I was kissed by the Countess, so pure and loving and the best of godmothers. It's the subject for a comedy, the time I fell asleep at her side, when I found her indisposed in bed. I had been sitting at her side, conversing for a while, when, overcome by heat and drowsiness, I let my head sink on to the feather pillow and was snoring when her husband, the dear old Count of Casal Po, shook me hard and roared: 'Undress yourself and climb into bed!'

My God, how our learned friend Messer Aurelio de la Fossa split his sides laughing when some ladies who were there recounted this to him, just as I did when the same Countess, on reading a letter I had brought her from Milan, turned to me and said: 'My husband writes to me that I should do for you all I would do for him: so will you sleep with me tonight?'

The uncomplicated exuberance of Aretino is in stark contrast to some of the more complicated, and often tortured, sexuality of less self-confident men. Dylan Thomas, perhaps less of a hero between the sheets than at the bar, wrote a curious letter, a mixture of bragging and cringing, to Pamela Hansford Johnson in 1934. His relations with the girl, who was later to become a distinguished novelist and marry the politician and writer C. P. Snow, were as platonic as they were passionate. He seems to have been more than a little frightened of her:

. . . I never want to lie to you. You'll be terribly angry with me I know and you'll never write to me again perhaps. But darling you want me to tell you the truth don't you. I left Laugharne on Wednesday morning and went down to a bungalow in Gower. I drank a lot in Laugharne & was feeling a bit grim even then. I stayed in Gower with a friend of mine in the waster days of the reporter's office. On Wednesday evening his fiancée came down. She was tall and thin and dark and a loose red mouth and later we all went out and got drunk. She tried to make love to me all the way home. I told her to shut up because she was drunk. When we got back she still tried to make love to me, wildly like an idiot in front of Cliff. She went to bed and my friend and I drank some more and then very modernly he decided to go and sleep with her. But as soon as he got into bed with her she screamed and ran into mine. I slept with her that night and for the next three nights. We were terribly drunk day and night. Now I can see all sorts of things. I think I've got them.

Oh darling, it hurts me to tell you this but I've got to tell you because I always want to tell you the truth about me. And I never want to share. It's you and me or nobody, you and me and nobody. But I have been a bloody fool and I'm going to bed for a week. I'm just on the borders of D.T.s darling and I've wasted some of my tremendous love for you on a lank, red-mouthed girl with a reputation like a hell. I don't love her a bit. I love you Pamela always and always. But she's a pain on the nerves. For Christ knows why she loves me. Yesterday morning she gave her ring back to Cliff. I've got to put a hundred miles between her and me. I must leave Wales for ever & never see her. I see bits of you in her all the time and tack on to those bits. I've got to be drunk to tack on to them. I love you Pamela and must have you. As soon as all this is over I'm coming straight up. If you'll let me. No, but better or worse I'll come up next week if you'll have me. Don't be too

cross or too angry. What the hell am I to do? And what the
hell are you going to say to me? Darling I love and think of
you all the time. Write by return and don't break my heart by
telling me I mustn't come up to London to you becos I'm such
a bloody fool.

xxxxx Darling. Darling oh

Sexual tastes are notoriously a matter for moralizing, hypocrisy
and quaint notions of propriety. Although Marie Stopes was a
liberating influence on sexual mores insofar as she endeavoured
to free women from the tyranny of unplanned and unwanted
pregnancies, it shouldn't be thought that her views on what was
appropriate in sexual intercourse were anything other than
conventional. Certainly she did not condone what she evidently
regarded as 'perversions'. In this respect she was as prudish as
some of her most vociferous critics, as her reply to an inquiry, in
1921, reveals:

> In the present attitude of public opinion, I think that not
> only would a wife be justified in bringing a charge of cruelty
> on two of the acts you mention (not the third) but that it
> would really be something of a public service to bring such a
> charge . . . she should confine it to the two points which are
> really disgusting and cruel, namely oral and rectal coitus. As
> such a large number of men use hand masturbation, any
> mention of that in addition would be like a red herring
> dragged across the path because no judge would dare to base
> a charge of cruelty on such a point as it would involve too
> revolutionary a change. The other two points, however,
> namely the use or even the attempt to use oral and rectal
> coitus are acts of such gross indecency that they undoubtedly
> amount to cruelty mentally to any refined or sensitive
> woman . . .

Dr Stopes was frank and sympathetic where she felt the
circumstances demanded it. In the following exchange of June
1926 she is perhaps encouraged to drop the governessy tone
that she often adopted towards the uneducated, by the fact that
a titled lady had been bold enough to write to her. This was
rather a coup, for her views were not always so well received in
the higher echelons of society: the copy of her book *Mother
England* that she tried to present to King George V three years

later was returned with a diplomatic note from the Private Secretary.

Lady KM to MCS

I have just been reading your *wonderful* book Married Love, and I am writing to beg you to help me. I am 61 years old, I was married in 1907 to an old man of 73 years of course he could do nothing. Last December I married a man of 58. My husband has not yet been able to consummate our marriage, he seems anxious to do so, he lies all over me and nearly smothers me, I don't think it is my age for other men have been very passionate if I would let them, my husband never tries to get me ready he just gets into bed and is on the top of me at once; he never kisses me or touches me first, and I *do* want it so much I have longed for it all my life. Can you help me?

MCS in reply

I shall be only too pleased to help you, and should advise you to get your husband to read the book, and after that you might suggest to him that you should try union, lying each on your sides. You will find if you put one leg under his waist that this position is very easy for both, and in the circumstances you describe should, I think, be useful and make matters possible for you. Perhaps if you knew more of the structure of the body it might help. Perhaps the book I have just published, *The Human Body*, might be of assistance . . .

The dangers of indulgence in sex, shrewdly exploited by moralists down the ages, do not stop short at the corruption of virtue and the ravages of disease. If some artists are to be believed, sex interferes with the creative process, a view which sounds remarkably akin to those of chaplains in English public schools. The following letter has been attributed to Chopin, but is now thought to be a forgery. The writer berates his mistress for having lured him into excessive love-making, and thus having drastically reduced his creativity:

. . . To me inspiration and creativity come only when I have abstained from a woman for a longish period. When, with passion, I have emptied my fluid into a woman until I am pumped dry then inspiration shuns me and ideas won't crawl

into my head. Consider how strange and wonderful it is that
the same forces which go to fertilise a woman and create a
human being should go to create a work of art! Yet a man
wastes this life-giving precious fluid for a moment of ecstasy.

The same is true of scholars who devote themselves to
scientific pursuits or men who make discoveries. The formula
is apparently a simple one: whatever the field, the creator
must abjure woman—then the forces in his body will accu-
mulate in his brain in the form of inspiration and he may give
birth to a pure work of art.

Just think of it—sexual temptation and desire can be
transmitted into inspiration! Of course I am speaking only of
those who have ability and talent. A fool, living without a
woman, will merely be driven insane by frustration. He can't
create anything worthy of God or man.

On the other hand unrequited love and unfulfilled passion,
sharpened by the image of one's beloved and carrying
unbearable frustration with it, can contribute to creativity . . .

What about Mozart? I don't know, but I think his wife
became ordinary food for him, his love and passion cooled,
and he was therefore able to compose a great deal. I haven't
heard of any love-affairs in Mozart's life.

Sweetest Fidelina, how much of that precious fluid, how
many forces have I wasted on you! I have not given you a
child and God only knows how many excellent inspirations,
how many musical ideas have gone to perdition!

Operam et oleunsa perdidi (I wasted the work and the
labour)!!! Who knows what ballades, polonaises, perhaps an
entire concerto, have been forever engulfed in your little D flat
major. . . .

The Middle Ages had a very different attitude to the married
state from that which has arisen in later times. Adultery became
institutionalized in the courtly love tradition, though much of it
was symbolic and platonic rather than real. But Abélard and
Héloïse, in their letters, share the unexalted view of marriage
derived from St Paul and St Jerome, which sees it largely as a
legal outlet for carnal desire. 'It is better to marry than to burn',
says St Paul, not very encouragingly, and his words have
echoed down the ages. Even the happily married Robert Louis
Stevenson observed that, putting it at its lowest, 'marriage is a
form of friendship recognized by the police'. After the secret

marriage of Peter Abélard to Héloïse and the dreadful revenge that her uncle Fulbert took in having the scholar castrated by his servants, both retired to religious houses and exchanged the letters that have become so famous. In the following extracts Héloïse's remembrance of sensual joys, and her efforts to forget them, are contrasted with Abélard's determination to push his former passion back into the realm of sin and shame:

Héloïse to Abélard

. . . In my case, the pleasures of lovers which we shared have been too sweet—they can never displease me, and can scarcely be banished from my thoughts. Wherever I turn they are always there before my eyes, bringing with them awakened longings and fantasies which will not even let me sleep. Even during the celebration of the Mass, when our prayers should be purer, lewd visions of those pleasures take such a hold upon my unhappy soul that my thoughts are on their wantonness instead of on prayers. I should be groaning over the sins I have committed, but I can only sigh for what I have lost. Everything we did and also the times and places are stamped on my heart along with your image, so that I live through it all again with you. Even in sleep I know no respite. Sometimes my thoughts are betrayed in a movement of my body, or they break out in an unguarded word. . . .

Men call me chaste; they do not know the hypocrite I am. They consider purity of the flesh a virtue, though virtue belongs not to the body but to the soul.

Abélard to Héloïse

. . . After our marriage, when you were living in the cloister with the nuns at Argenteuil and I came one day to visit you privately, you know what my uncontrollable desire did with you there, actually in a corner of the refectory, since we had nowhere else to go. I repeat, you know how shamelessly we behaved on that occasion in so hallowed a place, dedicated to the most holy Virgin. Even if our other shameful behaviour was ended, this alone would deserve far heavier punishment. Need I recall our previous fornication and the wanton impurities which preceded our marriage, or my supreme act of betrayal, when I deceived your uncle about you so disgracefully, at a time when I was continuously living with him in his own house? Who would not judge me justly treated by the man whom I had first shamelessly betrayed? Do you think that the momentary pain of that wound is sufficient punishment for such crimes? Or rather, that so great an advantage was fitting for such great wickedness? What wound do you suppose would satisfy God's justice for the profanation such as I described of a place so sacred to his own Mother? Surely, unless I am much mistaken, not that wound which was wholly beneficial was intended as a punishment for this, but rather the daily unending torment I now endure. . . .

In our own century the attitudes of official Christianity towards sexuality were frequently challenged and satirized by Bertrand Russell. Eventually his remarks became too much for the Bishop of Rochester. In 1957 Russell received a solemn letter from the Bishop, pointing out to the great philosopher what was his Achilles' heel. Omitting the Bishop's address and signature, Russell passed it on to the Freudian Ernest Jones for his comments:

Dear Dr Jones
I enclose a copy of a letter from an eminent Anglican divine. It seems to me a document worthy to go into your case-book. I should be very grateful if you felt inclined to send me any comments on it.

Yours sincerely
RUSSELL

Dear Lord Russell
It has been laid upon my conscience to write to you, after your article in the *Sunday Times* on the 'Great Mystery' of survival after death; seeing that you at 84 stand yourself upon that threshold.

Your contemporaries, like myself, acclaim you the greatest brain of our generation. And many must believe, with me, that if only your moral stature had matched your intellectual power and other singular endowments, you could have saved us from a second World War. Instead, in your book on Companionate Marriage, *Marriage and Morals* (1929), the cloven hoof of the lecher cannot be disguised; and it is lechery that has been your Achilles' heel, blinding your great mind from discerning that infinitely greater Mind behind all phenomena, such as has formed your enthralling study. Only the pure in heart can see God; and four wives, with three divorces, must be an awful and bitter humiliation, showing the man himself, entrusted with such a magnificent brain.

Moreover, I cannot but believe that you must at times be haunted by the remembrance of the murder, suicide, and untold misery, between the wars, caused by the experiments of young people with Companionate Marriage, of which you were the Apostle, with all the immense authority of your fame. I am an old man myself of 72, but with no outstanding gifts or learning; and yet I would, in humble sincerity, make my own, to you, what that Dr M. J. Routh, who died in his hundredth year as President of Magdalen, Oxford, (1854), wrote to a Quaker acquaintance in the condemned cell:

'Sir, this comes from one who, like yourself, has not long to live, being in his ninetieth year. He has had more opportunity than most for distinctly knowing that the scriptures of the New Testament were written by the Apostles of the Saviour of mankind. In these Scriptures it is expressly said that the blood of Jesus Christ cleanses from all sin, and that if we confess our sins, God, being merciful and just, will forgive us our sins on our repentance. Think, say, and do everything in your power to save your soul, before you go into another life.'

You may know that the great Bishop Joseph Butler of Durham, your peer as regards intellect, died with this verse from I John, I. 7, in his ears, and whispering: 'Oh! but this is comfortable.'

I pray God that you will recognise that, for some reason, I have been filled with a deep concern for you.

Yours sincerely
CHRISTOPHER ROFTEN

Dear Russell
I am a little surprised that you should find the Anglican's letter at all odd. I should have thought you received many such, and indeed I even wonder how many masses are already being said for your soul.

The interest of such letters is of course the calm identification of wickedness with sexual activity. Freud used to think that the main function of religion was to check man's innate aggressivity (the obvious source of all wickedness), but it is curious how often religious teachers bring it back again to sexuality. That makes one think there must be some deep connection between the two, and we believe nowadays that much aggressivity, possibly all, can ultimately be traced to the innumerable forms of sexual frustration. It remains noteworthy, however, that you, our leading apostle of true morality (love, charity, tolerance, etc) should be cast into perdition for not accepting the Catholic view of marriage.

If you want a psycho-analytic comment on the letter there is a clue in the omnipotence he attributes to you (ability to stop wars, etc). That can only point to a gigantic father figure (an earthly God), whose only sin, much resented by the son, was his sleeping with the mother. It is curious that such people are never shocked at God's adulterous behaviour with the Virgin Mary. It needs a lot of purification.

Yours sincerely
ERNEST JONES

Dear Jones
Thank you for your very pleasant letter of February 4. Ever since I got it, I have been luxuriating in the pleasure of seeing myself as a formidable father figure inspiring terror in the Anglican hierarchy. What surprised me about the letter I sent you was that I had imagined eminent Anglican Divines to be usually fairly civilized people. I get hundreds of letters very similar to the one I sent you, but they are generally from people with very little education. I cannot make up my mind whether the writer of the letter is gnawed with remorse for the sins he has committed or filled with regret for those that he has not committed.

Yours sincerely
RUSSELL

If Russell's bishop may seem to have had sex on the brain or, rather, imagined that Russell had, D. H. Lawrence in 1922 did his best to relocate it where he felt it should be:

> . . . The tragedy is, when you've got sex in your head, instead of down where it belongs, and when you have to go on copulating with your ears and your nose. It's such a confession of weakness, impotence. . . .

But there's the trouble; men have most of them got their sex in their head nowadays, and nowhere else. They all start their deeper reactions in their heads, and work themselves from the top downwards, which of course brings disgust, because you're only having yourself all the time, no matter what other individual you take as *machine à plaisir*, you're only taking yourself all the time.

Why don't you *jeunesse* let all the pus of festering sex out of your heads, and try to act from the original centres? The old, dark religions understood. 'God enters from below,' said the Egyptians, and that's right. Why can't you darken your minds, and know that the great gods pulse in the dark, and enter you as darkness through the lower gates. Not through the head. Why don't you seek again the unknown and invisible gods who step sometimes into your arteries, and down to the phallos, to the vagina, and have strange meetings there? . . . why don't you leave off your old white festerings in silence, and let a light fall over your mind and heal you? . . .

The nexus between sex and tenderness in Lawrence's work brings us back to the perennial problem of how much the former can exist without the latter, and all the problems that always have and always will bedevil sexual relationships. Rose Macaulay, in 1927, has something to say about it in a letter to her sister Jeanie:

> *Dearest Jeanie,*
> . . . I quite agree that the mind is the *important* part of the human affair—the only question is, which causes which. However, as you say, we shall never know. Your argument is weak about importance. Love (between man & woman) is the important part of the desire for each other, but the originator of it, which called love into being in man, is mere animal desire. I mean, the important factor often comes chronologically second. Similarly (as Socrates used to put it) the important part of an electric lamp is the light it gives, but the light is a function of the physical structure, and operates strictly within it, and would perish if the lamp were smashed. However, I am myself uncertain about body and soul!
> . . . Your loving E.R.M.

Body and soul; or just body; or just soul? In 1912, Virginia
Stephen in a frank letter to her future husband Leonard Woolf,
examines all the pressures in her own mind for and against
marrying him. It is a complicated letter from a complicated
person that tries to be honest about the lack of physical desire
she feels for him, notwithstanding her growing love:

Dearest Leonard,
   To deal with the facts first (my fingers are so cold I can
hardly write) I shall be back about 7 tomorrow, so there will be
time to discuss—but what does it mean? You can't take the
leave, I suppose, if you are going to resign certainly at the end
of it. Anyhow, it shows what a career you're ruining!
   Well then, as to all the rest. It seems to me that I am giving
you a great deal of pain—some in the most casual way—and
therefore I ought to be as plain with you as I can, because half
the time I suspect, you're in a fog which I don't see at all. Of
course I can't explain what I feel—these are some of the
things that strike me. The obvious advantages of marriage
stand in my way. I say to myself, Anyhow, you'll be quite
happy with him; and he will give you companionship, children, and a busy life—then I say By God, I will not look upon
marriage as a profession. The only people who know of it, all
think it suitable; and that makes me scrutinise my own
motives all the more. Then, of course, I feel angry sometimes
at the strength of your desire. Possibly, your being a Jew
comes in also at this point. You seem so foreign. And then I
am fearfully unstable. I pass from hot to cold in an instant,
without any reason; except that I believe sheer physical effort
and exhaustion influence me. All I can say is that in spite of
these feelings which go chasing each other all day long when I
am with you, there is some feeling which is permanent, and
growing. You want to know of course whether it will ever
make me marry you. How can I say? I think it will, because
there seems no reason why it shouldn't—But I don't know
what the future will bring. I'm half afraid of myself. I
sometimes feel that no one ever has or ever can share
something. It's the thing that makes you call me like a hill, or
a rock. Again, I want everything—love, children, adventure,
intimacy, work. (Can you make any sense out of this ramble? I
am putting down one thing after another). So I go from being
half in love with you, and wanting you to be with me always,

and know everything about me, to the extreme of wildness and aloofness. I sometimes think that if I married you, I could have everything—and then—is it the sexual side of it that comes between us? As I told you brutally the other day, I feel no physical attraction in you. There are moments—when you kissed me the other day was one—when I feel no more than a rock. And yet your caring for me as you do almost over- whelms me. It is so real, and so strange. Why should you? What am I really except a pleasant attractive creature? But it's just because you care so much that I feel I've got to care before I marry you. I feel I must give you everything; and that if I can't, well, marriage would only be second-best for you as well as for me. If you can still go on, as before, letting me find my own way, as that is what would please me best; and then we must both take the risks. But you have made me very happy too. We both of us want a marriage that is a tremendous living thing, always alive, always hot, not dead and easy in parts as most marriages are. We ask a great deal of life, don't we? Perhaps we shall get it; then, how splendid!

One doesn't get much said in a letter does one? I haven't touched upon the enormous variety of things that have been happening here—but they can wait.

. . . Yrs
VS

Virginia Woolf's letter is that of one honest and intelligent person to another; but in matters of sex honesty is too often a prey to cynicism. Some men will go to extraordinary lengths and expense to get physical gratification, often managing to deceive themselves about their feelings in the process. But some women have been strategists as good as, or better than the men. What could be more puncturing to the recipient's self-esteem than this letter of severe practicality from Marie de Vaubernier, later Comtesse du Barry, to an infatuated Monsieur Duval:

April 6th, 1761
Yes, my dear friend, I have told you, and repeat it: I love you dearly. You certainly said the same thing to me, but on your side it is only impetuousness; directly after the first enjoyment, you would think of me no more. I begin to know the world. I will tell you what I suggest, now: pay attention. I don't want to remain a shop girl, but a little more my own

mistress, and would therefore like to find someone to keep me. If I did not love you, I would try to get money from you; I would say to you, You shall begin by renting a room for me and furnishing it; only as you told me that you were not rich, you can take me to your own place. It will not cost you any more rent, not more for your table and the rest of your housekeeping. To keep me and my headdress will be the only expense, and for those give me one hundred livres a month, and that will include everything. Thus we could both live happily, and you would never again have to complain about my refusal. If you love me, accept his proposal; but if you do not love me, then let each of us try his luck elsewhere. Good-bye, I embrace you heartily.

Madame du Barry had a good run for her money as Louis XV's favourite, but her past caught up with her when the Revolution came. She was put on trial for 'wasting state treasure' and for wearing mourning for the Royal Family. She went to the guillotine, as it was said, 'vainly whimpering'.

Perhaps the most cynical discourse on sexual matters ever recorded is Benjamin Franklin's famous advice to an unknown correspondent recommending him to take an old mistress for reasons that are elegantly set out in the letter. It is a sustained exercise in outrageousness, though he does begin by advising the young man that much the best thing for him would be simply to get married. Having satisfied conventional mores with this piece of advice, Franklin sets out the alternative:

. . . But if you will not take this Counsel, and persist in thinking a Commerce with the Sex inevitable, then I repeat my former Advice, that in all your Amours you should *prefer old Women to young ones*. You call this a Paradox, and demand my Reasons. They are these:

1 Because as they have more Knowledge of the World and their Minds are better stor'd with Observations, their Conversation is more improving and more lastingly agreeable.

2 Because when Women cease to be handsome, they study to be good. To maintain their Influence over Men, they supply the Diminution of Beauty by an Augmentation of Utility. They learn to do a 1000 Services small and great, and are the most tender and useful of all Friends when you are sick. Thus they continue amiable. And hence there is hardly

such a thing to be found as an old Woman who is not a good Woman.

3   Because there is no hazard of Children, which irregularly produc'd may be attended with much Inconvenience.

4   Because thro' more Experience, they are more prudent and discreet in conducting an Intrigue to prevent Suspicion. The Commerce with them is therefore safer with regard to your Reputation. And with regard to theirs, if the Affair should happen to be known, considerate people might be rather inclin'd to excuse an old Woman who would kindly take care of a young Man, form his Manners by her good Counsels, and prevent his ruining his Health and Fortune among mercenary Prostitutes.

5   Because in every Animal that walks upright, the Deficiency of the Fluids that fill the Muscles appears first in the highest Part: The Face first grows lank and wrinkled; then the Neck, then the Breast and Arms; The lower Parts continuing to the last as plump as ever: so that covering all above with a Basket, and regarding only what is below the Girdle, it is impossible of two women to know an old from a young one. And as in the dark all Cats are grey, the Pleasure of corporal Enjoyment with an old Woman is at least equal, and frequently superior, every Knack being by Practice capable of Improvement.

6   Because the Sin is less. The debauching a Virgin may be her Ruin, and make her for Life unhappy.

7   Because the Compunction is less. The having made a young Girl *miserable* may give you frequent bitter Reflections; none of which can attend the making an old Woman *happy*.

8   (thly and Lastly) They are *so grateful!!* Thus much for my Paradox. But still I advise you to marry directly; being sincerely Your affectionate Friend.

After the tepid bath of Franklin's sly rationality it is refreshing to turn to a writer who movingly evoked the transcendental element in human sexuality in one of his limpid and inspiring letters to a young poet. His name was Rainer Maria Rilke:

> . . . Those who come together in the night time and entwine in swaying delight perform a serious work and gather up sweetness, depth and strength for the song of some poet that is to be, who will rise to tell of unspeakable bliss.

And they summon the future; and even though they go astray and embrace blindly, yet the future comes, a new human being arises, and on the basis of the chance occurrence which here seems consummated, awakens the law by which a resistant vigorous seed forces its way to the egg-cell that advanced openly to meet it. Do not let yourself be misled by outward appearances; in the depths everything becomes law. And those who live the secret falsely and badly (and they are very many) only lose it for themselves and yet hand it on like a sealed letter, without knowing it.

6

Contemplating Matrimony

A perennial hazard in embarking upon matrimony has been that of incurring parental wrath—the wrong person has been selected, or the wrong time, or the wrong place. After Wolfgang Amadeus Mozart married secretly he faced the delicate task of breaking the news to his father, Leopold. The latter was not best pleased at seeing his money-spinning offspring slipping from his grasp, and perhaps devoting much of his time to a wife and children. Mozart does his best, but there is an air of desperation about his touching letter:

Vienna, 15 December 1781

Dearest Father,

You ask me for an explanation of the words with which I ended my last letter! Oh, how gladly would I have opened my heart to you long since; but I held back lest you should reproach me for *thinking of such a thing unseasonably*—although thinking can never be unseasonable . . . To marry!—You are alarmed by the idea? But I entreat you, dearest, most beloved Father, to listen to me! I was obliged to disclose my intentions to you, now permit me also to disclose my reasons, which indeed are forcible ones. Nature's voice speaks within me as loudly as in any other man, and perhaps louder than in many a tall, strong lout. I cannot lead the same life as most young men do nowadays. Firstly, I have too much religion, secondly, too much love of my neighbour and sense of honour, to be able to seduce an innocent girl, and thirdly, too much horror and disgust, dread and fear of diseases, and too much regard for my health, to be running after whores. Thus I can swear that until now I have had no dealings of this kind with any woman. If it had happened I would not conceal it from you, for it is always natural enough for a man to err, and to err *once* would be mere weakness—though I would not trust myself to promise that I should be satisfied with a single error if I once indulged myself in this respect—but I can stake my life on this assurance to you. I am well aware that this reason, powerful though it always is, has not sufficient weight. But my temperament is more disposed towards a tranquil, domestic life than towards rowdiness; moreover from youth up I have never been accustomed to attend to my own affairs, such as linen, clothes, etc.—and I can think of nothing more necessary to me than a wife. I assure you that I am often put to needless expense because I do not give heed to anything—I am quite persuaded that with a wife (and the same income I have by myself) I should manage better than I do as it is. And how many needless expenses would be saved! One incurs others in their stead, that is true—but one knows what they are, one can allow for them—in short, one leads a well-ordered life. In my eyes a bachelor is only half alive—my eyes are like that, I cannot help it. I have considered and reflected sufficiently on the matter, and my mind is made up. But who then is the object of my love? Do not be alarmed again, I implore you; but surely she is not a Weber?—Yes, a Weber—but not Josepha—not Sophie.—It is *Konstanze*, the middle one. I never met such different natures in any family as in this one. The eldest daughter is a lazy, coarse, perfidious creature and as sly as a fox. Madame Lange [Aloysia, his former love] is a false, malicious creature and a coquette. The youngest—is still too young to be anything at all—is nothing more than a kind-hearted but too frivolous girl! May God preserve her from seduction. The middle one, however, namely my dear, kind Konstanze, is the martyr among them, and perhaps for that very reason the most warm-hearted, the cleverest, and in short the best of them all. She attends to everything in the house, and yet can do nothing right. Oh, dearest Father, I could fill whole pages if I were to describe to you all the scenes the two of us have witnessed in that house . . . She is not ugly, but she is far from beautiful. Her only beauties are a pair of little black eyes and a lovely figure. She has no wit, but enough good sense to be able to carry out her duties as wife and mother. She is not inclined to extravagance . . . and most of what a woman needs she can make for herself, and she dresses her own hair every day as well— understands housekeeping, has the kindest heart in the world—I love her, and she loves me with all her heart. Tell me, could I wish myself a better wife?

A business-like approach to marriage (the norm for most of history) didn't preclude affection, but affection by itself was not considered to be a sufficient reason for marrying. In the eyes of prudent parents it was a dangerous irrelevance if it encouraged a match that was unsuitable from the social and economic point of view. All the same, money was not the only consideration, at least for Michelangelo, who advises his nephew Lionardo in Florence about his marriage in the following letter. Having said that he is not in a position to give advice he characteristically goes on to give a lot of it. He clearly doesn't trust Lionardo not to botch matters:

> *1 February 1549*
>
> *Lionardo*: In my last I sent you a list of eligible girls, which was sent me from there, I believe by some broker, and he must be a man of little judgement, since he should have considered what sort of information I could have on the families of Florence after I have been living in Rome sixteen or seventeen years.
>
> So I tell you, if you want to get married do not be at my back, because I cannot advise you of the best; but I do tell you not to go after money, but only virtue and good reputation.
>
> I believe there are many poor and noble families in Florence with whom it would be a charity to become allied, even if there were no dowry, because there would also be no pride. You need one who will stay with you and whom you can command, and who will not put on airs and go to banquets and weddings every day; for where a court is it is easy to become a whore, and especially for one without relatives. And to say it seems you want to become ennobled shows a lack of respect, because it is known we are ancient Florentine citizens and as noble as any other house; so put your trust in God and pray Him to give you what you need, and I shall be very glad if when you find something you feel is suitable, you let me know before you close the alliance.

Sir William Stonor, the head of an influential family in medieval England, finding himself in the position of requiring a new wife after the death of his previous one, clearly took an unsentimental view of the business. He put out feelers through his relations for a suitable lady and had apparently issued a checklist of the necessary attributes of candidates. His cousin,

Thomas Restwold, writes back in reply to an inquiry from Stonor in 1480 or 1481, giving such intelligence as he had been able to obtain about one possible spouse. He is modestly encouraging:

> *Right worshipful Sir and Cousin*, I recommend me unto you. Sir, I moved my lord of the matter that ye desired me, and he told me that he had heard of her that she was so foul that Parker would none of her; wherefore my lord thought she were not for you, though she had 500 marks of land. Then I desired his lordship that he would send for Page, for I supposed he could tell the truth. My lord did so, and Page saith she is but little and somewhat round, a good woman and well disposed, save only that she is sometime vexed with the mother [womb], as ye have heard, and is 27 years of age. My lord thinketh she were for you, if you be pleased, for his opinion is that bearing of children should ease her infirmity and so ye be much beholden unto my lord.
>
> In haste at London.
>
> > Your own
> > THOS. RESTWOLD

From this rather bleak epistle it is refreshing to turn to a prospectus that G. K. Chesterton issued about himself to Frances Blogg. Although a little whimsical it is full of charm:

> . . . I am looking over the sea and endeavouring to reckon up the estate I have to offer you. As far as I can make out my equipment for starting on a journey to fairyland consists of the following items.
>
> 1st. A straw Hat. The oldest part of this admirable relic shows traces of pure Norman work. The vandalism of Cromwell's soldiers has left us little of the original hat-band.
>
> 2nd. A Walking Stick, very knobby and heavy: admirably fitted to break the head of any denizen of Suffolk who denies that you are the noblest of ladies, but of no other manifest use.
>
> 3rd. A copy of Walt Whitman's poems, once nearly given to Salter, but quite forgotten. It has his name in it still with an affectionate inscription from his sincere friend Gilbert Chesterton. I wonder if he will ever have it.
>
> 4th. A number of letters from a young lady, containing

everything good and generous and loyal and holy and wise that isn't in Walt Whitman's poems.

5th. An unwieldy sort of a pocket knife, the blades mostly having an edge of a more varied and picturesque outline than is provided by the prosaic cutler. The chief element however is a thing 'to take stones out of a horse's hoof'. What a beautiful sensation of security it gives one to reflect that if one should ever have money enough to buy a horse and should happen to buy one and the horse should happen to have a stone in his hoof—that one is ready; one stands prepared, with a defiant smile!

6th. Passing from the last miracle of practical foresight, we come to a box of matches. Every now and then I strike one of these, because fire is beautiful and burns your fingers. Some people think this a waste of matches: the same people who object to the building of Cathedrals.

7th. About three pounds in gold and silver, the remains of one of Mr Unwin's bursts of affection; those explosions of spontaneous love for myself, which, such is the perfect order and harmony of his mind, occur at startlingly exact intervals of time.

8th. A book of Children's Rhymes, in manuscript, called the 'Weather Book' about ¾ finished, and destined for Mr Nutt. I have been working at it fairly steadily, which I think jolly creditable under the circumstances. One can't put anything interesting in it. They'll understand those things when they grow up.

9th. A tennis racket—nay, start not. It is a part of the new régime, and the only new and neat-looking thing in the Museum. We'll soon mellow it—like the straw hat. My brother and I are teaching each other lawn tennis.

10th. A soul, hitherto idle and omnivorous but now happy enough to be ashamed of itself.

11th. A body, equally idle and quite equally omnivorous, absorbing tea, coffee, claret, sea-water, and oxygen to its own perfect satisfaction. It is happiest swimming, I think, the sea being about a convenient size.

12th. A Heart—mislaid somewhere. And that is about all the property of which an inventory can be made at present. After all, my tastes are stoically simple. A straw hat, a stick, a box of matches and some of his own poetry. What more does a man require? . . .

In the following letter Evelyn Waugh proposed to his second wife. Evelyn (née Gardner), his first wife, had left him, and the marriage was eventually annulled. Waugh was savagely hurt by this, and such references as there are to it in his letters are bitter ones. His new wife, Laura Herbert, was in fact a cousin of his first wife. Waugh's analysis of himself as a potential husband is pretty frank; indeed his entire sales pitch is startlingly negative:

Tell you what you might do while you are alone at Pixton. You might think about me a bit & whether, if those wop priests ever come to a decent decision, you could bear the idea of marrying me. Of course you haven't got to decide, but think about it. I can't advise you in my favour because I think it would be beastly for you, but think how nice it would be for me. I am restless & moody & misanthropic & lazy & have no money except what I earn and if I got ill you would starve. In fact it's a lousy proposition. On the other hand I think I could do a Grant and reform & become quite strict about not getting drunk and I am pretty sure I should be faithful. Also there is always a fair chance that there will be another bigger economic crash in which case if you had married a nobleman with a great house you might find yourself starving, while I am very clever and could probably earn a living of some sort somewhere. Also though you would be taking on an elderly buffer, I am without fixed habits. You wouldn't find yourself confined to any particular place or group. Also I have practically no living relatives except one brother whom I scarcely know. You would not find yourself involved in a large family & all their rows & you would not be patronized & interfered with by odious sisters in law & aunts as often happens. All these are very small advantages compared with the awfulness of my character. I have always tried to be nice to you and you may have got it into your head that I am nice really, but that is all rot. It is only to you & for you. I am jealous & impatient—but there is no point in going into a whole list of my vices. You are a critical girl and I've no doubt that you know them all and a great many I don't know myself. But the point I wanted to make is that if you marry most people, you are marrying a great number of objects & other people as well; well if you marry me there is nothing else involved, and that is an advantage as well as a disadvantage. My only tie of any kind is my work. That means that for several months each year we shall have to separate or you would have to share some very lonely place with me. But apart from that we could do what we liked & go where we liked—and if you married a soldier or stockbroker or member of parliament or master of hounds you would be more tied. When I tell my friends that I am in love with a girl of 19 they look shocked and say 'wretched child' but I don't look on you as very young even in your beauty and I don't think there is any sense in the line that you cannot possibly commit yourself to a decision that affects your whole life for years yet. But anyway there is no point in your deciding or even answering. I may never get free of your cousin Evelyn. Above all things, darling, don't fret at all. But just turn the matter over in your dear head.

Courtship and proposal in Victorian times seems to have been a traumatic affair, and often conducted in the full glare of a censorious family. It is hardly surprising that the Earl of Airlie, a shy man, should nearly have made a mess of things in wooing a daughter of the formidable Stanleys of Alderley. But he got himself launched at last, and on 4 August 1851 Lady Alderley wrote to her husband with the dramatic details that led to the big moment.

After some talk I left him to go to Blanche, & found her on her knees in her room, very nervous, but much happier, & then she told me how it all happened, that they went off walking & he never spoke all the time till she grew so faint & cold she said she must sit down. He then said he hoped she would not be angry but he must speak—she covered her face with her hands & he went on & said he was neither as good nor as clever as she was, but that he loved her very much, & she never answering till she says he took her hand & spoke in such agony & told her she frightened him, & then she answered that she would try to make him happy, but she said her voice sounded cold and different to his. She then asked him if he cld give up the thing he liked best for her, meaning racing, & he said he would, & she asked him if he had ever loved Lady Rachel at which he laughed & said never. She also asked him if he had ever liked anyone & he said he had been in love with Martia Fox, & she was kind enough to say that she did not mind that as she was dead.

. . . She told me tonight she was afraid when she met him

something dreadful would happen, meaning he would kiss her which he has not ventured to do & that he called her Blanche, all of which she will get used to. I think her conscience smote her for the rude way she spoke when he remarked on Bacon's essays, a book she is very fond of, that it was a deep book; she said, 'Oh yes, one you would not care to look into' & he answered 'You seem to think I cannot understand any book, & yet I know that one well' in a very quiet tone.

Perhaps the best thing to do when proposing is to keep matters as brief as possible. This was the course adopted by Samuel Parr, an eighteenth-century schoolmaster who was for a while suspected of being 'Junius', the composer of seventy satirical letters on political and social matters of the day which appeared in Woodfall's *Public Advertiser* from 21 January 1769 to 21 January 1772. (There are, however, some forty other possible condidates for authorship, of whom Sir Philip Francis seems to get the most votes.) One can see why knowing who 'Junius' was might have been one inducement to matrimony for the sharp-tongued Jane Morsingale—though surely not the clinching one. But she accepted him, and one commentator has observed: 'There is little doubt that in married life she made up in talking what had been missed when they were courting':

> *Madam*, You are a very charming woman, and I should be happy to obtain you as a wife. If you accept my proposal I will tell you who was the author of Junius.
>
> S.P.

In contrast to Parr, Franz Kafka, must have been the most vacillating 'lover' ever. Page after page of neurotic prose is poured out to the long-suffering Felice Bauer. It is mostly obsessive self-analysis. At one point they are engaged, then Kafka has one of his '*crises*' and it seems they are not. This happened twice. Corresponding with him was like riding in the big dipper at a fairground where you suspect they have inadequate safety precautions. In the letter that follows he makes a proposal—of sorts—keeping a medical trump card up his sleeve in case Felice should accept too enthusiastically and he should have to beat a tactical retreat. In the continuation of the letter he tries another tack—his intellectual inadequacy. It seems Felice was not deceived, knowing that Kafka, as usual, was merely soliciting 24-hour-a-day reassurance.

> By now you must realize my peculiar position. What comes between you and me is, above all, the doctor. What he will have to say is doubtful, the medical diagnosis is not the most decisive factor in these decisions; if it were, it wouldn't be worth obtaining. As I said, I have not actually been ill, and yet I am. It is possible that different circumstances might make me well, but it is impossible for these different circumstances to be created. The medical decision (which I can say at once won't necessarily be decisive for me) will depend solely on the unknown doctor's character. My family doctor, for instance, with his stupid irresponsibility, wouldn't see the slightest objection, on the contrary. Another and better doctor might throw up his hands in dismay.
> Now consider, Felice, in view of this uncertainty, it is difficult to say the word, and indeed it is bound to sound rather strange. Clearly, it's too soon to say it. But afterwards, it would be too late: there wouldn't be any time to discuss matters of the kind you mentioned in your last letter. But there also isn't time for endless hesitations, at least this is what I feel about it, and so I ask: in view of the above—alas, irremediable—conditions, will you consider whether you wish to be my wife? Will you do that?

It is hard to envisage marriage to Kafka as anything other than an act of self-sacrifice. Marriage to Tolstoy was also no bed of roses and got progressively less attractive as the old man grew steadily crankier and more dogmatic. But in a letter to his son Ilya written in 1887 Tolstoy has some penetrating things to say about what he sees as healthy and unhealthy motives for getting married. He illustrates his point by means of what teachers call a 'visual aid'.

> . . . This is what I think: to marry in order to enjoy oneself more will never work. To put marriage—union with the person you love—as your main aim, replacing everything else, is a big mistake. And it's obvious if you think about it. The aim is marriage. Well, you get married, and then what? If you have no other aim in life before marriage, then later on it will be terribly difficult, almost impossible for the two of you,

to find one. It's almost certain that if you have no common aim before marriage, nothing will bring you together afterwards, and you will always be falling out. Marriage only brings happiness when there is a single aim—people meet on the road and say, 'Let's walk on together'; 'yes, let's'; and offer one another their hands—and not when people are attracted to one another and then both turn off the road in different directions. In the first case it will be like this:

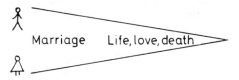

In the second, like this:

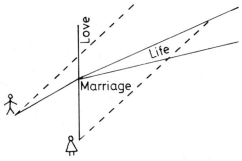

I say all this because the idea many people have that life is a vale of tears is just as false as the idea which the great majority have, and to which youth, health and wealth incline you, that life is a place of entertainment. Life is a place of service, where one sometimes has occasion to put up with a lot that is hard, but more often to experience a great many joys. Only there can only be real joys when people themselves understand their life as service: have a definite aim in life outside themselves and their own personal happiness. Usually married people forget this completely. Marriage and the birth of children offer so many joyful things to look forward to that it seems that these things actually constitute life itself, but this is a dangerous delusion. If parents live and produce children without having any aim in life, they only put off the question of the aim of life and the punishment to which people are subjected when they live without knowing why—they only put it off, but they can't avoid it, because they will have to bring up and guide children and there will be nothing to guide them by. And then parents lose their human qualities and the happiness linked with them, and become pedigree cattle. . . .

The inevitably finite nature of passion was much discussed in the eighteenth century. Miss Mulso, or Mrs Hester Chapone as she became, had plenty of advice on the subject. Mrs Chapone was one of the Bluestockings, an intellectual circle founded by Mrs Montagu in 1750. ('Blue-stocking' as a name for the club was derived from the fact that a male member of it, Mr Benjamin Stillingfleet, was famous for his blue stockings. The Bluestocking Club and its precursors in the Paris of 1590 and the Venice of 1400 all included women *and* men in their ranks.)

In the following extract from a letter to a newly-married lady, Mrs Chapone puts passion in its place:

> Swift (and almost every male writer on the subject) pronounces that the passion of love in men is infallibly destroyed by possession, and can subsist but a short time after marriage. What a dreadful sentence must this appear to you at this time! Your heart, which feels its own affection increased, knows not how to support the idea of such a change in the beloved object: but, my dear friend, the God of Nature, who provided the passion of love as the incitement to marriage, has also provided resources for the happiness of this his own institution, which kind and uncorrupted natures will not fail to find. It is not, indeed, intended that we should pass our lives in the delirium of passion, but whilst this subsides, the habit of affection grows strong. The tumult and anxiety of desire must of course be at an end when the object is secure; but a milder and more serene happiness succeeds, which in good hearts creates a tenderness that is often wanting amidst the fervours of violent passion. Before this palls, your business is to build the solid foundation of a durable friendship.

Unfortunately the 'milder, more serene happiness' does not necessarily ensue. Marriages rot as well as ripen. In the following grim letter—perhaps the only means of communicating with each other that they could by then bear—from Noël Coward's mother to his father, the final stage seems to have been reached:

Dear Arthur, This letter will probably come as a shock to you, I have made friends so often and it has taken a long time to kill my affection for you, but you have at last succeeded in doing so . . . As long as I can remember, not once have you ever stood up for me or the boys when we have been in any little trouble, you have *always* taken the opposite side and been against us. I remember so many times when you have failed me: and this has been the last straw. How *dare* you behave as you have been doing lately. I have never been so miserable in my life since I came from Ceylon, and who are you to dare to make my life so unhappy. What have you ever done for me or for either of your fine boys to help them on in life. You have never done anything to help anybody, and everything has been done for you. And yet you are so far from being ashamed of yourself that you plump yourself down on us, full of conceit, selfishness and self appreciation and spoil our lives for us. No one with any pretensions to being a gentleman could ever bully any woman as you bully my sister. It is *shameful* in front of those children too. [Presumably Noël and Erik.] She has as great a right to be here as you have. Noël chose to give her a home before he gave you one, and why are you not earning your living? You are strong and healthy and will no doubt live to be 100, a burden on Noël, not to speak of putting your wife on him too. Now I have come to a decision. I am going to add still more to poor Noël's burden and ask him to provide you with another home. If he agrees I will find you a cottage somewhere, with a little less grandeur than you have here which will do you good. Noël has always understood your character and what I have been through, and will do anything he can to make me happy again. For the present things must remain as they are and I must put up with you, but in a different way. I shall never stand up for you again as I have always done, and I tell you definitely, everything is over between you and me. The last scrap of my affection for you has gone and it is entirely your own fault. Violet.

In contrast to the bleak conjugal relations of the Cowards, Mr and Mrs Martin Luther had a lively relationship. Although Luther can hardly have been a restful sort of husband, Catharine Luther was not the kind of person to be daunted by his erratic temper and earthy language. What they shared was a strong sense of humour, an almost essential ingredient in any marriage. It can be seen in this delightful letter from husband to wife written in 1546:

> Grace and peace in Christ. Most holy lady doctoress! I thank you kindly for your great anxiety which keeps you awake. Since you began to worry we have almost had a fire at the inn, just in front of my door, and yesterday, due to your anxiety no doubt, a stone nearly fell on my head which would have squeezed it up as a trap does a mouse. For in my bedroom lime and cement had dribbled down on my head for two days, until I called attention to it, and then the people of the inn just touched a stone as big as a bolster and two spans wide, which thereupon fell out of the ceiling. For this I thank your anxiety, but the dear angels protected me. I fear that unless you stop worrying the earth will swallow me up or the elements will persecute me. Do you not know the catechism and the creed? Pray, and let God take thought as it is written: 'Cast thy burden on the Lord and he shall sustain thee,' both in Psalm 55 and other places.
>
> I am, thank God, well and sound, except that the business in hand disgusts me, and Jonas takes upon himself to have a bad leg, where he hit himself on a trunk; people are so selfish that this envious man would not allow me to have the bad leg. God bless you. I would willingly be free of this place and return home if God will. Amen. Amen. Amen.
>
> Your holiness's obedient servant,
MARTIN LUTHER

Almost as important as a sense of humour in close human relationships is a sense of realism. A striking example of this in action is provided by Lady Mary Wortley Montagu's account of a lady kidnapped into the Ottoman Empire who decided to make a virtue of necessity and married her captor. She describes the situation in an amusing letter to the Countess of Bute in 1718, making the story sound like a novel by E. M. Hull, a true tale of Turkish delight:

> I am well acquainted with a Christian Woman of Quality who made it her choice to live with a Turkish Husband, and is a very agreeable sensible Lady. Her story is so extraordinary I cannot forbear relating it, but I promise you it shall be in as

few words as I can possibly express it. She is a Spaniard, and was at Naples with her family when that Kingdom was part of the Spanish Dominion. Coming from thence in a Feloucca, accompany'd by her Brother, they were attack'd by the Turkish Admiral, boarded and taken; and now, how shall I modestly tell you the rest of her Adventure? The same Accident happen'd to her that happen'd to the fair Lucretia so many Years before her, but she was too good a Christian to kill her selfe as that heathenish Roman did. The Admiral was so much charm'd with the Beauty and long-suffering of the Fair Captive that as his first compliment he gave immediate Liberty to her Brother and attendants, who made haste to Spain and in a few months sent the sum of £4,000 sterling as a Ransom for his sister. The Turk took the Money, which he presented to her, and told her she was at Liberty, but the Lady very discreetly weigh'd the different treatment she was likely to find in her native Country. Her Catholic Relations, as the kindest thing they could do for her in her present Circumstances, would certainly confine her to a Nunnery for the rest of her Days. Her Infidel Lover was very handsome, very tender, fond of her, and lavish'd at her feet all the Turkish Magnificence. She answer'd him very resolutely that her Liberty was not so precious to her as her Honnour, that he could no way restore that but by marrying her. She desir'd him to accept the Ransom as her Portion and give her the satisfaction of knowing no Man could boast of her favours without being her Husband. The Admiral was transported at this kind offer and sent back the Money to her Relations, saying he was too happy in her Possession. He marry'd her and never took any other wife, and (she says her selfe) she never had any reason to repent the choice she made. He left her some years after one of the richest widoes in Constantinople, but there is no remaining honnourably a single woman, and that consideration has oblig'd her to marry the present Capitan Bassa (i.e. Admiral), his Successor. I am afraid you'l think that my Freind fell in love with her Ravisher, but I am willing to take her word for it that she acted wholly on principles of Honnour, tho I think she might be reasonably touch'd at his Generosity, which is very often found amongst the Turks of Rank.

Lady Mary Wortley Montagu's acquaintance clearly took a relaxed and sensible view of the marital state. Much the same

could be said of the historian Lecky writing to his friend
Knightley Wilmot-Chetwoode (the Alice in the letter is
Wilmot-Chetwoode's sister). His attitude to his proposed marriage is, like his prose style, exceedingly leisured; he is certainly
not swept away by the winds of passion, which, as one of the
least biased of historians, he no doubt deeply mistrusted. But he
does appear rather to like the lady. Their honeymoon consisted
of an extensive Continental tour, and lasted some nine months;
not, one supposes, nine months of torrid passion.

> . . . I have a piece of news about myself which may perhaps
> interest you a little, but hating gossip on such matters greatly I
> should rather it did not pass just yet outside your family
> circle. I rather think I am going to launch upon the great sea of
> matrimony. On the whole I think for various reasons it may
> be better. The lady is Dutch, a Baroness de Dedem, Maid of
> Honour to the Queen of Holland. She is more like Alice than
> anyone else I know, though not quite so argumentative, and
> like her a little mystical. She is nearly twenty-nine, speaks
> English as well as I do, and French, German and her own
> tongue equally well. She is very poor which I am sorry for, but
> between saving and literature and Church property I hope to
> have enough for both. I mean to go for a little to the Hague
> towards the end of the year and we will then make out
> whether the matter is definitely come to pass. . . .

Uxoriousness, while doubtless agreeable for the participants,
can be an awful bore for bystanders. One of the aspects of
Browning's love poetry and his letters that demands much
patience of the reader is his tendency to overdo things in this
respect. All the same, uxoriousness has its charming side, as in
this vignette of Victoria and Albert at home in a letter from Lady
Lyttelton, one of Victoria's Ladies-in-Waiting, to her daughter in
1840:

> . . . The Queen was cold (as indeed had long been all Her
> Majesty's loving subjects and servants then with her) the
> other evening—the great drawing-room having but one of its
> fires burning, and few people in it. She said, 'I am sadly cold.
> I should like the other fire lighted.' Then low to me, 'Tell Lord
> Poltimore to go and ask the Prince if he would like the other

fire lighted.' Of course the Prince did like it, but the thing tho'
small, struck me as a pretty bit of *wifeism*.

Lady Lyttelton reports another bit of *wifeism* a few days later:

> . . . Then at bedtime the Queen, evidently much tired and
> sleepy, won my heart over again by saying to me, 'Tell Lord
> Alfred to let the Prince know that it is eleven o'clock' (he was
> at his everlasting double chess, very deep); 'Tell him the
> Prince should *merely* be told the hour. The Prince *wishes* to be
> told, I know. He does not see the clock.' And quite fussy she
> seemed for fear of a disrespectful message or anything like a
> command being sent.

Arranged or dynastic marriages do not preclude warmth and
intimacy. Margaret and John Paston seem to have been close
even though their marriage was chiefly planned to further the
interests of the Paston family. Writing to her absent husband
only shortly after their marriage in 1441, Margaret happily
reveals what had become an open secret:

> Right reverend and worshipful husband, I commend
> myself to you, desiring heartily to hear of your welfare,
> thanking you for the token that you sent me by Edmund
> Perys. Please let me tell you that my mother sent to my father
> in London for some grey woollen gown cloth, to make me a
> gown, and he told my mother and me when he came home
> that he had instructed you to buy it after you left London. If it
> is not yet bought, please be so kind as to buy it and send it
> home as soon as you can, for I have no gown to wear this
> winter except my black and green one with tapes, and that is
> so cumbersome that I am tired of wearing it.
> As to the girdle that my father promised me, I spoke to him
> about it a little while before he last went to London, and he
> said to me that it was your fault, because you would not think
> about having it made: but I expect that it is not so—he said it
> just as an excuse. I ask you, if you dare take it upon you, to be
> so good as to have it made in time for your return home, for I
> never needed it more than I do now, for I have grown so fat
> that no belt or girdle that I have will go round me . . .
> John Damme was here, and my mother revealed my secret
> to him and he said by his troth that he was not so pleased by

arrything he had heard for the last twelve months as he was by that news. I can no longer live by cunning; my secret is revealed to everyone who sees me. I sent you word of all the other things that you desired me to send word of in a letter I wrote on Our Lady's day last [8 December].

The Holy Trinity have you in their keeping. Written at Oxnead in very great haste on the Thursday before St Thomas's day.

Please wear the ring with the image of St Margaret that I sent you as a keepsake until you come home. You have left me such a keepsake as makes me think of you both day and night when I want to sleep.

Yours, M.P.

Even a broken marriage sometimes leaves an afterglow of the happiness and intimacy that we see in Margaret Paston's letter to her husband. A pleasantly sentimental story of a broken marriage with a legacy of continuing friendship may serve to remind us that divorces are not always conducted in a welter of bitterness. Rupert Hart-Davis, writing to his friend George Lyttelton relates a dream; not a dream of fair women exactly, but of happier times and shared pleasures:

Other people's dreams are always tedious, but I shall tell you a recent one of mine nevertheless. When we were both twenty-two I married an enchanting actress called Peggy Ashcroft: it was a sad failure: we were much too young to know what we wanted, and actresses should never marry, especially young ones. Anyhow, after much agony we parted and were duly divorced. Nowadays Peggy and I lunch together perhaps once or twice a year in a Soho restaurant and have a lovely nostalgic-romantic talk of shared memories of long ago. She is a lovely person and the best actress living—did you see her Hedda Gabler? Some months ago, when I hadn't seen or consciously thought of her for months, I dreamed that we were lunching together as usual, and she asked me: 'Do you think you could ever be in love with me again as you were when we were young?' I answered: 'The lightning never strikes twice in the same place, but the sun shines on for ever.' Then I woke up. Next day I remembered the dream and wrote to tell P. of it. She was much pleased. I tremble to think what Freud would make of it, but it strikes me as beautiful. You needn't fear a spate of dream-recital, for I scarcely ever remember one. Do you? Now I must go to bed. Goodnight, dear George. You don't know what a godsend you are.

To lose a wife or a husband after only a few years of shared happiness is a numbing experience that few find the words to express. But the simplest are often the most powerful, as in this moving letter from a bereaved wife, remembering her husband who had been killed in a mining disaster at Whitehaven in 1914:

> . . . God took my man but I could never forget him he was the best man that ever lived at least I thought that, maybe it was just that I got the right kind of man. We had been married for 25 years and they were hard years at that, many a thing we both done without for the sake of the children. We had 11 and if I had him back I would live the same life over again. Just when we were beginning to stand on our feet I lost him I can't get over it when I think of him how happy he was that morning going to work and telling me he would hurry home, but I have been waiting a long time now. At night when I am sitting and I hear clogs coming down the street I just sit and wait hoping they are coming to my door, then they go right on and my heart is broke.

The grief of separation and loneliness expressed in this letter echoes down the ages. In the following letter, another wife writes her last letter to her husband before his death. John Penruddock was to be executed on Cromwell's orders for his part in a Royalist uprising at Exeter. The eloquent love of the letter suggests that Penruddock was no ordinary husband, and Arundel was no ordinary wife, but that they were two rather unusually sensitive and noble people:

May 3, 1655

My Dear Heart,—My sad parting was so far from making me forget you, that I scarce thought upon myself since, but wholly upon you. Those dear embraces which I yet feel, and shall never lose, being the faithful testimonies of an indulgent husband, have charmed my soul to such a reverence of your remembrance, that were it possible, I would, with my own blood, cement your dead limbs to live again, and (with reverence) think it no sin to rob Heaven a little longer of a martyr. Oh! my dear, you must now pardon my passion, this being my last (oh fatal word!) that ever you will receive from me; and know, that until the last minute that I can imagine you shall live, I shall sacrifice the prayers of a Christian, and the groans of an afflicted wife. And when you are not (which sure by sympathy I shall know), I shall wish my own dissolution with you, that so we may go hand in hand to Heaven. 'Tis too late to tell you what I have, or rather have not done for you; how being turned out of doors because I came to beg mercy; the Lord lay not your blood to their charge. . .

My dear,

Your sad, but constant wife, even to love your ashes when dead,

ARUNDEL PENRUDDOCK

May 3rd, 1655, eleven o'clock at night. Your children beg your blessing, and present their duties to you.

7

All In The Family

What more delicate letter is there to be written than that of a son to his father requesting an injection of funds? Depending on the father, it requires tact, humility, possibly a recognition of past improvidence and a determination to do better in the future, and a frank appeal to the parent's most noble qualities. Robert Louis Stevenson provides as good a model as any in this thoughtfully phrased request written in 1866:

> *Torquay*
> *Respected Paternal Relative*: I write to make a request of the most moderate nature. Every year I have cost you an enormous—nay, elephantine—sum of money for drugs and physician's fees, and the most expensive time of the twelve months was March.
> But this year the biting Oriental blasts, the howling tempests, and the general ailments of the human race have been successfully braved by yours truly.
> Does not this deserve remuneration?
> I appeal to your charity, I appeal to your generosity, I appeal to your justice, I appeal to your accounts, I appeal, in fine, to your purse.
> My sense of generosity forbids the receipt of more—my sense of justice forbids the receipt of less—than half-a-crown.— Greeting from, Sir, your most affectionate and needy son.

This would have been hard to resist. Perhaps in order to ward off the possibility of mellifluous and ingratiating letters, Lord Chesterfield in a letter to his son outlines what expenses he will undertake to bear with some precision. With even more precision he details those activities which he *declines* to subsidize:

. . . Having thus reckoned up all the decent expenses of a gentleman, which, I will most readily defray, I come now to those which I will neither bear nor supply. The first of these is gaming, which, though I have not the least reason to suspect you of, I think it necessary eventually to assure you that no consideration in the world shall ever make me pay your play-debts; should you ever urge to me that your honour is pawned, I should not immovably answer you, that it was your honour, not mine, that was pawned, and that your creditor might even take the pawn for the debt.

Low company and low pleasures are always much more costly than liberal and elegant ones. The disgraceful riots of a tavern are much more expensive, as well as dishonourable, than the (sometimes pardonable) excesses in good company. I must absolutely hear of no tavern scrapes and squabbles.

I come now to another and very material point; I mean women; and I will not address myself to you upon this subject, either in a religious, a moral, or a parental style. I will even lay aside my age, remember yours, and speak to you, as one man of pleasure, if he had parts too, would speak to another. I will, by no means, pay for whores, and their never-failing consequences, surgeons; nor will I, upon any account, keep singers, dancers, actresses, and *id genus omne*; and, independently of the expense, I must tell you, that such connections would give me, and all sensible people, the utmost contempt for your parts and address: a young fellow must have as little sense as address, to venture, or more properly to sacrifice his health, and ruin his fortune, with such sort of creatures; in such a place as Paris especially, where gallantry is both the profession and the practice of every woman of fashion. To speak plainly, I will not forgive your understanding c——s and p——s; nor will your constitution forgive them you. These distempers, as well as their cures, fall nine times in ten upon the lungs. This argument, I am sure, ought to have weight with you; for I protest to you, that if you meet with any such accident, I would not give one year's purchase for your life.

Lastly, there is another sort of expense that I will not allow, only because it is a silly one; I mean the fooling away your money in baubles at toyshops. Have one handsome snuff-box (if you take snuff) and one handsome sword; but then no more very pretty and very useless things . . .

In contrast to Lord Chesterfield's tough-minded approach, the following letter from a resigned Duke of Argyll to his son Lord Lorne in 1804 is as generous as his admonitions are just:

My Dear George,
For still I must call you so, in spite of Your extreme folly and unkindness to me as well as to Your Brother and Sisters, who must be deprived in part of what my affection would allot for them in support of their expences. I have signed the deeds brought to me by Ferrier, and with this, I sign my forgiveness, for anger or resentment is not in my composition, especially with respect to my children. In return I expect your solemn promise and declaration that you will never again play for any higher sum than twenty pounds in one day. This will be some satisfaction to me during the few months I probably have to live.

Never forget how much we are both obliged to Ferrier, who by the greatest diligence and from Attachment to the Family has extricated you a second time from the most unpleasant situation, and will point out to you in future how with common prudence you may live in affluence and even splendour of all your life. The principal cause of Your misfortunes is the habit you have long been in, of keeping very bad hours. They tend to drunkenness, and that to Gambling and every ruinous folly. The best remedy is marriage, which if you can find a Woman to your mind would keep you at home. I most earnestly recommend it to you. I do not make a point of money. I will share everything with You for the short time I have to linger here. Adieu.

Most affectionately Yours,
ARGYLL

The long-suffering Ferriers attached to great families were indeed indispensable. They watched over their charges, extricated them from financial scrapes and sexual entanglements, and reported back to their employers in terms that were sometimes candid in the extreme. Thirty years before the Duke's letter printed above, another young Argyll, the Duke of Hamilton, was being taken round the continent under the watchful eye of Dr Moore, the father of John Moore, the hero of Corunna. In a letter to the Duchess of Argyll dated 28 September 1772, Dr Moore gives a sort of end-of-term report on the Duke's progress with his studies—'he has a great Talent in deceiving the Lecturer and appearing to listen when his mind is in Reality employed about a very different matter'—and then turns to the young man's social life and his relationships with women. The Duke, it appears, was very susceptible, but the Doctor clearly thinks there is no cause for alarm:

. . . The Duke danced French Countery Dances till three in the Morning, and a few Minuets. There were some who perhaps a Dancing Master would have thought danced the Minuet more correctly, but none had so much easy Careless gracefulness as the Duke. I begin to think his Stoop has a good effect. The Women seem'd to be of the same opinion. He attached himself to a Madam Cozenof, a Lady with the Blackest and finest eyes in the world. The Duke says the Devil's own Eyes cannot possibly be blacker. I believe he is a little Catched by this Lady. Since he must have a flame (for his heart is like tinder) he cannot be better fixed. The Woman fortunately is Marryed. They say She is fond of her Husband. However, he ought not to trust too much to that.

This is the third Passion the Duke has had since we cross'd the Sea. They generally affect his appetite, and I can make a pretty good guess of the highth of his Love by the Victuals he Refuses to eat. A Slight touch of Love puts him immediately from Legumes and all kind of Jardinage. If it arises a degree higher he turns up his nose at Fricasses and Ragouts. Another degree and he will Rather go to bed supperless as taste plain Roasted Veal or Poulets of any sort. This is the utmost length his passion has ever come hitherto, for when he was at the worst with Madamoisel Marchenville, tho's she put him intirely from Greens, Ragouts, and Veal, yet she made no impression on his Roast Beef or Mutton appetite. He fed plentifully upon those in spite of all her charms. I intend to make a Thermometer for the Duke's Passion with four degrees: (1) Green, (2) Fricassees and Ragouts, (3) Roast Veal and fowls, (4) plain Roast Mutton or Beef. And if ever the Mercury mounts so high as the last I shall think the Case alarming and inform your Grace.

I remain with the greatest Respect
Your Grace's most obed't and
most humble Serv't
J. Moore

The indulgence of parents towards sons is not always replicated in attitudes towards daughters. An example of a father writing coldly to his daughter is to be seen in a letter of 1819 of William Godwin to Mary Shelley. She had recently lost her child and had written to him in a state of depression bemoaning her situation. By most people's standards his reply is very harsh. As C. Kegan Paul put it in his life of Godwin: 'The stoicism which is so admirable in repressing his own feelings, is less beautiful when used to condole with Mrs Shelley . . .'

My dear Mary,—Your letter of August 19 is very grievous to me, inasmuch as you represent me as increasing the degree of your uneasiness and depression.

You must, however, allow me the privilege of a father, and a philosopher, in expostulating with you on this depression. I cannot but consider it as lowering your character in a memorable degree, and putting you quite among the commonality and mob of your sex, when I had thought I saw in you symptoms entitling you to be ranked among those noble spirits that do honour to our nature. What a falling off is here! How bitterly is so inglorious a change to be deplored!

What is it you want that you have not? You have the husband of your choice, to whom you seem to be unalterably attached, a man of high intellectual attainments, whatever I, and some other persons, may think of his morality, and the defects under this last head, if they be not (as you seem to think) imaginary, at least do not operate as towards you. You have all the goods of fortune, all the means of being useful to others, and shining in your proper sphere. But you have lost a child: and all the rest of the world, all that is beautiful, and all that has a claim upon your kindness, is nothing, because a child of two years old is dead.

The human species may be divided into two great classes: those who lean on others for support, and those who are qualified to support. Of these last, some have one, some five, and some ten talents. Some can support a husband, a child, a small but respectable circle of friends and dependants, and some can support a world contributing by their energies to advance their whole species one or more degrees in the scale of perfectibility. The former class sit with their arms crossed, a prey to apathy and languor, of no use to any earthly creature, and ready to fall from their stools if some kind soul, who might compassionate, but who cannot respect them, did not come from moment to moment, and endeavour to set them up again. You were formed by nature to belong to the best of these classes, but you seem to be shrinking away, and voluntarily enrolling yourself among the worst.

Above all things, I entreat you, do not put the miserable delusion on yourself, to think there is something fine, and beautiful, and delicate, in giving yourself up, and agreeing to be nothing.

Remember, too, that though at first your nearest connections may pity you in this state, yet that when they see you fixed in selfishness and ill-humour, and regardless of the happiness of everyone else, they will finally cease to love you, and scarcely learn to endure you.

The other parts of your letter afford me much satisfaction. Depend upon it, there is no maxim more true or more important than this, Frankness of communication takes off bitterness . . . True philosophy invites all communication, and withholds none . . .

A less frigid letter of remonstrance, and perhaps a more justified one, was written by a provoked Michelangelo to his brother. It actually reads more like a letter from a father to a wayward son, and not unnaturally so since Michelangelo had taken on all the responsibilities of a head of the family. Of course Michelangelo was an irascible character and often overbearing with his relations and associates. The exact cause of the outburst given below is not known—perhaps it is as much the consequence of a personality clash as his brother's lack of thrift and respect for their father. At any rate it is a fine example of what Michelangelo's contemporaries described as his *terribilita*:

Rome, June 1509

Giovansimone: They say that those who do good to the good make them better, and to the bad, make them worse. I have been trying for some years now, with good words and deeds, to get you to the point of living decently and in peace with your father and the rest of us, and you continually get worse. I'm not telling you you're bad, but you're acting in a way I don't like any more than the others do. I could make you a long speech about your affairs, but they would be words, like the others I've spoken to you. To make it short, I can tell you for certain you haven't a thing in the world, and your spending money and household necessities are what I give you and have given you for some time now, for the love of God and thinking you were my brother like the rest. Now I know for certain you are not my brother because if you were you would not threaten my father; no, you are an animal, and I shall treat you like an animal. Let me tell you that whosoever sees his father threatened or stuck is obligated to interpose his own life, and that's all. I tell you you have nothing in the world, and if I hear the slightest thing about your activities, I shall come posthaste all the way there and show you your mistake, and teach you to tear up your things and set fires in the house and farms you didn't earn; you are not where you think. If I come there, I'll show you something to make you cry hot tears, and you'll know on what it is you base your pride. . .

8

First And Second Childhoods

The shortest entry in the *Dictionary of National Biography* is devoted to Marjorie Fleming, a Scottish child prodigy who died of measles in 1811 aged eight. Sir Walter Scott was delighted with her, and she became something of a cult. Her first letter was written to her cousin Isabella Keith just over half way through her life when she was five:

> *My Dear Isa*, I now sit down on my bottom to answer all your kind and beloved letters which you was so good as to write to me. This is the first time I ever wrote a letter in my life.
> There are a great number of Girls in the Square and they cry just like a pig when we are under the painfull necessity of putting it to Death.
> Miss Potune, lady of my acquaintance, praises me dreadfully. I repeated something out of Deen Swift and she said I was fit for the stage, and you may think I was primmed up with majestick Pride, but upon my word I felt myselfe turn a little birsay—birsay is a word which is a word that William composed which is as you may suppose a little enraged. This horid fat Simpliton says that my Aunt is beautiful which is intirely impossible for that is not her nature.

Precocious children cannot usually be prevented from voicing their (many) opinions, and letters give them a useful forum in which to lecture others. Thomas Hayley, the twelve-year-old-son of William Cowper's future biographer, wrote to the poet in 1973 pointing out the errors in his recently published translation of Homer (1791):

> *Honoured King of Bards*,—Since you deign to demand the observations of an humble and unexperienced servant of

yours, on a work of one who is so much his superior (as he is ever ready to serve you with all his might) behold what you demand! but let me desire you not to censure me for my unskilful and perhaps (as they will undoubtedly appear to you) ridiculous observations; but be so kind as to receive them as a mark of respectful affection from your obedient servant,

THOMAS HAYLEY

Book.	Line.	
I.	184.	I cannot reconcile myself to these expressions, 'Ah, cloth'd with impudence, etc.'; and 195, 'Shameless wolf'; and 126 'Face of flint'.
I.	508.	'Dishonor'd foul', is, my opinion, an uncleanly expression.
I.	651.	'Reel'd', I think makes it appear as if Olympus was drunk.
I.	749.	'Kindler of the fires in Heaven', I think makes Jupiter appear too much like a lamplighter.
II.	317–319.	These lines are, in my opinion, below the elevated genius of Mr. Cowper.
XVIII.	300–304.	This appears to me to be rather Irish, since in line 300 you say, 'No one sat', and in 304, 'Polydamas rose'.

Cowper replied that Thomas's critique had 'instructed him as much and entertained him more than all the other strictures of our public judges in these matters'.

When child letter-writers are not exhibiting erudition, they are most likely to be asking for something; like Piero de Medici, in 1479, whose father Lorenzo the Magnificent seemed to be unaccountably forgetful about supplying a previously promised pony:

Magnificent Father, Lucrezia and I are trying who can write best. She writes to grandmother Lucrezia, I, my Father, to you. The one who obtains what he asks for will win. Till now Lucrezia has had all she wished for. I, who have always written in Latin in order to give a more literary tone to my letters, have not yet had that pony you promised me; so that I am laughed at by all. See to it therefore, Your Magnificence, that she should not always be the winner.

Later:

> *Magnificent Father mine,*—That pony does not come, and I am afraid that it will remain so long with you that Andrea will cause it to change from a beast to a man, instead of curing its hoof.—We are all well and studying. Giovanni is beginning to spell. By this letter you can judge where I am writing; as for Greek I keep myself rather in exercise by the help of Martino than make any progress. Guilano laughs and laughs and thinks of nothing else; Lucrezia sews, sings, and reads; Maddalena knocks her head against the wall, but without doing herself any harm; Luisa begins to say a few little words; Contessina fills the house with her noise . . . Nothing is wanting to us save your presence.

Later still:

> *Magnificent Father mine,*—I fear that some misfortune has happened to that pony, for had it been well I know you would have sent it to me as you promised. I beg of you therefore as a grace that you will take this fear from me; for I think of it night and day, and until the pony comes I shall have no peace. In case that one cannot come be pleased to send me another. For, as I have already written to you, I am here on foot, and sometimes it is necessary for me to go in the company of my friends. See to this therefore, Your Magnificence.

And finally:

> *Magnifico Patri meo,*—I cannot tell you, Magnificent Father, how glad I am to have the pony, and how his arrival incites me to work. If I desire to praise him, *Ante diem clauset componet vesper Olympo.* He is so handsome and so perfect that the trumpet of Maronius would hardly suffice to sing his praises. You may think how I love him; particularly when his joyous neighs resound and rejoice all the neighbourhood. I owe you and I send you many thanks for such a fine gift and I shall try and repay you by becoming what you wish. I promise you that I shall try with all my heart.

Another request for a pony is recorded in a recently published collection of children's letters to God. The hopeful applicant has thought of a persuasive back-up argument to support his case:

Dear God
Please send me pony. I never asked for anything before you
can look it up

BRUCE

Deciding what presents to give to children is seldom difficult,
given the guidance that the potential recipients are usually more
than willing to give. In the following letter Henry James bestows
in 1897 a gift on his godson, an object which must have been as
foreign to the great novelist's personal experience as snow to a
Nubian; his godson was Guy Millar, grandson of George Du
Maurier, the illustrator and author of *Trilby*:

My dear Godson Guy,
I learned from your mother, by pressing her hard, some time
ago that it would be a convenience to you and a great help in
your career to possess an Association football— whereupon, in
my desire that you should receive the precious object from no
hand but mine I cast about me for the proper place to procure it.
But I am living for the present in a tiny, simpleminded country
town, where luxuries are few and football shops unheard of, so
I was a long time getting a clue that would set me on the right
road. Here at last, however, is the result of my terribly belated
endeavour. It goes to you by parcel post—not, naturally, in
this letter. I am awfully afraid I haven't got one of the right size:
if so, and you will let me know, you shall have a better one next
time. I am afraid I don't know much about the sorts and sizes
since they've all been invented since I was of football age. I'm
an awful muff, too, at games—except at times I am not a bad
cyclist, I think—and I fear I am only rather decent at playing at
godfather. Some day you must come down and see me here
and I'll do in every way the best I can for you. You shall have
lots of breakfast and dinner and tea—not to speak of lunch and
anything you like in between—and I won't ask you a single
question about a single one of your studies, but if you think
that is because I can't—because I don't know enough—I *might*
get up subjects on purpose.
                    Your most affectionate Godfather,
                                          HENRY JAMES

Henry James's graceful and touching letter to one so much his
junior in years reveals his humanity and humour. Lewis Carroll's

letters to children are certainly humorous, but more than a little strange. Take for example the one on the subject of penknives; the Hallam addressed was Lord Alfred Tennyson's son:

Ch. Ch. Oxford, 1862.

My Dear Hallam,

Thank you for your nice little note. I am glad you liked the knife, and I think it a pity you should not be allowed to use it 'till you are older. However, as you are older now, perhaps you have begun to use it by this time: if you were allowed to cut your finger with it, once a week, just a little, you know, till it began to bleed, and a good deep cut every birthday, I should think that would be enough, and it would last a long time so. Only I hope that if Lionel ever wants to have his fingers cut with it, you will be kind to your brother, and hurt him as much as he likes.

If you will send one word, some day, when your two birthdays are, perhaps I may send him a birthday present, if I can only find something that will hurt him as much as your knife: perhaps a blister, or a leech, or something of the sort.

Give him half my love, and take the rest yourself.

Your affectionate friend,
CHARLES L. DODGSON

Another fairly regular correspondent with the young was the witty parson Sydney Smith. He was in many ways the reverse of Lewis Carroll, outgoing, gregarious, and married. All the same, I somehow think a modern grandfather writing to his grand-daughter wouldn't phrase his remarks quite as in the following letter; (the reference to fourpence is because the little girl had failed to stamp her letter to Smith with the correct amount):

Oh, you little wretch! your letter cost me fourpence. I will pull all the plums out of your puddings; I will undress your dolls and steal their under petticoats; you shall have no currant-jelly to your rice; I will kiss you till you cannot see out of your eyes; when nobody else whips you, I will do so; I will fill you so full of sugar-plums that they shall run out of your nose and ears; lastly, your frocks shall be so short that they shall not come below your knees. Your loving grandfather,

SYDNEY SMITH

A constant feature of children's letters is the wail of anguish that is set up when they are left behind by their parents when they go travelling. Here is an example that has come down to us from about the 2nd century AD:

> Theon to his father Theon, greeting. It was a fine thing not to take me with you to town! If you won't take me with you to Alexandria I won't kiss you, or speak to you, or say goodbye to you. If you go to Alexandria, I won't ever take your hand nor greet you again. That is what will happen if you won't take me. Mother said to Archelaus: 'It quite upsets him to be left behind.' It was good of you to send me a present the day you sailed. Send me a lyre, now, I beg you. If you don't, I won't eat, I won't drink. That's that.

A sad instance of a genuinely deserted child was Allegra, Byron's daughter by Claire Clairmont. Claire was a daughter of William Godwin's second wife and Godwin was Shelley's father-in-law. Some time after Allegra's birth some ex-servants of Shelley put it about that he was actually the father, Claire having stayed with the Shelleys for a long period. This reached Lord Byron—indeed it could hardly not have done as the scandalmongers were busy circulating letters about it; and Mary Shelley wrote asking his assistance in stamping out the rumour, the truth of which she passionately denied. Byron seems to have done nothing, even perhaps half believing the tale. Shelley, in Ravenna, went to visit Allegra in her convent in 1821 and wrote this rather touching account of his visit to his wife:

> I went the other day to see Allegra at her convent, and stayed with her about three hours. She is grown tall and slight for her age, and her face is somewhat altered. The traits have become more delicate, and she is much paler, probably from the effect of improper food. She yet retains the beauty of her deep blue eyes and of her mouth, but she has a contemplative seriousness which, mixed with her excessive vivacity, which has not yet deserted her, has a very peculiar effect in a child. She is under very strict discipline, as may be observed from the immediate obedience she accords to the will of her attendants. This seems contrary to her nature, but I do not think it has been obtained at the expense of much severity. Her hair, scarcely darker than it was, is beautifully profuse,

and hangs in large curls on her neck. She was prettily dressed in white muslin, and an apron of black silk, with trousers. Her light and airy figure and her graceful motions were a striking contrast to the other children there. She seemed a thing of a finer and a higher order. At first she was very shy, but after a little caressing, and especially after I had given her a gold chain which I had bought at Ravenna for her, she grew more familiar, and led me all over the garden, and all over the convent, running and skipping so fast that I could hardly keep up with her. She showed me her little bed, and the chair where she sat at dinner, and the carozzina in which she and her favourite companions drew each other along a walk in the garden. I had brought her a basket of sweetmeats, and before eating any of them she gave her companions and each of the nuns a portion. This is not much like the old Allegra. I asked her what I should say from her to her mamma, and she said:

'Che mi manda un bacio e un bel vestituro.'

'E come vuoi il vestituro sia fatto?'

'Tutto di seta e d'oro,' was her reply. . .

Byron's attitude to Allegra was equivocal. The following letter about her purports to have been written to Augusta Leigh; however, it is probably one of the many forgeries satirizing Byron's character:

I shall be glad to hear from you, and of your children and mine. By the way, it seems that I have got another—a daughter, by that same lady, whom you will recognise by what I said of her in former letters.—I mean her who returned to England to become a Mamma incog., and who I pray the Gods to keep there. I am a little puzzled how to dispose of this new production (which is two or three months old, though I did not receive the accounts till at Rome) but shall probably send for and place it in a Venetian convent, to become a good Catholic, and (it may be) a Nun, being a character somewhat wanted in our family . . . I must love something in my old age. and probably circumstances will render this poor creature a great, and perhaps my only comfort.

Separation that is not by intention can be equally sad, though warmth and affection can bridge the gaps of time and place. Antonio Gramsci, the Italian communist leader and theoretician, was imprisoned by the Fascists in 1926 and died, still in prison, in 1937. During this period he wrote his famous *Notebooks* which contained elaborations of his social and political ideas and which amounted to thirty in all, occupying 2,350 pages in print; this, despite his health having been completely broken, and the usual difficulties about obtaining books and writing materials. He also wrote a vast number of letters to his wife who was living in Russia, and other members of his family and colleagues. He did not neglect to write to his children as well. The first of the following two letters is a charming example of his capacity to relate to his son, of whom he saw so little during his life:

Turi
February 22, 1932

Dear Delio,
I was delighted to hear about your 'little live corner', with its bullfinches and fish. If the bullfinches escape from their cage from time to time, don't grab them by the wings or the legs—these delicate parts might break or get dislocated. You have to take them in one handful—the whole body—without squeezing it. When I was young I raised birds and animals, such as falcons, owls, cuckoos, magpies, rooks, goldfinches, canaries, bullfinches and larks, a small snake, a weasel, porcupines and turtles. This is how I saw porcupines harvest apples; one autumn evening after dark, under a splendid bright moon, a friend of mine and I went into an orchard in which there were many apple trees, and hid behind a bush against the wind. All of a sudden the porcupines came out— five of them, two big ones and three small ones, and in Indian file moved toward the apples. They strolled about a bit first in the grass and then started working. Using their pretty little faces and legs, they rolled the apples the wind had shaken down into a small clearing and packed them close.

But it was clear that the apples lying around weren't enough for them: the largest porcupine looked around, his nose in the air and, choosing a tree that bent low, climbed upward and was followed by his wife. They sat down on a heavily loaded branch and began to swing rhythmically. The branch began to sway ever more violently, as apple after apple fell to the ground. When they had pushed these others into the pile, all of the porcupines, big and little, rolled over and, stretching out over the fruit, impaled it on their rigid needles. The baby porcupines carried off only a few, while the mother and father succeeded in fastening on seven or eight each. As they were returning to their hole, we came out of our hiding place, caught them with a bag and took them home. I kept the father and the two baby porcupines many months, letting them run free in the courtyard. They used to hunt down all the tiny animals—cockroaches, cockchafers, and so on—and eat fruit and lettuce leaves. Fresh salad greens were their favorite dish. This enabled me to train them a little, so they stopped rolling up into balls when they spied people coming. But they were terribly afraid of dogs. I used to amuse myself by bringing live snakes to the courtyard to see the porcupines run them down. As soon as a porcupine caught sight of the snake, he'd hop up quickly on all four legs and get ready to attack. The snake would lift up its head, stick its tongue out, and hiss. The porcupine, after a faint yelp, would hold onto the snake with his front legs, bite the neck, then eat it piece by piece. One day the porcupines disappeared, and I suspect someone ate them in turn.

The second letter is to his wife Guilia (Iulca,) and relates an incident that reveals the absurdity as well as the unpleasantness of the task confronting political goalers:

> *Clinica Quisisana*
> *Rome*
> *November 24, 1936*

Dear Iulca,

 . . . Let me tell you a little story that will make you laugh and also illustrate my state of mind. One time, when Delio was little, you wrote a charming letter to show me how he was beginning to learn about geography and to have a sense of direction. You described him lying in bed in a north-south position, repeating that in the direction of his head lived races who used dog carts, to the left was China and to the right Austria, the legs pointed to the Crimea and so on. In order to have this letter in my possession, I had to defend it without having even read it to see what the whole issue was about! The director of the prison kept me for an hour, wanting to know what secret messages were contained in it! 'What is Kitai, and what's this about Austria?' 'Who are these men who make dogs drag their carts?' I had quite a time trying to offer a plausible explanation for all this, without having even glanced at the letter. Finally, I asked the man brusquely, 'But aren't you married? Surely, you understand how a mother might write to her distant husband about their child.' He gave me the letter on the spot. (He was married but had no children.)

DOWNHILL ALL
THE WAY

1

Diseases, Real and Imagined

Pliny the Younger, unable to resist drawing philosophical edification from events as they were reported to him, once reminded his friend, Valerius Marcinius, of the links between ill health and good behaviour:

> The poor health of a friend of mine has lately reminded me that we are never so virtuous as when we are ill. Has a sick man ever been tempted by greed or lust? He is neither a slave to his passions nor ambitious for office; he cares nothing for wealth and is content with the little he has, knowing that he must leave it. It is then that he remembers the gods and realises that he is mortal: he feels neither envy, admiration, nor contempt for any man: not even slanderous talk can win his attention or give him food for thought, and his dreams are all of baths and cool springs. These are his sole concern, the object of all his prayers; meanwhile he resolves that if he is lucky enough to recover he will lead a sober and easy life in future, that is, a life of happy innocence.
>
> So here for our guidance is the rule, put shortly, which the philosophers seek to express in endless words and volumes: in health we should continue to be the men we vowed to become when sickness prompted our words.

Pliny's view of disease is that it is a humbling experience, sent by the gods to remind us that we are mortal. Yet the arbitrary choice of victims of the most terrible afflictions hardly suggests any master plan to improve the moral character of man. One of the bitterest blows that can be suffered is when the very skill or developed sense that someone lives by is the one to be attacked by disease—an artist who goes blind, a cellist who develops muscular dystrophy, or a composer like Bedřich Smetana, who goes deaf. 'The nerves of my ears are paralysed', he wrote to his friend Jan Vlastimir Karel in January of 1880, 'so that sound cannot penetrate to the brain and I cannot hear a thing. Believe me I need all my courage and force to keep myself from falling into despair and from putting a violent end to my suffering. Only the sight of my family and the thought that I must go on working for my people and country keeps me alive and inspires me to new work!' And in May 1883 he explains in a letter to Anna Trnobranska how he set to and completed such magnificent works as the symphonic poem *Má Vlast* (*My Fatherland*), imagining them as if he could hear them being played:

My disease is drawing a host of others in its wake, troublesome additional complaints which are all due to nervous irritation; this is the main reason why I have not been able for nearly a whole year to read anything that might irritate the fantastic side of my brain. This would cause other morbid conditions, and the doctors have forbidden me to read, write, think, etc. They have not, however, been able to forbid me to listen to what is happening around me, for one mightier than they has done so: 'Fate'. Forgive me for referring to my deafness which has lasted now for nine years, and which has robbed me of everything which makes our life beautiful. I, a musician, have had my hearing destroyed! Why, I have never even heard the little voices of my grandchildren . . . In this affliction I called to my spirit, and it made it possible for me to imagine my compositions as if I heard them. And I wrote long and difficult works throughout that period, great compositions such as *The Kiss*, an opera, *The Secret*, also an opera, and *The Devil's Wall*: then symphonic works, six large orchestral works under the title *My Fatherland*. And in this way I was able to bear my unbearable fate! If martyrs are still born today, then I am the unhappiest of them, for fate has sentenced me to a silent tomb where the sound of human voices does not penetrate . . .

In October 1802 Ludwig van Beethoven wrote to his brothers describing the onset of ill health and his own steadily increasing deafness. This famous *Heiligenstadt Testament* reveals Beethoven attempting to face his probable fate with resignation. But his physical and mental distress and his periods of despair are painfully evident:

. . . Alas! how could I possibly refer to the impairing *of a sense* which in me should be more perfectly developed than in other people, a sense which at one time I possessed in the greatest perfection, even to a degree of perfection such as assuredly few in my profession possess or have ever possessed—Oh, I cannot do it; so forgive me, if you ever see me withdrawing from your company which I used to enjoy. Moreover my misfortune pains me doubly, inasmuch as it leads to my being misjudged. For me there can be no relaxation in human society, no refined conversations, no mutual confidences. I must live quite alone and may creep into society only as often as sheer necessity demands; I must live like an outcast. If I appear in company I am overcome by a burning anxiety, a fear that I am running the risk of letting people notice my condition—And that has been my experience during the last six months which I have spent in the country. My sensible doctor by suggesting that I should spare my hearing as much as possible has more or less encouraged my present natural inclination, though indeed when carried away now and then by my instinctive desire for human society, I have let myself be tempted to seek it. But how humiliated I have felt if somebody standing beside me heard the sound of a flute in the distance and *I heard nothing*, or if somebody heard *a shepherd sing* and again I heard nothing— Such experiences almost made me despair, and I was on the point of putting an end to my life—The only thing that held me back was *my art*. For indeed it seemed to me impossible to leave this world before I had produced all the works that I felt the urge to compose; and thus I have dragged on this miserable existence—a truly miserable existence, seeing that I have such a sensitive body that any fairly sudden change can plunge me from the best spirits into the worst of humours—*Patience*—that is the virtue, I am told, which I must now choose for my guide; and I now possess it—I hope that I shall persist in my resolve to endure to the end, until it pleases the inexorable Parcae to cut the thread . . .

It is astonishing what artistic masterpieces and other human feats of leadership and courage have been achieved in the midst of physical pain and debilitation. One of the most powerful descriptions of what pain is actually like is given by Coleridge in a letter of 1796 to Thomas Poole. The fact that the basis of the pain may well have been psychosomatic, as Coleridge hints at the end of the letter, does not make the sensation of pain any more tolerable. The letter also shows that Coleridge is well on the way to his morally and mentally destructive reliance on opium—the 'laudanum' with which he dosed himself:

> . . . I wanted such a letter as yours, for I am very unwell. On Wednesday night I was seized with an intolerable pain from my right temple to the tip of my right shoulder, including my right eye, cheek, jaw, and that side of the throat. I was nearly frantic, and ran about the house naked, endeavouring by every means to excite sensations in different parts of my body, and so to weaken the enemy by creating division. It continued from one in the morning till half past five, and left me pale and fainting. It came on fitfully, but not so violently, several times on Thursday, and began severer threats towards night; but I took between sixty and seventy drops of laudanum, and *sopped* the Cerebus, just as his mouth began to open. On Friday it only *niggled*, as if the chief had departed from a conquered place, and merely left a small garrison behind, or as if he had evacuated the Corsica, and a few straggling pains only remained. But *this morning* he returned in full force, and his name is Legion. Giant-fiend of a hundred hands, with a shower of arrowy death-pangs he transpierced me, and then he became a wolf, and lay a-gnawing at my bones! I am not mad, most noble Festus, but in sober sadness I have suffered this day more bodily pain than I had before a conception of. My right cheek has certainly been placed with admirable exactness under the focus of some invisible burning-glass, which concentrated all the rays of a Tartarean sun. My medical attendant decides it to be altogether nervous, and that it originates either in severe application, or excessive anxiety . . .

Being immobilized in bed with an incurable disease provokes rather different thoughts from those provoked by stabs of acute pain, as the reality of death looms on the horizon. Here is a wistful letter to Mrs Belloc Lowndes from the consumptive Katherine Mansfield writing from her Swiss clinic in 1922, the year before her death:

> I have such a romantic vision in my mind of your house in Barton Street. Thank Heaven for dreams. I have been there on a

warm spring afternoon, and there has been a room with open windows where you have sat talking, wearing the same embroidered jacket. . . . But it's all far away from my cursed Swiss balcony where I'm lying lapping up the yellow of eggs and taking my temperature in the eye of Solemn Immensities—mobled kings.

Illness is a great deal more mysterious than doctors imagine. I simply can't afford to die with a very half-and-half little book and one bad one and a few stories to my name. In spite of everything, in spite of all one knows and has felt— one has this longing to *praise life*, to sing one's minute song of praise.

Will one ever be able to say how marvellously beautiful it all is? I long, above everything, to write about *family love*—the love between growing children—and the love of a mother for her son, and the father's feeling. But warmth, vivid, intimate—not 'made up', not self-conscious . . . Goodbye, I hope you are happy—I hope you are well?

In contrast to the dignity of fatal disease bravely borne, hypochondria is itself a sort of undignified disease, and certainly an important weapon in the fight to attract attention and sympathy. The following letter presents an amusing vignette of a hypochondriac in action. Its author, Sydney Smith, was an affectionate observer of Lady Holland's foibles:

Jan. 14th, 1835
Knowing (as you do my dear Lady Grey) Lady Holland so well, and having known her so long, you will I am sure be sorry to hear the misfortune which has befallen her. You know how long she has been alarmed by diseases of the heart; terrified to an agony by some recent death from that cause, she was determined that Brodie should examine the chest thoroughly with a stethoscope. He spent a long time there, bestowed the greatest attention upon the case, and ended with saying that in the course of his practice he had never witnessed a more decided case of healthy circulation, and that she had not a single complaint belonging to her. I have seen her since, and never saw anyone so crestfallen and desponding. She did all she could to get me to help her to some fresh complaint, but I was stubborn.

There is one category of persons who, whether or not they have a compulsive interest in their own state of health, certainly have an abiding interest in disease.. It is the business of doctors to pursue such an interest, and although the relish that is sometimes taken in dispassionate descriptions of repulsive symptoms may alarm the layman at a gathering of medical students, their dispassion is a necessary concomitant of efficiency and the acquisition of knowledge. Thomas Sydenham's letter to Robert Boyle written from Pall Mall on 2 April 1688 lovingly describes smallpox symptoms to his fellow scientist. Boyle, an Irishman, was the 'father of English chemistry' and best known for Boyle's Law which states that the pressure and volume of a gas are inversely proportional. Sydenham (1624–89) was known as 'The English Hippocrates', such was the fame of his medical knowledge. He stressed the importance of observation for diagnosis in clinical medicine. His achievements included distinguishing the symptoms of venereal disease and he wrote the classical account of gout, a complaint from which he himself suffered. His discoveries were immediately hailed on the Continent, one foreign colleague subsequently remarking that he never referred to Sydenham without raising his hat. In England, it is not very surprising to learn, he faced much professional opposition. This would not have been diminished by his occasional advocacy of bizarre 'remedies', including that of treating senile decrepitude by putting the patient in bed with a vital youngster. Perhaps he had King David in mind when he proposed this. Referring to his book on smallpox, Sydenham writes:

> I confess, some accidents there are incident to that disease which I never was able to master, till towards the end of last summer, and which, therefore could not be mentioned by me, as a phrenitis coming on the eighth day, where the patient is in the vigour of his youth, hath not been blooded, and hath been kept in a dose from the first decumbiture; as likewise (which is wont to be no less fatal) a great dosing, accompanied with a choking respiration, coming on from the tenth day (reckoning from the rigour and horror, which is my way of accounting) and occasioned by the matter of a ptyalism in a flux-pox, baking and growing thick, as it declines and comes to a concoction in those days. But which is observable, the small-pox never fluxes or runs together, but it hath been thrust out before the fourth day; and where you see any

eruption the first, second or third day from the decumbiture, you may safely pronounce it will be a flux-pox or a measle, for that sort, in its first appearance is like it. And, which is likewise observable in the highest flux of all, as that which comes out on the first or second day, it is in vain to endeavour the raising them to an height, for it is both impossible and unsafe to attempt, but all the discharge there can be, must be either from ptyalism, in a grown person, or a diarrhoea, in an infant, to whom the same is no more dangerous than the other to the former; and, wherever they flux, their discharge must be made one of those two ways. . . .

The town stands well in health, and at our end not anybody sick, that I hear, of the small-pox. I have much business about other things, and more than I can do, who yet am not idle. I have the happiness of curing my patients, at least of having it said of me, that few miscarry under me; but cannot brag of my correspondency with some other of the faculty, who, notwithstanding my profoundness in palmistry and chemistry, impeach me with great insufficiency, as I shall likewise do my tailor, when he mades my doublet like a hopsack, and not before, let him adhere to what hypothesis he will.

2

A Courageous Front

In 1943 the imprisoned Dietrich Bonhoeffer, wrote to Eberhard Bethge these compassionate thoughts about personal suffering:

> . . . Some people have been so violently shaken in their lives from their earliest days that they cannot now, so to speak, allow themselves any great longing or put up with a long period of tension, and they find compensation in short-lived pleasures that offer readier satisfaction. That is the fate of the proletarian classes, and it is the ruin of all intellectual fertility. It's not true to say that it is good for a man to have suffered heavy blows early and often in life; in most cases it breaks him. True, it hardens people for times like ours, but it also greatly helps to deaden them. When *we* are forcibly separated for any considerable time from those whom we love, we simply *cannot*, as most can, get some cheap substitute through other people—I don't mean because of moral considerations, but just because we are what we are. Substitutes repel us; we simply have to wait and wait; we have to suffer unspeakably from the separation, and feel the longing till it almost makes us ill. That is the only way, although it is a very painful one, in which we can preserve unimpaired our relationship with our loved ones. A few times in my life I've come to know what homesickness means. There is nothing more painful, and during these months in prison I've sometimes been terribly homesick. And as I expect you will have to go through the same kind of thing in the coming months, I wanted to write and tell you what I've learnt about it, in case it may be of some help to you. The first result of such longing is always a wish to neglect the ordinary daily routine in some way or other, and that means that our lives become disordered. I used to be tempted sometimes to stay in bed after six in the morning (it would have been perfectly possible), and to

sleep on. Up to now I've always been able to force myself not to do this; I realised that it would have been the first stage of capitulation, and that worse would probably have followed. An outward and purely physical régime (exercises and a cold wash down in the morning) itself provides some support for one's inner discipline. Further, there is nothing worse in such times than to try to find a substitute for the irreplaceable. It just does not work, and it leads to still greater indiscipline, for the strength to overcome tension (such strength can come only from looking the longing straight in the face) is impaired, and endurance becomes even more unbearable . . .

'The heavy blows early and often in life' in Bonhoeffer's terse phrase are nowhere more chillingly evoked than in an illiterate letter to Marie Stopes, one of many such she received. It is so sad that it leaves little room for anything but the hope that death will release the woman concerned from her imprisonment in life:

. . . I married a man in the year 1912 at the age of 18, he being 22 years older year after I found I was to become a Mother (the child was still born which Was cause throught fright 3 or 4 days before. And that nearly corst me my life) My Husband having to chrilder of his own at the time boy 3 and a girl 7, which are now 18 and 21. After that it was not till 1917 that I was in London and there waiting to go in the City Rd Hospital to be confined. (I was a lone in Lodging and had to Walk a mile in Angoing while the Air Raids was on. I just got to the Door and Callopsed, the Child beining bone almost at once. 13 months after I had a nother girl bone a hour before I could sent for help. 2 year later a boy, and 2 year later another boy, this last boy have shutter my nerves (for 2 months before he was Born I had nurses from the Guild Hall to dress my Varcass Vain. The last month I walk on Sticks and they came trice aday (the Weaight of the child cause the Vain to come to such a terrible size that the chair bottom had to be removed I had to sleep with legs up) he was born on the 6th of Oct and 24 hours after I found I had got to be stitched. When I got up I had a large lump form in the Brest. I went to the Hospital and they operated 16 stitches I had. I was there 4 weeks all my chrilen being in the Wookhouse I cam out to fetch the chrilden, and 2 months after the other brest was very bad I went up at 1 oclock to have to opration 12 stiches and walk home at 5. I could not have a days rest I still had to keep on, after I had to go for the Dressings Twice a day pushing 2 kiddies in the pram till at the week end my leg gave way and I had to stay four hours and wait for a letter, to say that I could go in the Calvasing Homes. I said yes, I did not go; the worry brought on a groth in my ear, I have to have it Lance. My trouble are my own, I have no simpathy hear the last day I saw was the 15th of Dec; It was on Boxing Night I conceived I have tried many Pills but Have not seen the desired effect. Please Help me! I have Had my share . . . My life is only a living Hell.

Illness, old age, and mental torment are the sort of afflictions which can only be borne with stoicism and courage. While some of the sufferings of Marie Stopes's correspondent could have been alleviated with better health care and less vindictive and mindless social attitudes, a fatal illness or simple old age have to be endured with patience. Here is James Agate writing to his brother in 1947, the year of his death at the age of seventy, bruised but unbroken by years of literary and artistic controversy (admittedly most of it stirred up by himself). He manages to adopt a philosophical attitude towards the onset of ill health and the decline of his physical and mental powers:

One thing, my dear Whiskers, that irks me is the extraordinary combination of fatigue and insomnia. Owing to the pain all my body cries out for sleep, and I just can't catch it— probably something to do with the asthma. Fortunately, however, my flat faces two ways, so that I can put an extremely comfortable, high-backed, well-pillowed chair in the windows of two rooms with different aspects. Both windows have ledges which will take a cushion. I go to what I call bed at eleven o'clock, sit in the dark, and get amusement out of Holborn's cats and other late *noceurs*. Quite frequently, round about four, I put my head on the cushion and drop off for a couple of hours, after which there is the delight of seeing Holborn wake up. To get the best of this entertainment I go into the room which has a view of a lot of little shops, including a tyre-dealer's and it is fun to watch dust-carts jostling Rolls-Royces for priority. And when the doctor comes in the morning and asks what sort of night I have had, I say, 'Splendid!'

I can't read new books because of the fatigue, but I can still quote Micawber in chunks. I don't play the gramophone much, as I find the noise hurts, but I can sit and nurse the records and play them in my head. When friends come round I like them to be more or less silent, while I recall the witty things they have said in the past. I have an immense amount to be thankful for, and never cease marvelling that a contentious and truculent fellow like me can have acquired, without angling for it, so much that gives old age its value. To-day I have had telephone messages from Lilian Braithwaite and Helen Haye; Abel of the Ivy sent me a dozen peaches; Gwen Chenhall's kindness is not to be believed; my room is almost as full of flowers as Sarah Bernhardt's *loge* on a first night. I could have cars here every hour of the day, but the doctors say I am not strong enough to go for drives. So I sit and muse and am thankful that, so far as I can perceive, my intellectual vigour has not abated. It shows itself best in this, I think—the realisation that it is not within the power of present pain to lay a finger on past ecstasy. I thank God that He has made this world more perdurable than any but a poet's view of it—that a thousand poets could fall off a mountain without doing anything except add to its grandeur. What does it matter if my spirits droop a little now and then so long as the butcher-boy can whistle, or how many aches and pains I groan under so long as the cherry blossoms in the Park?

So don't worry about me, I have had enough happiness and excitement and joy of work to fill ten lifetimes. Don't come up to London to see me; so long as you stay put I shall feel that 'There's sap in't yet'.

My best love to yourself, Lizzie, and Mary.

Ever,
JIMMIE

Some three months before *his* death John Keats wrote a farewell letter to his friend Charles Brown. In it, he is candid but unselfpitying about the extent of his physical suffering, and does his best to make a graceful exit:

. . . I cannot answer anything in your letter which followed me from Naples to Rome, because I am afraid to look it over again. I am so weak (in mind) that I cannot bear the sight of any handwriting of a friend I love so much as I do you. Yet I ride the little horse, and, at my worst, even in quarantine, summoned up more puns, in a sort of desperation, in one week than in any year of my life. There is one thought enough to kill me; I have been well, healthy, alert, &c., walking with her, and now—the knowledge of contrast, feeling for light and shade, all that information (primitive sense) necessary for a poem, are great enemies to the recovery of the stomach. There, you rogue, I put you to the torture; but you must bring your philosophy to bear, as I do mine, really, or how should I be able to live? Dr Clark is very attentive to me; he says, there is very little the matter with my lungs, but my stomach, he says, is very bad. I am well disappointed in hearing good news from George, for it runs in my head we shall all die young. I have not written to Reynolds yet, which he must think very neglectful; being anxious to send him a good account of my health, I have delayed it from week to week. If I recover, I will do all in my power to correct the mistakes made during sickness; and if I should not, all my faults will be forgiven. Severn is very well, though he leads so dull a life with me. Remember me to all friends, and tell Haslam I should not have left London without taking leave of him, but from being so low in body and mind. Write to George as soon as you receive this, and tell him how I am, as far as you can guess; and also a note to my sister—who walks about my imagination like a ghost—she is so like Tom, I can scarcely bid you good-bye, even in a letter. I always made an awkward bow.

God bless you!
JOHN KEATS

The tragedy of Keats is that he was a young man of brilliant promise struck down before that promise could be fulfilled. But the tragedy of many others is to outlive their physical and mental powers and to decline into an old age that is neither dignified nor contented. The declining years become a long trial of courage as a lifetime's abilities and habits gradually slip out of their grasp and the business of living becomes more of a daily struggle. In the following letter, Deane Swift, a connection of the author of *Gulliver's Travels*, replies to an inquiry from Lord Orrery concerning Jonathan Swift. It was said of the Dean that in old age he had one day caught sight of himself in a looking-glass and exclaimed: 'Oh, poor old man!'

Dublin, April 4, 1744
MY LORD, As to the story of 'O poor old man!' I inquired into it. The Dean did say something, upon his seeing himself in the glass, but neither Mrs Ridgeway nor the lower servants could tell me what it was he said. I desired them to recollect it by the time when I should come again to the deanery. I have been there since, they cannot recollect it. A thousand stories have been invented of him within these two years, and imposed upon the world. I thought this might have been one of them, and yet I am now inclined to think there may be some truth in it, for on Sunday the 17th March, as he sat in his chair, upon the housekeeper's moving a knife from him as he was going to catch at it, he shrugged his shoulders, and rocking himself, said, 'I am what I am, I am what I am'; and about six minutes afterwards, repeated the same words two or three times over.

His servant shaves his cheeks, and all his face as low as the tip of his chin, once a week: but under the chin, and about the throat, when the hair grows long, it is cut with scissors.

Sometimes he will not utter a syllable, at other times he will speak incoherent words, but he never yet, as far as I could hear, talked nonsense, or said a foolish thing.

About four months ago he gave me great trouble; he seemed to have a mind to talk to me. In order to try what he would say, I told him I came to dine with him, and immediately his housekeeper, Mrs Ridgeway, said, 'Won't you give Mr Swift a glass of wine, sir?' He shrugged his shoulders, just as he used to do when he had a mind a friend should pass the evening with him. Shrugging his shoulders, your Lordship may remember, was as much as to say, 'You'll ruin me in wine.' I own, I was scarce able to bear the sight. Soon after, he again endeavoured, with a good deal of pain, to find words to speak to me. At last, not being able, after many efforts, he gave a heavy sigh, and, I think, was afterwards silent. This puts me in mind of what he said about five days ago. He endeavoured several times to speak to his servant (now and then he calls him by name), at last, not finding words to express what he would be at, after some uneasiness he said, 'I am a fool.' Not long ago the servant took up his watch that lay upon the table to see what o'clock it was, he said, 'Bring it here': and when it was brought, he looked very attentively at it; some time ago, the servant was breaking a large stubborn coal, he said, 'That's a stone, you blockhead.'

In a few days or some very short time after guardians had been appointed for him, I went into his dining-room, where he was walking. I said something to him very insignificant, I know not what; but, instead of making any kind of answer to it, he said, 'Go, go,' pointing with his hand to the door, and immediately afterwards, raising his hand to his head, he said, 'My best understanding,' and so broke off abruptly, and walked away. I am, my Lord, Your Lordship's most obedient and most humble servant,

DEANE SWIFT

Mental endurance in the face of disaster also makes enormous demands on courage and patience. Fortunately not many of us are tested as severely as was Sir Walter Scott. He, however, showed extreme strength of character in facing an adversity that was far from inevitable and indeed totally unexpected, when his printing and publishing interests collapsed in 1826. Scott, who had not been directly responsible for the failure, found himself a bankrupt at the age of fifty-five in the middle of his successful career as an historical novelist. His liabilities amounted to the huge sum of £130,000. Refusing all offers of assistance (one anonymous admirer pledged £30,000), he set to work to pay off his debts with his writing and in two years had made £40,000. The effort broke him however, and by 1832 he was dead. In the letter quoted he faces his misfortune with clear-sighted courage and still manages to laugh a little at himself and his misfortunes. He also describes his terrifying workload:

Edinburgh, 6 February 1826

My dear Morritt,

It is very true I have been, and am in danger, of a pecuniary loss and probably a very large one, which, in the uncertainty, I look at as to the full extent, being the manly way of calculating such matters, since one may be better, but can hardly be worse. I can't say I feel overjoyed at losing a large sum of hard-earned money in a most unexpected manner, for all men considered Constable's people secure as the Banker yet, as I have obtained an arrangement of payment convenient for everybody concerned, and easy for myself, I cannot say that I care much about the matter. Some economical restrictions I will make; and it happened oddly that they were such as Lady Scott and myself had almost determined upon without this compulsion. Abbotsford will henceforth be our only establishment; and during the time I must be in town, I will take my bed at the Albyn Club. We shall also break off the rather excessive hospitality to which we were exposed, and no longer stand host and hostess to all that do pilgrimage to Melrose. Then I give up an expensive farm, which I always hated, and turn all my odds and ends into cash. I do not reckon much on my literary exertions—I mean in proportion to former success because popular taste may fluctuate. But with a moderate degree of the favour which I have always had, my time my own, and my mind unplagued about other things, I may boldly promise myself soon to get the better of this blow.

In these circumstances, I should be unjust and ungrateful to ask or accept the pity of my friends. I for one, do not see there is much occasion for making moan about it. My womankind will be the greater sufferers,—yet even they look cheerily forward; and, for myself, the blowing off my hat in a stormy day has given me more uneasiness.

3

The Art of Dying

It is a melancholy fact that death stimulates more letter writing than most other events in our lives. In letters are to be found many touching, and some harrowing, descriptions of the last hours of loved ones. Some writers seem determined to re-create the moment of death in words as a way of coming to terms with it. The recipient of such a letter is sometimes spared no detail of the end: Robert Southey describing his mother calling for more laudanum as he measured out the dose with shaking hands— 'That's nothing, Robert! thirty drops—six and thirty!' Or E. B. White sourly recalling the obsequies for his mother: 'Today she received [the] extreme unction, with the electric organ, the state lilies, the old colored servants sitting silent and attentive in the little chapel, together with the neighbors from across the street, the doctor who didn't know she had cancer of the liver, and the minister who was sure her soul would go to heaven.'

But death also has its scenes of dignity and courage. Pliny in one of his letters relates how Corellius Rufus, after enduring unbearable pain for some time, calmly took his own life. 'When the doctor offered him food, he only said: "I have made up my mind." . . . I mourn for my lost guardian and mentor,' says Pliny sadly, and: 'I am afraid I shall be less careful how I live now.' Equally moving and courageous is Mark Twain's account of his wife Livy's death: 'I bent over her and looked in her face and I think I spoke. I was surprised and troubled that she did not notice me. Then we understood and our hearts broke. How poor we are today!'

An early letter (*circa* 735) from the monk Cuthbert describes the death of Bede. Although the writer apologizes for his 'lack of skill in speech', his account is very moving in its evocation of the dying scholar's serenity and resignation:

About two weeks before the day of the Resurrection, he was

afflicted with great weakness and with shortness of breath, although he was without pain; and so, happy and rejoicing, giving thanks to Almighty God every day and every night, indeed almost every hour, he lived until the day of our Lord's ascension, that is the seventh of the Kalends of June. To us, his pupils, he continued to give lessons every day, and the rest of the day he spent in singing psalms. Ever vigilant, he would spend the whole night in rejoicing and in giving thanks, except when a little sleep prevented. Upon awaking, however, he would again repeat the customary prayers and with hands uplifted continue to give thanks to God. Truly I may say that I have neither seen with my eyes nor heard with my ears any one give thanks so diligently to the living God.

When the third Tuesday before the Ascension of our Lord had come, he began to experience great difficulty in breathing, and a slight swelling developed in his feet. But he laboured all that day, and dictated happily, and among other things said, 'Learn quickly, for I know not how long I shall live, or whether in a little while my Maker shall take me.' To us, however, it seemed that he knew well the time of his going forth. Thus he spent the night in vigils and thanksgiving. And at dawn, that is on Wednesday, he commanded us to write diligently what we had begun; and this we did unto the third hour. From the third hour we walked with the relics of the saints, as the custom of the day demanded. One of us remained with him, who said to him, 'There is yet one chapter lacking. Does it not seem hard that you should be questioned further?' But he answered, 'It is easy. Take pen and ink, and write quickly.' He did so. At the ninth hour he said to me, 'In my chest I have a few little valuables, pepper, napkins, and incense. Go quickly and bring hither the priests of our monastery, that I may distribute among them what gifts God has granted me. The rich men, in this day, may wish to give gold and silver and the like treasures; I, with great charity and gladness, shall give to my brother what God has bestowed.' And with fear I did this. Then addressing one and all, he besought them to sing masses for him and to pray diligently; which they freely promised. They all continued to weep and mourn, especially because he had said that they should not see his face much longer in this life. But they rejoiced because he said, 'It is time that I return to Him who made me, who created me and formed me out of nothing. I have lived long, and my gracious Judge has ordered my life well; the time of my return is come, for I desire to die and be with Christ.'

The loss of a scholar and a saintly man is not just a personal tragedy but one that affects a whole community. Cuthbert's awareness of the importance of the occasion suffuses his long letter of praise and lamentation. But most people's experience of death is the sharp pain of personal and private grief giving rise to a feeling of utter desolation, nowhere better evoked than in the closing lines of a letter to Samuel Pepys in 1686 from his brother-in-law:

I am Sir Stopped with a Torent of Soroful Lamentation, for Oh God I have lost, oh I have lost such a loss, that noe man is or cann be sensible but my Selfe: I have lost my wife, Sir, I have lost my wife; and such a wife, as your Honour knows has (may be) not lefte her felow, I cannot say any more at present being overwhelmed . . .

To be forcibly reminded of mortality is a chastening experience. The next two letters show how two great writers, Dr Johnson and Boris Pasternak reacted to near brushes with the reaper's scythe. The year before his death Dr Johnson had a stroke, and his account of it, sent to Mrs Thrale, combines courage and pathos in a way that must surely have moved the lady:

Bolt-Court, Fleet-street,
June 19, 1783

Dear Madam
I am sitting down in no cheerful solitude to write a narrative which would once have affected you with tenderness and sorrow, but which you will perhaps pass over now with the careless glance of frigid indifference. For this diminution of regard however, I know not whether I ought to blame you, who may have reasons which I cannot know, and I do not blame myself, who have for a great part of human life done you what good I could, and have never done you evil.

I had been disordered in the usual way, and had been relieved by the usual methods, by opium and catharticks, but had rather lessened my dose of opium.

On Monday the 16th I sat for my picture, and walked a considerable way with little inconvenience. In the afternoon and evening I felt myself light and easy, and began to plan schemes of life. Thus I went to bed, and in a short time waked and sat up, as has long my custom, when I felt a confusion and indistinctness in my head, which lasted I suppose about half a minute; I was alarmed, and prayed God, that however he might afflict my body, he would spare my understanding. This prayer, that I might try the integrity of my faculties, I made in Latin verse. The lines were not very good, but I knew them not to be very good: I made them easily, and concluded myself to be unimpaired in my faculties.

Soon after I perceived that I had suffered a paralytick stroke, and that my speech was taken from me. I had no pain, and so little dejection in this dreadful state, that I wondered at my own apathy, and considered that perhaps death itself when it should come would excite less horrour than seems now to attend it.

In order to rouse the vocal organs I took two drams. Wine has been celebrated for the production of eloquence. I put myself into violent motion, and I think repeated it; but all was vain. I then went to bed, and, strange as it may seem, I think, slept. When I saw light, it was time to contrive what I should do. Though God stopped my speech he left me my hand, I enjoyed a mercy which was not granted to my dear Friend Lawrence, who now perhaps overlooks me as I am writing, and rejoices that I have what he wanted. My first note was necessarily to my servant, who came in talking, and could not immediately comprehend why he should read what I put into his hands.

I then wrote a card to Mr Allen, that I might have a discreet friend at hand to act as occasion should require. In penning this note I had some difficulty, my hand, I knew not how nor why, made wrong letters. I then wrote to Dr Taylor to come to me, and bring Dr Heberden, and I sent to Dr Brocklesby, who is my neighbour. My physicians are very friendly and very disinterested, and give me great hopes, but you may imagine my situation. I have so far recovered my vocal powers, as to repeat the Lord's Prayer with no very imperfect articulation. My memory, I hope, yet remains as it was; but such an attack produces solicitude for the safety of every faculty.

. . . I suppose you may wish to know how my disease is treated by the physicians. They put a blister upon my back, and two from my ear to my throat, one on a side. The blister on the back has done little, and those on the throat have not risen. I bullied and bounced (it sticks to our last sand) and compelled the apothecary to make his salve according to the Edinburgh Dispensatory, that it might adhere better. I have two on now of my own prescription. They likewise give me salt of hartshorn, which I take with no great confidence, but am satisfied that what can be done is done for me.

O God! give me comfort and confidence in Thee: forgive my sins; and if it be Thy good pleasure, relieve my diseases for Jesus Christ's sake. Amen.

I am almost ashamed of this querulous letter, but now it is written, let it go.

I am, Madam Your most humble servant
SAM: JOHNSON

For Boris Pasternak, the experience of going to the brink and being hauled back at the last moment aroused feelings of thankfulness for his gifts as a poet, and in his letter to Nina Tabidze in 1953 he blesses God for having as he puts it 'laid on the paints so thickly' in his life:

Ninochka, I am still alive, I am at home. Oh, there are so many things I have to tell you.

. . . Some may think: 'Yes, all those fine words, idealism, creative work, and all those speeches and toasts are all right for so long and no longer, at table with friends, until the first trouble and the first serious trial. Let us see what will be left of it at the first collision with the inevitable . . .'

When it happened and I was taken away and then spent the first five hours in the reception room and afterwards a night in the corridor of an ordinary, huge, overcrowded city hospital, I was seized by such a wonderful feeling of calm and bliss in the intervals between loss of consciousness and attacks of sickness and vomiting.

I kept thinking that in the event of my death nothing inopportune or irreparable would happen. Zina and Lyonochka would have enough to live on for six months, after which they would look round and find something to do. They will have friends. No one will treat them badly. The end will not come to me by surprise, in the middle of my work, before something is finished. The little that could be done among the obstructions caused by the events of our time has been done [the translations of Shakespeare, *Faust* and Baratashvili].

All about me everything went on as usual, things stood out so vividly, shadows fell so sharply! A mile-long corridor with bodies of sleeping patients plunged in darkness and silence, at the end of which a window looking out into the grounds through which one caught a glimpse of the inky haze of a rainy night with the reflection of the glow of the street lights of Moscow behind the treetops. This corridor, the green glow of the lampshade on the table of the night-nurse, the stillness, the shadows of the nurses, the proximity of death behind the window and behind my back—all this taken together was, by its concentration, such an unfathomable, such a superhuman poem!

At a moment which seemed to be the last in my life, I wanted more than ever to talk to God, to glorify everything I saw, to catch and imprint it on my memory. 'Lord,' I whispered, 'I thank you for having laid on the paints so thickly and for having made life and death the same as your language—majestic and musical, for having made me a creative artist, for having made creative work your school, and for having prepared me all my life for this night.' *And I rejoiced and wept* with joy.

The death of Keats in 1821 seemed to epitomize youthful brilliance being snuffed out at the moment when it was set to conquer the world. It was said that critical attacks made on him in *The Quarterly* and *Blackwoods* hastened his death; of this theory Byron commented drily that he never knew 'criticism could be so killing'. The ridicule heaped on Keats by some critics cannot have helped his fight against the consumption that finally killed him; but he had a number of loyal friends, most notably Joseph Severn, the artist, who wrote this letter to John Haslam the day before the poet died:

My dear Haslam, O, how anxious I am to hear from you! I have nothing to break this dreadful solitude but letters. Day after day, night after night, here I am by our poor dying friend. My spirits, my intellect, and my health are breaking down. I can get no one to change with me—no one to relieve me. All run away, and even if they did not, Keats would not do without me. Last night I thought he was going, I could hear the phlegm in his throat, he bade me lift him up on the bed or he would die with pain. I watched him all night, expecting him to be suffocated at every cough. This morning by the pale daylight, the change in him frightened me; he has sunk in the last three days to a most ghastly look. Though Dr Clark has prepared me for the worst, I shall ill bear to be set free even from this, my horrible situation, by the loss of him. I am still quite precluded from painting, which may be of consequence to me. Poor Keats has me ever by him, and shadows out the form of one solitary friend; he opens his eyes in great doubt and horror, but when they fall upon me they close gently, open quietly and close again, till he sinks to sleep. This thought alone would keep me by him till he dies; and why did I say I was losing my time? The advantages I have gained by knowing John Keats are double and treble any I could have won by any other occupation.

Keats himself in his *Ode To The Nightingale* exclaims that he is 'half in love with easeful death', and a letter to Fanny Brawne of July 1819 eloquently draws a connecting line between passion, sensuality and death: 'I have two luxuries to brood over in my walks, your loveliness and the hour of my death. O that I could have possession of them both in the same minute.' But this is a romantic intimation of mortality, not the despairing death-wish of a potential suicide. In contrast to a Keats luxuriating in the unity of love and death, suicide notes are usually brief and often apologetic. One of the most moving of such notes was written by Virginia Woolf to her husband Leonard before she drowned herself in the Sussex River Ouse on 28 March 1941:

Dearest,
I feel certain I am going mad again. I feel we can't go through another of those terrible times. And I shan't recover this time. I begin to hear voices, and I can't concentrate. So I am doing what seems to be the best thing to do. You have given me the greatest possible happiness. You have been in every way all that anyone could be. I don't think two people could have been happier till this terrible disease came. I can't fight any longer. I know that I am spoiling your life, that without me you could work. And you will I know. You see I can't even write this properly. I can't read. What I want to say is I owe all the happiness of my life to you. You have been

entirely patient with me and incredibly good. I want to say that—everyone knows it. If anybody could have saved me it would have been you. Everything has gone from me but the certainty of your goodness. I can't go on spoiling your life any longer.

I don't think two people could have been happier than we have been.

V.

Committing suicide, though formerly a crime (and ironically a capital one), is now more often regarded with sympathy and understanding. But one of the consequences of acts of suicide is the suffering caused to those whom the victim leaves behind, and especially those who felt some responsibility towards him. A feeling of impotence, and of self-blame, characterizes the following letter in which the American poet, Robert Frost laments the death of his unbalanced son, Carol, who shot himself with a hunting rifle on 9 October 1940. Frost is tortured by what he sees as his failure to be a better father. The letter is addressed to a fellow poet Louis Untermeyer:

Dear Louis:
I took the wrong way with him. I tried many ways and every single one of them was wrong. Something in me is still asking for the chance to try one more. There's where the greatest pain is located. I am cut off too abruptly in my plans and efforts for his peace of mind. You'll say it ought not to have come about that I should have to think for him. He really did most of his thinking for himself. He thought too much. I doubt if he rested from thinking day or night in the last few years. Mine was just an added touch to his mind to see if I couldn't make him ease up on himself and take life and farming off-hand. I got humbled. Three weeks ago I was down at Merrils [Merrill Moore] telling Lee [Simonson] how to live. Two weeks ago I was up at South Shaftsbury telling Carol how to live. Yesterday I was telling seven hundred Harvard freshmen how to live with books in college. Apparently nothing can stop us once we get going. I talk less and less however as if I knew what I was talking about. My manner will be intended to indicate henceforth that I acknowledge myself disqualified from giving counsel. Kay says I am not to give myself up. Well then I'll be brave about this failure

as I have meant to be about my other failures before. But you'll know and Kay will know in what sense I say things now . . .

I failed to trick Carol or argue him into believing he was the least successful. Thats what it came down to. He failed in farming and he failed in poetry (you may not have known). He was splendid with animals and little children. If only the emphasis could have been put on those. He should have lived with horses. This is a letterful . . .

Yours ROBERT

Losing a son or daughter is an experience that has often been movingly recorded in letters. Here is an example from Edmund Burke in his long satirical *Letter to a Noble Lord* in which he steps aside for a moment from his hostile intent and gives us a glimpse of his personal grief in a memorable simile:

> . . . He was made a public creature, and had no enjoyment whatever but in the performance of some duty. At this exigent moment, the loss of a finished man is not easily supplied.
>
> But a Disposer whose power we are little able to resist and whose wisdom it behoves us not at all to dispute, has ordained it in another manner, and (whatever my querulous weakness might suggest) a far better. The storm has gone over me; and I lie like one of those old oaks which the late hurricane has scattered about me. I am stripped of all my honours, I am torn up by the roots, and lie prostrate on the earth.

There is no mistaking the depth and sincerity of Burke's feelings; but all too often death is greeted with conventional eulogy that is either meaningless or paints a portrait that is unrecognizable as a description of the deceased. Lord Stanley voices his objections to this sort of thing in a letter to his wife in 1856, after he had been consulted about an epitaph:

> I have written to Holmwood about the Epitaph. It is an invidious task for me to make objections, but still I cannot avoid it when their proposed words are submitted to me for my opinion.
>
> '*Gifted with high intellect*' may be true in the estimation of

friends & relatives—it was however a private estimation & not the result of public acts or deeds.

'Advocate of freedom' every Englishman professes to be & there was no peculiar public act of his life which makes it necessary to record the fact.

'Love of truth' is very vague & not the subject matter for an inscription.

The next two letters are extremely harrowing but so powerfully written that they make fascinating reading. Gustave Flaubert lost his great friend, and sometime mentor, Alfred de Poittevin, in 1848. In a letter to Maxime DuCamp he records the scene of Le Poittevin's death-bed and his own reactions with all the disturbing realism to be expected of the author of *Madame Bovary*:

Alfred died on Monday at midnight. I buried him yesterday, and am now back. I watched beside him two nights (the second time, all night), I wrapped him in his shroud, I gave him the farewell kiss, and saw him sealed in his coffin. I was there two days—very full days. While I sat beside him I read Creuzer's *Religions of Antiquity*. The window was open, the night splendid. I could hear a cock crowing, and a night-moth circled around the tapers. I shall never forget all that, or the look on Alfred's face, or, the first night at midnight, the far-off sound of a hunting-horn that came to me through the forest.

On Wednesday I walked all afternoon, with a dog that followed me without being summoned. (It was a bitch that had become attached to Alfred and always accompanied him when he walked alone. The night before his death she howled frightfully and couldn't be quieted.) From time to time I sat on the moss; I smoked, I stared up at the sky, I lay down behind a heap of cut broom and slept.

The last night I read *Les Feuilles d'automne*. I kept coming upon poems that were his favourites or which had special meaning for me in the circumstances. Now and then I got up, lifted the veil covering his face, and looked at him. I was wrapped in a cloak that belonged to my father and which he had worn only once, the day of Caroline's wedding.

At daybreak, about four o'clock, the attendant and I began our task. I lifted him, turned him, covered him. The feeling of the coldness and rigidity of his limbs stayed in my fingertips all the next day. He was horribly decomposed; the sheets were stained through. We wrapped him in two shrouds. When it was done he looked like an Egyptian mummy in its bandages, and I was filled with an indescribable sense of joy and relief on his account. There was a whitish mist, the trees were beginning to be visible through it. The two tapers shone in the dawning whiteness; two or three birds sang, and I recited to myself this sequence from his *Bélial*: 'Il ira, joyeux oiseau, saluer dans les pins le soleil levant'—or rather I heard his voice saying it to me, and for the rest of the day was deliciously obsessed by it.

He was laid in the coffin in the entry, where the doors had been removed and where the morning air poured in, freshened by the rain that had started to fall. He was carried to the cemetery on men's shoulders. It was almost an hour's walk. From behind, I saw the coffin swaying like a rolling boat. The service was atrociously long. In the cemetery the earth was muddy. I stood by the grave and watched each shovelful as it fell: there seemed to be a hundred thousand of them. When the hole was filled I walked away, smoking, which Boivin didn't think proper.

I returned to Rouen on the box of a carriage with Bouilhet. The rain beat down, the horses went at a gallop. I shouted to urge them on, we were back in 43 minutes—5 leagues. The air did me much good. I slept all night and most of today, and had a strange dream, which I wrote down lest I lose it.

On one of his last days, when the windows were open and the sun was coming into the room, he said: 'Close it! It is too beautiful—too beautiful!' . . .

Even more bleak with its awful flashes of black comedy, is Robert Ross's long letter to More Adey describing the death in November 1900 of his friend Oscar Wilde, from which the following extracts are taken:

. . . Terrible offices had to be carried out into which I need not enter. Reggie [Turner] was a perfect wreck.

He and I slept at the Hotel d'Alsace that night in a room upstairs. We were called twice by the nurse, who thought Oscar was actually dying. About 5.30 in the morning a complete change came over him, the lines of the face altered, and I believe what is called the death rattle began, but I had never heard anything like it before; it sounded like the horrible turning of a crank, and it never ceased until the end. His eyes did not respond to the light test any longer. Foam and blood came from his mouth, and had to be wiped away by someone standing by him all the time. At 12 o'clock I went out to get some food, Reggie mounting guard. He went out at 12.30. From 1 o'clock we did not leave the room; the painful noise from the throat became louder and louder. Reggie and myself destroyed letters to keep ourselves from breaking down. The two nurses were out, and the proprietor of the hotel had come up to take their place; at 1.45 the time of his breathing altered. I went to the bedside and held his hand, his pulse began to flutter. He heaved a deep sigh, the only natural one I had heard since I arrived, the limbs seemed to stretch involuntarily, the breathing came fainter; he passed at 10 minutes to 2 P.M. exactly.

. . . It was in the afternoon the District Doctor called and asked if Oscar had committed suicide or was murdered. He would not look at the signed certificates of Klein and Tucker. Gesling had warned me the previous evening that owing to the assumed name and Oscar's identity, the authorities might insist on his body being taken to the Morgue. Of course I was appalled at the prospect; it really seemed the final touch of horror. After examining the body, and, indeed, everybody in the hotel, and after a series of drinks and unseasonable jests, and a liberal fee, the District Doctor consented to sign the permission for burial. Then arrived some other revolting official; he asked how many collars Oscar had, and the value of his umbrella. (This is quite true, and not a mere exaggeration of mine.) Then various poets and literary people called, Raymond de la Tailhade, Tardieu, Charles Sibleigh, Jehan Rictus, Robert d'Humières, George Sinclair, and various English people, who gave assumed names, together with two veiled women. They were all allowed to see the body when they signed their names . . .

I am glad to say dear Oscar looked calm and dignified, just as he did when he came out of prison, and there was nothing at all horrible about the body after it had been washed. Around his neck was the blessed rosary which you gave me, and on the breast a Franciscan medal given me by one of the nuns, a few flowers placed there by myself and an anonymous friend who had brought some on behalf of the children,

though I do not suppose the children know that their father is
dead. Of course there was the usual crucifix, candles and holy
water.

Gesling had advised me to have the remains placed in the
coffin at once, as decomposition would begin very rapidly,
and at 8.30 in the evening the men came to screw it down. An
unsuccessful photograph of Oscar was taken by Maurice
Gilbert at my request, the flashlight did not work
properly . . .

A plain tombstone was later set above the grave at Bagneux,
bearing these words from the twenty-ninth chapter of the
Book of Job: *Verbis meis addere nihil audebant et super illos stillabat
eloquium meum* ['To my words they durst add nothing, and my
speech dropped upon them.' (Douai version)]

Although the usual decencies are generally observed in matters
of death, a certain frankness is to be observed in some letters
whose writers do not trouble themselves too much to conceal
the defects of the deceased. Charlotte Brontë, writing to W. I.
Williams in 1842 was blunt about her feelings regarding the
death of her unstable, consumptive, and drunken brother,
Branwell:

I do not weep from a sense of bereavement—there is no prop
withdrawn, no consolation torn away, no dear companion
lost—but for the wreck of talent, the ruin of promise, the
untimely dreary extinction of what might have been a burning
and a shining light. My brother was a year my junior. I had
aspirations and ambitions for him once, long ago—they have
perished mournfully. Nothing remains of him but a memory
of errors and sufferings. There is such a bitterness of pity for
his life and death, such a yearning for the emptiness of his
whole existence as I cannot describe. I trust time will allay
these feelings.

And George Bernard Shaw in an effort to counter what he
regarded as the cant surrounding the death of Queen Victoria
wrote a marvellously deflating letter to the *Morning Leader*
whose Editor declined to publish it:

Sir
I am loth to interrupt the rapture of mourning in which the

nation is now enjoying its favourite festival—a funeral. But in a country like ours the total suspension of common sense and sincere human feeling for a whole fortnight is an impossibility. There are certain points in connection with the obsequies of Queen Victoria which call for vigorous remonstrance.

Why, may I ask, should the procedure in the case of a deceased sovereign be that which has long been condemned and discarded by all intelligent and educated persons as insanitary and superstitious? To delay a burial for a fortnight, to hermetically seal up the remains in a leaden coffin (and those who are behind the scenes at our cemeteries know well what will happen to that leaden coffin), is to exhibit a spectacle, not of reverent mourning, but of intolerable ignorance perpetuated by court tradition long after it has been swept away in more enlightened quarters. The remains of the Queen should have been either cremated or buried at once in a perishable coffin in a very shallow grave. The example set by such a course would have been socially invaluable. The example set by the present procedure is socially deplorable.

If at such a moment the royal family, instead of making each other Field-Marshals, and emphasizing every foolish unreality and insincerity that makes court life contemptible, were to seize the opportunity to bring its customs into some sort of decent harmony with modern civilization, they would make loyalty much easier for twentieth-century Englishmen.

That death should not be a matter for levity unless you are sure of the present company is, however, vividly demonstrated by the following letter from Coleridge to Miss Anne R. Scott in 1833 describing Dorothy Wordsworth's reaction to a heartless witticism:

Once, she, [Dorothy Wordsworth] being present, I told one of these good stories, the main drollery of which rests on their utter *unbelievability as actual fact*—viz—one a Surgeon, who having restored to life two or three persons who had attempted to hang or drown themselves; and having been afterwards importuned by them for Help and Maintenance on the plea, that having forced life upon them against their own will and wish, he was bound to support it; had ventured, that he would never interfere in any such accidents without having first ascertained whether the individual wished it or no. On a

summer day while on a water-party, one of the Rowers in
some unaccountable way fell over-board and disappeared.
But on his re-emersion the Surgeon caught hold of his Hair
and lifting his head and chest above the water said—Now,
my good Fellow! did you really mean to drown yourself! What
is your own wish?—O—o—o—! (sobbed out the man)—a
sickly *Wife*—and seven small children!—Ha! *poor* Fellow! No
Wonder Then!—exclaimed the Surgeon, and instantly
popped him under again. The party were all on the brink of a
loud Laugh, when Dorothy Wordsworth, with tears sparkling
in her eyes, cried out—Bless me! but was not that very
inhuman!—This stroke of exquisite Simplicity and true single-
ness of heart, made us almost roll off our chairs; but was there
one of the Party, that did not love Dorothy the more for it? I
trust not one . . .

Nonetheless, some deaths *are* more absurd than tragic. For
example, the poet Thomas Gray writing to Dr Clarke from
Pembroke Hall in 1760 describes the demise of a don in anything
but reverent terms:

Our friend Dr Chapman (one of [Cambridge's] nuisances) is
not expected here again in a hurry. He is gone to his grave
with five fine mackerel (large and full of roe) in his belly. He
ate them all at one dinner; but his fate was a turbot on Trinity
Sunday, of which he left little for the company besides bones.
He had not been hearty all the week; but after this sixth fish
he never held up his head more, and a violent looseness
carried him off.—They say he made a very good end.

It is often difficult to make a 'good end'. Perhaps the most we
can hope for is to make an entirely characteristic one. Poor
Hazlitt was short of money for most of his life so it is not
surprising that he wrote this final, sadly irrelevant note to the
Editor of the *Edinburgh Review* a few days before his death in
September 1830:

Dear Sir,
I am dying; can you send me 10£, and so consummate your
many kindnesses to me?

W. HAZLITT

4

In Time of Trouble

Apposite words of sympathy often evade the grasp of articulate and practised consolers; but in the following letter, Ivanov Macarius proves himself both eloquent and perceptive. Macarius lived from 1788 to 1860 and was a *staret* (spiritual director) in the Russian Orthodox Church. His words of comfort to a recently widowed lady are appropriate, as well as beautiful:

> I thank you for having unveiled to me the sadness of your grief-stricken heart; a great radiance comes over me when I share with others their sorrow. Complete, perfect, detailed compassion is the only answer I can give to your tender love of me that has led you, at such a time, to seek me out in my distant silent, humble hermitage.
>
> . . . In the ground of the Christian's heart, sorrow for the dead soon melts, illuminated by the light of the true wisdom. Then, in the place of the vanished grief, there shoots up a new knowledge made of hope and faith. This knowledge does not only wash the soul of all sadness; it makes it glad.
>
> Fanaticism shackles the mind; faith gives it the wings of freedom. This freedom is apparent in a quiet firmness, unruffled by any circumstances, fortunate or unfortunate. The sword that cuts us free of shackles is the purified mind; the mind that has learnt to discern the true, the secret, the mysterious cause and purpose of every occurrence. Purification of the mind is gained through frequently pondering on one's utter insignificance; but this pondering should always be veiled in a throbbing living prayer; for God's protection and his help.

A writer of enormous grace and precision was the Christian platonist Marsilio Ficino. He believed that philosophy and religion were not mutually antipathetic but parallel paths to truth. In his letter to Gismondo della Stufa written on 1 August 1473, he consoles his friend with the elegant conceit that Albiera degli Albizzi is reunited with her ideal form, the beautiful idea in the Creator's mind that fashioned her; and so may she remain in the mind of her earth-bound husband. A more charming and imaginative consolation would be hard to find, and surely it must have lightened Gismondo's burden:

> If each of us, essentially, is that which is greatest within us, which always remains the same and by which we understand ourselves, then certainly the soul is the man himself, and the body is but his shadow. Whatever wretch is so deluded as to think that the shadow of man is man, like Narcissus is dissolved into tears. You will only cease to weep, Gismondo, when you cease looking for your Albiera degli Albizzi in her dark shadow and begin to follow her by her own clear light. For the further she is from the mis-shapen shadow the more beautiful will you find her, past all you have ever known.
>
> Withdraw into your soul, I beg you, where you will possess her soul which is so beautiful and dear to you; or rather, from your soul withdraw to God. There you will contemplate the beautiful idea through which the Divine Creator fashioned your Albiera; and as she is far more lovely in her Creator's form than in her own, so you will embrace her there with far more joy.
>
> Farewell.

Mary Ann Evans, the novelist George Eliot, began her adult life enthusiastically evangelical, but became increasingly sceptical under the influence of social experience and the philosophical views of Charles Bray; so much so that she refused to attend church after a while, thus enraging her strong-minded father. He threatened to break up their household, over which Mary had presided since the death of her mother, and go and live with his married daughter. Mary Ann compromised, but her views were unchanged. F. W. H. Myers writing in 1881 relates how the novelist opened a conversation with him by pronouncing the three words 'God, Immortality and Duty'. She went on to observe with 'terrific earnestness', 'how inconceivable was the *first*, how unbelievable the *second*, and yet how peremptory and absolute the *third*.'

In the letter quoted below George Eliot offers condolence to

Mrs Bray on the death of her husband, eschewing religious or philosophical consolation, but demonstrating human warmth and sympathy. 'There is,' she says, 'no such thing as consolation, when we have made the lot of another our own':

> *The Priory, March 18, 1865*
>
> I believe you are one of the few who can understand that in certain crises direct expression of sympathy is the least possible to those who most feel sympathy. If I could have been with you in bodily presence, I should have sat silent, thinking silence a sign of feeling that speech, trying to be wise, must always spoil. The truest things one can say about great Death are the oldest, simplest things that everybody knows by rote, but that no one knows really till death has come very close. And when that inward teaching is going on, it seems pitiful presumption for those who are outside to be saying anything. There is no such thing as consolation when we have made the lot of another our own. I don't know whether you strongly share, as I do, the old belief that made men say the gods loved those who died young. It seems to me truer than ever, now life has become more complex, and more and more difficult problems have to be worked out. Life, though a good to men on the whole, is a doubted good to many, and to some not good at all. To my thought, it is a source of constant mental distortion to make the denial of this a part of religion—to go on pretending things are better than they are. To me early death takes the aspect of salvation; though I feel, too, that those who live and suffer may sometimes have the greater blessedness of *being* a salvation. But I will not write of judgments and opinions. What I want my letter to tell you is that I love you truly, gratefully, unchangeably.

Official letters of condolence are a more equivocal genre. The death of some blood-stained dictator has often to be marked with some official display of respect for the purposes of diplomacy. And then again, a politician may sometimes be more comfortable mourning an opponent's death than dealing with the living rival. The following letter from Elizabeth I to James VI is a good example of a somewhat suspect letter of condolence. It was sent after the execution of Mary Queen of Scots. Elizabeth's feelings on the matter were undoubtedly complex but her letter is as much a piece of diplomacy as one of deep sentiment. In any case the recipient was reputedly not too unhappy about the removal of one obstacle towards his own more rapid progress to the English throne—his mother:

14 February 1587

My dear brother,

I would you knew (though not felt) the extreme dolour that overwhelms my mind, for that miserable accident which (far contrary to my meaning) hath befallen. I have now sent this kinsman of mine, whom by now it has pleased you to favour, to instruct you truly of that which is too irksome for my pen to tell you. I beseech you, as God and many more know, how innocent I am in this case; so you will believe me that if I had bid ought I would have bid by it. I am not so base-minded that fear of any living creature or prince should make me afraid to do that were just; or done, to deny the same. I am not of so base a lineage, nor carry so vile a mind. But, as not to disguise fits not a king, so will I never dissemble my actions, but cause them show even as I meant them. Thus assuring yourself of me, that as I know this was deserved, yet if I had meant it I would never lay it on others' shoulder; no more will I not damnify myself that thought it not. The circumstance it may please you to have of this bearer. And for your part, think you have not in the world a more loving kinswoman, nor a more dear friend than myself; nor any that will watch more carefully to preserve you and your estate. And who shall otherwise persuade you, judge them more partial to others than you. And thus in haste I leave to trouble you; beseeching God to send you a long reign.

Your most assured loving sister and cousin
ELIZ. R

Totally unequivocal is the following letter on the death in December 1894 of a much-loved writer, written by Henry James to Mrs Robert Louis Stevenson. Although James's manner is very literary and interspersed with Jamesian periods, its depth of feeling is evident:

My dear Fanny Stevenson,

What can I say to you that will not seem cruelly irrelevant or vain? We have been sitting in darkness for nearly a fortnight,

but what is *our* darkness to the extinction of your magnificent
light? You will probably know in some degree what has
happened to us—how the hideous news first came to us via
Auckland, etc., and then how, in the newspapers, a doubt
was raised about its authenticity—just enough to give one a
flicker of hope; until your telegram to me via San
Francisco—repeated also from other sources—converted my
pessimistic convictions into the wretched knowledge. All this
time my thoughts have hovered round you all, around *you* in
particular, with a tenderness of which I could have wished
you might have, afar-off, the divination. You are such a
visible picture of desolation that I need to remind myself that
courage, and patience, and fortitude are also abundantly with
you. The devotion that Louis inspired—and of which all the
air about you must be full—must also be much to you. Yet as I
write the word, indeed, I am almost ashamed of it—as if
anything could be 'much' in the presence of such an abysmal
void. To have lived in the light of that splendid life, that
beautiful, bountiful being—only to see it, from one moment
to the other, converted into a fable as strange and romantic as
one of its own, a thing that *has* been and has ended, is an
anguish into which no one can enter with you fully and of
which no one can drain the cup for you. You are nearest to the
pain, because you were nearest the joy and the pride . . .

Writing in tribute to the dead and to comfort the living requires
great subtlety. An even more difficult task was attempted, and
successfully carried through, by James Agate, writing in July
1943 to an actress he admired and liked. An illness had made it
likely that her extremely promising career was to be cut short
since it had affected her legs with semi-paralysis. It is, in the
circumstances, rather a brave letter (paying her the painful
compliment of addressing her as 'Hedda', after her greatest
role), and perhaps elicited a corresponding bravery from its
recipient:

My dear Hedda
Do you remember Mr Nicodemus Dumps? He comes in
Sketches by Boz, the story called *The Bloomsbury Christening*.
Dumps is the godfather of Master Frederick Charles William
Kitterbell, and here is part of the speech he makes at the 'sit
down supper' after the ceremony. 'I hope and trust, ladies

and gentlemen, that the infant whose christening we have this evening met to celebrate may not be removed from the arms of his parents by premature decay; that his young and now *apparently* healthy form may not be wasted by lingering disease. You, I am sure, will concur with me in wishing that he may live to be a comfort and a blessing to his parents. But should he not be what we could wish—should he forget in after-times the duty which he owes to them—should they unhappily experience that distracting truth, "how sharper than a serpent's tooth it is to have a thankless child . . ."' In other words, I do not think that you can look forward to a time when your state of health will permit you to be whirled about the stage in the manner of Juanita and the Ganjou Brothers.

Dear Pam, let's face it, you may never return to the stage. Having squared up to this tragedy—for that it would be—let's look around and see if we can espy any comfort. I think we can. I'm not going to tell you that victories are not always won on battlefields. You are an artist, and any consolation to be found for you must be such as befits an artist. Very well, then, I am not discouraged.

I foresaw all this at Oxford, I said to myself, 'Here is a great little player who may, or may not, have the health to grow into a great big one.' I then bethought me of my favourite passage in all literature. It occurs at the end of Théophile Gautier's *Mademoiselle de Maupin*: 'Combien sont morts qui, moins heureux que vous, n'ont pas même donné un seul baiser à leur chimère!' I determined that you should have your heart's desire and greatly play a great part. This you did. Nothing can take from you the knowledge that, judged by the highest standards, you were as grand a Hedda Gabler as an actress of your age could hope to be. I am not lying to please you. I stake my critical reputation, such as it is, on the beauty and understanding of your performance. You followed this up by a glamorising tosh—a great triumph, since the mark of the second-rate actress is that she is no good in anything except the masterpieces. If you return to the stage, be sure that if I am alive I shall be there to welcome you. If you do not return, may I be a perpetual guest in the theatre of your mind? Attend first nights with me in spirit. Let me write you from time to time what I really think of that wan blossom, Miss X, and that splendacious orchid, Miss Y.

Now cheer up. The summer's flower is to the summer sweet, though to itself it only live and die. But it wasn't summer—it was February, if I remember aright. And your Hedda lived triumphantly.

Ever your sympathetic
JAMES AGATE

BRICKBATS AND
BOUQUETS

1

'A Word In Your Ear . . .'

Those who are very ready with unsolicited advice are not always
the best qualified to give it. Humility, a knowledge of the world
and an understanding of human nature, are the qualities
required of counsellors. This seems to have been true in any
age, whether it be Erasmus writing to his pupil Christian
Northoff in 1497:

> . . . Avoid nocturnal lucubrations and studies at unseason-
> able times. They exhaust the mind and seriously affect the
> health. The dawn, beloved of the Muses, is the fit time for
> study. After dinner either play, or walk, or take part in
> cheerful conversation. Possibly even among these amuse-
> ments some room may be found for improvement. Take as
> much food as is required, not for your pleasure, but for your
> health. Before supper take a short walk, and after supper do
> the same. Before going to bed read something exquisite and
> worth remembering, of which you will be thinking when
> overcome by sleep, and for which you will ask yourself again
> when you wake. Let this maxim of Pliny rest always in your
> mind: All your time is lost which you do not impart to study.
> Remember that nothing is more fugitive than youth, which,
> when once it has flown away, never returns. But I am
> beginning to preach, after promising to be nothing but a
> guide. Follow, sweetest Christian, the plan I have traced, or
> any better that you can. Farewell.

Or whether it be William Lecky writing to a friend about his son
in 1869:

> I know so very little about the practical side of the world and
> more particularly about Cambridge and Civil Engineering and

about Erskine that I greatly hesitate in expressing any opinion.

It seems to me that the success of men in life depends more than upon any other single thing on this—that they constantly set before them a clear definite aim to be attained and acquire the habit of working steadily towards its accomplishment. To form this habit early seems to me the supremely important object of education, and in early manhood a prolonged indecision about the future may and often does do irreparable injury, relaxing the energies, producing desultory and procrastinating habits and wasting the time in which the mind may be most easily set to a definite object. I believe very little in the plan of reading for its own sake, for the acquisition of knowledge and so forth. In the case of a very few minds it may be useful, but in the case of most very young men it only forms desultory and dilettante habits and produces a great incapacity for that drudgery which is absolutely essential to professional success, and besides a taste for reading is always most easily and at the same time most beneficially found in the intellectual atmosphere of a university. Only infinitesimally few persons acquire it before entering one.

There are many instances of free literary advice. In 1911 Sir Walter Scott in the following letter combined his debunking of exaggerated notions about the facility for writing poetry (which he describes as a 'knack'), with a pre-romantic lecture on the dangers of 'enthusiasm'. Poetry and belles-lettres were not, it seemed a serious occupation, but acceptable as an engaging pastime. He is replying to a fifteen-year-old schoolboy poet who had asked for Scott's opinion of his verses:

. . . Above all, sir, I must warn you against suffering yourself to suppose that the power of enjoying natural beauty and poetical description are necessarily connected with that of producing poetry. The former is really a gift of Heaven, which conduces inestimably to the happiness of those who enjoy it. The second has much more of a knack in it than the pride of poets is always willing to admit; and, at any rate, is only valuable when combined with the first . . . I would also caution you against an enthusiasm which, while it argues an excellent disposition and feeling heart, requires to be watched, and restrained, though not repressed. It is apt, if too much indulged, to engender a fastidious contempt for the ordinary business of the world, and gradually to render us unfit for the exercise of the useful and domestic virtues which depend greatly upon our not exalting our feelings above the temper of well-ordered and well-educated society. No man can ever be happy when he is unfit for the career of simple and commonplace duty; and I need not add how many melancholy instances there are of extravagance and profligacy being resorted to under pretence of contempt for the common rules of life . . .

Other writers who give advice seem more concerned to put people off writing altogether. In the following letter E. E. Cummings is anything but encouraging:

Dear Mr ——
thanks for the letter of February 14. It was an astonishing valentine! Being neither a scholar nor a critic, I don't read manuscripts or give advice. But in your case let me make a suggestion
why not learn to write English? It's one of the more beautiful languages. And (like any language) it has a grammar, syntax, etc: which can be learned. Nobody can teach you to write poetry, but only you can learn the language through which you hope to become a poet
trying to write poetry before you've learned all there is to learn about writing is like tackling the integral calculus without understanding arithmetic. It's even more like trying to build yourself a house from the ridgepole down; instead of laying the foundations first & then erecting a structure on them, story by story
there must be someone at your college who teaches English Composition. If you take this letter to him, he'll be glad (I'm sure) to help you

Andrew Lang, in his letter to a young journalist, gives a recital of the vices inherent in that calling designed to leave the recipient without any illusions about what was required of him:

. . . If you enter on this path of tattle, mendacity, and malice and if, with your cleverness and light hand, you are successful, society will not turn its back on you. You will be feared in many quarters, and welcomed in others. Of your paragraphs people will say that 'It is a shame, of course, but it is amusing.' There are so many shames in the world, shames not at all amusing, that you may see no harm in adding to the number. 'If I don't do it,' you may argue, 'someone else will.' Undoubtedly; *but why should you do it?*

You are not a starving scribbler; if you determine to write, you can write well, though not so easily, on many topics. You have not that last excuse of hunger, which drives poor women to the street, and makes unhappy men act as public blabs and spies. If *you* take to this *métier*, it must be because you like it, which means that you enjoy being a listener to and reporter of talk that was never meant for any ears except those in which it was uttered. It means that the hospitable board is not sacred for you; it means that, with you, friendship, honour, all that makes human life better than a low smoking-room, are only valuable for what their betrayal will bring. It means that not even the welfare of your country will prevent you from running to the Press with any secret which you may have been entrusted with, or which you may have surprised. It means, this peculiar kind of profession, that all things open and excellent, and conspicuous to all men, are with you of no account. Art, literature, politics, are to cease to interest you. You are to scheme to surprise gossip about the private lives, dress, and talk of artists, men of letters, politicians. Your professional work will sink below the level of servants' gossip in a public-house parlour. If you happen to meet a man of known name, you will watch him, will listen to him, will try to sneak into his confidence, and you will blab, for money, about him, and your blab will inevitably be mendacious. In short, like the most pitiable outcasts of womankind, and without their excuse, you will live by selling your honour. You will not suffer much, nor suffer long. Your conscience will very speedily be seared with a red-hot iron. You will be on the road which leads from mere dishonour to crime; and you may find yourself actually practising chantage, and extorting money as the price of your silence. This is the lowest deep: the vast majority, even of social mouchards, do not sink so low as this.

. . . The whole question for you is, Do you mind incurring this damnation? If there is nothing in it which appals and revolts you, if your conscience is satisfied with a few ready

sophisms, or if you don't care a pin for your conscience, fall
to!

Vous irez loin! You will prattle in print about men's private
lives, their hidden motives, their waistcoats, their wives, their
boots, their business, their incomes. Most of your prattle will
inevitably be lies. But go on! Nobody will kick you, I deeply
regret to say. You will earn money. You will be welcomed in
society. You will live and die content, and without remorse. I
do not suppose that any particular inferno will await you in
the future life. Whoever watches this world 'with larger other
eyes than ours' will doubtless make allowance for you, as for
us all. I am not pretending to be a whit better than you;
probably I am worse in many ways, but not in your way.
Putting it merely as a matter of taste, I don't like the way. It
makes me sick—that is all. It is a sin which I can comfortably
damn, as I am not inclined to it. You may put it in that light;
and I have no way of converting you, nor, if I have not
dissuaded you, of dissuading you from continuing, on a
larger scale, your practices in *The Bull-dog.*

The robustness and humour in Lang's letter are echoed in a
magnificent letter from Anton Chekhov to his brother in which
he remarks that, notwithstanding Nikolay's other qualities, he is
vitally lacking in the most important one: 'You have only one
fault . . . it is your utter lack of culture.'

Cultured people must, in my opinion, meet the following
conditions:
1. They respect human personality, and for this reason they
are always lenient, gentle, civil, and ready to give in to others.
They do not raise a rumpus over a hammer or a lost eraser;
when they live with you they do not make you feel that they
are doing you a favour, and on leaving they do not say,
'Impossible to live with you!' They overlook noise, cold
overdone meat, jokes, the presence of strangers in their
rooms.
2. They feel compassion not only for beggars and cats. Their
hearts ache over what the naked eye does not see. Thus, for
instance, if Pyotr knows that his parents do not sleep nights
because they see him seldom (and that when he is drunk), he
will spit on vodka and hasten to see them. They sit up nights

in order to help the Polevayevs, to keep their brothers at the university, and to buy clothes for their mother.

3. They respect the property of others and therefore pay their debts.

4. They are candid, and dread lying as they dread fire. They do not lie even about trifles. A lie insults the listener and debases him in the eyes of the speaker. They do not pose; they behave in the street as they do at home; they do not show off before their inferiors. They do not chatter and do not force uninvited confidences on others. Out of respect for the ears of other people they often keep silent.

5. They do not belittle themselves to arouse compassion in others. They do not play on other people's heartstrings so as to elicit sighs and be fussed over. They do not say, 'People do not understand me' or 'I have frittered away my talent! . . .' because all that is striving after cheap effect; it is vulgar, stale, false.

6. They are not vain. They do not care for such paste diamonds as familiarity with celebrities . . . the raptures of the first comer in a picture gallery, popularity in beer halls . . . When they have done a copeck's worth of work they do not strut about with their briefcases as though they had done a hundred roubles' worth, and they do not brag of having entree where others are not admitted. The truly talented always keep in the shade, among the crowd, far from the show. Even Krylov [Russia's La Fontaine] said that an empty barrel is noisier than a full one.

7. If they possess talent they respect it. They sacrifice peace, women, wine, vanity to it. They are proud of their talent. They do not carouse with riff-raff: they are aware that their calling is not just to live with such people but to have an educative influence on them. Besides, they are fastidious.

8. They cultivate their aesthetic sense. They cannot fall asleep in their clothes, see cracks in the wall full of insects, breathe foul air, walk on a spittle-covered floor, eat off a kerosene stove. They seek as far as possible to take and ennoble the sexual instinct. . . . The kitchen is not their main interest. What they want from a woman is not a bedfellow, not equine sweat, not a cleverness that shows itself in the ability to fake a pregnancy and to lie incessantly. What they need, especially, if they are artists, is freshness, elegance, humanity, the capacity for being not a——but a mother. They do not swill

vodka offhand. They do not sniff at cupboards, for they know that they are not pigs. They drink only when they are free, on occasion. For they need *mens sana in corpore sano*.

And so on. That is what cultivated people are like. In order to educate yourself and not be below the level of your surroundings it is not enough to read *The Pickwick Papers* and memorize a monologue from Faust . . .

What is needed is continuous work, day and night, constant reading, study, will power. Every hour counts.

. . . You must make a clean break. Come to us; smash the vodka bottle; lie down and read—Turgenev, if you like, whom you have not read—give up your conceit, you are not a child. You will soon be thirty. It is time!

I am waiting . . . We are all waiting . . .

Your A. CHEKHOV

Chekhov concentrates on social and aesthetic qualities, but of course these have a moral dimension which he illustrates anecdotally. Spiritual advisers start with the ethical dimension and place it in a context of faith and ultimate values. When one of them has to reprimand a member of his flock, the necessity of tactfully blending sympathy with rebuke can put considerable strain on his powers as a writer. He tries to censor without appearing censorious, demonstrate authority but exhibit humility, and be frank without being brutal. An attempt to combine all these elements is seen in John Henry Newman's letter of 1846 to J. B. Morris. Morris was a member of the religious community at Maryvale, Birmingham, and evidently his conduct left a good deal to be desired. Newman seized the opportunity of Morris's convalescence from mumps to write him a letter which may not have hastened his recovery but surely improved his spiritual health:

My dear Morris,

One is so seldom able in the common course of things to hear from others what concerns oneself, that I cannot bring myself to let slip the opportunity which now offers of begging you to hear me say about you what will be painful to me as well as to you, yet acceptable to you, I am sure, notwithstanding. Nay I feel confident, that, even though you should not see the justice of some things I am going to say, you will on the whole thank me still, from the chance of your learning something or other about yourself amid whatever I may say irrelevant or erroneous. Angel visits are said to be 'few and far between'; and speaking as I wish to do in Christian charity, I know, my dear Morris, you will pay me back that charity, and consider my words, in spite of their infirmity, as almost an Angel's, and a blessing.

Nor am I unmindful, as I do trust, of what may be the beam in my own eye while I venture to speak of the mote in another's; nor again do I forget the weakness of your general health, which may seem to account for the points which I am to notice. And here I am brought at once to my subject.

Weak health certainly has a tendency to make us selfish, unless we are watchful; and though I dare not use so hard a word of so good a person as you, yet I do think it has made you your own centre, more than is expedient . . .

. . . And now, my dear Morris, comes my great difficulty, how to bring this home to you; for at first you will not see things in my light. And again, the evidence of it depends on a number of very small details which it is difficult, and almost frivolous to set down on paper. Each by itself may be explained away, whatever be the cumulative force of all together. Accordingly I shall give up absolutely any attempt to prove to you my impression; I shall but seek to convey it, by means of instances, which, however minute, nay though exaggerated, distorted, or unfounded here or there, and though abrupt in their sound, may on the whole gradually let you into my meaning on reflection. And now I begin.

Your first object apparently when you came here, was to get suitable rooms for yourself, and you have got such as no one else has. You wanted your books brought upstairs—several men cheerfully undertook at once what was a considerable labour. You took their services as a matter of course; you did not thank them or feel that they were working for you. Then you set about carpentering for yourself; not for the house, except in one or two matters when you were directly asked, such as nailing down the parlour carpet. Then you ordered wood in my name at Mr Grove's; with my consent indeed, but you used it for yourself, not for the house. When we said you should be carpenter, you took the office, not as a duty towards the house, but as a sort of privilege. You kept the keys of the shop from us, while you made use of the shop only for yourself.

As you suffered your books to be brought up to you, so did you let us sweep your room, and attend to you when indisposed, as a matter of course, not showing that you felt the kindness. Each of us took his turn in the routine house business as septenarius; it seemed never to occur to you that you ought to have a week too. I took yours for you during Lent thinking you would be less wearied when Easter came. At Easter you were surprised to hear that you were to have two weeks together, nay that you were to have any week at all. You did not attend to either of them as a matter of duty. You went up to Oscott, leaving others to do your work, without asking them.

Instead of living with us, you have kept your own room. Nay, you grudged us your company for any time however short, for a quarter of an hour after dinner, though you could go up to Oscott for the whole of Sunday. You could give us nothing of you, and nothing struck you but surprise that others did not leave the house on Sundays too . . . At breakfast and supper your one object was to make your own cocoa or tea, and get your meal. When you were septenarius, you thought it enough to engage another to make the coffee instead of you.

These are illustrations, my dear Morris, of what I mean to point out to you; and it distresses me to pursue the tokens of a similar habit of mind into other matters. I am reluctantly led to think that you like your way, more than you ought, generally. You have before now done serious things which ever seemed to me to be marks of something faulty in you, and for which I have not been able to account. I refer especially to that old matter, the letters in the English Churchman about the Vice-Chancellor's election, as to which it avails very little to say that you consulted another person. You are apt too, without knowing it, to set up your own views as a standard, in indifferent matters, so as even to smile on those who measure things differently. You would be surprised to be made aware how frequent the word 'I' is in your mouth. E.g. your first remark on a book being mentioned is, 'This is a book I have never read', though it is *nihil ad rem* to say so; or 'I have read part of that book', or 'that is a book I don't think much of.' And as perhaps one remembers best what has been personal to oneself, I will add my feeling, that you have been bent, more than you are aware of, on forcing your own judgement on me in my matters. E.g. in the case of the new bookshelves in the small library, you insisted that they should be grooved in at Birmingham, though you knew my own contrary view on starting, and I could hardly bring you to end the discussion. So again you took a view that I ought to go up to Oscott for the functions, which was no concern of yours . . .

And now, my dear Morris, I beg your pardon if I have not written this as kindly as I might have done. I have been anxious to do it well, and have written it more than once over; but I know well that had I more of the spirit of love, I should have written it better. While then I am giving you pain, I am not without some feelings of humiliation myself. That our most Merciful Father and Guide may ever be with you, show you His will, and direct you in your vocation is the earnest prayer of

Your affte Friend JOHN H NEWMAN

Newman's remarks are in every respect well judged. Not all advice is. Pietro Aretino, who enjoyed outraging his correspondents and his fellow citizens, described himself as 'secretary of the whole world'. His shrewd perceptions and witty tongue were greatly feared, but he also flattered the powerful when it suited him; he was thus in line for preferment on the one hand, while on the other, he was in the market for bribes to stop his mouth. His impudence was unbounded and his letters sometimes read like those of a sixteenth-century Italian George Bernard Shaw. Here, in November 1537, he is advising Messer Battista Strozzi that if he *must* go to war he should keep well to the rear:

Some fellow or other swore to me that you had taken it into your head to embark once again on some splendid enterprise or other. Stay at Correggio, dear sir; do, I insist, stay put: or else, good God, you'll be looking for me to dash off some epitaph for your wretched tombstone. I thought that what went on at Montemurlo had made you wise, but you are madder than ever. And the reason for this is the Ciceronian argument in the treatise *On Tyranny*, which is the ABC of all you want to do. I tell you again that you should devote your time to conferring with your lyre at Signora Veronica's fireplace, plucking out a modest stanza or two in the heroic manner, and letting vagabonds do your wandering for you.

I am amazed that having found yourself at Prato, buried in a stack of hay, and having said to a cart-horse which, not knowing you were there, went to take a couple of mouthfuls: 'I surrender', you haven't vowed before all the holy pictures in the world never to talk again about a soldier's life. Come on, now! The devil and your own madness are tempting you and inciting you to go, therefore do so, but be cautious and keep in the rear, because when it comes to honour, *nos otros* [all of us] find it in the *Salvum me fac* ['Preserve me, O God'] and not in running risks in order to be wounded half a dozen times and held as a wild beast into the bargain.

. . . So therefore, when you return to the fray, fasten your steed's shoes with just a couple of nails, like the man with dysentery who held up his breeches with two bits of string. In that way, staying well to the rear and breathing fire and defiance, you can convince the mob that it would be all the worse for the enemy if your nag's shoes hadn't fallen off! And if the battle should be won, then spur your horse forward and mingle with the victors, and drinking in the cries of Hurrah! Hurrah! be among the first to enter the conquered town, looking not just like a captain but a giant. If the battle goes badly, draw back, take to your heels and flee for your life, because if you want to save your skin it's better that they should shout: 'Here's a man running away,' than: 'There's a man who's dead.'

Put glory in its place: when we are dead, mistress Fame can pipe her pavanes and galliards, but the man crowned with Laurel and returned to dust and ashes hears nothing.

Shaw himself, of course, gave copious advice to all and sundry; often it was full of robust common sense, frequently it was mischievous, and always it was entertaining. Here he explains to the actress Frances Dillon how she should play Ann Whitefield in *Man and Superman*:

. . . I strongly advise you to read the letters of Queen Victoria through from beginning to end. Then try to imagine yourself Queen Victoria every night in the 1st Act. You will notice that Queen Victoria, even when she was most infatuatedly in love with Prince Albert, always addressed him exactly as if he were a little boy of three and she his governess. That is the particularly kind of English ladylikeness in which you are deplorably deficient. An English lady in mourning is a majestic and awful spectacle. No matter how improperly she may behave, an English lady never admits she is behaving improperly. Just as there are lots of women who are good-hearted and honest and innocent in an outrageously rowdy way, so are there ladies who do the most shocking things with a dignity and gentility which a bishop might envy. Ann is one of the latter sort; and this is what you have not got in Ann. Ann's dignity, her self-control, her beautifully measured speed, her impressive grief for her father, which absolutely forbids her to smile until she is out of mourning, a sort of rich, chaste, noble self-respect about her which makes you feel that she belongs to carriage folk and is probably very highly connected, must be splendidly and very firmly handled on the stage in order to give effect to her audacity. In this you fail most hideously. From the moment of your entrance, you give Ann away as an easy-going, not particular sort of person. You smiled freely; and when you threw your boa round Tanner's neck, there was nothing in it, because it was just exactly what one would have expected you to do. I was perfectly shocked at your second-rate behaviour when I should have been thrilled and stupended by the lifting of the goddess's veil only to disclose a syren. Your view of yourself was simply 'With these pretty teeth, and this pretty smile, and these little ways, I can get round any man', whereas your view should have been, 'I am Miss Ann Whitefield, of Whitefield Court, Richmond, Surrey. I belong to a distinguished intellectual set; and although I do things that vulgar people might misunderstand because they are vulgar, the fact that I do them hallmarks them as eternally correct and right. Therefore be good enough not to shew your ignorance by sniggering.' What gave me a final blow was your going off the stage in the last act and coming back with a new make-up on and a general air of saying, 'Now I am going to shew you something. Now I'm going to get my teeth into the only scene that makes this rotten play worth playing.' You play it very well; but nobody on earth could play that scene badly if once they could play it at all. It is the 1st Act of Man and Superman that tests an actress; and I solemnly declare that your performance of the 1st act would have been dear at fifteen shillings a week. I believe this was the effect of uncertainty as to how to take Ann. Try whether you can get any more out of it on the lines I have sketched above . . .

Shaw's advice is constructive; he knew what actresses had to go through. The same warmth and identification with a fellow sufferer comes through in a typically elegant letter from Sydney Smith, written in 1820, to a melancholy Lady Georgiana Morpeth. Smith was languishing in his parish of Foston in Yorkshire—which hardly suited such a sociable and witty man. His twenty precepts, if followed, would contribute more to sociability and the banishment of gloom than whole books of more solemn instruction:

> *Dear Lady Georgiana,*
>   . . . Nobody has suffered more from low spirits than I have done—so I feel for you. 1st. Live as well as you dare. 2nd. Go into the shower-bath with a small quantity of water at a temperature low enough to give you a slight sensation of cold, 75° or 80°. 3rd. Amusing books. 4th. Short views of human life—not further than dinner or tea. 5th. Be as busy as you can. 6th. See as much as you can of those friends who respect and like you. 7th. And of those acquaintances who amuse you. 8. Make no secret of low spirits to your friends, but talk of them freely—they are always worse for dignified concealment. 9th. attend to the effects tea and coffee produce upon you. 10th. Compare your lot with that of other people. 11th. Don't expect too much from human life—a sorry business at the best. 12th. Avoid poetry, dramatic representations (except comedy) music, serious novels, melancholy sentimental people, and everything likely to excite feeling or emotion not ending in active benevolence. 13th. *Do good*, and endeavour to please everybody of every degree. 14th. Be as much as you can in the open air without fatigue. 15th. Make the room where you commonly sit, gay and pleasant. 16th. Struggle by little and little against idleness. 17th. Don't be too severe upon yourself, or underrate yourself, but do yourself justice. 18th. Keep good blazing fires. 19th. Be firm and constant in the exercise of rational religion. 20th. Believe me, dear Lady Georgiana,
>
>   Very truly yours,
>   SYDNEY SMITH

The Gentle Art of Making Enemies

Most public figures get hate mail, which is usually sterile and repetitive, and triumphantly works up to some crushing apothegm to which the writer believes there can be no answer; not that they require or desire one. 'What extraordinary letters people write to people they don't know!' wrote Rose Macaulay to her sister Jeanie after receiving the fall-out from one of her radio broadcasts:

> . . . I have got a *most* impertinent one from a man who is furious because I said on the 'Critics' that I saw no reason why children shouldn't see the X film we were discussing. Apparently I said that I had been allowed to read what books I liked as a child, and they had done me no harm. He said on the contrary, I flattered myself, they had obviously done me *great* harm, if I was willing that innocent children should see X films. I wonder in what mood people write these impertinent letters—I suppose indignation. But it is difficult to imagine such impulses being yielded to. I suppose Aunt Mary might. But she wouldn't write so vulgarly, being educated. I don't like getting rude letters; it is like having mud thrown at you. I never answer them, of course.

James Agate, in contrast to Dame Rose, was more than prepared to give as good as he got. He notes the following in his diary:

> A sergeant air-gunner writes: 'I don't suppose you have spent eighteen months in a desert. Or sat in a gun-turret for four hundred and fifty hours, eight hours at a stretch. Or been shot down and wounded. If you had, perhaps you would take a more kindly view of the enclosed poem.' I have replied: 'No, I shouldn't. Your poem, badly rhymed and worse scanned, did its job when it took your mind off the desert and the gun-turret. Having done this, it became waste paper.'

Another writer who was willing to have a go was Mark Twain. On one occasion he prepared a splendid piece of invective, but on reflection mailed a one-liner which was less overtly abusive but more crushing. It was in response to a gentleman who kept soliciting Twain's support for a new system of musical notation which, he claimed, was vastly superior to all the existing and inadequate ones. Twain explains the background to this row, and his mailed and unmailed answers follow:

An enthusiast who had a new system of musical notation wrote to me and suggested that a magazine article from me, contrasting the absurdities of the old system with the simplicities of his new one, would be sure to make a 'rousing hit'. He shouted and shouted over the marvels wrought by his system and quoted the handsome compliments which had been paid it by famous musical people but he forgot to tell me what his notation was like or what its simplicities consisted in. So I could not have written the articles if I had wanted to—which I didn't, because I hate strangers with axes to grind. I wrote him a courteous note explaining how busy I was—I always explain how busy I am—and casually dropped this remark:

'I judge the X-X notation to be a rational mode of representing music, in place of the prevailing fashion, which was the invention of an idiot.'

Next mail he asked permission to print that meaningless remark. I answered no—courteously but still no, explaining that I could not afford to be placed in the attitude of trying to influence people with a mere worthless *guess*. What a scorcher I got, next mail! Such irony! Such sarcasm, such caustic praise of my superhonorable loyalty to the public! And withal, such compassion for my stupidity, too, in not being able to understand my own language. I cannot remember the words of this letter broadside but there was about a page used up in turning this idea round and round and exposing it in different lights.

Unmailed Answer

Dear Sir,
What is the trouble with you? If it is your viscera, you cannot have them taken out and reorganized a moment too

soon. I mean, if they are inside. But if you are composed of them, that is another matter. Is it your brain? But it could not be your brain. Possibly it is your skull: you want to look out for that. Some people, when they get an idea, it pries the structure apart. Your system of notation has got in there and couldn't find room. Without a doubt that is what the trouble is. Your skull was not made to put ideas in, it was made to throw potatoes at.

Yours truly

Mailed Answer

Dear Sir,
Come, come—take a walk. You disturb the children.

Yours truly

Critics and writers who are partly in the business of sniping at others must expect a certain amount of ricochet, but their position is less perilous than that of social reformers who can be the target of particularly vicious letters from that sector of the population ironically described by Bertrand Russell as 'nice people'. The following exchange between a curate and the husband of Dr Marie Stopes (the writer was not prepared to demean himself by taking issue with Dr Stopes directly) is a good illustration of the psychological basis of many such letters. In November 1920 Marie Stopes had sent a questionnaire to two thousand Church of England incumbents chosen at random from Crockford's directory. It included questions about what methods of birth control were used by the recipients; unfortunately one questionnaire landed on the desk of a vicar 'too senile to read or fill it in', and provoked his curate to a violent response:

Dr Stopes apparently uses no care or discrimination to whom she sends her rotten communications—for no decent man could read such papers without loathing—If Dr Stopes could use her energies to prevent people marrying who were not fit and by having lunatics and weakminded castrated before leaving an asylum she would be doing a more useful work—leaving healthy young people to have children as a wise nature intended them, instead of having six or seven means of prevention plonked before their eyes by a person who unless strong evidence is brought to the contrary Mr S must believe to be an old whore.

In reply, Marie Stopes's husband, H. V. Roe, wrote:

> . . . It is quite evident you have rushed off your letter without giving it any Christian thought, otherwise I am sure it would not have been worded in so insolent and objectionable a fashion . . . That you may differ from Dr Stopes in your opinion is quite permissible but to write as you have done, makes it evident that you are unacquainted with the wonderful work she has done in making married life more sacred . . . If you do study her work you will, as a gentleman, suitably apologize to her for your disgusting letter. Yours faithfully

The curate's answer was: 'Can you not feel that if a man wrote to you on such topics, you would travel a long, long way to thrash him?'

Dr Stopes, at the time she was active, belonged to a profession that was barely respectable and indeed only recently invented. The legal profession, on the other hand, thinks of itself as highly respectable and resents any implications to the contrary. In 1973 lawyers were outraged when the Commissioner of the Metropolitan Police suggested that a few of them were criminal in every sense of the word. The parading of injured virtue was wonderful to behold. Bernard Levin printed in *The Times* a series of parodies of the letters of protest with which lawyers had immediately bombarded the newspapers. His imitations exactly capture the mixture of pomposity, mendacity and Uriah Heepishness that characterized their public protestations. The two that follow are good examples of Levin's unerring eye for humbug:

> *From Sir Preposterous Attorney, QC*
> *Sir,*
> When will people like Sir Robert Mark learn that criticism of lawyers cannot and must not be permitted? And the reason is a very simple and practical one. It is not that lawyers are in some mystical way sacrosanct (though they are), nor that the slightest criticism of them will almost certainly lead to the total destruction of civilization as we know it (though it will); it is

that lawyers, by reason of their training and the character with which they are imbued by it, are simply unable to do wrong. It makes no more sense to talk of a 'crooked lawyer' than it does to refer to a 'square circle'. Just as there is not, and cannot be, such a thing as a square circle, so there is not, never has been and never could be, any such thing as a lawyer who would, in any circumstances, do wrong. You do not have to take my word for it, either; ask any lawyer.

Yours faithfully,
PREPOSTEROUS ATTORNEY, QC

333¾ Lincoln's Inn, EC4
From Mr Understandably Shifty, QC
Sir,
The suggestion by Sir Robert Mark that we lawyers should ourselves seek out and deal with the crooked ones among us is absurd; how on earth would we find the time to take money if we carried on like that?

Yours faithfully,
UNDERSTANDABLY SHIFTY, QC

Groucho Marx, another master of casual abuse, enjoyed taking on whole corporations. After a memorable victory over the legal department of Warner Bros (see page 200), he had a go, in 1961, at the Franklin Corporation. As an investor, though a nervous and reluctant one, he had been sent the company's glossy annual report, which was designed to impress stockholders and give a reassuring picture of the trading prospects. The brochure had rashly printed pictures of the directors, and Groucho was alarmed:

Dear Mr Goodman:
I received the first annual report of the Franklin Corporation and though I am not an expert at reading balance sheets, my financial adviser (who, I assure you, knows nothing) nodded his head in satisfaction.
You wrote that you hope I am not one of those borscht circuit stockholders who get a few points' profit and hastily scram for the hills. For your information, I bought Alleghany Preferred eleven years ago and am just now disposing of it.
As a brand new member of your family, strategically you made a ghastly mistake in sending me individual pictures of

the Board of Directors. Mr Roth, Chairman of the Board, merely looks sinister. You, the President, look like a hard worker with not too much on the ball. No one named Prosswimmer can possibly be a success. As for Samuel A. Goldblith, PhD., head of Food Technology at MIT, he looks as though he had eaten too much of the wrong kind of fodder.

At this point I would like to stop and ask you a question about Marion Harper, Jr. To begin with, I immediately distrust any man who has the same name as his mother. But the thing that most disturbs me about Junior is that I don't know what the hell he's laughing at. Is it because he sucked me into this Corporation? This is not the kind of a face that inspires confidence in a nervous and jittery stockholder.

George S. Sperti, I dismiss instantly. Any man who is the President of an outfit called Institutum Divi Thomae will certainly bear watching . . . James J. Sullivan, I am convinced, is Paul E. Prosswimmer photographed from a different angle.

Offhand, I would say that I have summed up your group fairly accurately. I hope, for my sake, that I am mistaken.

In closing, I warn you, go easy with my money. I am in an extremely precarious profession whose livelihood depends upon a fickle public.

Sincerely yours,
GROUCHO MARX
(temporarily at liberty)

The most effective abuse is bland and relaxed, and thus more likely to make its victims squirm than any amount of scatological invective. However, there are a few examples of letters of the latter variety which succeed in damaging the opposition by their sheer energy and unforgiving venom. Swinburne, who had been attacked by some American journalists, hit back in his letter to Ralph Waldo Emerson of 1874. He must have worked on it, but it comes across as quite spontaneous:

I am informed that certain American journalists not content with providing filth of their own for the consumption of their kind, sometimes offer to their readers a dish of beastliness which they profess to have gathered from under the chairs of more distinguished men. While the abuse lavished on my name and writings could claim no higher than a nameless source, I have always been able to say with Shelley, 'I have neither curiosity, interest, pain nor pleasure, in anything, good or evil, they can say of me. I feel only a slight disgust, and a sort of wonder, that they presume to write my name.'

If I am to believe that that name has been made the mark for such vile language as is now publicly attributed to men of note in the world of letters, I, who am not sufficiently an expert in the dialect of the cesspool and the dung-cart to retort in their own kind on these venerable gentlemen—I, whose ears and lips are alike unused to the amenities of conversation embroidered with such fragments of flowery rhetoric as may be fished up by congenial fingers or lapped up by congenial tongues out of the sewage of Sodom, can return no better or more apt reply than was addressed by the servant of Octavia to the satellites of Nero, and applied by Lord Denman when counsel for Queen Caroline to the sycophants of George IV.

A foul mouth is so ill-matched with a white beard that I would gladly believe the newspaper-scribes alone responsible for the bestial utterances which they declare to have dropped from a teacher whom such disciples as these exhibit to our disgust and compassion as performing on their obscene platform the last tricks of tongue now possible to a gaptoothed and hoary-headed ape, carried at first into notice on the shoulder of Carlyle, and who now in his dotage spits and chatters from a dirtier perch of his own finding and fouling: coryphaeus or choragus of his Bulgarian tribe of autocoprophagous baboons, who make the filth they feed on . . .

It is something of a relief to turn to another literary quarrel, and to read Benjamin Franklin's characteristically deadpan satire against a rival newspaper. With low cunning he printed examples of stale news, as retailed in *The American Weekly Mercury*, in the form of a letter in 1732 to the Printer of his own organ, the *Pennsylvania Gazette*; this gave him an excuse to write in reply:

To the Printer of the Gazette.

As you sometimes take upon you to correct the Publick, you ought in your Turn patiently to receive publick Correction. My Quarrel against you is your Practice of publishing under the Notion of News, old Transactions which I suppose you hope we have forgot. For Instance, in your Numb. 669, you tell us from London of July 20, That the Losses of our Merchants are laid before the Congress of Soissons, by Mr

Stanhope, &c. and that Admiral Hopson died the 8th of May
last. Whereas 'tis certain, there has been no Congress at
Soissons nor any where else these three Years at least; nor
could Admiral Hopson possibly die in May last, unless he has
made a Resurrection since his Death in 1728. And in your
Numb 670 among other Articles of equal Antiquity, you tell us
a long Story of a Murder and Robbery perpetrated on the
Person of Mr Nath. Bostock, which I have read Word for Word
not less than four years since in your own Paper. Are these
your *freshest Advices foreign and domestick*? I insist that you insert
this in your next, and let us see how you justify yourself.

Memory

I need not say more in Vindication of my self against this
Charge, than that the Letter is evidently wrong directed, and
should have been to *the Publisher of the Mercury*: Inasmuch as
the Numb. of my Paper is not yet amounted to 669, nor are
those old Articles any where to be found in the *Gazette*, but in
the *Mercury* of the two last Weeks.

Political abuse is exemplified in a letter of 1843 written by Walter
Savage Landor to the Editor of the *Examiner*. Lord Brougham was
bringing a libel action against the paper for accusing him of
having insinuated that Cobden, the apostle of free trade, had
recommended political assassination. Brougham was a fiery
speaker, frequently wild in his pronouncements, and associated
with the *Examiner*'s rival paper *The Edinburgh Review*. He seems to
have been greatly mistrusted by his colleagues, but they could
not afford to ignore him because of his large following. Whatever
the rights and wrongs of his libel action, Landor's attack on him
as a vindictive humbug is really a fine performance:

> Sir,
> The prosecution with which you are threatened by Lord
> Brougham might well be expected from every facette of his
> polygonal character. He began his literary and political life
> with a scanty store of many small commodities. Long after he
> set out, the witty and wise Lord Stowell said of him that he
> wanted only a little law to fill up the vacancy. His shoulders
> were not over-burdened by the well-padded pack he bore on
> them; and he found a ready sale, where such articles find the
> readiest, in the town of Edinburgh. Here he entered into a
> confederacy (the word *conspiracy* may be libellous) to defend

the worst atrocities of the French, and to cry down every author to whom England was dear and venerable. A better spirit now prevails in the *Edinburgh Review*, from the generosity and genius of Macaulay. But in the days when Brougham and his confederates were writers in it, more falsehood and malignity marked its pages than any other Journal in the language. And here is the man who cries out he is wounded! the recreant who, screaming for help, aims a poisoned dagger at the vigorous breast that crushes him to the ground . . .

Landor was, to say the least, a difficult man, and always ready to react to real or imagined slights; in about 1858 he wrote to Lord Normanby:

> *My Lord*,
> Now I am recovering from an illness of several months' duration, aggravated no little by your lordship's rude reception of me at the Cascine, in presence of my family and innumerable Florentines, I must remind you in the gentlest terms of the occurrence.
> We are both of us old men, my lord, and are verging on decrepitude and imbecility. Else my note might be more energetic. I am not unobservant of distinctions. You by the favour of a minister are Marquis of Normanby. I by the grace of God am
>
> WALTER SAVAGE LANDOR

Quarrelling, of course, can be great fun for spectators. Humphrey Prideaux in a letter to John Ellis in 1682 goes so far as to lament the patching up of a promising squabble through the intervention of a bishop:

> We had great expectations of a tryall at the other court between ye Ld. Norris and Brome Whorwood, about their quarrel in the Town Hall at the election of ye Town Clerk. Broom brought an action of battery against my Ld. for beateing him, and my Ld. an action of *scandalum magnatum* against Broome for calleing him yong fool. But the Bp. of Oxford interposing spoild the sport and made up the matter between them; for in truth ye Ld. Norris first began the quarrel, and called Brome old fool before he called him yong

fool; and beside it was reather hypothetically then categori-
cally sayd, for my Ld. calleing him old fool, he replyed, 'If I
am an old fool you are a yong fool', and therefore I thinke his
Lordship did very wisely to submitt it to the Bps. arbitration.

Sadly, quarrels are often between friends, and rabid abuse not
infrequently arises from thwarted love. With some people you
can hardly be counted their friend at all, unless you have earned
the privilege of being insulted by them. The more refined the
insult, the deeper the affection—or so one is bound to hope. If
one was working for a man as obsessive but as humane as
Harold Ross of the *New Yorker* it would be inappropriate to send
him *billets doux* and flowers at Christmas. Much better to send
him an extremely modest practical article, gift-wrapped with
elegant abuse. E. B. White hit it off perfectly at Christmas 1927:

> *Dear Mr Ross:*
> Here is the address book you were hinting for. Perhaps a
> few words of explanation would not be amiss. It was bought
> at Brentano's and cost seven fifty, a little more than I had
> expected to pay. It is of hand-tooled leather, as opposed to the
> ordinary machine-tooled kind which is every bit as good
> probably. It is a 'red' book with a decorative border of 'gold'
> and has a little pencil at the side which you will never use
> because it isn't practical. There is a good chance that you will
> never use the book either, but I took that into consideration
> when I bought it and will not be emotionally affected one way
> or the other. The filler or 'pack' is removable, which is a
> handy wrinkle except that Brentano's have none of them in
> stock and it would be a lot of work to hunt one up any place
> else. The filler is indexed, the letters of the alphabet being
> alternately blue and red, possibly for some reason which you
> can figure out.
> Now as to spirit of the gift. The spirit of the gift is very
> good. At first I resented the idea of having to give anything to
> my employer. I don't owe you anything! Everything I have
> had at your hands I have worked for, often twice. But then it
> occurred to me that it might be worth my while to give you an
> address book in order to 'get in strong' with you. And I might
> add that all my previous employers, when Christmas came
> round, received from me a little package of ground glass and
> porcupine quills. But my relations with you have always been

pleasant, and as Ring Lardner so aptly put it you are a wonderful friend you. With a lot of hard work and honest effort on your part, I see no reason why we cannot continue on this friendly basis almost indefinitely. Please enter my name in your address book 12 W. 113 St Chelsea 5276 and believe me

Merry Christmas,
E. B. WHITE

Thank you for your many courtesies, which I often brood over.

(The address White gives was intentionally wrong—he was still living at 112 West 13th Street. The telephone number is scrambled, too.) All White's velvet insults are only made efficacious by the fact that a long intimacy existed between him and Ross. But the most frustrating type of abuse of all for the recipient is surely the completely impersonal one. A writer to *The Times* in February 1915 gives an example of what I mean:

Sir,
A little light might be shed, with advantage, upon the high-handed methods of the Passports department at the Foreign Office. On the form provided for the purpose I described my face as 'intelligent'. Instead of finding this characterization entered, I have received a passport on which some official utterly unknown to me, has taken it upon himself to call my face 'oval'.

Yours very truly,
BASSETT DIGBY

3

How to Say No

In his series of useful pro-forma letters delicately phrased to fit a number of common social situations, Max Beerbohm supplied the ideal begging letter under the title: *Letter from a Poor Man to Obtain Money from a Rich One*:

> *Dear Sir,*
> To-day, as I was turning out a drawer in my attic, I came across a letter which by a curious chance fell into my hands some years ago, and which, in the stress of grave pecuniary embarrassment, had escaped my memory. It is a letter written by yourself to a lady, and the date shows it to have been written shortly after your marriage. It is of a confidential nature, and might, I fear, if it fell into the wrong hands, be cruelly misconstrued. I would wish you to have the satisfaction of destroying it in person. At first I thought of sending it on to you by post. But I know how happy you are in your domestic life; and probably your wife and you, in your perfect mutual trust, are in the habit of opening each other's letters. Therefore, to avoid risk I would prefer to hand the document to you personally. I will not ask you to come to my attic, where I could not offer you such hospitality as is due to a man of your wealth and position. You will be so good as to meet me at 3.0 (sharp) to-morrow (Thursday) beside the tenth lamp-post to the left on the Surrey side of Waterloo Bridge; at which hour and place we shall not be disturbed.
>
> I am, dear Sir,
> Yours respectfully,
> JAMES GRIDGE

Replies to begging letters, if short and negative, are no doubt extremely unwelcome to the recipients. When the replies are not only negative but long and discursive, dwelling at length on the character defects that have brought the applicant to such a pass, they must be even more repellent. Abraham Lincoln's bluntly phrased reply in 1851 to a request from his nephew is one such, but perhaps the advice it contained was easily worth the monetary sum that failed to accompany it:

Dear Johnston, Your request for eighty dollars I do not think it best to comply with now. At the various times when I have helped you a little you have said to me, 'We can get along very well now;' but in a very short time I find you in the same difficulty again. Now, this can only happen by some defect in your conduct. What that defect is, I think I know. You are not lazy, and still you are an idler. I doubt whether, since I saw you, you have done a good whole day's work in any one day. You do not very much dislike to work, and still you do not work much, merely because it does not seem to you that you could get much for it. This habit of uselessly wasting time is the whole difficulty; it is vastly important to you, and still more so to your children, that you should break the habit. It is more important to them, because they have longer to live, and can keep out of an idle habit before they are in it, easier than they can get out after they are in.

You are now in need of some money; and what I propose is, that you shall go to work, 'tooth and nail', for somebody who will give you money for it. Let father and your boys take charge of your things at home, prepare for a crop, and make the crop, and you go to work for the best money wages, or in discharge of any debt you owe, that you can get; and, to secure you a fair reward for your labour, I now promise you, that for every dollar you will, between this and the first of May, get for your own labour, either in money or as your own indebtedness, I will then give you one other dollar. By this, if you hire yourself at ten dollars a month, from me you will get ten more, making twenty dollars a month for your work. In this I do not mean you shall go off to St Louis, or the lead mines, or the gold mines in California, but I mean for you to go at it for the best wages you can get close to home in Coles County. Now, if you will do this, you will be soon out of debt, and, what is better, you will have a habit that will keep you from getting in debt again. But, if I should now clear you out of debt, next year you would be just as deep in as ever. You say you would almost give your place in heaven for seventy or eighty dollars. Then you value your place in heaven very cheap, for I am sure you can, with the offer I make, get the seventy or eighty dollars for four or five months' work. You say if I will furnish you the money you will deed me the land, and, if you don't pay the money back, you will deliver possession. Nonsense! If you can't now live with the land, how will you then live without it? You have always been kind to me, and I do not mean to be unkind to you. On the contrary, if you will but follow my advice, you will find it worth more than eighty times eighty dollars to you.

Mark Twain also had some difficulty with a persistent debt-accumulator in the family. His brother Orion was a classic example of the type of character in which hope forever triumphs over experience. Each new project was going to be the making of him, and each new project was succeeded with bewildering rapidity by another. In the following letter of 1879 Mark Twain writes resignedly to his friend W. D. Howells about his feckless relation. Some of Orion's antics sound uncannily like those of ex-President Carter's dreadful brother Billy:

My dear Howells,
I have just received this letter from Orion. Take care of it, for it is worth preserving . . .
Observe Orion's career—that is, a little of it: 1. He has belonged to as many as five different religious denominations. Last March he withdrew from the deaconship in a Congregational Church and the Superintendency of its Sunday School, in a speech in which he said that for many months (it runs in my mind that he said 13 years) he had been a confirmed infidel and so felt it to be his duty to retire from the flock.
2. After being a republican for years, he wanted me to buy him a democratic newspaper. A few days before the Presidential election, he came out in a speech and publicly went over to the democrats. He prudently 'hedged' by voting for 6 state republicans also.
The new convert was made one of the secretaries of the democratic meeting and placed in the list of speakers. He wrote me jubilantly of what a ten-strike he was going to make with that speech. All right—but think of his innocent and

pathetic candor in writing me something like this, a week later:

'I was more diffident than I had expected to be, and this was increased by the silence with which I was received when I came forward, so I seemed unable to get the fire into my speech which I had calculated upon, and presently they began to get up and go out, and in a few minutes they all rose up and went away.'

How could a man uncover such a sore as that and show it to another? Not a word of complaint, you see—only a patient, sad surprise.

3. His next project was to write a burlesque upon *Paradise Lost*.

4. Then, learning that the *Times* was paying Harte $100 a column for stories, he concluded to write some for the same price. I read his first one and persuaded him not to write any more.

5. Then he read proof on the *N.Y. Eve. Post* at $10 a week and meekly observed that the foreman swore at him and ordered him around 'like a steamboat mate'.

6. Being discharged from that post, he wanted to try agriculture—was sure he could make a fortune out of a chicken farm. I gave him $900 and he went to a ten-house village 2 miles above Keokuk on the river bank. This place was a railway station. He soon asked for money to buy a horse and light wagon, because the trains did not run at church time on Sunday and his wife found it rather far to walk.

For a long time I answered demands for 'loans' and by next mail always received his check for the interest due me to date. In the most guileless way he let it leak out that he did not underestimate the value of his custom to me, since it was not likely that any other customer of mine paid his interest quarterly, and this enabled me to use my capital twice in 6 months instead of only once. But alas, when the debt at least reached $1800 or $2500 (I have forgotten which) the interest ate too formidably into his borrowings and so he quietly ceased to pay it or speak of it. At the end of two years I found that the chicken farm had long ago been abandoned, and he had moved into Keokuk. Later, in one of his casual moments, he observed that there was no money in fattening a chicken on 65 cents' worth of corn and then selling it for 50.

7. Finally, if I would lend him $500 a year for two years (this

was 4 or 5 years ago) he knew he could make a success as a lawyer, and would prove it. This is the pension which we have just increased to $600. The first year his legal business brought him $5. It also brought him an unremunerative case where some villains were trying to chouse some negro orphans out of $700. He still has this case. He has waggled it around through various courts and made some booming speeches on it. The negro children have grown up and married off, now, I believe, and their litigated town lot has been dug up and carted off by somebody, but Orion still infests the courts with his documents and makes the welkin ring with his venerable case. The second year he didn't make anything. The third he made $6 and I made Bliss put a case in his hands—about half an hour's work. Orion charged $50 for it. Bliss paid him $15. Thus four or five years of lawing has brought him $26, but this will doubtless be increased when he gets done lecturing and buys that 'law library'. Meantime his office rent has been $60 a year, and he has stuck to that lair day by day as patiently as a spider.

8. Then he by and by conceived the idea of lecturing around America as 'Mark Twain's Brother'—that to be on the bills. Subject of proposed lecture, 'On the Formation of Character'.

9. I protested, and he got on his warpaint, couched his lance, and ran a bold tilt against total abstinence and the Red Ribbon fanatics. It raised a fine row among the virtuous Keokukians.

10. I wrote to encourage him in his good work but I had let a mail intervene, so by the time my letter reached him he was already winning laurels as a Red Ribbon Howler.

11. Afterward he took a rabid part in a prayer meeting epidemic; dropped that to travesty Jules Verne, dropped that in the middle of the last chapter last March to digest the matter of an infidel book which he proposed to write; and now he comes to the surface to rescue our 'noble and beautiful religion' from the sacrilegious talons of Bob Ingersoll.

Now come! Don't fool away this treasure which Providence has laid at your feet, but take it up and use it. One can let his imagination run riot in portraying Orion, for there is nothing so extravagant as to be out of character with him.

Well—goodbye, and a short life and a merry one be yours.

Poor old Methusaleh, how did he manage to stand it so long?

Yrs ever,
MARK.

Twain's next letter to Orion began 'My dear Bro. . . . I enclose a draft on Hartford for $25. You will have abandoned the project you wanted it for by the time it arrives but no matter, apply it to your newer and present project, whatever it is.'

Probably the greatest effrontery ever offered by the writer of a begging letter was that of a Signor Prospero Bertani. He had been disappointed in *Aida* on a first visit to hear it at Parma in 1872 and so went a second time, when he was again disappointed. He therefore sat down and penned the following letter to the composer:

> *Much honoured Signor Verdi,*
> The 2nd of this month I went to Parma, drawn there by the sensation made by your opera *Aida*. So great was my curiosity, that half an hour before the commencement of the piece I was already in my place, No. 120. I admired the *mise en scène*, I heard with pleasure the excellent singers, and I did all in my power to let nothing escape me. At the end of the opera, I asked myself whether I was satisfied, and the answer was 'No.' I started back to Reggio and listened in the railway carriage to the opinions given upon *Aida*. Nearly all agreed in considering it a work of the first order.
> I was then seized with the idea of hearing it again, and on the 4th I returned to Parma; I made unheard-of efforts to get a reserved seat; as the crowd was enormous, I was obliged to throw away five lire to witness the performance in any comfort.
> I arrived at this decision about it: it is an opera in which there is absolutely nothing which causes any enthusiasm or excitement, and without the pomp of the spectacle, the public would not stand it to the end. When it has filled the house two or three times, it will be banished to the dust of the archives.
> You can now, dear Signor Verdi, picture to yourself my regret at having spent on two occasions thirty-two lire; add to this the aggravating circumstance that I depend on my family, and that this money troubles my rest like a frightful spectre. I

therefore frankly address myself to you, in order that you may send me the amount. The account is as follows:

	Lire
Railroad—going	2.60
Railroad—returning	3.30
Theatre	8
Detestable supper at the station	2
Twice	15.90
	31.80

Hoping that you will deliver me from this embarrassment, I salute you from my heart.

BERTANI

My address: Bertani Prospero, Via San Domenico, No. 5.

Verdi was prepared to pay up, but was careful to protect himself from future dunning by a shrewd stratagem. He wrote to his publishers, Messrs Ricordi in Milan, enclosing the preceding letter:

You may well imagine that to protect the son of a family from the spectres which pursue him, I will willingly pay the little bill which he sends me. I therefore beg you to forward by one of your correspondents to this M. Prospero Bertani at Reggio, Via San Domenico No. 5, the sum of 27 lire 80 centimes. It is not the amount he demands; but that in addition I should be expected to pay for his supper, certainly not! He might very well take his meals at home.

It is understood that he will give you an acknowledgement, and further a short letter in reply, undertaking to hear my new operas no more, exposing himself no more to the menace of spectres, and sparing me further travelling expenses . . .

In due course the receipt arrived:

I the undersigned acknowledge to have received from the maestro G. Verdi the sum of 27 liri 80 Centesimi, by way of repayment of my travelling expenses to Parma to hear *Aida*, the master having considered it fair that this sum should be returned to me, as I did not find his opera to my taste. It is at the same time agreed that in future I shall not make any journey to hear new operas of the maestro unless I undertake the entire expense, whatever may be my opinion of his works.

In faith of which I have signed,

BERTANI PROSPERO

The higher the profile of a public figure the more likely he is to be a target of epistolary gadflies. Bertrand Russell received an inquiry in 1930 which at least had a certain engaging effrontery. Its sender said he was preparing a free-lance article 'on the subject of parasitic nuisances who bedevil authors'—people like himself in fact. Russell played the game and sent this entirely characteristic reply:

Dear Mr Aiken

In common with other authors, I suffer a good deal from persons who think that an author ought to do their work for them. Apart from autograph hunters, I get large numbers of letters from persons who wish me to copy out for them the appropriate entry in *Who's Who*, or ask me my opinion on points which I have fully discussed in print.

I get many letters from Hindus, beseeching me to adopt some form of mysticism, from young Americans, asking me where I think the line should be drawn in petting, and from Poles, urging me to admit that while all other nationalism may be bad that of Poland is wholly noble.

I get letters from engineers who cannot understand Einstein, and from parsons who think that I cannot understand Genesis, from husbands whose wives have deserted them—not (they say) that that would matter, but the wives have taken the furniture with them, and what in these circumstances should an enlightened male do?

I get letters from Jews to say that Solomon was not a polygamist, and from Catholics to say that Torquemada was not a persecutor. I get letters (concerning whose genuineness I am suspicious) trying to get me to advocate abortion, and I get letters from young mothers asking my opinion of bottle-feeding.

I am sorry to say that most of the subjects dealt with by my correspondents have escaped my memory at the moment, but the few that I have mentioned may serve as a sample.

Yours very truly

BERTRAND RUSSELL

The category of those who 'think an author ought to do their work for them' must surely include the schoolchildren who are encouraged to embark on projects by their reckless teachers, which include gathering material from well-known people. Some might think this fairly harmless and even a benign intrusion on a celebrity's available time. Not so James Thurber, whose reply to one 'project' pusher in 1958 may possibly have decreased the flow of similar inquiries from that particular school thereafter:

Mr Robert Leifert
New York City, New York

Dear Robert,
Since a hundred schoolchildren a year write me letters like yours—some writers get a thousand—the problem of what to do about such classroom 'projects' has become a serious one for all of us. If a writer answered all of you he would get nothing else done. When I was a baby goat I had to do my own research on projects, and I enjoyed doing it. I never wrote an author for his autograph or photograph in my life. Photographs are for movie actors to send to girls. Tell your teacher I said so, and please send me her name . . .
One of the things that discourage us writers is the fact that 90 per cent of you children write wholly, or partly, illiterate letters, carelessly typed. You yourself write 'clarr' for 'class' and that's a honey, Robert, since s is next to a, and r is on the line above. Most schoolchildren in America would do a dedication like the following (please find the mistakes in it and write me about them):
To Miss Effa G. Burns
Without who's help
this book could never
of been finished it,
is dedicated with
gartitude by it's
arthur.
Show that to your teacher and tell her to show it to her principal, and see if they can find the mistakes . . .
Just yesterday a letter came in from a girl your age in South Carolina asking for biographical material and photograph. That is not the kind of education they have in Russia, we are told, because it's too much like a hobby or waste of time. What do you and your classmates want to be when you grow

up—collectors? Then who is going to help keep the United States ahead of Russia in science engineering, and the arts?

Please answer this letter. If you don't I'll write to another pupil.

Sincerely yours,
JAMES THURBER

On another occasion Thurber turned down a request to allow a 'condensation' of his work in terms which can only make all anthologists and abridgers bleed inwardly: 'I appreciate Omnibook's vast problem, which is to convince itself that there are too many lines in a sonnet and too many stars and one unnecessary color in the flag. It is a hell of a job and I send you my sympathy . . .'; but not, however, his permission.

Trying to enlist Evelyn Waugh's co-operation in journalistic projects was not a rewarding exercise. In January of 1946 *Life Magazine* had the bright idea of finding out from the master of English comedy who were the models for his most memorable characters, and then printing photographs of them. Whether the models themselves would not have raised objections to this proposal may be conjectured, but the first response from the author was certainly not encouraging:

Dear Madam:
I have read your letter of yesterday with curiosity and re-read it with compassion. I am afraid you are unfamiliar with the laws of my country. The situation is not that my co-operation is desirable, but that my permission is necessary, before you publish a series of photographs illustrating my books. I cannot find any phrase in your letter that can be construed as seeking permission.

You say: 'Without consulting you the project will be like blind flying'. I assure you it will be far more hazardous. I shall send a big blue incorruptible policeman to lock you up and the only 'monumental' work Mr Scherman is likely to perform is breaking stones at Dartmoor (our Zing Zing).

Yours faithfully,
EVELYN WAUGH

Undeterred the *Life* journalists evidently wrote again the following month, and Waugh gave an inch or two, but in terms that would encourage none but the bravest to pursue the matter:

Dear Mr Osborne:
I don't know how I have given you and Mrs Reeve and Mr
Scherman the impression that I seek popularity for my books
among those who cannot read. I have tried to give the literate
all the information they need about my characters. If I have
failed, I don't believe you can help me.

I am sure it is not your fault and that you are being bothered
by some boss in the United States. Take heart; he has
forgotten all about it already. I was once a journalist for seven
weeks and I know about bosses. They are volatile creatures.

But if this preposterous project has become a fixed idea with
the man and you would like to see me, by all means come. I
cannot ask you to stay as I have no cook or housemaids; there
is a neighbouring inn. Have you a bicycle? I live seven miles
from Stroud station. I am always here and can give you a glass
of port on your arrival and plenty of dry bread.

Please do not telephone.

Yours sincerely,
EVELYN WAUGH

The opposite situation to that of the foregoing arises when
authors are themselves supplicants. In 1774 a Rev. Mr Hawkins
tried to bully David Garrick into staging his plays, which Garrick
thought were rubbish; after a while he sufficiently exasperated
the actor to provoke the following crushing reply:

Sir, Though your threatening letter found me in a fit of the
gout, which is a very peevish disorder, yet I assure you it
added nothing to my ill-humour: nay I could have laughed,
though in pain, had not the more humane sensation of pity
prevented it.

Notwithstanding your former flattering letters to me, which
I have luckily preserved, you now accuse me of pride,
rancour, evil designs and the Lord knows what, because I
have refused your plays, which I most sincerely think unfit for
representation, and which (some of them if not all) have had
the same fortune with other managers. You are pleased to say
that 'of all animals a manager is the sorest'. Pray, Mr Hawkins, had you no feelings at the time you wrote this which
contradicted the assertion? Can you really believe that this
unprovoked, intemperate, behaviour can make me submit to
your inquisitorial menaces? 'Perform my plays or I'll appeal to

the public!' If you will publish your plays with your appeal, I will forgive you the rest. . . . May I, without offence, differ in opinion with a gentleman who was once a credit to the Professorship of Poetry in Oxford? 'It will be very hard, methinks' (these are your own words) 'if that should not be a proper foundation of a fable which happens to be a matter of fact.' Indeed, Sir, the best dramatic critics I have read tell me that matters of fact are *not* always proper foundations for dramatic fables.

In contrast to the blunt tone of Garrick, here is a Chinese publisher's rejection letter which is almost worth having instead of an advance and a contract:

> *Illustrious brother of the sun and moon*—Behold thy servant prostrate before thy feet. I kow-tow to thee and beg of thy graciousness thou mayest grant that I may speak and live. Thy honored manuscript has deigned to cast the light of its august countenance upon me. With raptures I have pursued it. By the bones of my ancestry, never have I encountered such wit, such pathos, such lofty thoughts. With fear and trembling I return the writing. Were I to publish the treasure you sent me, the Emperor would order that it should be made the standard, and that none be published except such as equaled it. Knowing literature as I do, and that it would be impossible in ten thousand years to equal what you have done, I send your writing back. Ten thousand times I crave your pardon. Behold my head is at your feet. Do what you will.
>
> Your servant's servant
THE EDITOR

That letter is reprinted in Robert Hendrickson's entertaining *The Literary Life and other Curiosities*, and Hendrickson also has some interesting statistics on spectacular rejections by publishers over the years. The wittiest rejection letter he discovered is surely one from Gertrude Stein's editor A. J. Fifield. Stein, who once said: 'Think of the Bible and of Homer, think of Shakespeare and think of me', attempted to apply the theories of abstract painting to the writing of prose; the results, however, did not always appeal to her readers. Her editor's letter captures her manner so delightfully that it might even have made his formidable correspondent smile:

> I am only one, only one, only. Only one being, one at the same time. Not two, not three, only one. Only one life to live, only sixty minutes in one hour. Only one pair of eyes. Only one brain. Only one being. Being only one, having only one pair of eyes, having only one time, having only one life, I cannot read your MS three or four times. Not even one time. Only one look, only one look is enough. Hardly one copy would sell here. Hardly one. Hardly one.

If dealing with editors seems frustrating to authors, dealing with film directors is doubly so even if you do get paid for the frustration. The substantial fees are perhaps designed to blunt the author's natural desire to seek revenge for the mutilation of his literary offspring. Raymond Chandler's letter of 1950 to Alfred Hitchcock must be one of many similar *cris du coeur*:

> *Dear Hitch,*
> In spite of your wide and generous disregard of my communications on the subject of the script of *Strangers on a Train* and your failure to make any comment on it, and in spite of not having heard a word from you since I began the writing of the actual screenplay—for all of which I might say I bear no malice, since this sort of procedure seems to be part of the standard Hollywood depravity—in spite of this and in spite of this extremely cumbersome sentence, I feel that I should, just for the record, pass you a few comments on what is termed the final script. I could understand your finding fault with my script in this or that way, thinking that such and such a scene was too long or such and such a mechanism was too awkward. I could understand you changing your mind about the things that you specifically wanted, because some of such changes might have been imposed on you from without. What I cannot understand is your permitting a script which after all had some life and vitality to be reduced to such a flabby mass of clichés, a group of faceless characters, and the kind of dialogue every screen writer is taught not to write— the kind that says everything twice and leaves nothing to be implied by the actor or the camera. Of course you must have had your reasons but, to use a phrase once coined by Max

Beerbohm, it would take a 'far less brilliant mind than mine' to guess what they were.

Regardless of whether or not my name appears on the screen among the credits, I'm not afraid that anybody will think I wrote this stuff. They'll know damn well I didn't. I shouldn't have minded in the least if you had produced a better script—believe me, I shouldn't. But if you wanted something written in skim milk, why on earth did you bother to come to me in the first place? What a waste of money! What a waste of time! It's no answer to say that I was well paid. Nobody can be adequately paid for wasting his time . . .

We don't know the quality of Chandler's original script, but we *do* know the quality of Tchaikovsky's Concerto in B flat minor. After he had composed it Tchaikovsky played it through to Nicolai Rubinstein, the founder of the Moscow Conservatoire. What followed is related by Tchaikovsky in a letter to Madame Von Meck dated 21st January 1878:

. . . I played the first movement. Never a word, never a single remark . . . Rubinstein's silence was eloquent . . . I pulled myself together and played the concerto straight through to the end. Still silence.

'Well?' I asked, and rose from the piano. Then a torrent broke from Rubinstein's lips. Gentle at first, gathering volume as it proceeded, and finally bursting into the fury of a *Jupiter tonans*. My concerto was worthless, absolutely unplayable; the passages so broken, so unskilfully written, that they could not even be improved; the work itself was bad, trivial, common; here and there I had stolen from other people; only one or two pages were worth anything; all the rest had better be destroyed . . . The chief thing I cannot reproduce: the *tone* in which all this was said. An independent witness of this scene could have concluded I was a talentless maniac, a scribbler with no notion of composing, who had ventured to lay his rubbish before a famous man . . . I left the room without a word . . . Presently Rubinstein came to me and, seeing how upset I was, called me into another room. There he repeated that my concerto was impossible, pointed out many places where it needed to be completely revised, and said if I would suit the concerto to his requirements, he would bring it out as his concert. 'I shall not alter a single note,' I replied. 'I shall publish the work precisely as it stands.' This intention I actually carried out . . .

Personal rejection where our talents are found to be unwanted distresses even the strongest characters. The art of writing a rejection letter in such circumstances therefore demands more than ordinary tact. I'm not sure if the Vicar of Baulking has quite got it right in the following letter to Penelope Betjeman, but he is certainly trying:

> *My Dear Penelope,*
> I have been thinking over the question of the playing of the harmonium on Sunday evenings here and have reached the conclusion that I must now take it over myself.
> I am very grateful to you for doing it for so long and hate to have to ask you to give it up, but, to put it plainly, your playing has got worse and worse and the disaccord betwen the harmonium and the congregation is becoming destructive of devotion. People are not very sensitive here, but even some of them have begun to complain, and they are not usually given to doing that. I do not like writing this, but I think you will understand that it is my business to see that divine worship is as perfect as it can be made. Perhaps the crankiness of the instrument has something to do with the trouble. I think it does require a careful and experienced player to deal with it.
> Thank you ever so much for stepping so generously into the breach when Sibyl was ill; it was the greatest possible help to me and your results were noticeably better then than now.
> > Yours ever,
> > F. P. Harton

It is easier to write a letter of rejection if you have something to justify your dislike of the other party. The most famous example of such a letter must surely be Dr Johnson's to Lord Chesterfield, the author of the famous letters of advice to his son. In February 1755 Chesterfield belatedly offered the lexicographer his support after he had struggled with his great dictionary for eight years, and all but completed it: this, though he must surely have known of Johnson's continuing labours and difficulties. It is hard to make a dignified letter out of wounded pride, but

Johnson's crushing invective, coupled with his genuine sense of injury, just about carry it off:

My Lord,
I have been lately informed, by the proprietor of *The World*, that two papers, in which my Dictionary is recommended to the public, were written by your lordship. To be so distinguished, is an honour, which, being very little accustomed to favours from the great, I know not well how to receive, or in what terms to acknowledge.

When, upon some slight encouragement, I first visited your lordship, I was overpowered, like the rest of mankind, by the enchantment of your address, and could not forbear to wish that I might boast myself *Le Vainqueur du Vainqueur de la terre:*—that I might obtain what regard for which I saw the world contending; but I found my attendance so little encouraged, that neither pride nor modesty would suffer me to continue it. When I had once addressed your lordship in public, I had exhausted all the art of pleasing which a retired and uncourtly scholar can possess. I had done all that I could; and no man is well pleased to have his all neglected, be it ever so little.

Seven years, my lord, have now passed, since I waited in your outward rooms, or was repulsed from your door; during which time I have been pushing on my work through difficulties, of which it is useless to complain, and have brought it, at last, to the verge of publication, without one act of assistance, one word of encouragement, or one smile of favour. Such treatment I did not expect, for I never had a patron before.

The shepherd in Virgil grew at last acquainted with Love, and found him a native of the rocks.

Is not a patron, my lord, one who looks with unconcern on a man struggling for life in the water, and, when he has reached ground, encumbers him with help? The notice which you have been pleased to take of my labours, had it been early, had been kind; but it has been delayed till I am indifferent, and cannot enjoy it: till I am solitary, and cannot impart it; till I am known, and do not want it. I hope it is no very cynical asperity not to confess obligations where no benefit has been received, or to be unwilling that the public should consider me as owing that to a patron, which Providence has enabled me to do for myself.

Having carried on my work thus far with so little obligation to any favourer of learning, I shall not be disappointed though I should conclude it, if less be possible, with less; for I have been long wakened from that dream of hope, in which I once boasted myself with so much exultation, my lord, your lordship's most humble, most obedient servant,

SAM: JOHNSON

Another letter which is written with some moral force and acidly rejects the implied view of the author that an invitation to him had contained, is that of John Henry Newman to George Talbot. Monsignor Talbot had hoped to capture the celebrated theologian to preach to a fashionable Rome congregation. Newman's response, dated July 1864, is admirably brief:

Dear Monsignor Talbot,
I have received your letter, inviting me to preach next Lent in your Church at Rome, to 'an audience of Protestants more educated than could ever be the case in England.'
However, Birmingham people have souls; and I have neither taste nor talent for the sort of work, which you cut out for me: and I beg to decline your offer.

I am &c JHN

In similar vein, but very different circumstances, the following magnificent rejection exhibits immense dignity. It was written by the Earl of Derby, a Royalist civil war commander, who was holding out in the Isle of Man. In a letter to General Henry Ireton, Cromwell's son-in-law, he refuses to surrender the island or to recognize the Commonwealth. Of course in the end he had to surrender and was beheaded in 1650; but the defiant courage of the note must have impressed even General Ireton:

Sir,—I have received your letter with indignation, and with scorn return you this answer, that I cannot but wonder whence you should gather any hopes that I should prove like you, treacherous to my sovereign; since you cannot be ignorant of the manifest candour of my former actings in his late Majesty's service, from which principles of loyalty I am not a whit departed. I scorn your proffer; I disdain your favour; I abhor your treason; and am so far from delivering up this island to your advantage, that I shall keep it to the utmost of my power, and, I hope, to your destruction. Take this for your final answer, and forbear any further solicitations; for if you trouble me with any more messages of this nature, I will burn your paper, and hang up your messenger. This is the immutable resolution, and shall be the undoubted practice, of him who accounts it his chiefest glory to be his Majesty's most loyal and obedient subject,

DERBY

Brevity and simplicity unite in Derby's letter to devastating effect. But it is possible to be even more brief, and even more plain, as in this letter of March 1855 from Flaubert to his now unwanted mistress Louise Colet:

> *Madame*: I was told that you took the trouble to come here to see me three times last evening.
> I was not in. And, fearing lest persistence expose you to humiliation, I am bound by the rules of politeness to warn you that *I shall never be in.*

Yours,
G.F.

Colet scribbled on the note, *lâche, couard et canaille.*

4

Fan Mail

An absolutely shameless writer of fan mail was Pietro Aretino. A lot of it was self-interested, being the prelude to touching a prospective patron for a share of those assets that Aretino felt sure were surplus to his requirements. In addressing Henry VIII of England in 1542, he obviously feels he has nothing to lose by pulling out all the stops. The flattery is so outrageous that the King, knowing the satirical nature of much of Aretino's work, might have been expected to smell a rat; but Henry's armour-plating of self-esteem appears to have allowed Aretino to get away with almost anything. He begins modestly enough, I suppose:

> TO THE GREAT AND MAGNANIMOUS
> HENRY THE EIGHTH
> *The divine King of England*
> Since you, great King, excelling in every virtue like the eagle which is sovereign over all the birds, deserve all honour and glory, I come to honour and glorify you with the offering of this little work of mine. And as I honour and glorify you by this means, I realize, as does the whole world, that by God's will Nature produced you not just by chance like other princes but with care and deliberation. And this was in order that the stars should have a subject capable of receiving their exalted influences, whose marvellous effects, assembled in the sacred breast of your eternal regality, exercise the same authority that the stars impose above . . .

By the second paragraph Aretino is already in the higher realms of hyperbole ('you are rightly called divine, since all your deeds are immortal'), though he humbly confesses that 'what I have said of you is little or nothing compared with what I should say':

. . . This is because you are so fashioned that only by your fame and reputation, only by the shadow of your majesty, only by your miraculous prudence, you force all people to venerate the very traces of your steps, to kneel at your feet and to kiss your right hand, the one which when it draws the sword strikes terror in the infidel and when it takes the pen disperses the rabble of heretics, and in the generosity of faith reassures the minds of the doubters. And in recompense for such merit, both this present age and all times to come are bound to offer you sweat, ink, years and thoughts, preaching your fame eternally in such a celestial way that their voices cannot be stilled by any earthly accident, any reversal of fortune or the passing of time . . .

This is rather rich, coming from a man who was once said to be in the running for a cardinal's hat, and being addressed to one who, by 1542, had carried out the dissolution of the monasteries and was about to execute his fifth wife before acquiring a sixth.

But the history of fan mail is not entirely one of self-interest and sycophancy. One of the most delightful examples of the genre, hitting exactly the right grace notes, is the following by Sydney Smith to Lady Dacre in 1837 complimenting her on her translations of Petrarch which had been published in November 1836:

Many thanks, dear Lady Dacre, for your beautiful translations in your beautiful book—

I read forthwith several beautiful sonnets upon Love, which paint with great fidelity some of the worst symptoms of that terrible disorder, than which none destroys more completely the happiness of common existence, and substitutes for the activity which Life demands a long and sickly dream with moments of pleasure and days of intolerable pain. The Poets are full of false views: they make mankind believe that happiness consists in falling in love, and living in the country—I say: live in London; like many people, fall in love with nobody. To these rules of life I add: read Lady Dacre's Translations, and attend her Monday evening parties.

Ever yours,
SYDNEY SMITH

In turning from Sydney Smith's *billet doux* to the overripe exchange of letters in 1935 between Lawrence Durrell in Corfu and Henry Miller in Paris, the reader is transported abruptly from the sublime to the ridiculous. Durrell starts off with a missive that would have made a lesser man than Miller hide his blushes:

Dear Mr Miller:

I have just read *Tropic of Cancer* again and feel I'd like to write you a line about it. It strikes me as being the only really man-size piece of work which this century can really boast of. It's a howling triumph from the word go; and not only is it a literary and artistic smack on the bell for everyone, but it really gets down on paper the blood and bowels of our time. I have never read anything like it. I did not imagine anything like it could be written; and yet, curiously, reading it I seemed to recognize it as something which I knew we were all ready for. The space was all cleared for it. *Tropic* turns the corner into a new life which has regained its bowels. In the face of it eulogy becomes platitude; so for Godsake don't blame me if this sounds like the bleat of an antique reviewer, or a cold-cream ad. God knows, I weigh the words as well as I am able, but the damn book has rocked the scales like a quake and muddled up all my normal weights and measures. I love its guts. I love to see the canons of oblique and pretty emotion mopped up; to see every whim-wham and bagatelle of your contemporaries from Eliot to Joyce dunged under. God give us young men the guts to plant the daisies on top and finish the job.

Tropic is something they've been trying to do since the war. It's the final copy of all those feeble, smudgy rough drafts— *Chatterley, Ulysses, Tarr*, etc. It not only goes back, but (which none of them have done) goes forward as well.

It finds the way out of the latrines at last. Funny that no one should have thought of slipping out via the pan during a flush, instead of crowding the door. I salute *Tropic* as the copy-book for my generation. It's man-size, and goes straight up among those books (and they are precious few) which men have built out of their own guts. God save me, that sounds pompous, but what can one say?

Perish the Rahuists! Skoal to the stanchless flux!

Yours sincerely
LAWRENCE DURRELL

Happily, Miller is equal to the occasion and is able to compliment Durrell on his perception:

Dear Mr Durrell:
Your letter rocks me a bit too. You're the first Britisher who's written me an intelligent letter about the book. For that matter, you're the first anybody who's hit the nail on the head. I particularly prize your letter because it's the kind of letter I would have written myself had I not been the author of the book. That isn't just sheer vanity and egotism, believe me. It's curious how few people know what to admire in the book.

The phrase that struck me particularly, in your letter, was, 'I seemed to recognize it as something we were all ready for.' That's just it. The world *is* ready for something different, something new, but it seems that it requires a war or some colossal calamity to make people realize it.

Your letter is so vivid, so keen, that I am curious to know if you are not a writer yourself. How did you come by the book—through Barclay Hudson?

Cordially yours,
HENRY MILLER

In fairness it should be said that Durrell was equally capable of writing a fierce critique of Miller's work, at any rate when the first glow of mutual admiration had worn off. He did just that when he had read *Sexus*, inquiring sadly of his friend, 'What on earth possessed you to leave so much twaddle in? . . . The new mystical outlines are all there; but they are lost, lost, damn it, in this shower of lavatory filth which no longer seems tonic and bracing, but just excrementious and sad.' The stanchless flux had evidently flooded the living room.

I doubt if anyone would have dared to write a Durrell-type letter, laudatory or critical, to Evelyn Waugh. Those who did venture to embark on what was likely to be a one-sided correspondence, might have got any of thirteen types of reply according to the level at which Waugh considered their impertinence to have been pitched. He explained his system in a letter of July 1952 to Nancy Mitford, who had inquired of him how he handled such matters:

Dearest Nancy
I am not greatly troubled by fans nowadays. Less than one a day on the average. No sour grapes when I say they were an infernal nuisance. I divide them into
(a) Humble expressions of admiration. To these a post-card

saying: 'I am delighted to learn that you enjoyed my book. E.W.'

(b) Impudent criticism. No answer.

(c) Bores who wish to tell me about themselves. Post-card saying. 'Thank you for interesting letter. E.W.'

(d) Technical criticism. eg. One has made a character go to Salisbury from Paddington. Post-card 'Many thanks for your valuable suggestion E.W.'

(e) Humble aspirations of would-be writers. If attractive a letter of discouragement. If unattractive a post-card.

(f) Requests from University Clubs for a lecture. Printed refusal.

(g) Requests from Catholic Clubs for lecture. Acceptance.

(h) American students of 'Creative Writing' who are writing theses about one & want one, virtually, to write their theses for them. Printed refusal.

(i) Tourists who invite themselves to one's house. Printed refusal.

(j) Manuscript sent for advice. Return without comment.

I also have some post-cards with my photograph on them which I send to nuns.

In case of very impudent letters from married women I write to the husband warning him that his wife is attempting to enter into correspondence with strange men.

Oh and of course

(k) Autograph collectors: no answer.

(l) Indians & Germans asking for free copies of ones books: no answer.

(m) Very rich Americans: polite letter. They are capable of buying 100 copies for Christmas presents.

I think that more or less covers the field.

Love
E

Item (k) is an interesting item in this list and must be one of the commonest irritations for the famous. American presidents have solved the problem by having automatic pens; but this will hardly satisfy the really persistent autograph collector, like the one who wrote to Bertrand Russell asking him for his. He said he had all the other important ones, including that of Jesus Christ, which was obtainable from a fundamentalist evangelist who broadcast from Del Rio in Mexico.

Rose Macaulay in whom the milk of human kindness flowed a little more strongly than in Evelyn Waugh, was also troubled with unwanted but persistent admirers. She has some sharp things to say about them in the postscript of a letter to her sister Jeanie in 1926 and analyses the psychology of such people very shrewdly:

> P.S. what do you do with mawkish female admirers who vent their passion by leaving you expensive flowers and begging you to have meals etc. with them? I get them through my books, and they are becoming (one in particular) a problem. I don't like being rude, yet it bores me to see her, and I haven't time either. Yet, as she says, I must have lunch somewhere, and can she join me at it. I think I must pretend to have gone abroad or something. She asks if she may become, if possible, one of my friends. *What do I say?* She mayn't, but I must convey this politely if possible. So far I've not answered the letter. She called to see me, with lilies of the valley, and I went out to lunch to get rid of her, and she had it with me. Writing books is a terrible magnet for such as her. They are so very boring, as a rule. I suppose no-one who wasn't would force their way into people's lives like that. Now that she has seen me, she is *worse* than ever. Do you have them too, or is everyone you know too busy? I'm really too busy myself, but one's own busyness doesn't deter people. Anyhow I have enough friends already, and I do resent people thinking they can become friends merely by pushing their way in. As a matter of fact I select my friends with great care, and only have those who please me a great deal. There must be a way out of these problems, I wish I could hit on it. I must ask other novelists what they do.

Some enthusiastic ladies have been known to pursue men in the public eye with a tenacity that is astonishing and that would, if it were applied to some other activity, surely bring them to the top of their profession. A girl called Erica Cotterill conceived a highly inappropriate passion for George Bernard Shaw after seeing one of his plays in 1905. She sent him a fan letter signed 'Miss Charmer' and gave an answering address of 'Poste Restante, Godalming'. Shaw replied, something he may later have regretted doing. Dan H. Laurence, the Editor of Shaw's letters, describes her as subsequently 'bombarding him with letters—strange, effervescent rambling effusions, often unintelligible and generally illegible'. She seems, however, to have appealed to Shaw's vanity and he wrote to her quite frequently in reply to the effusions, and even introduced her to his friends. Eventually she began to get completely out of hand, trying to install herself in his life by arriving at Ayot St Lawrence on a motorbike and taking charge of the household, in Laurence's words, 'as if she were in her own home and Shaw her spouse'. Naturally Mrs Shaw had reservations about this. In the following letter, dated April 1908, Shaw gives her a magisterial ticking off; not that it did the slightest bit of good. The reference to Rupert Brooke is interesting, as Erica Cotterill was his aunt.

> . . . Now that I have taught you some respect for business and law, let me assure you that marriage is more sacred than either, and that unless you are prepared to treat my wife with absolute loyalty, you will be hurled into outer darkness for ever. The privilege of pawing me, such as it is, is hers exclusively. She has to tolerate worshipping females whose efforts to conceal the fact that they take no interest in her are perfunctory, and who bore her to distraction with their adoration of me; but it is my business to see that her patience is not abused. You are a luxurious young devil, with the ethics, and something of the figure, of an anteater; and I have no doubt you can coax your mother & your Rupert [Brooke] by crawling all over them; but if you dare to try those tactics with me in my wife's house, you will be very startlingly awakened to the iron laws of domestic honour. Also, it is not sensible nor decent to write about such demonstrations except to men of your own time of life, and with some assurance that they are equally infatuated, and will read it all as touching poetry . . .

The behaviour of admirers need not be all slushy self-indulgence. To get a letter from an informed colleague must be one of the greatest pleasures for an academic, or a creative artist. And to get one from an informed member of his potential audience, must be the ultimate satisfaction, for then at least it means that his work is getting through. Sir Edward Elgar must surely have been pleased to receive this pleasantly unassuming letter from Aircraftman Shaw, alias T. E. Lawrence, in 1933:

Dear Sir Edward, This is from my cottage and we have just been playing your 2nd Symphony. Three of us, a sailor, a Tank Corps soldier, and myself. So there are all the Services present: and we agreed that you must be written to and told (if you are well enough to be bothered) that this Symphony gets further under our skins than anything else in the record library at Clouds Hill. We have the Violin Concerto, too; so that says quite a lot. Generally we play the Symphony last of all, towards the middle of the night, because nothing comes off very well after it. One seems to stop there.

You would laugh at my cottage, which has one room upstairs (gramophone and records) and one room downstairs (books): but there is also a bath, and we sleep anywhere we feel inclined. So it suits me. A one-man house, I think.

The three of us assemble there nearly ever week-end I can get to the cottage, and we wanted to say 'thank you' for the Symphony ever so long ago; but we were lazy, first: and then you were desperately ill, and even now we are afraid you are too ill, probably, to be thinking of anything except yourself: but we are hoping that you are really getting stronger and will soon be able to deal with people again.

There is a selfish side to our concern: we want your Symphony III: if it is wiser and wider and deeper than II we shall very sadly dethrone our present friend, and play it last of the evening. Until it comes, we shall always stand in doubt if the best has really yet happened.

Imagine yourself girt about by a mob of young pelicans, asking for III: and please be generous to us, again!

Yours sincerely
T. E. SHAW

A far more rhetorical fan letter, and one that is characteristically self-conscious, was written by the eighteen-year-old James Joyce to Henrik Ibsen in 1901. It followed Joyce's first published article which was devoted to Ibsen and appeared the previous year. Joyce's sense of cultural and spiritual exile provides a point of identification with Ibsen. Like most of Joyce's letters, it is principally an exercise in exploring himself:

. . . What shall I say more? I have sounded your name defiantly through the college where it was either unknown or known faintly and darkly. I have claimed for you your rightful place in the history of the drama. I have shown what, as it seemed to me, was your highest excellence—your lofty impersonal power. Your minor claims—your satire, your technique and orchestral harmony—these, too, I advanced. Do not think me a hero-worshipper—I am not so. And when I spoke of you in debating societies and so forth, I enforced attention by no futile ranting.

But we always keep the dearest things to ourselves. I did not tell them what bound me closest to you. I did not say how what I could discern dimly of your life was my pride to see, how your battles inspired me—not the obvious material battles but those that were fought and won behind your forehead, how your wilful resolution to wrest the secret from life gave me heart and how in your absolute indifference to public canons of art, friends and shibboleths you walked in the light of your inward heroism. And this is what I write to you of now. Your work on earth draws to a close and you are near the silence. It is growing dark for you. Many write of such things, but they do not know. You have only opened the way—though you have gone as far as you could upon it—to the end of 'John Gabriel Borkman' and its spiritual truth—for your last play stands, I take it, apart. But I am sure that higher and holier enlightenment lies—onward.

As one of the young generation for whom you have spoken I give you greeting—not humbly, because I am obscure and you in the glare, not sadly, because you are an old man and I a young man, not presumptuously, nor sentimentally—but joyfully, with hope and with love, I give you greeting.

Faithfully yours,
JAMES A. JOYCE

5

Complaints

It is difficult to be original in writing letters of complaint but the following one addressed to a French typewriter shop by an extremely dissatisfied customer surely succeeds:

Monsixur,
Il y a quxlquxs sxmainxs jx mx suis offxrt unx dx vos machinxs à écrirx. Au début j'xn fus assxz contxnt. Mais pas pour longtxmps. Xn xffxt, vous voyxz vous-mêmx lx défaut. Chaqux fois qux jx vxux tapxr un x, c'xst un x qux j'obtixns. Cxla mx rxnd xnragé. Car quand jx vxux un x, c'xst un x qu'il mx faut xt non un x. Cxla rxndrait n'importx qui furixux. Commxnt fairx pour obtxnir un x chaqux fois qux jx desirx un x? Un x xst un x, xt non un x. Saisissxz-vous cx qux jx vxux dirx?
Jx voudrais savoir si vous êtxs xn mxsurx dx mx livrxr unx machinx à écrirx donnant un x chaqux fois qux j'ai bxsoin d'un x. Parcx qux si vous mx donnxz unx machinx donnant un x lorsqu'on tapx un x, vous pourrxz ravoir cx damné instrumxnt. Un x xst très bixn tant qux x, mais, oh xnfxr!
Sincèrxmxnt à vous, un dx vos clixnts rxndu xnragé.
XUGÈNX X . . .

A more conventional complaint of the 'more in sorrow than in anger' type was once written by Mark Twain to the gas and electric company of Hartford:

Gentlemen,
There are but two places in our whole street where lights could be of any value, by any accident, and you have measured and appointed your intervals so ingeniously as to leave each of those places in the center of a couple of hundred yards of solid darkness. When I noticed that you were setting

one of your lights in such a way that I could almost see how to
get into my gate at night, I suspected that it was a piece of
carelessness on the part of the workmen and would be
corrected as soon as you should go around inspecting and
find it out. My judgment was right. It is always right when
you are concerned. For fifteen years, in spite of my prayers
and tears, you persistently kept a gas lamp exactly half-way
between my gates so that I couldn't find either of them after
dark, and then furnished such execrable gas that I had to hang
a danger signal on the lamp post to keep teams from running
into it, nights. Now I suppose your present idea is to leave us
a little more in the dark.

Don't mind us—out our way. We possess but one vote
apiece, and no rights which you are in any way bound to
respect. Please take your electric light and go to—but never
mind, it is not for me to suggest. You will probably find the
way. And anyway you can reasonably count on divine
assistance if you lose your bearings.

S. L. CLEMENS

Manufacturers and public utility companies must grow used to
getting letters from would-be humorists and ignoring them.
Letters from professional humorists, such as E. B. White,
perhaps give greater cause for concern; there is, after all, the
danger of publication and public ridicule. White once received a
communication from the vice-president of the manufacturers of
his refrigerator informing him that it might be discharging
poison gas and that he should therefore keep a window open in
the house. This provoked White into the following reply:

Dear Mr Aiken:

I am a stockholder in the Consolidated Edison Company,
and I rent an apartment at 229 East 48 Street in which there is
a gas refrigerator. So I have a double interest in your letter of
December 19. It seems to me a very odd letter indeed.

You say that my refrigerator, even if it seems to be operat-
ing properly, may be producing poison gas, and you suggest
that I open a window. I do not want to open a window. It
would be a very unpopular move with the cook. Furthermore,
I haven't the slightest intention of living under the same roof
with a machine that discharges poison gas. Your recommen-

dation is that I get plenty of fresh air—enough to counteract the effect of the gas. But I cannot believe that you are serious.

Will you be good enough to let me know what sort of poison gas is generated by a Servel gas refrigerator, and in what quantity, and how discharged. I know that there is a vent at the top of the machine and that some sort of warm air flows from the vent. I have always assumed it was hot air. Is it something else?

I also know that a gas refrigerator poses a carbon problem, and I ask the landlord to remove the carbon about once a year, which he does. But your letter makes me think that the matter is not so simple and I am anxious to be enlightened.

If gas refrigerators are, as your letter suggests, discharging poison gases into people's homes I don't want to own a gas refrigerator and I shall certainly sell my stock.

Sincerely,
E. B. WHITE.

On another occasion White had problems placing a public notice in the *New York Times*. All he wanted to do was send greetings to his old friend Clarence Day; but the paper's advertisement department was suspicious:

Dear Clarence:
    . . . I called up the NY Times on Tuesday morning, when I received your letter, and said I wanted to insert a Public Notice. 'How does it go?' the clerk asked. 'It goes,' I replied, '"E. B. White sends New Year's greetings to Clarence Day exactly."' Well, the clerk said, you will have to come into the office, we can't take that over the telephone. Come in and see either Mr McNamara or Mr Kaufman. This sounded like a challenge, so I went around to the Times office and gained an audience with Mr McNamara. I showed him the typewritten copy. 'E. B. White sends New Year's greetings to Clarence Day exactly.' He studied it a long time. 'What does it mean?' he asked finally. 'Means what it says,' I snapped. 'It's kind of a greeting.' 'Well,' he said, 'we can't run that as a Public Notice; it might mean something.' Then he got up and took the matter up with Mr Kaufman. I saw Mr Kaufman study the slip of paper for a long time, then shake his head. Mr McNamara came back. 'What does this mean here—Clarence Day *exactly*? What do you mean "exactly"?' 'I put that in,' I

explained, 'to prevent a great many inconsiderable and nosey people, in whom I haven't the slightest charitable interest, from horning in on the New Year's wishes I am sending my good friend Mr Day.' Mr McNamara gazed at me in alarm. 'However,' I went on, 'if you object to the word "exactly" I will take it out. Just make it read: "E. B. White sends New Year's greetings to Clarence Day."' Again Mr McNamara studied the notice, in a kind of reverie. He shook his head. 'You mean,' I asked, 'that the Times won't accept my greetings?' 'We can't,' he said. 'It might mean something.' 'Really,' I said, 'the Times is magnificent!' I rose, shook hands and departed. Happy new year *anyway*!

ANDY

Complaints that involve a personal grievance are not always attractive to read, but very revealing of their author. James Joyce was doubtless a difficult employee and his acute sense of pride may have complicated his relationships with ordinary colleagues. Yet some of the grievances aired in the following letter are very real and one can just imagine the vindictive attitude of the Triesteans towards his unmarried and pregnant companion, Nora Barnacle. He was writing to his brother Stanislaus in July 1905. Joyce was then twenty-three years old:

I must, first of all, tell you that Trieste is the rudest place I have ever been in. It is hardly possible to exaggerate the incivility of the people. The girls and women are so rude to Nora that she is afraid to go out in the street. Nora can speak about thirty words of Triestine dialect (I tried and failed to teach her French) and so whenever she goes out I must accompany her and I have often to spend an afternoon looking for a simple thing at a reasonable price. I must tell you also that as soon as she began to be any way noticeable we were turned out of our lodgings. This happened three times until I conceived the daring plan of living in the house next the school and astonishing the landlady by the glamour of that wonderful establishment. This ruse has succeeded so far but we are still in imminent danger of being put out. The director of the school and the sub-director (vegetarian, and a German) have both wives but—no children. The director when he saw Nora said he thought I must be stark mad. The sub-director is also appalled. He has written in German and published at his own expense a 'booklet of spring flowers' in which there is a poem which begins:

'In drinking I did never lag'

and another (a pure feat of the imagination in the circumstances) which begins:

'O, can there be for mother's heart
A fairer poem
Than when her child after many an effort
Lisps the first word.'

You will see from this what an interesting atmosphere I breathe but—to go on. Nora is almost always complaining. She can eat very few of the sloppy Italian dishes and whatever she eats gives her a pain in her chest. She drinks beer but the least thing is enough to make her sick. In Pola during the winter she suffered dreadfully from the cold and now (the thermometer being at 100°F or so) she lies nearly all day on the bed powerless with fatigue. The Trieste people are great 'stylists' in dress, often starving themselves in order to be able to flaunt good dresses on the pier and she with her distorted body (Eheu! peccatum?) and her short four crown skirt and hair done over the ears is always nudged at and sniggered at. I was thinking lately of renting a quarter (that is, two or three rooms and a kitchen) but a house-agent told me that it was very difficult to get into a quarter in Trieste if you have children . . .Trieste is not very cheap and the difficulties of an English teacher living with a woman on a salary fit for a navvy or a stoker and expected to keep up a 'gentlemanly' appearance and to ease his intellectual heart by occasional visits to a theatre or a bookshop are very great. Having heard the first part of the story you can understand that the régime of these schools is a reign of terror and that I should be in a much more terrorised position were it not that many of my pupils (noblemen and signori and editors and rich people) have praised me highly to the director who being a socialist is very sensible of my deservingness in consequence . . .

Complaints about towns, climates and people are the common coin of private intercourse. Complaints about being misrepresented demand a public forum. The following two letters to *Time* Magazine, in 1941 and 1948 respectively, try and put the record straight with some good humour:

Many thanks for the flattering reference to my gaudily crowned head but may I file a gentle demurrer to your repeated use of the adjective 'dwarfish' in describing my person. Although I actually stand five feet four inches in socks, I have never objected to being ribbed about my size. Your pet word, however, strikes me as inappropriate as it carries a connotation of the monstrous and stunted. Let me suggest that such phrases as 'smallish', 'minute', 'miniature', and even 'pocket-size' Billy Rose would be considerably more appetizing.

BILLY ROSE
New York City

It has come to my attention that in your Current & Choice section, Lauren Bacall has consistently been left out of the cast of *Key Largo*.

Inasmuch as there are those of us in Hollywood, Miss Bacall among them, who would rather make Current & Choice than win an Academy Award or make Men of Distinction, won't you please include her in the cast of *Key Largo* in Current & Choice just once, as she is my wife and I have to live with her. Miss Bacall is extremely tired of being labeled *et al*.

HUMPHREY BOGART
Beverly Hills

6

Ripostes

Long complex ripostes to insult or insinuations are less effective
than those that are brief and to the point. Indeed, as likely or
not, such lengthy missives will have been drafted by lawyers
who pay themselves by the hour and tend to make them prolix,
evasive, and full of impenetrable language. It is better to deal
with impertinence in a few well chosen words, as Benjamin
Franklin did in writing to his former friend William Strahan.
Franklin had played a leading role in trying to negotiate with the
British on behalf of the American colonies, but after the bombardment of Boston and the battle of Bunker Hill, his patience
was exhausted. Strahan, an English MP, had been pestering
him with letters urging him to continue to act as mediator; the
American was eventually provoked into this magnificently
robust letter, which he did not send, but published in the press
in July 1775:

> *Mr Strahan*,
> You are a Member of Parliament, and one of that Majority
> which has doomed my Country to Destruction.—You have
> begun to burn our Towns, and murder our People.—Look
> upon your Hands! They are stained with the Blood of your
> Relations!—You and I were long Friends:—You are now my
> Enemy,—and I am
>
> > Yours,
> > B FRANKLIN

The majesty of this compares very favourably with another
famous riposte, that from Elizabeth I to a recalcitrant bishop.
One feels a little sorry for Dr Richard Cox, as he had been a keen
supporter of the Church of England and had suffered imprisonment under Mary. Before that he had been tutor to Edward VI,
and Elizabeth raised him to the see of Ely on her accession.

However, Sir Christopher Hatton, who had become a favourite of Elizabeth's chiefly because of his dancing prowess, coveted Ely Palace and its gardens in Holborn. Elizabeth said he should have it. Dr Cox said he should not. The Queen therefore wrote to Dr Cox:

> Proud Prelate,
> You know what you were before I made you what you are now. If you do not immediately comply with my request, I will unfrock you, by God.
>
> ELIZABETH

Politics and diplomacy provide the ideal forum for ripostes. These are often necessarily sent through third parties, but they need not be any the less effective for that; ambassadors become masters of the art of implying with heavy irony and veiled belligerence what would or would not be likely to be acceptable to their principals. In 1840, and not for the first time, the British were having trouble with the French. Both countries had imperialistic Foreign Secretaries, Palmerston for the British and Thiers for the French. Palmerston's policy, up to then successful, had been to involve the French in alliances which sought to maintain the integrity of the Ottoman Empire; but Thiers now tried to revive Napoleonic ambitions of French supremacy in the Levant and looked like being prepared to set Europe alight in the furtherance of these aims. Palmerston decided that the French policy was bluff and wrote to the British ambassador in Paris the following blueplan for a riposte to the sabre-rattling of M. Thiers. It had the desired effect:

> My dear Bulwer,—Notwithstanding the mysterious threatening with which Thiers has favoured us, I still hold to my belief that the French Government will be too wise and prudent to make war; and various things which come to me from different quarters confirm me in that belief. Besides, bullies seldom execute the threats they deal in; and men of trick and cunning are not always men of desperate resolves. But if Thiers should again hold to you the language of menace, however indistinctly and vaguely shadowed out, pray retort upon him to the full extent of what he may say to you, and with that skill of language which I know you to be

the master of, convey to him in the most friendly and unoffensive manner possible, that if France throws down the gauntlet we shall not refuse to pick it up; and that if she begins a war, she will to a certainty lose her ships, colonies, and commerce before she sees the end of it; that her army of Algiers will cease to give her anxiety, and that Mehemet Ali will just be chucked into the Nile.

Palmerston's unequivocal approach is echoed in a far more celebrated riposte, that of Dr Johnson to James Macpherson, who had unwisely sent the great man a threatening letter. Macpherson claimed to have collected many originals of Gaelic folk poems, which he obligingly rendered in translations for a gullible literary public, amongst whom they achieved a great vogue. In Europe they were even more of a success, and the Germans became very enthusiastic, seeing the poems of 'Ossian' (Macpherson's supposed Celtic bard) as the first flowering of third-century lyric poetry in Europe. German scholars ranked his work with Homer, and Goethe even made Werther and Charlotte weep over 'Ossian's' ballads. On the first appearance of the Ossian poems Dr Johnson was not for a moment deceived, describing them crisply as 'impudent forgeries'. When asked by Dr Blair whether he thought any man of a modern age could have written such poems, he replied: 'Yes, Sir, many men, many women, and many children.'
Macpherson had quite an extensive career with the British Government, despite his emotional attachment to the Jacobite cause. He was for a while agent to the Nabob of Arcot, and surveyor-general of the Floridas. He paid rather a lot to be buried in Poets' Corner of Westminster Abbey. In later life he exhausted himself cobbling up further evidence for the existence of Ossian, as the public became daily more sceptical; and no doubt he continued to write hostile letters to his critics:

(January 1775)

Mr James Macpherson—
I received your foolish and impudent note. Whatever insult is offered me I will do my best to repel, and what I cannot do for myself, the law will do for me. I will not desist from detecting what I think a cheat, from any fear of the menaces of a Ruffian.
You want me to retract. What shall I retract? I thought your

book an imposture from the beginning. I think it upon yet
surer reasons an imposture still. For this opinion I give the
publick my reasons which I here dare you to refute.

But however I may despise you, I reverence truth and if you
can prove the genuineness of the work I will confess it. Your
rage, I defy, your abilities since your Homer are not so
formidable, and what I have heard of your morals disposes
me to pay regard not to what you shall say, but to what you
can prove.

You may print this if you will.

SAM: JOHNSON

Forgery is not very common as a source of literary controversy,
but plagiarism is a hardy perennial. 'Bad poets imitate,' wrote T.
S. Eliot in one of his essays, 'good poets steal'; but the sort of
stealing he had in mind was rather different from the sort of
stealing that provokes charges of plagiarism, the difference
being that between quotation and representing another person's
writing as your own. This was the charge offered against Oscar
Wilde by his persistent enemy James McNeill Whistler. Whistler
is celebrated for his lawsuit against Ruskin who had criticized
his painting in most opprobious terms, remarking in print that
he had flung 'a pot of paint in the public's face'. The litigant was
awarded a farthing's damages. The story of his (many) disputes
and artistic quarrels is told in his autobiographical *The Gentle Art
of Making Enemies*. Sporadically witty, it is for the most part a
wearisome exercise in sarcasm and invective. Whistler and
Wilde ought to have been on the same side on many issues,
particularly their dislike of sentimentality passed off as fine
painting. But doubtless the art world wasn't big enough to
contain two combative egos of such ample proportions.

Truth
Jan. 9, 1890
Sir,—I can hardly imagine that the public are in the very
smallest degree interested in the shrill shrieks of 'Plagiarism'
that proceed from time to time out of the lips of silly vanity or
incompetent mediocrity.

However, as Mr James Whistler has had the impertinence
to attack me with both venom and vulgarity in your columns,
I hope you will allow me to state that the assertions contained

in his letters are as deliberately untrue as they are deliberately offensive.

The definition of a disciple as one who has the courage of the opinions of his master is really too old even for Mr Whister to be allowed to claim it, and as for borrowing Mr Whistler's ideas about art, the only thoroughly original ideas I have ever heard him express have had reference to his own superiority as a painter over painters greater than himself.

It is a trouble for any gentleman to have to notice the lucubrations of so ill-bred and ignorant a person as Mr Whistler, but your publication of his insolent letter left me no option in the matter.—I remain, Sir, faithfully yours,

OSCAR WILDE

In a further exchange Wilde writes that: 'with our James vulgarity begins at home, and should be allowed to stay there'; to which Whistler retorted with a single observation: '"A poor thing", Oscar!—"but", for once, I suppose "your own".'

A splendid literary fracas involving accusations of plagiarism was provoked by Edith Sitwell when she published *Aspects of Modern Poetry* in 1934. She took the opportunity to deliver a few well-aimed swipes at some of the contemporary arbiters of poetic taste, in particular Dr Leavis, who was once aptly described by J. B. Priestley as the 'keeper of literary passports'. Of the Doctor's prose style she wrote:

The Doctor has a transcendental gift, when he is writing sense, for making this appear to be nonsense . . .

The sound of a great deal of Milton . . . affects Dr Leavis much as the sound of a motor bicycle affects my less sensitive nervous system . . . as for his interpretation of the stressing, it is sad to see Milton's great lines bobbing up and down in the sandy desert of Dr Leavis's mind with the grace of a fleet of weary camels.

She also swiped at Geoffrey Grigson, the pugnacious editor of *New Verse*, ('A Paper . . . of Inordinate and Notorious Funniness') and at an old enemy, Wyndham Lewis. One of his poems provided an ideal target:

Mr Lewis suffers from various other little troubles that he would like us to understand and to sympathise with. There is

for instance the worry about back and fronts . . . and this, at
moments, grows to such a pitch that he seems scarcely to
know if he is coming or going. (*This in reference to the poem
beginning*:
> Try and walk backwards: you will quickly see
> How you were meant only one-way to be!
> Attempt to gaze out of your bricked-up back:
> You will soon discover what we one-ways lack!)

The situation you describe must be most trying, but these
little things will occur, you know. And we want you not to
fret about the seriousness of the symptoms.

The response of this somewhat solemn trio of literary con-
troversialists to Edith Sitwell's stirring was very encouraging. Dr
Leavis observed in print that the Sitwells 'belonged to the
history of publicity'. Wyndham Lewis blasted away in *Time &
Tide*, and an ally, G. W. Stonier did a hatchet review of her book
in the *New Statesman and Nation* which accused her of 'borrowing' from Dr Leavis's work and that of Geoffrey Grigson without
acknowledgement. Her riposte was masterly. She wrote to the
New Statesman and Nation as follows:

> *Sir*, With regard to Mr G. W. Stonier's review of my book
> *Aspects of Modern Poetry*, may I reply that had I known that Dr
> Leavis was the author of Andrew Lang's sonnet *The Odyssey*
> (and I think him capable of it), I should have acknowledged
> my debt to him. Had I known that he was the author of Mr
> Arthur Symons's book on the French Symbolists, of Villiers de
> l'Isle Adam's *Axel*, of Mr Yeats's *Autobiographies* and *Essays*,
> and of the *Oxford Book of English Verse*, I should have acknow-
> ledged my debt. But this is the first I have heard of it. Before
> we know where we are, we shall find that Dr Leavis is the
> Dark Lady of the Sonnets!
>
> Again, Mr Stonier says that, whilst attacking Mr Grigson, I
> 'appropriate, with acknowledging' (sic) 'an exceedingly apt
> quotation from Yeats's *Packet for Ezra Pound*, which Mr Grig-
> son used in a review in *New Verse*, October, 1933 . . . I have
> not read Mr Grigson's review. Mr Yeats, with great kindness,
> sent me the *Packet for Ezra Pound* when it first appeared, with
> most interesting annotations in his own handwriting. The
> book is one of my most treasured possessions. I was unaware

that I had to thank Mr Grigson for this. I thought my debt was
to Mr Yeats, who sent me the book!

It is right and natural that Mr Stonier should admire Dr
Leavis. It reminds me of Miss Nellie Wallace's appeal to her
slightly denuded feather boa: 'For God's sake, hold together,
boys!'

As, Sir, you have published Mr Stonier's quite unwarranted
remarks about me, I hope that you will also publish my letter,
without alterations.

All of which goes to show that accusations of plagiarism can
sometimes boomerang. A particularly enjoyable example of this
was when the legal department of Warner Brothers, the huge
American film company, decided to try and establish copyright
in the name 'Casablanca', having previously produced a celebrated film under this title starring Humphrey Bogart and Ingrid
Bergman. Five years after the great *Casablanca*, the Marx
Brothers decided to do a film entitled *A Night in Casablanca*. The
litigious moguls, egged on by their characteristically unscrupulous and voracious lawyers, decided to take legal action to crush
this piece of Marxian effrontery. But they had reckoned without
Groucho Marx, who fired off the following broadside:

> *Dear Warner Brothers:*
> Apparently there is more than one way of conquering a city
> and holding it as your own. For example, up to the time that
> we contemplated making this picture, I had no idea that the
> city of Casablanca belonged exclusively to Warner Brothers.
> However, it was only a few days after our announcement
> appeared that we received your long, ominous legal docu-
> ment warning us not to use the name Casablanca.
>
> It seems that in 1471, Ferdinand Balboa Warner, your
> great-great-grandfather, while looking for a shortcut to the
> city of Burbank, had stumbled on the shores of Africa and,
> raising his alpenstock (which he later turned in for a hundred
> shares of the common), named it Casablanca.
>
> I just don't understand your attitude. Even if you plan on
> re-releasing your picture, I am sure that the average movie fan
> could learn in time to distinguish between Ingrid Bergman
> and Harpo. I don't know whether I could, but I certainly
> would like to try.
>
> You claim you own Casablanca and that no one else can use

that name without your permission. What about 'Warner Brothers'? Do you own that, too? You probably have the right to use the name Warner, but what about Brothers? Professionally, we were brothers long before you were. We were touring the sticks as The Marx Brothers when Vitaphone was still a gleam in the inventor's eye, and even before us there had been other brothers—the Smith Brothers; the Brothers Karamazov; Dan Brothers, an outfielder with Detroit; and 'Brother, Can You Spare a Dime?' (This was originally 'Brothers, Can You Spare a Dime?' but this was spreading a dime pretty thin, so they threw out one brother, gave all the money to the other one and whittled it down to, 'Brother, Can You Spare a Dime?')

Now Jack, how about you? Do you maintain that yours is an original name? Well, it's not. It was used long before you were born. Offhand, I can think of two Jacks—there was Jack of 'Jack and the Beanstalk', and Jack the Ripper, who cut quite a figure in his day.

As for you, Harry, you probably sign your checks, sure in the belief that you are the first Harry of all time and that all other Harrys are imposters. I can think of two Harrys that preceded you. There was lighthouse Harry of Revolutionary fame and a Harry Appelbaum who lived on the corner of 93rd Street and Lexington Avenue. Unfortunately, Appelbaum wasn't too well known. The last I heard of him, he was selling neckties at Weber and Heilbroner.

. . . This all seems to add up to a pretty bitter tirade, but I assure you it's not meant to. I love Warners. Some of my best friends are Warner Brothers. It is even possible that I am doing you an injustice and that you yourselves know nothing at all about this dog-in-the-Wanger attitude. It wouldn't surprise me at all to discover that the heads of your legal department are unaware of this absurd dispute, for I am acquainted with many of them and they are fine fellows with curly black hair, double-breasted suits and a love of their fellow man that out-Saroyans Saroyan.

I have a hunch that this attempt to prevent us from using the title is the brainchild of some ferret-faced shyster, serving a brief apprenticeship in your legal department. I know the type well—hot out of law school, hungry for success and too ambitious to follow the natural laws of promotion. This bar sinister probably needled your attorneys, most of whom are fine fellows with curly black hair, double-breasted suits, etc., into attempting to enjoin us. Well, he won't get away with it! We'll fight him to the highest court! No pasty-faced legal adventurer is going to cause bad blood between the Warners and the Marxes. We are all brothers under the skin and we'll remain friends till the last reel of 'A Night in Casablanca' goes tumbling over the spool.

Sincerely,
GROUCHO MARX

A puzzled legal department replied asking for details of the film's plot. This was provided, and of course vastly complicated everything as it was quite inconsequential. It puzzled the legal department even more, so they asked for more detail. Groucho supplied it. Unfortunately the new plot bore no relation at any point to the one previously submitted . . .

Dear Brothers:
Since I last wrote you, I regret to say there have been some changes in the plot of our new picture, 'A Night in Casablanca'. In the new version I play Bordello, the sweetheart of Humphrey Bogart. Harpo and Chico are itinerant rug peddlers who are weary of laying rugs and enter a monastery just for a lark. This is a good joke on them, as there hasn't been a lark in the place for fifteen years.

Across from this monastery, hard by a jetty, is a waterfront hotel, chockful of apple-cheeked damsels, most of whom have been barred by the Hays Office for soliciting. In the fifth reel, Gladstone makes a speech that sets the House of Commons in uproar and the King promptly asks for his resignation. Harpo marries a hotel detective; Chico operates an ostrich farm. Humphrey Bogart's girl, Bordello, spends her last years in a Bacall house.

This, as you can see, is a very skimpy outline. The only thing that can save us from extinction is a continuation of the film shortage.

Fondly,
GROUCHO MARX

Perhaps not surprisingly, there was no reply to this from Warner Brothers.

Groucho Marx did not exactly share the qualities of Bertrand

Russell, but they were both masters of the epistolary riposte. Both display a vein of impish humour which must have been highly disconcerting to the opposition who had to disentangle serious observations from those made in possibly malicious jest. In 1957 Russell received a bubbly, self-confident letter from an American professor who told him that he had devised a computer which could make philosophers redundant:

> The enclosed [paper] will indicate our progress in simulating human problem-solving processes with a computer . . . we obtain rather striking improvements in problem-solving ability . . . in one case [the machine] created a beautifully simple proof to replace a far more complex one in [*Principia Mathematica*] . . . The machine required something less than five minutes to find the proof. I am not sure that these facts should be made known to schoolboys. You may also be interested in the evidence of our paper that the learned man and the wise man are not always the same person . . .

Russell was impressed:

> Thank you very much for your letter, and for the enclosure. I am delighted by your example of the superiority of your machine to Whitehead and me. I quite appreciate your reasons for thinking that the facts should be concealed from schoolboys. How can one expect them to learn to do sums when they know that machines can do them better? I am also delighted by your exact demonstration of the old saw that wisdom is not the same thing as erudition.
>
> Yours sincerely,
BERTRAND RUSSELL

An intellectual controversy that provided a trenchant exchange in letter form was that between H. L. Mencken and Ezra Pound. The latter conceived a violent enthusiasm for the political programme known as 'social credit' which was briefly fashionable in the 1930s. Pound found it difficult to see why others were not instantly converted to his latest intellectual fad, and began bombarding editors with long and dogmatic letters on the subject. Mencken despatched a brilliantly crushing reply to one of Pound's blockbusters:

My dear Pound:
You are something behind-hand with that tirade, but if you
want to print it I surely have no objection. Everything you say
has been said before, first by the war patriots, then by the Ku
Kluxers, then by the Anti-Saloon League brethren, then by
the Harding visionaries, then by the Coolidge ditto, then by
the apostles of Hoover's New Economy, and now by the New
Dealers and Union Square Communists, with applause all
along the line by the Single Taxers, chiropracters, anti-
vivisectionists, sur-realists, anti-Darwinians, Rotarians,
Kiwians, thought-transferers, Fundamentalists, Douglasites,
pacifists, New Thoughters, one-crop farmers, American
Legionaires, osteopaths, Christian scientists, labor skates,
and kept idealists of the *New Republic*.
In brief, you come to the defense of quackery too late. All
you say or can say has been said 10,000 times before, and by
better men. I say better men because there is plainly a
quantitative if not a qualitative difference between quackeries,
and hence between the gullibility of their customers . . .
. . . when you fell into the hands of those London logrol-
lers, and began to wander through pink fogs with them, all
your native common sense oozed out of you, and you set up a
caterwauling for all sorts of brummagem Utopias, at first in
the aesthetic region only but later in the regions of political
and aesthetic baloney. Thus a competent poet was spoiled to
make a tin-horn politician.
Your acquaintance with actual politics, and especially with
American politics, seems to be pathetically meagre . . . Very
little real news seems to penetrate to Rapallo. Why not
remove those obscene and archaic whiskers, shake off all the
other stigmata of the Left Bank, come home to the Republic,
and let me show you the greatest show on earth? If, after six
months of it, you continue to believe in sorcery, whether
poetical, political or economic, I promise to have you put to
death in some painless manner . . .
Meanwhile, please don't try to alarm a poor old man by
yelling at him and making faces. It has been tried before.

Perhaps the best ever riposte was sent by Charles Mathews the
elder, the nineteenth-century entertainer who made a big hit in
two tours of America. Not, however, with the Reverend Paschal
Strong, a minister of the Dutch Reformed Church. In a

fire-and-brimstone sermon on the subject of the yellow-fever peril, the text of which was *Pestilence—A Punishment for Public Sins*, he denounced the theatrical profession in terms that would have made John Knox sound like an anaemic Anglican curate. In particular it seemed that Mathews was personally responsible for the dreadful outbreak of fever that had occurred in July 1823 and lasted until November. On leaving the USA, Mathews wrote the following letter to Rev. Strong as his parting shot:

Sir,—Ingratitude being in my estimation a crime most heinous and most hateful, I cannot quit the shores of America without expressing my grateful sense of services which you have gratuitously rendered.

Other professors in '*that school of Satan,* that *nursery of hell!*' as you most appropriately style the theatre, have been, *ex necessitate,* content to have their merits promulgated through the medium of the public papers; but mine you have graciously vouchsafed to blazon from the pulpit. You have, as appears in your recently published sermon, declared me to be (what humility tells me I only am in your partial and prejudiced estimation) 'an actor whom God Almighty sent here as a man better qualified than any other in the world to dissipate every serious reflection!'

What man! what woman! what child! could resist the effects of such a description, coming from such a quarter? particularly as you, at the same time, assured the laughter-loving inhabitants of this city that the punishment incident to such a 'thirst after dissipation' had been already inflicted by 'their late calamity', the pestilence, 'voracious in *its thirst of prey!*' and you might have added, thirsty in its *hunger* for *drink.* No wonder that the theatre has since been crowded, the manager enriched, and the most sanguine expectations of him whom you have perhaps improperly elevated to the rank of the avenging angel so beautifully described by Addison, completely realized.

For each and all of these results accept, reverend sir, my cordial and grateful thanks. Nor deem me too avaricious of your favours, if I venture to solicit more. As you have expressly averred, in the sermon before me, that 'God *burnt the theatre of New York,* to rebuke the *devotees of pleasure there resident*', permit me, your humble avenging angel to inquire, by whom and for what purpose the cathedrals at Rouen and

Venice were recently destroyed by fire, and in a manner which more especially implicated the hand of Providence? But beware, most reverend sir, I conjure you, lest your doctrines of special dispensations furnish arguments and arms to the scoffer and atheist . . .

I have sir, the honour to be, most gratefully your obliged, angelic, yellow-fever-producing friend,

C. MATHEWS

ENGAGING ECCENTRICS

1

Larger Than Life

People who are somewhat larger than life are often a magnet for other strong personalities; Lord Byron, for instance, apart from having to fend off the innumerable feeble-minded women who were constantly flinging themselves at him, was also courted, if that is the word, by a lady made of sterner stuff. Once Maria Cogni had become his mistress, she showed herself to be fiercely demanding and loyal, so much so that even the cynical and easy-going poet of *Don Juan* had some difficulty in preventing her from getting completely out of control. He tells the story in a letter to John Murray of 1819 in the manner of a hilarious burlesque:

. In the summer of 1817, Hobhouse and myself were saunter-ing on horseback along the Brenta one evening—when amongst a group of peasants we remarked two girls as the prettiest we had seen for some time. —About this period there had been great distress in the country—and I had a little relieved some of the people. —Generosity makes a great figure at very little cost in Venetian livres—and mine had probably been exaggerated—as an Englishman's—— Whether they remarked us looking at them or no—I know not—but one of them called out to me in Venetian—'Why do not you who relieve others—think of us also?'—I turned round and answered her—'Cara—tu sei troppo bella e giovane per aver' bisogno del' soccorso mio'—she answered—'if you saw my hut and my food—you would not say so'—All this passed half jestingly—and I saw no more of her for some days —A few evenings after—we met with these two girls again—and they addressed us more seriously— assuring us of the truth of their statement. —They were cousins—Margarita married—the other single. —As I doub-ted still of the circumstances—I took the business up in a different light—and made an appointment with them for the next evening. —Hobhouse had taken a fancy to the single lady—who was much shorter—in stature—but a very pretty girl also. —They came attended by a third woman—who was cursedly in the way—and Hobhouse's charmer took fright (I don't mean at Hobhouse but at not being married—for here no woman will do anything under adultery), and flew off—and mine made some bother—at the propositions—and wished to consider of them. —I told her 'if you really are in want I will relieve you without any conditions whatever—and you may make love with me or no just as you please—*that* shall make no difference—but if you are not in absolute necessity—this is naturally a rendezvous—and I presumed that you understood this—when you made the appointment.'—— She said that she had no objection to make love with me—as she was married—and all married women did it—but that her husband (a baker) was somewhat ferocious—and would do her a mischief. —In short—in a few evenings we arranged our affairs—and for two years—in the course of which I had more women than I can count or recount—she was the only one who preserved over me an ascendancy—which was often disputed & never impaired. —As she herself used to say publicly—'It don't matter—he may have five hundred—but he will always come back to me.'——The reasons of this were firstly—her person—very dark—tall—the Venetian face—very fine black eyes—and certain other qualities which need not be mentioned. —She was two & twenty years old—and never having had children—had not spoilt her figure—nor *anything else*—which is I assure you—a great desideration in a hot climate where they grow relaxed and doughy and *flumpity* in a short time after breeding. . . . [She] used to walk in whenever it suited her—with no very great regard to time, place, nor persons—and if she found any women in her way she knocked them down. —When I first knew her I was in *'relazione'* (liaison) with la Signora Segati—who was silly enough one evening at Dolo—accompanied by some of her female friends—to threaten her—for the Gossips of the Villeggiature—had already found out by the neighing of my horse one evening—that I used to 'ride late in the night' to meet the Fornarina. —Margarita threw back her veil (*fazziolo*) and replied in very explicit Venetian—'*You* are *not* his *wife*: I

am *not* his *wife*—*you* are his Donna—and *I* am his *donna*—*your*
husband is a cuckold—and mine is another;—for the rest,
what *right* have you to reproach me?—if he prefers what is
mine—to what is yours—is it my fault? if you wish to secure
him—tie him to your petticoat-string—but do not think to
speak to me without a reply because you happen to be richer
than I am.——Having delivered this pretty piece of eloquence
(which I translate as it was related to me by a bystander) she
went on her way—leaving a numerous audience with Madam
Segati—to ponder at her leisure on the dialogue between
them . . . At last she quarrelled with her husband—and one
evening ran away to my house. —I told her this would not
do—she said she would lie in the street but not go back to
him—that he beat her (the gentle tigress) spent her
money—and scandalously neglected his Oven. As it was
Midnight—I let her stay—and next day there was no moving
her at all.——Her husband came roaring & crying—&
entreating her to come back, *not* She! —He then applied to the
Police—and they applied to me—I told them and her husband to *take* her—I did not want her—she had come and I
could not fling her out of the window—but they might
conduct her through the door if they chose it——She went
before the Commissary—but was obliged to return with that
'*becco Ettico*' (consumptive cuckold), as she called the *poor* man
who had a Ptisick. —In a few days she ran away again. —
After a precious piece of work she fixed herself in my
house—really & truly without my consent. . . . She was a fine
animal—but quite untameable. *I* was the only person that
could at all keep her in any order—and when she saw me
really angry—(which they tell me is rather a savage sight), she
subsided. —But she had a thousand fooleries—in her
fazziolo—the dress of the lower orders—she looked
beautiful—but alas! she longed for a hat and feathers and all I
could say or do (and I said much) could not prevent this
travestie.—I put the first into the fire—but I got tired of
burning them before she did of buying them—so that she
made herself a figure—for they did not at all become her.—
Then she would have her gowns with a *tail*—like a lady
forsooth—nothing would serve her—but 'l'abito colla *coua*',
or *cua*, (that is the Venetian for 'la *Coda*' the tail or train) and as
her cursed pronunciation of the word made me laugh—there
was an end to all controversy—and she dragged this diaboli-

cal tail after her every where.——In the meantime she beat the women—and stopped my letters.—I found her one day pondering over one—she used to try to find out by their shape whether they were feminine or no—and she used to lament her ignorance—and actually studied her Alphabet—on purpose (as she declared) to open all letters addressed to me and read their contents . . .

Byron made several attempts to get rid of this fiery creature which she thwarted by such expedients as fighting her way into the house with a knife and throwing herself into the canal outside his windows; but at length he succeeded by means of a round-the-clock guard. He remarks that she was very devout and 'would cross herself if she heard the prayer-time strike— sometimes—when that ceremony did not appear to be much in unison with what she was then about.'

Another vivid character who would undoubtedly have appealed to Byron was the Greek writer and *raconteur* George Katsimbalis. In a letter to Henry Miller written on board a Greek steamer in 1940, Lawrence Durrell describes the night of Katsimbalis's salute to the cocks of Attica. This occasion was immortalized in the opening pages of Miller's lyrical hymn to Greece and the Greeks, *The Colossus of Marousi*. The 'Colossus' was Katsimbalis himself.

The peasants are lying everywhere on deck eating watermelons; the gutters are running with the juice. A huge crowd bound on a pilgrimage to the Virgin of Tinos. We are just precariously out of harbour, scouting the skyline for Eyetalian subs. What I really have to tell you is the story of the cocks of Attica; it will frame your portrait of Katsimbalis which I have not yet read but which sounds marvellous from all accounts. It is this. We all went up to the Acropolis the other evening very drunk and exalted by wine and poetry; it was a hot black night and our blood was roaring with cognac. We sat on the steps outside the big gate, passing the bottle, Katsimbalis reciting and Georgakis weeping a little, when all of a sudden he was seized with a kind of fit. Leaping to his feet he yelled out, 'Do you want to hear the cocks of Attica, you damned moderns?' His voice had a hysterical edge to it. We didn't answer, and he wasn't waiting for one. He took a little run to the edge of the precipice, like a fairy queen, a heavy black fairy queen, in his black clothes, threw back his head, clapped the crook of his stick into his wounded arm, and sent out the most blood-curdling clarion I have ever heard. Cock a doodle doo. It echoed all over the city—a sort of dark bowl dotted with lights like cherries. It ricocheted from hillock to hillock and wheeled up under the walls of the Parthenon. Under the winged victory this horrible male cockcrow—worse than Emil Jannings. We were so shocked that we were struck dumb. And while we were still looking at each other in the darkness, lo, from a distance silvery clear in the darkness a cock drowsily answered—then another, then another. This drove K. wild. Squaring himself, like a bird about to fly into space, and flapping his coattails, he set up a terrific scream—and the echoes multiplied. He screamed until the veins stood out all over him, looking like a battered and ravaged rooster in profile, flapping on his own dunghill. He screamed himself hysterical and his audience in the valley increased until all over Athens like bugles they were calling and calling, answering him. Finally between laughter and hysteria we had to ask him to stop. The whole night was alive with cockcrows—all Athens, all Attica, all Greece, it seemed, until I almost imagined you being woken at your desk late in New York to hear these terrific silver peals: Katsimbaline cockcrow in Attica . . .

Another engaging literary eccentric is described by Lord Chesterfield in one of the celebrated letters to his son, whom he counsels to follow the same practice as the gentleman in his anecdote.

> . . . I knew a gentleman, who was so good a manager of his time, that he would not even lose that small portion of it which the calls of nature obliged him to pass in the necessary-house, but gradually went through all the Latin poets in those moments. He bought, for example, a common edition of Horace, of which he tore off gradually a couple of pages, carried them with him to that necessary place, read them first, and then sent them down as a sacrifice to Cloacina; this was so much time fairly gained; and I recommend to you to follow his example. It is better than only doing what you cannot help doing at those moments; and it will make any book which you shall read in that manner, very present to your mind . . .

Not to lose a moment in the cause of enriching the mind is characteristic of scholars and those who interpret life through their art. The ability to do so implies another indispensable ingredient in the writer's makeup, the capacity for drudgery. Indeed, without that, Shaw tells his biographer Archibald Henderson in a letter of 1904, he himself would not have become a genius:

. . . I advise you in anything you write to insist on this training of mine, as otherwise you will greatly exaggerate my natural capacity. It has enabled me to produce an impression of being an extraordinarily clever, original, & brilliant writer, deficient only in feeling, whereas the truth is that though I am in a way a man of genius—otherwise I suppose I would not have sought out & enjoyed my experience, and been simply bored by holidays, luxury & money—yet I am not in the least naturally 'brilliant' and not at all ready or clever. If literary men generally were put through the mill I went through & kept out of their stuffy little coteries, where works of art breed in and in until the intellectual & spiritual product becomes hopelessly degenerate, I should have a thousand rivals more brilliant than myself. There is nothing more mischievous than the notion that my works are the mere play of a delightfully clever & whimsical hero of the salons: they are the result of perfectly straightforward drudgery, beginning in the ineptest novel writing juvenility, and persevered in every day for 25 years. Anybody can get my skill for the same price; and a good many people could probably get it cheaper. Man & Superman no doubt sounds as if it came from the most exquisite atmosphere of art. As a matter of fact, the mornings I gave to it were followed by afternoons & evenings spent in the committee rooms of a London Borough Council, fighting questions of drainage, paving, lighting, rates, clerk's salaries &c, &c, &c, &c; and that is exactly why it is so different from the books that are conceived at musical at homes. My latest book, The Common Sense of Municipal Trading, is in its way one of the best and most important I have ever written. I beg you, if you write about my 'extraordinary career', to make it clear to all young aspirants, that its extraordinariness lies in its ordinariness—that, like a greengrocer & unlike a minor poet, I have lived instead of dreaming and feeding myself with artistic confectionery. With a little more courage & a little

more energy I could have done much more; and I lacked these
because in my boyhood I lived on my imagination instead of
on my work.
    . . . It is quite true that the best authority on Shaw is Shaw.
My activities have lain in so many watertight compartments
that nobody has yet given anything but a sectional and
inaccurate account of me except when they have tried to piece
me out of my own confessions.

Shaw being the best authority on Shaw, it followed that, if you
wanted to know the truth about him, you had to brave the lion's
den, and take up some of the genius's valuable time. But visiting
literary lions can be rather alarming. In a letter to Violet
Dickinson of 1907, Virginia Woolf, then still Virginia Stephen,
describes the unnerving experience of tea with Henry James at
Rye Golf Club:

    . . . Henry James fixed me with his staring blank eye—it is
    like a childs marble—and said 'My dear Virginia, they tell
    me—they tell me—they tell me—that you—as indeed being
    your fathers daughter nay your grandfathers grandchild—the
    descendant I may say of a century—of a century—of quill
    pens and ink—ink—ink pots, yes, yes, yes, they tell
    me—ahm m m—that you, that you, that you *write* in short.'
    This went on in the public street, while we all waited, as
    farmers wait for the hen to lay an egg—do they?—nervous,
    polite, and now on this foot now on that. I felt like a
    condemned person, who sees the knife drop and stick and
    drop again. Never did any woman hate 'writing' as much as I
    do. But when I am old and famous I shall discourse like Henry
    James. We had to stop periodically to let him shake himself
    free of the thing; he made phrases over the bread and butter
    'rude and rapid' it was, and told us all the scandal of Rye. 'Mr
    Jones has eloped, I regret to say, to Tasmania; leaving 12 little
    Jones, and a possible 13th to Mrs Jones; most regrettable,
    most unfortunate, and yet not wholly an action to which one
    has not a private key of ones own so to speak.' . . .

In a letter to her family in 1774, Sally More, the sparkling
daughter of Hannah More, gave a wonderfully evocative
account of meeting another literary lion. The great lexicographer
was apparently in benign, even waggish, mood:

. . . Miss Reynolds told the Doctor of all our rapturous exclamations on the road. He shook his scientific head at Hannah, and said, 'She was *a silly thing.*' When our visit was ended, he called for his hat (as it rained), to attend us down a very long entry to our coach, and not Rasselas could have acquitted himself more *en cavalier*. We are engaged with him at Sir Joshua's, Wednesday evening—what do you think of us? I forgot to mention that, not finding Johnson in his little parlour when we came in, Hannah seated herself in his great chair, hoping to catch a little ray of his genius; when he heard it, he laughed heartily, and told her it was a chair in which he never sat. He said, it reminded him of Boswell and himself, when they stopped a night at the spot (as they imagined) where the weird sisters appeared to Macbeth; the idea so worked upon their enthusiasm, that it quite deprived them of rest; however, they learned the next morning, to their mortification, that they had been deceived, and were quite in another part of the country . . .

A more bizarre visit with a literary motive is described by Rupert Hart-Davis in one of his letters to George Lyttelton. Hart-Davis was the editor of Oscar Wilde's letters and the occasion he describes was an episode in his quest for unpublished letters, a cache of which was said to be in the hands of an eccentric and very queer Wilde fan:

. . . My French week-end was delightful. After lunch on Monday Diana drove me into Paris (Chantilly is about as far as Windsor is from London) through forked lightning and tropical rain. High up in the Boulevard Beaumarchais, near the Bastille, I ran to earth the old Wilde fan. His flat was indeed murky as a fox's earth: every window, and most shutters, tightly fastened on a stifling Turkish-Bath afternoon. All the time I was there (about 1½ hours) sweat was trickling down inside my shirt. He is a short man of seventy-something, with a thick white beard, masses of white hair, and spectacles. He received me dressed in trousers, a very *décolleté* pyjama-jacket and a dressing gown. At great length he described how he had been knocked down crossing the road, was now permanently lame, and moreover sometimes lost his memory in the middle of the lectures by which I imagine he earns his living. You can imagine the law-suit he is conducting against all and sundry. He told me that since 1903 he had collected every book, cutting, photograph and anecdote of Oscar, and he has shelves and cupboards and shelves and cupboards to prove his assiduity. Telling me he had written or translated more than 200 plays, he showed me glass cases full of puppets that belonged to D'Annunzio, also signed photographs of Sarah Bernhardt and goodness knows who. When I steered him back to Oscar in my halting French, he read me, with much emphasis and emotion, long extracts from his translations of *The Ballad of Reading Gaol* and the other poems. Then he produced two enormous files, which contained the programme of *every* production of *Salome* all over the world, together with photographs of lightly clad but hideous actresses in the name-part. At last I got him on to the letters, and he fished out a thick folder stuffed with copies of letters, all in his illegible old-Frenchman's hand, and all in French. After some discussion I promised to send him a list of what we've got, and he promised to recopy and send me any of his that we lack, though I very much doubt how many of them are authentic. Beyond touching hands a little more than was necessary when handing me books to look at, he made no advances, and was I think genuinely pleased to have someone to talk and show his treasures to. The whole flat was dark, stuffy, hung with oriental hangings, full of books, pictures and *bibelots*—very ninetyish . . .

The English are perhaps better known for eccentricity as a way of life than the French. A whole line that has contributed significantly to the field are the Bosanquets whose remarkable achievements and the manner of their attainment were chronicled by novelist Nigel Dennis in a corrective letter to *The Times* in 1963. It seems that the man who gave the world the 'googly' had been traduced by a previous correspondent:

Sir,

Do you want to be torn to pieces by nettled Bosanquets? That family claims two major innovations: (1) the introduction into Oxford of Hegel and 'German idealism', (2) the introduction into cricket of the googly. It is obvious that (2) was merely the sporting consequence of (1): but just as Bradley must be granted to have helped with the philosophical juggle, so must my dear mother (*née* Louise Bosanquet) be allowed her share in the bowling one.

As a little girl she hero-worshipped her cousin, 'BJT', and paid for it in the 1890s by being made to stand at one end of a lawn for hours, retrieving his experimental googlies. A tennis ball was always used—'Not a *billiard* ball, a *tennis* ball' were among my mother's last words to me. As she knew nothing about German idealism, I must append the following highly significant dates off my own bat:

1886. Publication of B. Bosanquet's *The Introduction to Hegel's Philosophy of Fine Art.*

1890. The googly idea conceived by B. J. T. Bosanquet.

1893. Publication of Bradley's *Appearance and Reality.*

1893–1900. Intensive work, helped by my mother, to hide the reality behind the googly's appearance.

1903. The Ashes regained by the googly—German idealism's first and last sporting victory.

Yours faithfully

NIGEL DENNIS

(Reality insists the Ashes were regained on 3 March 1904. The late Reginald Bosanquet came from the same distinguished family.) Eccentricities that might be forgivable on the cricket field or in the columns of *The Times*, are considerably less so on the stage, at least during a performance. In a letter to an unknown correspondent of 1840 Miss Fanny Kemble explains the hazards of working with the great Macready. According to George Henry Lewes the actor used to 'spend some five minutes behind the scenes, lashing himself into an imaginative rage by cursing *sotto voce* and shaking violently a ladder fixed against the wall'. The process, if Fanny Kemble is to be believed, was all too effective:

> . . . Macready is not pleasant to act with, as he keeps no specific time for his exits or entrances, comes on while one is in the middle of a soliloquy, and goes off while one is in the middle of a speech to him. He growls and prowls, and roams and foams, about the stage in every direction, like a tiger in his cage, so that I never know on what side of me he means to be: and keeps up a perpetual snarling and grumbling like the aforesaid tiger, so that I never feel quite sure that he *has done*, and that it is my turn to speak . . .

I do not know how Desdemona might have affected me under other circumstances, but my only feeling about acting it with Mr Macready is dread of his personal violence. I quail at the idea of his laying hold of me in those terrible, passionate scenes; for in *Macbeth* he pinched me black and blue, and almost tore the point lace from my head. I am sure my little finger will be rebroken, and as for that smothering in bed, 'Heaven have mercy upon me!' as poor Desdemona says. If that foolish creature wouldn't persist in talking long after she has been smothered and stabbed to death, one might escape by the off side of the bed, and leave the bolster to be questioned by Emilia, and apostrophised by Othello; but she will uplift her testimony after death to her husband's amiable treatment of her, and even the bolster wouldn't be stupid enough for that . . .

Miss Kemble's very sensible objections to the posthumous speeches of Desdemona put one in mind of one writer who was merciless about asking awkward questions concerning works of literature and art, the ones that the critics persistently overlooked. Rupert Hart-Davis, in another of his letters to George Lyttelton, recalls meeting the irrepressible Beachcomber (whose real name was J. B. Morton), and rashly consenting to take a walk with him:

. . . Reverting to Beachcomber, I daresay you never see the *Daily Express*, but twenty years ago when I used to see a lot of B in London (he is an Old Harrovian called J. B. Morton) he was immensely gay and amusing. One day when we were walking down an extremely crowded Fleet Street, he suddenly went up to a pillar-box and shouted into the slot: 'YOU CAN COME OUT NOW!' I liked very much his poem on Tolstoy, of which the refrain ran:
He ran away from home when he was ninety,
     And his golden hair was hanging down his back.
And he summed up the jargon-bosh of art- and music-critics beautifully by announcing: 'Wagner is the Puccini of music.' He always told me that the readers of the *Daily Express* were (often understandably) unable to distinguish between his funny column and the rest of the paper. In proof he told how one day, short of a paragraph and late with his copy, he filled up the space with these words: '*Stop Press*. At 3.55 pm

yesterday there was a heavy fall of green Chartreuse over South Croydon.' Next morning he received *six* letters from six people assuring him he was mistaken: they had all spent that afternoon in South Croydon and were positive that not so much as a drop of green Chartreuse had fallen! After that he gave up . . .

2

Mistaken Identity

In August 1698 the antiquary Humphrey Wanley wrote this readable piece of reportage to a colleague concerning an impostor who claimed to be the Duke of Monmouth. As that unfortunate gentleman had already been dead for thirteen years, it suggests considerable effrontery on the impostor's part, an impression that is not contradicted by his performance at his inevitable trial:

We have an account from the Assizes of Horsham in Sussex that on Monday se'nnight last a fellow was indicted and tried there for personating and pretending himself to be the late Duke of Monmouth, and by that means drawing considerable sums of money out of the zealots of that country. It appeared that he lodged at the house of one Widow Wickard (tho' with seeming privacy), where his true friends visited him and were admitted to kiss his hand upon their knees. He said he was the true legitimate son of King Charles II, and that his Uncle King James had such honour for him as to execute a common criminal in his stead to satisfy the Priests and to send him out of the way. And that the Prince of Orange was a very honest Gentleman and his deputy, and would surrender the crown to him when things were ripe, etc. Happy was he that could by any interest be introduced to his Highness to have the honour of his hand. It happened that one of his trusty friends one morning coming to pay him a visit with a stranger with him found him in bed. At the sight of the stranger he seemed much surprised and offended, and turning himself quick to the wall, sighing, said 'Oh! my friends will undo me.' At which the Gentleman assured his Highness that the person he had brought with him was life and fortune in his interest. Upon which he returned about and gave him his hand to kiss. Presently after, came into his lodgings a wench with a basket of chickens as a present from her mistress, and another with a letter to him, at the reading of which he seemed a little discontented. Upon which they desired to know if his Highness had received any bad news. He answered, No, 'twas indifferent, 'twas from Lord Russell to acquaint him that he was come with his fleet to Torbay and wanted some further direction. But that which troubled him was that he wanted a horse and money to carry him thither. At which they bid him not trouble for that he should be supplied immediately with both, which accordingly he was, and was away a fortnight, till he had spent both money and horse, and then returned. 'Tis said he has received above £500 thus, and lain with at least 50 of their wives. Upon his trial he declared himself to be the son of him that keeps the Swan Inn at Leicester, adding that he could not help it if the people would call him the Duke of Monmouth, he never bid them do so but told two Justices of the Peace, who had sent for him, his true name. He made so cunning a defence, and none of his zealots coming in against him (being prosecuted only by Major Brewer), that he was cleared of the indictment. Only the Lord Chief Justice afterwards bound him to good behaviour, for which he soon found bail amongst his party, who maintained him like a prince in prison, and three or four of the chief of them attended him to the Bar at his Trial and believe him still to be the true Duke of Monmouth. The Gaoler got, the first day he was committed, 40s. of people that came to see this imposter at 2d. a piece.

Deliberate impersonation of another man is a risky business, whatever the ephemeral profits to be gained. The person who is misrepresented very reasonably objects to the infringement of the copyright he feels he has in himself, and the drain on his bank account occasioned by someone deciding to share it with him. But how much more alarming to be told that one doesn't exist at all, or alternatively, that one is somebody else. Edward Lear explained how this happened to him, in a letter to Lady Waldegrave of 1866:

   . . . A few days ago in a railway as I went to my sister's a gentleman explained to two ladies (whose children had my 'Book of Nonsense'), that thousands of families were grateful to the author (which in silence I agreed to) who was not generally known—but was really Lord Derby: and now came a showing forth, which cleared up at once to my mind why that statement has already appeared in several papers. Edward Earl of Derby (said the Gentleman) did not choose to publish the book openly, but dedicated it as you see to his relations, and now if you will transpose the letters LEAR you will read simply EDWARD EARL.—Says I, joining spontaneous in the conversation—'That is quite a mistake: I have reason to know that Edward Lear the painter and author wrote and illustrated the whole book.' 'And I,' says the Gentleman, says he—'have good reason to know Sir, that you are wholly mistaken. *There is no such a person* as Edward Lear.' 'But,' says I, 'there *is*—and I am the man—and I wrote the book!' Whereupon all the party burst out laughing and evidently thought me mad or telling fibs. So I took off my hat and showed it all round, with Edward Lear and the address in large letters—also one of my cards, and a marked handker- chief: on which amazement devoured those benighted indi- viduals and I left them to gnash their teeth in trouble and tumult.

Believe me, Dear Lady Waldegrave,

Yours sincerely
EDWARD LEAR

The problem of not existing at all in other people's conscious- ness is paralleled by another: that of being two (or more) persons at once. But it can be politic to have an alternative persona, as John Adams, the second president of the United States, once demonstrated. He got a rousing reception when he was sent to France as commissioner for the New Republic in 1777; but were his hosts welcoming him or *another* Mr Adams?

. . . the Pamphlet entitled Common sense, had been prin- ted in the *Affaires de L'Angleterre et De L'Amérique*, and expressly ascribed to M. Adams the celebrated Member of Congress, *le célèbre Membre du Congrès*. It must be further known, that altho the Pamphlet Common sense, was received in France and in all Europe with Rapture: yet there were certain Parts of it, that they did not choose to publish in France. The Reasons of this, any Man may guess. Common sense undertakes to prove, that Monarchy is unlawful by the old Testament. They therefore gave the Substance of it, as they said, and paying many Compliments to Mr Adams, his sense and rich imagination, they were obliged to ascribe some Parts to Republican Zeal. When I arrived at Bordeaux, all that I could say or do, would not convince any Body, but that I was the *fameux* Adams.—*Cette un homme célèbre. Votre nom est bien connu ici.*—My Answer was—it is another Gentleman, whose Name of Adams you have heard. It is Mr Samuel Adams, who was excepted from Pardon by Gen. Gage's Proclamation.—*O Non Monsieur, cette votre Modestie.*

But when I arrived at Paris, I found a very different Style. I found great Pains taken, much more than the question was worth to settle the Point that I was not the famous Adams. There was a dread of a sensation—Sensations at Paris are important Things. I soon found too, that it was effectually settled in the English News Papers that I was not the famous Adams. No body went so far in France or England, as to say I was the infamous Adams. I make no scruple to say, that I believe, that both Parties, for Parties there were, joined in declaring that I was not the famous Adams. I certainly joined both sides in this, in declaring that I was not the famous Adams, because this was the Truth.

It being settled that he was not the famous Adams, the Consequence was plain—he was some Man that nobody had ever heard of before—and therefore a Man of no Consequence—a Cypher. And I am inclined to think that all Parties both in France and England—Whiggs and Tories in England—The Friends of Franklin, Deane and Lee, differing in many other Things agreed in this—that I was not the *fameux* Adams . . .

Adams was tactfully prepared to settle for being the Mr Adams they wanted. But giving people what they want can have disreputable motives, as may be seen in the following bit of mischief concocted by Edith Sitwell. The Sitwells were very aristocratic, very intolerant and very witty. Some of their eccentricity was clearly calculated, some, perhaps, not. It is hard to know into which category would fall her assertion to Evelyn Waugh that port was made of methylated spirits, something she knew for a fact because her charlady had told her so. Her treatment of the gushing lady in the French hotel here described is vintage Sitwell. She is writing to James Agate from Paris in 1934:

Dear Mr Agate,

I should have written to you much sooner, but no letters were forwarded to me as I was motoring about France. Before that, I was at Brides-les-Bains, a scene of much desolation, and the temporary haunt of people who have eaten so much that nature has supervened, and driven them to this desert where they can eat nothing. Here, my brother Osbert and I were much afflicted by the conversation of a Swiss lady who babbled of D. H. Lawrence and Aldous Huxley. Eventually, she asked me if I wrote under my own name, and if she ought to have heard of me. This annoyed me—it shows how conceited I am—and I replied: 'I do, and you could not have heard of me. But my brother writes under the name of Clemence Dane.' Unfortunately, the news spread like wildfire, and the Swiss lady, clasping her hands and turning up her eyes, kept on saying: 'How *great* she is, your Dane! She is great as your Barrie! She is great as your Galsworthy, or your Walpole!' Told everybody. So that Osbert, looking very angry, sat surrounded by quite a little court of admirers of *Will Shakespeare*. He was perfectly furious, especially when photographers tried to take snapshots of him for the English newspapers. On one occasion, to my unconcealed delight, the Swiss lady, who was the high priestess of his admirers, spoke of him as the Great Dane. She is going to marry an Englishman and live in England, so there will be an awful scandal—especially as I have told her that *Will Shakespeare* was the result of automatic writing, and that Osbert wrote it in his sleep and must not be questioned about it as the doctor says the shock will be too much for his brain if he finds he has written it. This was because she wanted him to give a reading. I told her a lot about 'literary life' in England. Oh, a lot! I have never met Miss Dane, but hear on all sides that she is a delightful woman, so I hope this scandal will not touch her too nearly.

Yours sincerely
EDITH SITWELL

Mischievous Sitwells notwithstanding, experience suggests that it is quite unnecessary to invent alternative versions of oneself, since others are happy to do it for you. This is James Joyce's complaint, expressed with his usual sour humour in a letter to Harriet Shaw Weaver in 1921:

. . . A nice collection could be made of legends about me. Here are some. My family in Dublin believe that I enriched myself in Switzerland during the war by espionage work for one or both combatants. Triestines, seeing me emerge from my relative's house occupied by my furniture for about twenty minutes every day and walk to the same point the G.P.O. and back (I was writing *Nausikaa* and *The Oxen of the Sun* in a dreadful atmosphere) circulated the rumour, now firmly believed, that I am a cocaine victim. The general rumour in Dublin was (till the prospectus of *Ulysses* stopped it) that I could write no more, had broken down and was dying in Yew York. A man from Liverpool told me he had heard that I was the owner of several cinema theatres all over Switzerland. In America there appear to be or have been two versions: one that I was almost blind, emaciated and consumptive, the other that I am an austere mixture of the Dalai Lama and Sir Rabindranath Tagore. Mr Pound described me as a dour Aberdeen minister. Mr (Wyndham) Lewis told me he was told that I was a crazy fellow who always carried four watches and rarely spoke except to ask my neighbour what o'clock it was. Mr Yeats seemed to have described me to Mr Pound as a kind of Dick Swiveller. What the numerous (and useless) people to whom I have been introduced here think I don't know. My habit of addressing people whom I have just met for the first time as 'Monsieur' earned for me the reputation of a *tout petit bourgeois* while others consider what I intend for politeness as most offensive. I suppose I now have the reputation of being an incurable dispomaniac. One woman here originated the rumour that I am extremely lazy and will never do or finish anything. (I calculate that I must have spent nearly 20,000 hours in writing *Ulysses*.) A batch of people in Zurich persuaded themselves that I was gradually going mad and actually endeavoured to induce me to enter a sanatorium where a certain Doctor Jung (the Swiss Tweedledum who is not to be confused with the Viennese Tweedledee, Dr Freud) amuses himself at the expense (in every sense of the word) of ladies and gentlemen who are troubled with bees in their bonnets . . .

Of course Joyce's personal identity is tied up with his literary identity, one good reason why he is sensitive to his image. His anger at the outside world's neglect of him was an anger compounded of contempt for the world's values together with a desire to be recognized for his achievements. It is typical of him, as in the letter quoted, to combine, in Richard Ellmann's phrase, 'aloofness with self-advertisement', having 'his own press notices printed and sent . . . with chilling formality, to possible reviewers'.

Another hazard in the path of writers is the possible misidentification of characters in their works by unsympathetic readers. They get used to being asked whether their books are 'autobiographical' or not, but it is more difficult to cope with the person who is sure he has been represented—usually to his detriment—in some novel. Thomas Mann was for many years pursued in print and in private by an irate Arnold Schoenberg who claimed that Leverkühn in Mann's *Doctor Faustus* was a malicious portrait of himself because Leverkühn used the twelve-tone system of composition. And Henry James, in the following letter of October 1896, deals graciously with Anton Capadose, a curious, rather than aggrieved correspondent:

My Dear Sir,
You may be very sure that if I had ever had the pleasure of meeting a person of your striking name I wouldn't have used the name, especially for the purpose of the tale you allude to.
. . . 'Capadose' must be in one of my old note-books. I have a dim recollection of having found it originally in the first columns of *The Times*, where I find almost all the names I store up for my puppets. It was picturesque and rare and so I took possession of it. I wish—if you care at all—that I had applied it to a more exemplary individual! But my romancing Colonel was a charming man, in spite of his little weakness.
I congratulate you on bearing a name that is at once particularly individualizing and not ungraceful (as so many rare names are). I am, my dear Sir,

Yours very truly
HENRY JAMES

It may be better to head off trouble with mistaken identities before they occur. Rather than have a nasty spat on his hands, Sir Charles Snow wrote to Edith Sitwell after his wife had finished a novel in which a character appeared who was thought by some readers to be a malicious parody of Edith. The character concerned was an Australian housewife who wrote bad verse dramas about her seven children and gave lectures at the British Council; which certainly doesn't sound like a very close portrait of Dame Edith. Still, Sir Charles was taking no chances, politician that he was, and his letter elicited a fine Sitwellian reply addressed to Lady Snow:

> *Dear Lady Snow,*
> How much I laughed when I received Sir Charles' letter.
> I am, at the same time, alarmed, for I am at the moment finishing a book called *The Queens and the Hive* which is about Queen Elizabeth I and Mary Queen of Scots and contains a rousing account of Catherine de Medici planning the massacre of St Bartholomew's Eve. I am now terrified that this may be supposed, by any readers I may have, to be a lascivious portrait of you. After all, you are not Italian, do not persecute Protestants, and are not the mother-in-law of Mary Queen of Scots, so the likeness springs to the eyes!
> What do you suppose I have done with my seven offspring? Eaten them?

But some cases of mistaken identity are just that. The following two letters demonstrate alternative solutions to the problem of receiving the correspondence and/or abuse of one's namesake (no relation). Mr Winston Churchill to Mr Winston Churchill in 1899:

> Mr Winston Churchill presents his compliments to Mr Winston Churchill and begs to draw attention to a matter which concerns them both. He has learnt from the Press notices that Mr Winston Churchill proposes to bring out another novel, entitled 'Richard Carvel', which is certain to have a considerable sale both in England and America. Mr Winston Churchill is also the author of a novel now being published in serial form in *Macmillan's Magazine*, and for which he anticipates some sale both in England and America. He also proposes to publish on the 1st of October another Military Chronicle on the Soudan War. He has no doubt that Mr Winston Churchill will recognize from this letter—if indeed by no other means—that there is grave danger of his works being mistaken for those of Mr Winston Churchill. He feels sure that Mr Winston Churchill desires this as little as he does himself. In future to avoid mistakes as far as possible, Mr

Winston Churchill has decided to sign all published articles, stories, or other work, 'Winston Spencer Churchill', and not 'Winston Churchill' as formerly. He trusts that this arrangement will commend itself to Mr Winston Churchill, and he ventures to suggest, with a view to preventing further confusion which may arise out of this extraordinary coincidence, that both Mr Winston Churchill and Mr Winston Churchill should insert a short note in their respective publications explaining to the public which are the works of Mr Winston Churchill and which those of Mr Winston Churchill. The text of this note might form a subject for future discussion if Mr Winston Churchill agrees with Mr Winston Churchill's proposition. He takes this occasion of complimenting Mr Winston Churchill upon the quality and success of his works, which are always brought to his notice whether in magazine or book form, and he trusts that Mr Winston Churchill has derived equal pleasure from any work of his that may have attracted his attention.

Bertrand Russell and Lord Russell of Liverpool created a similar confusion in the public mind, which also required sorting out after a while. In 1959, after some to-ing and fro-ing they decided on a majestic announcement in *The Times*:

Dear Lord Russell,
Many thanks for your letter of the 18th.
I am not sure whether you are in earnest or joking about a joint letter to *The Times* but, in either event, I think it is a good idea. Even were it not effective it would provide a little light amusement, and if you would care to write such a letter I would gladly add my signature below yours . . .

Yours sincerely
RUSSELL OF LIVERPOOL

Dear Lord Russell of Liverpool
Thank you for your letter of February 20. I was both serious and joking in my suggestion of a joint letter. I enclose a draft which I have signed, but I am entirely willing to alter the wording if you think it too frivolous. I think, however, that the present wording is more likely to secure attention than a more solemn statement.

Yours sincerely
RUSSELL

To the Editor of *The Times*:

Sir
In order to discourage confusions which have been constantly occurring, we beg herewith to state that neither of us is the other.

Yours etc.
RUSSELL OF LIVERPOOL
(Lord Russell of Liverpool)
RUSSELL
(Bertrand, Earl Russell)

INTERPRETATIONS

1

Inspirations

Among the most interesting letters of creative writers are those that reveal background situations from which a great work of imagination subsequently developed. The experience can be mundane or even, as in the case of Flaubert, sordidly banal, but it is still grist to the artistic mill. Here is D. H. Lawrence writing in 1912 to the critic and editor, Edward Garnett about the genesis of *Sons and Lovers*:

Your letter has just come. I hasten to tell you I sent the MS of the Paul Morel novel to Duckworth, registered, yesterday. And I want to defend it, quick. I wrote it again, pruning it and shaping it and filling it in. I tell you it was good form—*form*: haven't I made it patiently, out of sweat as well as blood. It follows this idea: a woman of character and refinement goes into the lower class, and has no satisfaction in her own life. She has had a passion for her husband, so the children are born of passion, and have heaps of vitality. But as her sons grow up she selects them as lovers—first the eldest, then the second. These sons are *urged* into life by their reciprocal love of their mother—urged on and on. But when they come to manhood, they can't love, because their mother is the strongest power in their lives, and holds them.—It's rather like Goethe and his mother and Frau von Stein and Christiana—.As soon as the young men come into contact with women, there's a split. William gives his sex to a fribble, and his mother holds his soul. But the split kills him, because he doesn't know where he is. The next son gets a woman who fights for his soul—fights his mother. The son loves the mother—all the sons hate and are jealous of the father. The battle goes on between the mother and the girl, with the son as object. The mother gradually proves stronger, because of the tie of blood. The son decides to leave his soul in his mother's hands, and, like his elder brother, go for passion. He gets passion. Then the split begins to tell again. But, almost unconsciously, the mother realises what is the matter, and begins to die. The son casts off his mistress, attends his mother dying. He is left in the end naked of everything, with the drift towards death.

It is a great tragedy, and I tell you I've written a great book. It's the tragedy of thousands of young men in England.

The early emotional and sensual experiences of Robert Burns were also grist to the artistic mill. In a candid autobiographical letter he remarks that he began to write poetry not as a result of anything he had read, but as a further outlet for his sensuality:

. . . This kind of life, the cheerless gloom of a hermit with the unceasing moil of a galley-slave,[1] brought me to my sixteenth year; a little before which period I first committed the sin of RHYME.—You know our country custom of coupling a man and woman together as Partners in the labors of Harvest.—In my fifteenth autumn, my Partner was a bewitching creature who just counted an autumn less.—My scarcity of English denies me the power of doing her justice in that language; but you know the Scotch idiom, She was a bonie, sweet, sonsie lass.—In short, she altogether unwittingly to herself, initiated me in a certain delicious Passion, which in spite of acid Disappointment, gin-horse Prudence and bookworm Philosophy, I hold to be the first of human joys, our dearest pleasure here below.—How she caught the contagion I can't say; you medical folks talk much of infection by breathing the same air, the touch, &c. but I never expressly told her that I loved her.—Indeed I did not well know myself, why I liked so much to loiter behind with her, when returning in the evening from our labours; why the tones of her voice made my heartstrings thrill like an Eolian harp; and particularly, why my pulse beat such a furious ratann when I looked and fingered over her hand, to pick out the nettle-stings and thistles.—Among her other love-inspiring qualifications, she sung sweetly; and 'twas her favorite reel to which I attempted giving an embodied vehicle in rhyme.—I was not so presum-

---

[1] Burns is here referring to the fact that his family was at the mercy of a grasping factor.

tive as to imagine that I could make verses like printed ones, composed by men who had Greek and Latin; but my girl sung a song which was said to be composed by a small country laird's son, on one of his father's maids, with whom he was in love; and I saw no reason why I might not rhyme as well as he, for excepting smearing sheep and casting peats, his father living in the moors, he had no more Scholarcraft than I had.—

Thus with me began Love and Poesy; which at times have been my only, and till within this last twelvemonth have been my highest enjoyment.

While Burns is sometimes a sentimentalist, and Lawrence could not keep polemic out of his writing, Gustave Flaubert is a master of detached manipulative realism. Here, writing to Louise Colet in August 1853, he describes a seaside scene in a manner that is cruelly deflating to human dignity. The disgust is reminiscent of certain passages in Orwell's fiction, notably *Coming Up For Air*.

I spent an hour yesterday watching the ladies bathe. What a sight! The two sexes used to bathe together here. But now they are kept separate by means of signposts, wire netting, and a uniformed inspector: (what an atrociously lugubrious object, this grotesque figure!) And so, yesterday, from the place where I was standing in the sun, with my spectacles on my nose, I could contemplate the bathing beauties at my leisure. The human race must indeed have become completely moronic to have lost all sense of elegance to this degree. Nothing is more pitiful than these bags in which women encase their bodies, and these oilcloth caps! What faces! And how they walk! Such feet! Red, scrawny, covered with corns and bunions, deformed by shoes, long as shuttles or wide as washerwomen's paddles. And in the midst of it all, scrofulous brats screaming and crying. Farther off, grandmas knitting and respectable old gentlemen with gold-rimmed spectacles reading newspapers, looking up from time to time between the lines to survey the vastness of the horizon with an air of approval. The whole thing made me long all afternoon to escape from Europe and go to live in the Sandwich Islands or the forests of Brazil. There, at least, the beaches are not polluted by such ugly feet, by such foul-looking specimens of humanity.

The day before yesterday, in the woods near Touques, in a

charming spot beside a spring, I found old cigar butts and scraps of pâté. People had been picnicking. I described such a scene in *Novembre*, eleven years ago: there it was entirely imagined, and the other day it was experienced. Everything one invents is true, you may be sure. Poetry is as precise as geometry. Induction is as good as deduction; and besides, after reaching a certain point one no longer errs about matters of the soul. My poor Bovary, without a doubt, is suffering and weeping at this very hour in twenty villages of France.

More sinister than Flaubert's controlled disgust is this account of a demonic laughing fit by Franz Kafka in a letter to his patient fiancée, Felice Bauer. The slightly mad tone of the letter only adds to the satirical effect of his description of the pompous middle-class businessman going through his patronizing routine with his employees, and being only mildly disconcerted by the behaviour of his strange underling. The air of unreality about the occasion recalls the scenarios and atmosphere of Kafka's fiction:

I can also laugh, Felice, have no doubt about this; I am even known as a great laugher, although in this respect I used to be far crazier than I am now. It even happened to me once, at a solemn meeting with our president—it was two years ago, but the story will outlive me at the office—that I started to laugh, and how! It would be too involved to describe to you this man's importance; but believe me, it is very great: an ordinary employee thinks of this man as not on this earth, but in the clouds. And as we usually have little opportunity of talking to the Emperor, contact with this man is for the average clerk—a situation common of course to all large organizations—tantamount to meeting the Emperor. Needless to say, like anyone exposed to clear and general scrutiny whose position does not quite correspond to his achievements, this man invites ridicule; but to allow oneself to be carried away by laughter at something so commonplace and, what's more, in the presence of the great man himself, one must be out of one's mind. At that time we, two colleagues and I, had just been promoted, and in our formal black suits had to express our thanks to the president—here I must not forget to add that for a special reason I owed the president special gratitude. The most dignified of us (I was the youngest) made the speech of thanks—short, sensible, dashing, in accordance with his character. The president listened in his usual posture adopted for solemn occasions, somewhat reminiscent of our Emperor when giving audience—which, if one happens to be in a certain mood, is a terribly funny pose. Legs lightly crossed, left hand clenched and resting on the very corner of the table, head lowered so that the long white beard curves on his chest, and, on top of all this, his not excessively large but nevertheless protruding stomach gently swaying. I must have been in a very uncontrolled mood at the time, for I knew this posture well enough, and it was quite unreasonable for me to be attacked by fits of the giggles (albeit with interruptions), which so far however could easily be taken as due to a tickle in the throat, especially as the president did not look up. My colleague's clear voice, eyes fixed straight ahead—he was no doubt aware of my condition, without being affected by it—still kept me in check. But at the end of my colleague's speech the president raised his head, and then for a moment I was seized with terror, without laughter, for now he could see my expression and easily ascertain that the sound unfortunately escaping from my mouth was definitely not a cough. But when he began his speech, again the usual one, all too familiar, in the imperial mould, delivered with great conviction, a totally meaningless and unnecessary speech; and when my colleague with sidelong glances tried to warn me (I was doing everything in my power to control myself), and in so doing reminded me vividly of the joys of my earlier laughter, I could no longer restrain myself and all hope that I should ever be able to do so vanished. At first I laughed only at the president's occasional delicate little jokes; but while it is a rule only to contort one's features respectfully at these little jokes, I was already laughing out loud; observing my colleagues' alarm at being infected by it, I felt more sorry for them than for myself, but I couldn't help it; I didn't even try to avert or cover my face, but in my helplessness continued to stare straight at the president, incapable of turning my head, probably on the instinctive assumption that everything could only get worse rather than better, and that therefore it would be best to avoid any change. And now that I was in full spate, I was of course laughing not only at the current jokes, but at those of the past and the future and the whole lot together, and by then no one knew what I was really laughing about. A general embarrassment set in; only the president remained relatively unconcerned, as behoves a great man accustomed to the ways of the world and to whom the possibility of irreverence towards his person would not even occur. Had we been able to slip out at this moment (the president had evidently shortened his speech a little), everything might still have gone fairly well; no doubt my behaviour would have remained discourteous, but this discourtesy would not have been mentioned, and the whole affair, as sometimes happens with apparently impossible situations, might have been dealt with by a conspiracy of silence between the four of us. But unfortunately my colleague, the one hitherto unmentioned (a man close to forty, a heavy beer drinker with a round, childish, but bearded face), started to make a totally unexpected little speech. Now, the president in all innocence had said something to which this colleague of mine took exception . . . So now, as he started to hold forth, brandishing his arms, about something absurdly childish (even in general, but here in particular), it was too much for me: the world, the semblance of the world which hitherto I had seen before me, dissolved completely, and I burst into loud and uninhibited laughter of such heartiness as perhaps only schoolchildren at their desks are capable of. A silence fell, and now at last my laughter and I were the acknowledged centre of attention. While I laughed my knees of course shook with fear, and my colleagues on their part could join in to their hearts' content, but they could never match the full horror of my long-rehearsed and practised laughter, and thus they remained comparatively unnoticed. Beating my breast with my right hand, partly in awareness of my sin (remembering the Day of Atonement), and partly to drive out all the suppressed laughter, I produced innumerable excuses for my behaviour, all of which might have been very convincing had not the renewed outbursts of laughter rendered them completely unintelligible. By now of course even the president was disconcerted; and in a manner typical only of people born with an instinct for smoothing things out, he found some phrase that offered some reasonable explanation for my howls—I think an allusion to a joke he had made a long time before. He then hastily dismissed us. Undefeated, roaring with laughter yet desperately unhappy, I was the first to stagger out of the hall. —By writing a letter to the president immediately afterwards and through the good offices of one of the president's sons whom I know well, and thanks also to the passage of time, the whole thing calmed down considerably. Needless to say, I did not achieve complete absolution, nor shall I ever achieve it. But this matters little; I may have behaved in this fashion at the time simply in order to prove to you later that I am capable of laughter.

Humour, usually black humour, is of course a central ingredient of Evelyn Waugh's novels. Writing to his wife Laura in February 1940, he gives an account of a hilarious weekend spent with his superior officer at Bisley, one of the novelist's postings during the Second World War. All the ingredients of Wavian comedy are there—eccentricity, black comedy, a wonderful eye for detail and ear for dialogue:

Darling Laura
. . . Yesterday was an alarming day. The Brigadier suddenly accosted Messers Bennets & me & said, 'I hear you are staying in camp for the week-end. You will spend the day with me.' So at 12.30 he picked us up in his motor-car and drove all over the road to his house which was the lowest type of stockbroker's Tudor and I said in a jaggering way, 'Did you build this house, sir?' and he said, 'Build it! It's 400 years old!' The Brigadier's madam is kept very much in her place and ordered about with great shouts 'Woman, go up to my cabin and get my boots'. More peculiar, she is subject to booby- traps. He told us with great relish how the night before she had had to get up several times in the night to look after a daughter who was ill and how, each time she returned, he had fixed up some new horror to injure her—a string across the door, a jug of water on top of it etc. However she seemed to thrive on this treatment & was very healthy & bright with countless children.
So after luncheon we were taken for a walk with the Brigadier who kept saying 'Don't call me "sir".' He told us how when he had a disciplinary case he always said, 'Will you be court martialled or take it from me.' The men said, 'Take it from you, sir,' so 'I bend 'em over and give 'em ten of the best with a cane.'
When we came back from our walk he showed me a most embarrassing book of rhymes & drawings composed by

himself and his madam in imitation of *Just So Stories*, for one of his daughters. I had to read them all with him breathing stertorously down my neck. Then we did the cross-word puzzle until a daughter arrived from London where she is secretary to a dentist. She told me she had been a lift girl at the Times Book Club and had lost her job because at Christmas time, she hung mistletoe in the lift. The Brigadier thought this a most unsuitable story to tell me. When he is in a rage he turns slate grey instead of red. He was in an almost continuous rage with this daughter who is by a previous, dead madam. After that she & I talked about low night clubs until I thought the Brigadier's colour so unhealthy that I ought to stop. Most of the madam's reminiscences dealt with appalling injuries to one or other member of the family through their holiday exercises. The Brigadier says that the only fault he has to find with the war is that he misses his hockey. A very complex character. A lot of majors & their madams came to dinner; oddly enough all foreign—a Russian, a German and a Swede—a fact on which the Brigadier never ceased to comment adding 'I suppose I can't really tell 'em what I think of their benighted countries.' Then he asked very loudly whether it was true that he ought not to smoke his pipe with vintage port and if so why, so I told him and he got a bit grey again.

He said, 'There's only one man in Egypt you can trust. Hassanin Bey. Luckily he's chief adviser to the King. He is a white man. I'll tell you something that'll show you the kind of chap he is. He and I were alone in a carriage going from Luxor to Suez—narrow gauge, single track line, desert on both sides, blazing heat. Ten hours with nothing to do. I thought I should go mad. Luckily I had a golf ball with me. So I made Hassanin stand one end of the corridor and we threw that ball backwards & forwards as hard as we could the whole day— threw it so that it really hurt. Not many Gyppies would stand up to that. Ever since then I've known there was at least one Gyppy we could trust.'

. . . He also said, 'I hope you aren't taking a lot of notes about us all to make fun of us in a book. There was a nasty bloke called Graves wrote a book called *Goodbye To All That*. Made fun of his brigadier.' Bad show! I thought it lucky he did not know what was in this letter.

All love
EVELYN

Another novelist who drew copiously on personal experience was C. P. Snow; he managed to be a don, a civil servant and a politician, as well as a novelist. In this account of academic in-fighting in Christ's College, Cambridge, he reveals some of the inspiration for his novel of university life, *The Masters*. He was writing in 1938 to his brother in Fiji, and allows himself some waspish and sardonic vignettes of colleagues:

The main interest here has, of course, been in the high jinks over the Mastership. As soon as Raven knew that Darwin was going, he set to work single-mindedly and rather naively to get it for himself . . . [Sydney] Grose [in the novels, Arthur Brown], who supported R. warmly in 1936, of course, looked very pink when Raven approached him and said that, though his own opinion of Raven was unchanged, the opinion of important sections of the College [i.e. Wyatt, the bursar] had changed drastically: and so Grose couldn't vote for Raven if it meant a complete lack of harmony between Raven and Wyatt.

So Raven went off irresponsibly to see Wyatt, and asked him whether he could explain why his (Wyatt's) opinion of him (Raven) had changed. Wyatt told him. Raven asked for his frank opinion. Wyatt gave it. He thought R. dishonest in College politics, of negative judgement, and personally unscrupulous. 'I gave him chapter and verse,' said Wyatt afterwards. 'It made him think.'

R. went away and immediately wrote the following letter. 'My dear Wyatt, I was extremely grateful for our talk this afternoon. When a relationship like ours, personally so friendly, is interrupted by misunderstandings about outside affairs, there is nothing like an intimate talk. I believe that some of the faults you point out in my behaviour I shall be able to remedy, and I owe you much for your help. Not, however, that I admit that all the faults are on one side. Of all the men I have ever met, you are the most impossible to carry on a controversy with. You become hot and violent at the slightest sign of opposition. You think anyone who disagrees with you is either a fool or a knave. You are a born dictator: and I don't like dictators. Let me say that this difference of opinion will make no difference in my mind to our personal friendship.'

To which Wyatt replied: 'My dear Raven. When I agreed to talk to you yesterday I had no idea or intention of letting myself in for a correspondence. And I might point out that, though you asked for my frank opinion of you, I did not for a moment ask for your opinion of me. I can only repeat what I told you yesterday. You are a dishonest man in College politics. Our standards are not the same. We do not talk the same language. You may persuade yourself that this is another case of my becoming "hot and violent". You are capable of persuading yourself of anything. All this makes it only more certain that we could not work smoothly in double harness. Like you, I have not the slightest intention of letting this interfere with our personal friendship. P. S. Have you seen Vol. 2 of Witherby's British Birds?'

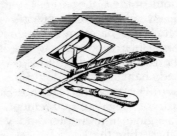

2

Portraits of Painters

'I want to paint humanity, humanity and again humanity,' says
Vincent Van Gogh in one of his letters. 'I love nothing better than
this series of bipeds, from the smallest baby in long clothes to
Socrates, from the woman with black hair and a white skin to the
one with golden hair and a brick-red sun-burnt face.'

In Van Gogh's vivid and passionate letters the impulse to paint
is explored again and again. It is one that often springs from his
identification with ordinary people, and especially with human
suffering—the sort of impulse J. B. Yeats, writing from New York
in July 1913, describes in this letter to his poet son:

> . . . portraiture in art or poetry [is] the effort to keep the pain
> alive and intensify it, since out of the heart of the pain comes
> the solace, as a monk scourges himself to bring an ecstasy.
> Some time ago I saw a young mother with a sick infant in her
> arms. I need not go into circumstances, but I know that I put
> the question to her and that I was haunted by what I saw and
> heard for days and days. Why did I put these questions and
> why did I try constantly to recall and keep alive the incident? I
> regretted that I could not take my canvas and paint a portrait of
> her and her child. She was soft spoken, Irish and young and
> very pretty, from Donnybrook, and all her children had died in
> infancy. She was *ashamed* of her sick child and *tried to hide it from
> me*. She was not many years over and her father and mother
> dead since she left Ireland—her face full of goodness. I would
> fain scourge myself spiritually, and it pained me that the image
> should fade. The mediaeval artists lived among such sights and
> sounds and had nothing to console them but their art and their
> religion, unless like Raphael they averted their eyes . . .

The passion and accuracy of vision need not be expended on an
explicitly social subject. As Van Gogh struggled to reproduce the

absolute freshness of the elemental colour in the environment, so Monet describes his struggle in old age to match up to his task as a painter when his physical powers were failing. The letter is a moving description of the unending struggle of the artist for perfection:

. . . Colours no longer looked as brilliant to me as they used to do, I no longer painted shades of light so correctly. Reds looked muddy to me, pinks insipid, and the intermediate or lower notes in the colour scale escaped me. As for forms, I could see them as clearly as ever, and render them as decisively. At first I tried pertinacity. How many times I have remained for hours near the little bridge, exactly where we are now, in the full glare of the sun, sitting on my camp-stool, under my sunshade, forcing myself to resume my interrupted task and to re apture the freshness my palette had lost! A waste of effort. What I painted was more and more mellow, more and more like an 'old picture', and when the attempt was over and I compared it with what I used to do in the old days, I would fall into a frantic rage, and I slashed all my pictures with my penknife . . .

Though I remained insensitive to the subtleties and delicate gradations of colour seen at close quarters, my eyes at least did not deceive me when I drew back and looked at the subject in its broad lines, and this was the starting-point of new compositions. A very modest starting-point, to tell the truth. I distrusted myself, I was resolved to leave nothing to chance. Slowly I tried my strength in innumerable rough sketches which convinced me, in the first place, that the study of bright light was now, once and for all, impossible for me— but also reassured me by showing that while I could no longer go in for playing about with shades or for landscapes in delicate colours, I could see as clearly as ever when it came to vivid colours isolated in a mass of dark tones.

How was I to put this to use?

My intentions gradually became clearer. Ever since I entered my sixties I had had the idea of setting about a kind of 'synthesis' in each of the successive categories of themes that held my attention—of summing up in one canvas, sometimes in two, my earlier impressions and sensations. I had given up the notion. It would have meant travelling a great deal and for a long time, revisiting, one by one, all the places through which my life as a painter had taken me, and verifying my former emotions. I said to myself, as I made my sketches, that a series of general impressions, captured at the times of day when I had the best chance of seeing correctly, would not be without interest. I waited for the idea to consolidate, for the grouping and composition of the themes to settle themselves in my brain little by little, of their own accord; and the day when I felt I held enough cards to be able to try my luck with a real hope of success, I determined to pass to action, and did so.

Monet's patience and ability to let the scene gell before he worked on it is evident in the letters of another painter: Keats's pictorial imagination might have responded to the language of the following letter by Camille Corot, in which he describes the beginning of a landscape painter's day in a way that lyrically evokes nature and man in the setting of nature.

Gruyères, 1857

You know, a landscape painter's day is delightful. You get up early, at three o'clock in the morning, before sunrise; you go and sit under a tree; you watch and wait. At first there is nothing much to be seen. Nature looks like a whitish canvas with a few broad outlines faintly sketched in; all is misty, everything quivers in the cool dawn breeze. The sky lights up. The sun has not yet burst through the gauze veil that hides the meadow, the little valley, the hills on the horizon. The nocturnal vapours are still creeping in silvery flakes over the frozen green of the grass. Ah! a first ray of sunshine! The tiny flowers seem to wake up happily. Each has its tremulous dewdrop. The leaves shiver with cold in the morning breeze. Invisible birds are singing beneath the leaves. It seems as though the flowers were saying their prayers. Little butterfly-winged cupids frolic over the meadow, making the tall grass ripple. One sees nothing. Everything is there! The whole landscape lies behind the transparent gauze of the fog that now rises, drawn upwards by the sun, and, as it rises, reveals the silver-spangled river, the fields, the trees, the cottages, the further scene. At last one can discern all that one could only guess at before.

The sun is up! There is a peasant at the end of the field, with his waggon drawn by a yoke of oxen. You can hear the little bell round the neck of the ram, the leader of the flock. Everything is bursting into life, sparkling in the full light— light which as yet is still soft and golden. The background, simple in line and harmonious in colour, melts into the infinite expanse of sky, through the bluish, misty atmosphere. The flowers raise their heads, the birds flutter hither and thither. A countryman on a white horse rides away down the steep-banked lane. The little rounded willows on the bank of the stream look like birds spreading their tails. It's adorable! and one paints! and paints! . . .

In February 1888 Vincent Van Gogh moved to Arles, and was joined there by Gauguin. In this vivid letter to his brother Theo he describes his surroundings in terms that recall his marvellous paintings:

My house here is painted the yellow colour of fresh butter on the outside with glaringly green shutters; it stands in the full sunlight in a square which has a green garden with plane trees, oleanders and acacias. And it is completely whitewashed inside, and the floor is made of red bricks. And over it there is the intensely blue sky. In this I can live and breathe, meditate and paint. And it seems to me that I might go still farther into the South, rather than go up to the North again, seeing that I am greatly in need of a strong heat, so that my blood can circulate normally. Here I feel much better than I did in Paris.

You see, I can hardly doubt that you on your part would also like the South enormously. The fact is that the sun has never penetrated us people of the North. It is already a few days since I started writing this letter, and now I will continue it. In point of fact I was interrupted these days by my toiling on a new picture representing the outside of a night café. On the terrace there are the tiny figures of people drinking. An enormous yellow lantern sheds its light on the terrace, the house front and the side-walk, and even casts a certain brightness on the pavement of the street, which takes a pinkish violet tone. The gable-topped fronts of the houses in a street stretching away under a blue sky spangled with stars are dark blue or violet and there is a green tree. Here you have a night picture without any black in it, done with nothing but beautiful blue and violet and green, and in these surroundings the light square acquires a pale sulphur and greenish citron-yellow colour. It amuses me enormously to paint the night right on the spot. They used to draw and paint the picture in the daytime after the rough sketch. But I find satisfaction in painting things immediately.

Monet, Corot and Van Gogh record their unending struggle to satisfy personal standards; but many artists have also had to reckon with another set of standards and tastes—that of their patrons. In the following letter Benozzo Gozzoli, the brilliant painter of the frescoes in the Palazzo Medici Riccardi in Florence, writes a business letter to his paymaster Piero de' Medici, and tries to accommodate himself to his benefactor's wishes. Of course, one of the easiest ways of keeping difficult patrons quiet was to depict them in flattering terms as the protagonists of historical or biblical scenes. Gozzoli, who was not in the least religious himself, produced a famous representation of the Medici family as the Magi. And one cherub more or less was nothing to him:

Florence, 10 July 1459

This morning I received a letter from Your Magnificence, by the hand of Roberto Martelli. From which it appears that you do not find that the cherubim I have painted are suitable. One of these I have set in a corner, among clouds, of which only the tips of the wings are visible; and he is so much concealed, and the clouds cover him in such manner, that he causes no uncomeliness, but rather gives beauty. That is the one that is beside the column. I made another on the other side of the altar, but concealed after the same manner. Roberto Martelli saw them, and declared that the thing was of no consequence. Nevertheless, I will do as you shall command; two clouds will quickly dispose of them.

I would have come to speak with you; but this morning I began to lay on the azure, and that cannot be left. The heat is great, and the plaster is spoiled in an instant. I believe that during the next week I shall have done with this scaffolding, and I suppose that you will desire to see the work before the scaffold is removed. I have also heard that you have given order to Roberto Martelli to furnish me with whatever I may need. I have caused him to give me two florins, and that suffices me for the present. I pursue the work as zealously as I

may; whatsoever I may leave undone, it will be for lack of
skill, for God knows that no thought so much torments me;
and I am continually searching for means to do some thing
that shall please you, at least in a good degree; it is my only
concern. I commend me to your Magnificence,

Your servant

An even more exacting patron was Pope Julius II for whom
Michelangelo executed his frescoes for the ceiling of the Sistine
Chapel in the Vatican. Apart from the artistic difficulties,
Michelangelo worked under appalling physical stress and had
to complete the task at considerable speed while being badgered
by his impatient patron. He dismissed his usual assistants
whom he considered had shown themselves inadequate for the
job, and undertook the vast project alone. It took him four years
of backbreaking work, the pressures of which he describes in a
letter of 1510 to Giovanni da Pistoia in the form of an amusing
poem. When the ceiling was finished in 1512, Michelangelo, at
the age of thirty-seven, was acclaimed as the greatest living
artist; this at a time when Leonardo was still alive, and Raphael
had begun his climb to fame. But he paid a high price for his
success. Vasari says that the work caused such injury to his eyes
that 'thereafter he could not read a letter or observe any object
without holding it above his head to see it the better'.

> I've grown a goitre by dwelling in this den—
>> As cats from stagnant streams in Lombardy,
>> Or in what other land they hap to be—
>> Which drives the belly close beneath the chin:
> My beard turns up to heaven; my nape falls in,
>> Fixed on my spine: my breast-bone visibly
>> Grows like a harp: a rich embroidery
>> Bedews my face from brush-drops thick and thin.
> My loins into my paunch like levers grind:
>> My buttock like a crupper bears my weight;
>> My feet unguided wander to and fro;
> In front my skin grows loose and long; behind,
>> By bending it becomes more taut and strait;
>> Crosswise I strain me like a Syrian bow:
>>> Whence false and quaint, I know,
>> Must be the fruit of squinting brain and eye;
>> For ill can aim the gun that bends awry.

Come then, Giovanni, try
To succour my dead pictures and my fame;
Since foul I fare and painting is my shame.

A good many of Michelangelo's projects, or those thought up
for him by prospective patrons, did not come to fruition. There
is an amusing account by him of one such, a statue of colossal
dimensions which would certainly have given today's rubber-
necks something to talk about during their trip round Florence.
In a letter to a priest of Santa Maria del Fiore, Michelangelo
discusses the siting of the proposed statue with an irreverence
that did not amuse the papal authorities:

From Rome, December 1525

As to the colossus eighty feet high that you inform me of;
which has to go or, rather, is to be put on the corner of the
loggia of the Medici garden opposite Master Luigi della
Stufa's corner, I have thought about it, and not a little, as you
tell me; and it seems to me it doesn't go well on the aforesaid
corner, because it would take up too much of the street; but
on the other, where the barber shop is, it would turn out
much better in my opinion, because it has the square in front
and wouldn't disturb the street so much. And since maybe
removing the aforesaid shop will not be tolerated, for the sake
of the income, I thought the aforesaid figures might be made
seated, and the seat might be made high enough so the barber
shop would go underneath, by making the aforesaid work
hollow inside, since it is most appropriate to make it in pieces,
and the rent would not be lost. And also, since the aforesaid
shop ought to have a way to expel the smoke, as it does now, I
feel the aforesaid statue should have a horn of plenty in its
hand, hollow inside, which would serve it for a chimney.
Then, since I would have the head of the figure hollow inside
like the other members, I think some use ought to be got out
of that too, since there is a shopkeeper here on the square, a
great friend of mine, who has told me in secret he would
make a fine dovecote inside. Then too another notion occurs
to me that would be much better, but the figure would have to
be made much bigger, and it could be done, since a tower is
made up of pieces, and this is that the head could serve as a
bell tower for San Lorenzo, which badly needs one, and if the
bells were stowed inside and the sound came out of the

mouth, the aforesaid colossus would seem to be crying mercy, and especially on feast days when the ringing is more frequent and with bigger bells.

As for getting the marble blocks brought for the outside of the said statue, and to keep anybody from knowing, I feel they should be brought at night and well shrouded, so they won't be seen. There will be a little danger at the gate, and for this we can take measures; at worst there is always the Sangallo gate, which keeps ajar until daylight . . .

A few weeks later Michelangelo got a rather indignant reply from a papal minion: '. . . About the statue to be made, his Holiness would have you to understand it is the truth and not a joke, and he wishes it to be made . . .'

A love-hate relationship is often the best that can be expected between sponsors or patrons and their protégés. Walter Sickert has some acid remarks on the subject in one of the long rambling letters which he used to send to *The Times*; (Graham Greene recalls in his autobiography how, as a young sub-editor on the letters page, much of his time had to be devoted to editing down Sickert's 'savage non-sequiturs'). Opinionated and provocative, Sickert did a lot to stimulate interest and controversy in artistic matters:

. . . Now I will describe to you, briefly, the *modus operandi* of many a patron in this country.

Long, long after a painter's battle is lost or won, long after his stock has been safely housed in the dealer's cellars, our patron, being slightly deaf, and very slow-moving, and extremely suspicious, meets at dinner someone who tells him, what everyone has known for twenty years, that works signed with such-and-such names have gone up strangely in value.

'Dear me!' he says. 'You surprise me! Tut, tut, tut! I must see if I can't get some. What did you say was the name? Degas, Monet. Really?'

Scenting a profit, off he goes to the biggest dealers. 'I want to see some pictures by So-and-so, and So-and-so. What! Thousands of pounds? Impossible! Dear me! Well, let me have half a dozen at my house to look at for a while, so that I may choose at leisure.'

'Certainly, sir, if you will pay carriage and insurance.'

That is arranged to the satisfaction of both sides. Our
patron then marches every expert he has ever met past this
little 'appro' collection. Some of the experts are painters, some
writers, some dealers, some ladies who have sat to a
portrait-painter, and so rank as 'artistic'. One and all, having a
sprat or two of their own to fry, crab the 'appro' collection,
nicely, but unmistakably. Our patron, slightly discouraged,
ends by picking out a very minor work by a name of the
second rank, and pays a few hundreds for it. These hundreds
include the original artist's price, interest on it for a matter of
fifteen or twenty years, part rent of premises in Bond Street,
or the Rue Laffitte for the same time, plus what the French call
'false expenses', postage, cabs, telegrams, and odds and ends
of that kind. And note that patrons of this type consider
themselves as real friends of the arts, that they generally
frequent and prefer the society of artists, and are always
slightly puzzled and aggrieved that they are not regarded
with positive enthusiasm by the whole artistic profession . . .

A patron who was definitely not 'deaf' or 'slow-moving', and
not blind either, was the Earl of Rochester, the seventeenth-
century courtier, wit, and composer of obscene verse. In a letter
to his Countess he comments unfavourably on three attempts at
her likeness which he has just seen:

Madam,
  I received three pictures and am in a great fright lest they
should be like you. By the bigness of the head, I should
apprehend you far gone in the rickets: by the severity of the
countenance, somewhat inclined to prayer and prophecy. Yet
there is an alacrity in your plump cheeks that seems to signify
sack and sugar, and your sharp-sighted nose has borrowed
quickness from the sweet swelling eye. I never saw a chin
smile before, a mouth frown, or a forehead mump. Truly the
artist has done his part (God keep him humble) and a fine
man he is if his excellences don't puff him up like his pictures.
  The next impertinence I have to tell you is that I am coming
into the country. I have got horses, but want a coach: when
that defect is supplied you shall quickly have the trouble of
Your humble servant
ROCHESTER

Patrons can take a collective form, committees that award prizes or decide who shall hang in the Royal Academy Summer Exhibition. One such body in Munich rashly awarded J. McNeill Whistler a medal for his work, an action tantamount to offering a lobster your bare finger. They received the following acknowledgement:

> *Sir*,—I beg to acknowledge the receipt of your letter, officially informing me that the Committee award me a second-class gold medal.
> Pray convey my sentiments of tempered and respectable joy to the gentlemen of the Committee, and my complete appreciation of the second-hand compliment paid me.
> And I have, Sir,
>
> > The honour to be
> > Your most humble, obedient servant,
> > J. McNEILL WHISTLER

From this it will be seen that a sure touch is required when dealing with artists. J. A. Ackerley developed one in his days as Editor of *The Listener*, during which time he was foolhardy enough to commission a series of articles by painters and sculptors on their own work. His most difficult contributor proved to be the French Expressionist, Georges Rouault. Rouault had strong feelings about artistic theory which he expressed in impenetrable prose. The article was quite unpublishable, and in the following letter of 1937, a by now desperate Ackerley attempts to get himself off the hook with the help of a friend, art critic Douglas Cooper:

> *Dear Douglas*,
> Without previous enquiry or any warning I am sending you, under this cover, some material which I am very anxious for you to help me with as quickly as possible, for I think you are really the only person who can do for me this very tiresome and, I think, very difficult work.
> As you know, in this series of articles from the artists themselves, I invited a contribution from Rouault. I asked him to give something about his early work in stained glass window design. He sent me, in fact, a series of what he called 'Soliloques', which had practically no bearing whatever on the subject. I then returned to the attack and asked him if he

could possibly furnish me with a few more of his 'soliloquies', a little less abstract in nature and more concerned with his own work. He politely consented and sent me an article on Cézanne.

I did not know what to do with these articles and sent them to Vyvyan Holland, asking him whether he would read them for me and tell me (a) which was the better for me to use, or, (b) whether, if both were bad, a kind of mélange could be made out of them with as free a translation as he liked. He replied that he did not see how to combine the two, as they were written in quite different styles; that Rouault appeared to mistake confusion of thought for depth of thought; that however much one tinkered with the 'Soliloques', he thought that nothing readable would emerge; and, that the second article about Cézanne was written in such a strange style and in such odd grammar as to be practically meaningless. He ended by saying that he really thought that both contributions were rubbish.

I therefore thought that the only thing I could do would be to conceal from the general reader the rubbish of this writing by publishing one of the articles—and I chose the 'Soliloques'—in the more decent obscurity of its difficult French; for my main object, as you know, in this series was to publish the original paintings or drawings I was extracting from the contributors—the text seeming to me of supernumerary importance. And of all the original designs I have received, Rouault's is the most beautiful.

My Editor, however, now intervenes and says he will not publish rubbish—even by Rouault, and even in French; that he will not have an article on Rouault to present the special painting, since we have already had one article on him recently, and, that the only way, therefore, in which I can use and publish this special painting by Rouault in my series in *The Listener* is to get somebody who will take the trouble to write an article, the main object of which will be to present to our readers as much of Rouault's thought as is intelligible in these two manuscripts, in a kind of introductory article . . .

Now, will you be an angel and do this for me and let me have it back at the latest by Monday morning, September 20? I don't mind how liberally (*sic*) you translate the extracts from Rouault's scripts, nor do I mind how short the article is—it could be anything from 1000 to 1500 words—presenting

Rouault, his work and his thoughts to the public. I shall publish with it, the charming original sketch, 'Head of a Clown', and also another of the pictures he has sent me—I expect a rather stained glass window 'Christ' . . .

Yours
JOE

3

Harmonies and Discords

It would be naive to claim that composers are exceptionally nice people (Wagner wasn't, for a start), but the profession has contained some who were remarkably honourable (Verdi), or charming and companionable (Schubert), and even genuinely modest (Bruckner). This is in stark contrast to the serpent-toothed tribe of musical critics. If that gloomy volume *The Lexicon of Musical Invective* is to be believed, they seem mostly to have been baptized in wormwood and fed on gall. It is pleasant, therefore, to find an example of a critic—admittedly himself an artist of renown—who changed his mind, and wrote gracefully to Giuseppe Verdi apologizing for his former musical prejudice:

>   *Hamburg, 7 April 1892*
> *Illustre Maestro,*
> Please deign to listen to the confession of a contrite sinner! It is now eighteen years since the undersigned was guilty of a great . . . great journalistic *bestiality* . . . towards the last of the five Kings of modern Italian music. He has repented in bitter shame—how many times! When the sin in question was committed (in your generosity you may have quite forgotten it) he was really not in control of his own mind—forgive me if I remind you of what may be called an attenuating circumstance. His mind was clouded by an ultra-Wagnerian fanaticism. Seven years later, the light gradually dawned on him. His fanaticism was purified into enthusiasm. Fanaticism is an oil lamp, enthusiasm an electric light. In the intellectual and moral world, light means justice. Nothing is more destructive than injustice, nothing more intolerable than intolerance, as the most noble Leopardi once said . . .
> I have begun to study your latest works, *Aida*, *Otello*, and the *Requiem*, a rather feeble performance of which was

recently enough to move me to tears: I have been studying them not only in the letter which kills, but in the spirit which gives life! Well, *illustre Maestro,* now I admire you, love you! . . .

To which Verdi wrote an equally graceful reply:

> *Illustre Maestro Bülow,*
> There is no taint of sin in you!—and no need to talk of repentance and absolution!
> If your former views were different from what they are today, you were perfectly right to express them, and I would never have ventured to complain of that. Besides, who knows . . . perhaps you were right then.
> Be that as it may, such an unexpected letter from a musician of your quality and importance in the world of art has given me great pleasure! Not out of personal vanity, but because it shows me that really fine artists form their opinions unprejudiced by schools, by nationality or by period.
> If artists in the North and those in the South have different tendencies, then let them be *different*! They should all preserve the *characteristics proper to their respective nations*, as Wagner so well expressed it.
> Happy you, to be still the sons of Bach! And we? We too, the sons of Palestrina, once had a great school—of our own! Now it has become bastardized and is in danger of collapsing! If only we could turn back again?! . . .

No doubt every artist yearns for recognition; but the price to be paid for it was sometimes very high. A constant refrain of composers has been the violation of the artistic integrity of their works by singers intent on making a name for themselves, or conductors who knew better than the composers what was required of their music. There were too many of them, who, as Shaw put it, 'volunteered various improvements on . . . the score'. The cult of the conductor is still with us, as is the cult of the singer, though the liberties taken with the original work are usually more in the realm of production than scores. An excessive puritanism in such matters is not appropriate, but Verdi's complaints in a letter to his publisher Giulio Ricordi must have echoed those of many other composers:

Genoa, 11 April 1871

I have read your article on the orchestra, which I return herewith, and I think it is open to criticism:

1. On the subject of the intentions of those of our composers to whom you refer, and their skill in instrumentation.

2. On the perceptivity of conductors . . . and on the idea that *every performance is a fresh creation* . . . This is a principle that leads to exaggeration and artificiality. It was the path that led the art of music into exaggeration and artificiality at the end of the last century and the beginning of this, when singers took it upon themselves to *create* their roles (as they still say in France) and consequently served up all kinds of muddle and nonsense. No: I want to have one single creator, and all I ask is that what is written down shall be performed simply and accurately; the trouble is that this is never done. I often read in the newspapers about *effects undreamt of by the composer*; but I myself have never come across them. I appreciate everything you say about Mariani. We are all agreed as to his merits; but the question here is not one individual, however great, but art itself. I do not admit that either singers or conductors have the power to *create*; that, as I said before, is a principle that leads to disaster . . . Shall I give you an example? You once spoke to me in praise of an effect drawn by Mariani from the overture to *La Forza del Destino*, when he brought in the *brass* in G with a *fortissimo*. Well, I do not approve of that effect. My idea was that the brass, coming in *mezzo forte*, was to express the religious chanting of the Friars and only that. Mariani's *fortissimo* altered the whole character and turned the passage into something by a military band: something which has nothing to do with the plot, where the warlike part is quite secondary. And so we are led into the exaggerated and the artificial . . .

But even entirely sympathetic and scrupulous study of a score might leave a conductor perplexed and unable to respond to it, thus rendering Verdi's desire that the music as written down should be performed 'simply and accurately' all but impossible. The following letter of September 1887 is a *cri du coeur* from Hermann Levi to one of Bruckner's supporters, Josef Schalk. The result of his complaints was that once again poor Bruckner set to work to remove the matter to which his critics objected and substitute something more acceptable:

I am at my wits' end and I must appeal to you for advice and help. To put it briefly, I am completely at sea in Brucker's Eighth Symphony, and haven't the courage to present it.

I am quite sure it would meet with intense opposition among the orchestra and the public. That would not matter to me, if I myself were fascinated by it as I was by the Seventh—if I could say to the orchestra, as I did then, 'By the fifth rehearsal you will have come to like it.' But I am terribly disappointed! I have studied the work for days on end, but I cannot grasp it. Far be it from me to criticize—it is quite possible that I am wrong, that I am too stupid or too old—but I find the instrumentation impossible, and what particularly shocks me is the great resemblance to the Seventh Symphony, almost amounting to mechanical copying. The opening passage of the first move-ment is grand, but I am nonplussed by the development.

As for the last movement, it is Greek to me.

What is to be done? It makes me shudder to think of the effect of this news on our friend! I cannot write to him. Should I suggest that he come here to listen to a rehearsal? In my despair I showed the score to a musician friend of mine, and he agreed that it could not possibly be performed. Do please write at once to tell me how I should approach Bruckner. If it were merely a question of his thinking me an ass, or worse still, a faithless friend, I would make the best of it. But I am afraid of something worse, I am afraid the disappointment may quite dash his courage. Do you happen to know the Symphony well? And can you make anything of it? Help me, I really do not know what to do!

Composers are not alone in being misunderstood. Performers also suffer. In a letter to *The Times* in January 1955, Sir Thomas Beecham fought back after being accused of rushing through the Third Brandenburg Concerto. However his affable dismissal of the charge may have been justified in this case, he did occa-sionally dismay even his warmest admirers by his erratic con-ducting. Sir John Barbirolli once said of him that he 'conducted like a dancing dervish', and Neville Cardus remarked sombrely that 'the finale of the Seventh Symphony of Beethoven acted on him as red rag to a bull'.

Sir,
I believe that it is generally well known that I have much

respect for and sympathy with those brave fellows who attempt the hazardous task of musical criticism. More particularly does this partiality of mine apply to *The Times*, which alone among London journals of the present day devotes adequate space to the consideration of music in its various aspects. For these good reasons I refrain from uttering a word of reproach when I read something that strikes me as being unusually inexplicable.

But last Tuesday, 18 January, I played with my orchestra at Festival Hall a minor work of Johann Sebastian Bach, by no means representative either of his greatness or of his period. The following morning I was positively dazzled to read in one of your esteemed columns that my performance of this trifle was a positive travesty, and that the nature of the crime was to be discovered in the headlong speed adopted by me; comparable, according to the genial writer of the critique, with the famous ride of John Gilpin or it might have been Richard Turpin, Esq.

Now, Sir, I hope that you will agree with me that 'travesty' is a mighty word to use when belabouring an executive artist in respect of some alleged offence. I therefore am emboldened to enter a modest defence against such a grave charge. What is the truth of the matter? It is that my tempi on this occasion differed in no way from those adopted by 19 out of 20 conductors throughout the world during the past 50 years. All my concert programmes are recorded and each one is played to me on the day after the event. On this occasion I was able to verify that the respective tempi employed by me in the two movements of this concerto were—in metronomic language—92 and 80. Since then I have obtained the gramophone records of four other orchestras playing under their regular conductors the same piece, and what do I find? (Incidentally these other records were played in the presence of four skilled and grimly independent witnesses.) They are:

1 Boston Symphony Orchestra	92 and 76
2 Danish Orchestra	92 and 76
3 Boyd Neel Orchestra	92 and 84
4 Stuttgart Chamber Orchestra	88 and 80

From this it will be seen that four of us adopted exactly the same tempo in the first of the two movements, three likewise in the second movement, and where there was any difference it did not exceed one point of metronomic indication. (In the metronomic calculation there is nothing between 76 and 80, this slight difference being hardly distinguishable.) I think then, if I am to be convicted of the misdemeanour of 'travesty', there must stand in the dock beside me the vast majority of my colleagues and their orchestras over the long period of time to which I have referred.

What is the explanation of this apparent mystification? I think, if I may so suggest, that it lies in the comparative inability of nearly all listeners to distinguish correctly between the three separate entities of speed, rhythm and accent. I freely admit that I play this particular piece with a great deal more vigour and emphasis than any of my distinguished colleagues, and it is possible that there are those that do not care for this treatment of it. But their complaint, if they made it, cannot be directed against me on the ground of excessive speed. Long ago I commented in a book of mine upon the tendency of so many persons to imagine that I was an apostle of rapid tempi, although I was able through the evidence of gramophone records to establish that the majority of my interpretations might have erred in the contrary direction.

I trust that both you and the writer of the notice in question will look upon this little remonstrance of mine as having been uttered in a spirit of friendliness and respect.

I am your obedient servant,
THOMAS BEECHAM

Beecham chastised inaccurate criticism with his customary aplomb. So also does Rossini reveal his delightful personality and sense of humour in a letter to the director of the Théâtre Italien in Paris in 1859. The commercially minded management were evidently trying to exploit the Rossini name without scruple:

Monsieur,
I am told that your theatre is announcing on its posters a new opera by me, entitled *Un curioso Accidente*. I do not know whether I have the right to prevent the performance of a medley in two acts (more or less) of old pieces of mine; I have never concerned myself with such questions in respect of my works (of which none, be it said in passing, bears this title of *Un curioso Accidente*). In any case I have not opposed the performance of this *curioso Accidente* and do not intend to do

so. But I cannot allow the audiences who will visit your theatre, or your subscribers, to believe, firstly, that this is a new opera by me, and secondly, that I have any hand in whatever arrangement is to be made. I am therefore writing to request you to remove from your poster the word *new* and my name as composer, and to replace them by the following: *Opera put together by M. Berrettoni from pieces by M. Rossini.* I must insist that this alteration appears on tomorrow's poster; otherwise I shall be obliged to appeal to the law instead of, as at present, to your sense of justice . . .

Sometimes the activities of unscrupulous managements, the infighting of rival claques, and critical imbecility almost induced a composer to give up altogether. Opera was particularly bad for intrigue and politics, and perhaps still is. But we must be grateful that the composer of *Orpheus and Eurydice* didn't throw in the sponge, as he threatens to in a letter to Countess Von Fries. The terrific war between the Gluckists and Piccinnists, representing French and Italian opera styles respectively, was finally decided in favour of the Gluckists two years after this letter. In 1779 *Iphigénie en Tauride* was staged and swept the opposition before it.

Paris, 16 November 1777

Madame,
    I have been so plagued about music, and am so much disgusted with it, that at present I would not write one single note for a louis; by this you may conceive, Madame, the degree of my devotion to you, since I have been able to bring myself to arrange the two songs for the harp for you, and have the honour to send them herewith. Never has a more terrible and keenly-contested *battaglia* been waged, than the one I began with my opera *Armide*. The cabals against *Iphigénie*, *Orfeo* and *Alceste* were no more than little skirmishes of light horse by comparsion. The Neapolitan Ambassador, to ensure great success for Piccinni's opera, is tirelessly intriguing against me, at Court and among the nobility. He has induced Marmontel, La Harpe and several members of the Academy to write against my system of music and my manner of composing. The Abbé Arnaud, M. Suard and several others have come to my defence, and the quarrel grew so heated that from insults they would have passed to blows, but that

friends of both sides brought them to order. The *Journal de Paris*, which comes out every day, is full of it. This dispute is making the Editor's fortune, for he already has more than 2,500 subscribers in Paris. That's the musical revolution in France, amid the most brilliant pomp. Enthusiasts tell me: Sir, you are fortunate to be enjoying the honour of persecution; every great genius has had the same experience. —I wish them to the devil with their fine speeches. The fact is that the opera, which was said to have fallen flat, brought in 37,200 *livres* . . . The pit was so tightly packed that when a man who had his hat on his head was told by the guard to take it off, he replied: 'Come and take it off yourself, for I cannot move my arms'; which caused laughter . . .

The factionalism and backbiting amongst musical audiences does not always spring from a passionate love of music for its own sake. Berlioz's *Memoirs* demonstrate that money also had a lot to do with it, and even today some European opera houses are plagued by the antics of paid or unpaid claques. It is refreshing therefore to read of a music lover who could not possibly be accused of any ulterior motivation in a letter to *The Times* from Sir John Squire in 1936. This was Thomas Hardy's dog who, though not a musical connoisseur, clearly knew what he liked and was determined to get it:

. . . A good many years ago I was staying with the late Mr Thomas Hardy at Max Gate. He possessed then, and for long, a delightful fox terrier who nonchalantly supported the name of Wessex. His owner said of him that he bit bad poets and nuzzled good ones: I was let off, so naturally was flattered. During dinner Mr Hardy, a man of free mind who was willing to admit any fact if it was demonstrably a fact, remarked casually that the dog had a passion for the wireless. 'He won't,' he said, 'let us leave this room (the wireless, as Dr Watson might deduce, was in the dining room) until he's had a few minutes of it. He insists on it, even when we don't want it ourselves.' I listened, not incredulous, for Mr Hardy had one of the most accurate minds that ever I encountered. The ladies left the room, and I and that gentlest and most modest of great old poets were left alone with our (or, at that date, it may have been my) port. We talked a little about Chesil Bank, Dead Man's Bay, geology, and the Cerne Abbas giant (the dog meanwhile couched comfortably beneath the silent loud-speaker), and then, as manners bade, but forgetfully, we rose to go and I was graciously ushered towards the door.

Not a bit of it! Wessex's ears were pricked. He would no more go without his Sir (or was it then Mr?—historians must be exact about these things) John Reith than he would go without his breakfast. As Mr Hardy was about to pass out of the room the dog sprang at him, and gave him a fierce nip in the trouser-leg. Mr Hardy turned with that smile that wrinkled all his country face, and said: 'Well, well, Wessex, we forgot you, didn't we?' He closed the door and switched on what was then, I suppose, Daventry: and we resumed our seats. Melodiously forth came—well, I won't say a Bach Fugue, for I do not remember asking Mr Hardy whether his dog's Bach was worse than his bite. We watched the dog with affectionate and solicitous eyes, while the dog, squatting on his haunches with his jaws wide and his tongue hanging out, intently watched the 'set'. After five minutes he had had his ration, and he made no complaint when he was asked to join the general company in another room.

Sir, I am not saying or suggesting that all dogs' tastes in music are the same. One dog's Bartok is another dog's poison. Even among humans there are the tone-deaf: we remember the classic Victorian instance of the man who confessed that he could not tell 'Pop goes the Queen' from 'God save the Weasel'. But is there not a scientific field for investigation here? What percentage of dogs like music? Do particular breeds like particular kinds of music? What variations are there within the breeds themselves? Which kinds of dogs sing best? A hundred such problems await the attentions of research—and we must have many thousands of proved instances before we can draw the most provisional of deductions.

Mr Wodehouse's Ukridge, in the course of his many optimistic efforts to turn some kind of a penny, started a farm in Kent where dogs, which their owners thought had developable intelligences, could have their intelligences developed—probably on Montessori lines. Could not some scientist, or body of scientists, more competent and better endowed than Mr Ukridge, attack a more limited sphere in a more practical manner, collect a large number of dogs of various kinds, and assist dogowners who wish to have the sort of dogs who like the sort of music that they like themselves?

I forgot to add that when Mr Hardy was describing his terrier's passion to me he added (with a poet's exactitude): 'Mind you, he doesn't like the talks.'

I replied: 'I can't tell you how I agree with him!' I had just delivered some myself.

Yours faithfully,
J. C. SQUIRE

4

In Touch With The Muse

The painter J. B. Yeats wrote this to his son the poet, W. B. Yeats, on 6 April 1913:

> . . . I have just finished an article in which I maintain that art embodies not this or that feeling, but the whole totality—sensations, feeling, intuitions, everything—and that when everything within us is expressed there is peace and what is called beauty—this totality is personality. Now a most powerful and complex part of the personality is *affection* and affection *springs straight out of the memory*. For that reason what is new whether in the world of ideas or of fact cannot be subject for poetry, tho' you can be as rhetorical about it as you please—rhetoric expresses other people's feelings, poetry one's own . . .

This attempt to discover what poetry should be about, like all such attempts, is only partially successful, but it hits hard at the idea of poetry as something that tries to conform to the intellectual fashions of the age in which it is written. Poetry, says Yeats, is not original but eternal—'What oft was thought but ne'er so well expressed'. This view has inescapable implications for those who write poetry. Robert Graves, in a letter to *The Times* of 1962, remarks caustically that they should concentrate on writing the stuff, rather than 'being poets'.

At the risk of offending my friend Cecil Day-Lewis, let me offer 'Ignore the Poet!' as more salutary advice to public-spirited organizations than 'Don't Forget the Poet!'

A true poet writes because he must, not because he hopes to make a living from his poems. Obsession with principle keeps him out of literary gang-warfare, commerce and patronage. He never considers himself affronted by neglect, and treats whatever money comes from the sale of his poems as laughably irrelevant to their making. If neglected enough and obsessed enough, he buys a hand-press and publishes his own work, despising any form of whipped-up public charity. He knows that 'who pays the piper, calls the tune'. How to reconcile poetic principle with earning a livelihood is for him to settle, and no one else.

A pretended poet with nothing urgent to say, joins a movement, studies fashion, courts publishers, badgers elder poets for testimonials and expects the nation to support him. I beg the directors of all public-spirited organizations to ignore him. He is one of many idle thousands. There are never more than four or five poets in any country at the same time who are worth reading, and all tend to be fanatically independent. It is far better for a poet to starve than to be pampered. If he remains true to his obsession, then the older he is when fashions change and money suddenly pours in (often with a rush that would have made Alfred Lord Tennyson gasp) the less self-reproach will he feel, and laugh the louder.

The business of being 'a poet' was perfected by the American Carl Sandburg, of whom Gore Vidal unkindly remarks that he belonged to the 'Mount Rushmore' school of literature. Robert Frost, writing to Lincoln MacVeagh in May 1922, sourly notes how image-making has taken over from poetry in Sandburg's career:

> . . . We've been having a dose of Carl Sandburg. He's another person I find it hard to do justice to. He was possibly hours in town and he spent one of those washing his white hair and toughening his expression for his public performance. His mandolin pleased some people, his poetry a very few and his infantile talk none. His affectations have almost buried him out of sight. He is probably the most artificial and studied ruffian the world has had. Lesley says his two long poems in The New Republic and The Dial are as ridiculous as his carriage and articulation. He has developed rapidly since I saw him two years ago. I heard someone say he was the kind of writer who had everything to gain and nothing to lose by being translated into another language . . .

Carl Sandburg was rapidly transforming the occupation of poet into a branch of show business. But for most writers the vocation of poetry is as demanding as it can be financially unrewarding. Those who have it seem to know their destiny at an early age and have an inborn certainty about their gifts.

This sort of self-confidence and dedication are evident in a bold letter from the schoolboy Shelley to publishers Longman and Co:

> *Eton College, May 7, 1809*
> Gentlemen,—It is my intention to complete and publish a Romance, of which I have already written a large portion, before the end of July. My object in writing it was not pecuniary, as I am independent, being the heir of a gentleman of large fortune in the county of Sussex, and prosecuting my studies as an Oppidan at Eton; from the many leisure hours I have, I have taken an opportunity of indulging my favourite propensity in writing. Should it produce any pecuniary advantages, so much the better for me, I do not expect it. If you would be so kind as to answer this, direct it to me at the Rev. George Bethell's. Might I likewise request the favour of secrecy until the Romance is published.—I am, your very humble servant,
>
> PERCY SHELLEY
>
> Be so good as to tell me whether I shall send you the original manuscript when I have completed it or one corrected, etc.

Criticism demands empathy, not didacticism, on the part of the critic if his remarks are not to be beside the point. True poets write in the only way they can; and those who are not true poets are unlikely to become ones by simply following rules. This was roughly the stance of Byron, replying to the scholar Sir Francis Palgrave's objections to *Don Juan* in a letter to his publisher John Murray in 1819. The letter is full of provocative Byronic touches, and his implied contention that milk and water poetry is the only suitable fare for timid and conventional critics is a robust counter-punch to Palgrave:

> . . .—But nevertheless—I will answer your friend C. V. who objects to the quick succession of fun and gravity—as if in that case the gravity did not (in intention at least) heighten the fun.—His metaphor is that 'we are never scorched and

drenched at the same time!'—Blessings on his experience!—
ask him these questions about 'scorching and drenching'.—
Did he never play at Cricket or walk a mile in hot
weather?—did he never spill a dish of tea over his testicles in
handing the cup to his charmer to the great shame of his
nankeen breeches? —did he never swim in the sea at Noon-
day with the Sun in his eyes and on his head—which all the
foam of ocean could not cool? did he never draw his foot out
of a tub of too hot water damning his eyes & his valet's? did
he never inject for a Gonorrhea?—or make water through an
ulcerated Urethra?—was he ever in a Turkish bath—that
marble paradise of sherbet and sodomy?—was he ever in a
cauldron of boiling oil like St John?—or in the sulphurous
waves of hell? (where he ought to be for his 'scorching and
drenching at the same time') did he never tumble into a river
or lake fishing—and sit in his wet cloathes in the boat—or on
the bank afterwards 'scorched and drenched' like a true
sportsman? . . .

The inspiration for individual poems or even a whole corpus of
poetry is often to be found in a poet's journals and letters. In the
case of Thomas Gray, the celebrated author of the 'Elegy in a
Country Churchyard', the manner as well as the matter of his
verse is often apparent in his letters. The scene he here describes
overlooking the Bristol Channel is unfolded in terms reminiscent of Stoke Poges churchyard. There is even an ancient Abbey
with a ghostly reputation to lend exactly the right touch of
restrained 'horror' to the proceedings:

   . . . So I proceed to tell you that my health is much
improved by the sea, not that I drank it, or bathed in it, as the
common people do: no! I only walked by it and looked upon
it. The climate is remarkably mild, even in October and
November; no snow has been seen to lie there for these thirty
years past; the myrtles grow in the ground against the houses,
and Guernsey lillies bloom in every window: the town, clean
and well-built, surrounded by its old stone walls, with their
towers and gateways, stands at the point of a peninsula, and
opens full south to an arm of the sea, which, having formed
two beautiful bays on each hand of it, stretches away in direct
view, till it joins the Bristol Channel; it is skirted on either side
with gently-rising grounds, clothed with thick wood, and

directly cross its mouth rise the high lands of the Isle of Wight at distance, but distinctly seen. In the bosom of the woods (concealed from profane eyes) lie hid the ruins of Netley Abbey; there may be richer and greater houses of religion, but the abbot is content with his situation. See there, at the top of that hanging meadow, under the shade of those old trees that bend into a half circle about it, he is walking slowly (good man!) and bidding his beads for the souls of his benefactors, interred in that venerable pile that lies beneath him. Beyond it, (the meadow still descending) nods a thicket of oaks that mask the building, and have excluded a view too garish and luxuriant for a holy eye; only on either hand they leave an opening to the blue glittering sea. Did you not observe how, as that white sail shot by and was lost, he turned and crossed himself to drive the tempter from him that had thrown that distraction in his way? I should tell you that the ferryman who rowed me, a lusty young fellow, told me that he would not for all the world pass a night at the Abbey (there were such things near it) though there was a power of money hid there.

In contrast to the restraint of Thomas Gray, Robert Burns's account of the origin of his famous poem 'Tam o'Shanter' is as rumbustious and comic as the poem itself. 'Tam o'Shanter' published in 1790, was written in a single day; considering it is 228 lines long, this suggests remarkable stamina on Burns's part. The poem relates an alarming encounter with warlocks, witches, and Old Nick himself. At any rate, that is Tam's story, but he is not entirely a reliable witness, as the poet remarks:

> The swats sae reamed in Tammie's noddle,
> Fair play, he cared na de'ils a boddle:

Dumfries, 1792

Among the many witch stories I have heard relating to Alloway Kirk, I distinctly remember only two or three.

Upon a stormy night, amid whistling squalls of wind and bitter blasts of hail,—in short, on such a night as the devil would choose to take the air in,—a farmer, or farmer's servant, was plodding and plashing homeward, with his plough irons on his shoulder, having been getting some repairs on them at a neighbouring smithy. His way lay by the Kirk of Alloway, and being rather on the anxious look-out in approaching a place so well known to be a favourite haunt of the devil, and the devil's friends and emissaries, he was struck aghast by discovering through the horrors of the storm and stormy night a light, which, on his nearer approach, plainly showed itself to proceed from the haunted edifice. Whether he had been fortified from above, on his devout supplication, as is customary with people when they suspect the immediate presence of Satan, or whether according to another custom, he had got courageously drunk at the smithy, I will not pretend to determine; but so it was that he ventured to go up to, nay into, the very kirk. As luck would have it, his temerity came off unpunished.

The members of the infernal junto were all out on some midnight business or other, and he saw nothing but a kind of kettle or cauldron, depending from the roof over the fire, simmering some heads of unchristened children, limbs of executed malefactors, etc., for the business of the night. It was in for a penny in for a pound with the honest ploughman; so, without ceremony, he unhooked the cauldron from off the fire, and pouring out the damnable ingredients, inverted it on his head, and carried it fairly home, where it remained long in the family, a living evidence of the truth of the story.

Another story, which I can prove to be equally authentic, was as follows:—

On a market day, in the town of Ayr, a farmer from Carrick, and consequently whose way lay by the very gate of Alloway Kirkyard, in order to cross the river Doon at the old bridge, which is about two or three hundred yards farther on than the said gate, had been detained by his business, till by the time he reached Alloway it was the wizard hour, between night and morning.

Though he was terrified with a blaze streaming from the kirk, yet it is a well-known fact that to turn back upon these occasions is running by far the greatest risk of mischief; he prudently advanced on his road. When he had reached the gate of the kirkyard he was surprised and entertained through the ribs and arches of an old gothic window, which still faces the highway, to see a dance of witches, merrily footing it round their old sooty blackguard master, who was keeping them all alive with the power of his bagpipe. The farmer, stopping his horse to observe them a little, could plainly descry the faces of many old women of his acquaintance and neighbourhood. How the gentleman was dressed tradition does not say, but that the ladies were all in their smocks; and one of them, happening unluckily to have a smock which was considerably too short to answer all the purposes of that piece of dress, our farmer was so tickled that he involuntarily burst out with a loud laugh: 'Weel luppen, Maggy wi' the short sark!' and recollecting himself, instantly spurred his horse to the top of his speed. I need not mention the universally known fact, that no diabolical power can pursue you beyond the middle of a running stream. Luckily it was for the poor farmer that the river Doon was so near, for, notwithstanding the speed of his horse, which was a good one, against he reached the middle of the arch of the bridge, and consequently the middle of the stream, the pursuing, vengeful hags were so close at his heels, that one of them actually sprung to seize him; but it was too late, nothing was on her side of the stream but the horse's tail, which immediately gave way at her infernal grip, as if blasted by a stroke of lightning; but the farmer was beyond her reach. However, the unsightly, tailless condition of the steed was, to the last hour of the noble creature's life, an awful warning to the Carrick farmer not to stay too late in Ayr markets.

The last relation I shall give, though equally true, is not so well identified as the two former with regard to the scene; but as the best authorities give it for Alloway, I shall relate it.

On a summer's evening, about the time that nature puts on her sable to mourn the expiring of the cheerful day, a shepherd boy, belonging to a farmer in the immediate neighbourhood of Alloway Kirk, had just folded his charge and was returning home. As he passed the kirk, in the adjoining field he fell in with a crew of men and women, who were busy pulling stems of the plant ragwort. He observed that as each person pulled a ragwort, he or she got astride of it, and called out, 'Up, horsee,' on which the ragwort flew off, like Pegasus, through the air, with its rider. The foolish boy likewise pulled his ragwort, and cried with the rest, 'Up, horsee,' and, strange to tell, away he flew with the company. The first stage at which the cavalcade stopped was a merchant's wine-cellar in Bordeaux, where, without saying by your leave, they quaffed away at the best the cellar could afford, until the morning, foe to the imps and works of darkness, threatened to throw light on the matter, and frightened them from their carousals.

The poor shepherd lad being equally a stranger to the scene and the liquor, heedlessly got himself drunk; and when the rest took horse he fell asleep, and was found so next day by some of the people belonging to the merchant. Somebody that understood Scotch, asking him who he was, he said such-a-one's herdboy in Alloway, and by some means or other getting home again, he lived long to tell the world the wondrous tale. I am, etc.,

R.B.

The inspiration and ideas that may be found in Keats's letters lack the specificity of Burns; instead they spiral into the abstract where visual beauty becomes an expression of sublime thought. A letter to George and Georgiana Keats memorably embodies the notion of the self-sufficiency of the poet who has Beauty and Solitude to entrance him:

. . . Though the most beautiful Creature were waiting for me at the end of a Journey or a Walk; though the carpet were of Silk, the Curtains of the morning Clouds; the chairs and Sofa stuffed with Cygnet's down; the food Manna, the Wine beyond Claret, the Window opening on Winander mere, I should not feel—or rather my Happiness would not be so fine. My Solitude is sublime. Then instead of what I have described, there is a sublimity to welcome me home. The roaring of the wind is my wife and the Stars through the window pane are my Children. The mighty abstract Idea I have of Beauty in all things stifles the more divided and minute domestic happiness—an amiable wife and sweet Children I contemplate as a part of that Beauty—but I must have a thousand of those beautiful particles to fill up my heart. I feel more and more every day, as my imagination strengthens, that I do not live in this world alone but in a thousand worlds. No sooner am I alone than shapes of epic greatness are stationed around me, and serve my Spirit the office which is equivalent to a King's body guard—then 'tragedy with scepter'd pall, comes sweeping by'.[1] According to my state of mind I am with Achilles shouting in the Trenches, or with Theocritus in the Vales of Sicily. Or I throw my whole being into Troilus, and repeating those lines, 'I

---

[1] Milton, 'Il Penseroso', 11. 97–8.

wander, like a lost Soul upon the Stygian Banks staying for waftage',[1] I melt into the air with a voluptuousness so delicate that I am content to be alone. These things combined with the opinion I have of the generality of women—who appear to me as children to whom I would rather give a Sugar Plum than my time—form a barrier against Matrimony which I rejoice in. I have written this that you might see I have my share of the highest pleasures and that though I may choose to pass my days alone I shall be no Solitary. You see there is nothing spleenical in all this. The only thing that can ever affect me personally for more than one short passing day, is any doubt about my powers for poetry—I seldom have any, and I look with hope to the nighing time when I shall have none . . .

[1] Shakespeare, *Troilus & Cressida*, III, ii, 8–10.

Scribble, Scribble, Scribble . . .

Embarking on a literary career is a form of masochism involving patience, penury and persistence. A major hazard is that
the average publisher's reader may neither understand nor like
an original work, especially if it is revolutionary in form or
approach. If a writer is lucky, an existing literary eminence
may come to his aid. While James Joyce's 'dogged attempt to
cover the universe with mud' (E. M. Forster) naturally met
with a good deal of resistance, he had his supporters, one of
whom was Ezra Pound. In a letter dated January 1916 to the
literary agent, James B. Pinker, Pound castigates the reader's
report prepared for the publishing firm of Duckworth that had
complained that *A Portrait of the Artist as a Young Man* was 'too
discursive, formless, unrestrained', and that 'ugly things, ugly
words, are too prominent; indeed at times they seem to be
shoved in one's face on purpose unnecessarily':

> Dear Mr Pinker
> I have read the effusion of Mr Duckworth's reader with no
> inconsiderable disgust. These vermin crawl over and be-s-
> lime our literature with their pulings, and nothing but the
> day of judgement can, I suppose, exterminate 'em. Thank
> god one need not, under ordinary circumstances, touch
> them. Hark to his puling squeak: too 'unconventional'. What
> in hell do we want but some change from the unbearable
> monotony of the weekly six shilling pears soap annual novel;
> (and the George Robey-Gaby mixture) 'Carelessly written',
> this of the sole, or almost sole piece of contemporary prose
> that one can enjoy sentence by sentence and re-read with
> pleasure . . .
> It is with difficulty that I manage to write to you at all on
> being presented with the . . ., the dungminded dungbear-
> ded, penny a line, please the mediocre-at-all-cost doctrine.

You English will get no prose till you enterminate [sic] this breed . . . to say nothing of the abominable insolence of the tone.

I certainly will have nothing to do with the matter. The Egoist was willing to publish the volume, Lane would have read it a while ago.

I must repeat my former offer, if this louse will specify exactly what verbal changes he wants made I will approach Joyce in the matter. But I most emphatically will not forward the insults of an imbecile to one of the very few men for whom I have the faintest respect.

Canting, supercilious, blockhead . . . I always supposed from report that Duckworth was an educated man, but I can not reconcile this opinion with his retention of the author of the missive you send me. If you have to spend your life in contact with such minds, God help you, and do accept my good will and sympathy in spite of the tone of this note.

God! 'a more finished piece of work'.

Really, Mr Pinker, it is too insulting, even to be forwarded to Joyce's friend, let alone Joyce.

And the end . . . also found fault with . . . again, O God, O Montreal[1] . . .

Why can't you send the publishers readers to the serbian front, and get some good out of the war . . .

Serious writers will certainly give up the use of english altogether unless you can improve the process of publication.

In conclusion, you have given me a very unpleasant quarter of an hour, my disgust flows over, though I suppose there is no use in spreading it over this paper. If there is any phrase or form of contempt that you care to convey from me to the reeking Malebolge of the Duckworthian slum, pray, consider yourself at liberty to draw on my account (unlimited credit) and transmit it.

Please, if you have occasion to write again, either in regard to this book or any other, please do not enclose the publisher's readers opinions. Sincerely yours,

EZRA POUND

They pour out Elinor Glyn and pornography after pornography, but a piece of good writing they hate.

---

[1] 'O God, O Montreal!', a poem by Samuel Butler, lampooning prudish tastelessness in art.

P.S. I am reminded that Landor had equal difficulty in getting published—yet he is the best mind in your literature.

. . . as for altering Joyce to suit Duckworth's readers—I would like trying to fit the Venus de Milo into a piss-pot . . . a few changes required.

If Pound's language seems somewhat excessive, it is less so when one realizes what Joyce was up against. During his attempts to get *Dubliners* published he fell into the hands of Grant Richards, a financially unstable publisher (he went into liquidation twice) with a flare for spotting the new generation of talented writers. But remonstrating with him was like shouting down a well, and attempting to elicit some response to complaints about his astonishing incompetence was like plunging a fist into cotton wool. George Bernard Shaw ends one letter to him: 'If you won't be businesslike with other people, you *shall* with me: I'll make you, if only for the sake of your education. *Do* wake up.' In refusing to publish *Dubliners* without alterations, to the original list of which he kept adding as his nervousness increased, Richards wrote Joyce what must be the classic publisher's letter attempting to justify artistic mutilation:

> . . . If I had written your stories I should certainly wish to be able to afford your attitude; but as I stand on the publisher's side, I feel most distinctly that for more than one reason you cannot afford it . . . You won't get a publisher—a real publisher—to issue it as it stands . . . After all, remember, it is only words and sentences that have to be altered; and it seems to me that the man who cannot convey his meaning by more than one set of words and sentences has not yet realized the possibilities of the English language. That is not your case.

Joyce wrote to Grant Richards, at the end of long and abortive negotiations for Richards to publish the book, as follows: 'It is not my fault that the odour of ashpits and old weeds and offal hangs around my stories. I seriously believe that you will retard the course of civilization in Ireland by preventing the Irish people from having a good look at themselves in my nicely polished looking glass.' In an earlier letter he explains more specifically why cuts and changes are unacceptable.

As for my part and share in the book I have already told all I have to tell. My intention was to write a chapter of the moral history of my country and I chose Dublin for the scene because that city seemed to me the centre of paralysis. I have tried to present it to the indifferent public under four of its aspects: childhood, adolescence, maturity and public life. The stories are arranged in this order. I have written it for the most part in a style of scrupulous meanness and with the conviction that he is a very bold man who dares to alter in the presentment, still more to deform, whatever he has seen and heard. I cannot do any more than this. I cannot alter what I have written. All these objections of which the printer is now the mouthpiece arose in my mind when I was writing the book, both as to the themes of the stories and their manner of treatment. Had I listened to them I would not have written the book. I have come to the conclusion that I cannot write without offending people. The printer denounces *Two Gallants* and *Counterparts*. A Dubliner would denounce *Ivy Day in the Committee-Room*. The more subtle inquisitor will denounce *An Encounter*, the enormity of which the printer cannot see because he is, as I said, a plain blunt man. The Irish priest will denounce *The Sisters*. The Irish boarding-house keeper will denounce *The Boarding-House*. Do not let the printer imagine, for goodness' sake, that he is going to have all the barking to himself . . .

Joyce's literary antecedents include Gustave Flaubert, who also had trouble with his editors and publishers. Even Flaubert's friend Maxime DuCamp, in editing *Madame Bovary* for serialization in the *Revue de Paris*, was capable of writing a letter in which he solemnly urged his friend to let them correct his 'muddled work': 'Be brave, close your eyes during the operation, and have confidence—if not in our talent, at least in the experience we have acquired in such matters, and also in our affection for you . . .' Flaubert scrawled on the letter, '*Gigantesque!*'
The giveaway word in DuCamps letter is 'experience', by which was meant experience of what the public (and the police) would stand. Flaubert had no illusions about such matters, as he showed in a letter to his sometime mistress, Louise Colet, in 1846:

Sculptors who create real women, with breasts that can contain milk and thighs that suggest fecundity, are accused of sensualism. Whereas, were they to carve wads of drapery and figures

flat as signboards, they would be called idealists, spiritualists.
'Yes, he does neglect form, it's true,' people would say, 'but
he is a thinker!' Whereupon the bourgeois, with cries of joy,
would outdo themselves to admire what bores them. It's easy,
with the help of conventional jargon, and two or three ideas
acceptable as common coin, to pass as a socialist humanitarian
writer, a renovator, a harbinger of the evangelical future
dreamed of by the poor and the mad. Such is the modern
mania: one blushes to be a writer. If you merely write verse or
a novel, merely carve marble, shame! That was acceptable
previously, before the poet had a 'social mission'. Now every
piece of writing must have its moral significance, must teach
its lesson, elementary or advanced; a sonnet must be
endowed with philosophical implications, a play must rap the
knuckles of royalty, and a watercolour contribute to moral
progress. Everywhere there is pettifoggery, the craze for
spouting and orating: the muse becomes a mere pedestal for a
thousand unholy desires. Poor Olympus! They'd be capable
of planting a potato patch on its summit!

Flaubert's letters are wonderfully rich in such insights and his
understanding is often extremely prescient. 'A play must rap
the knuckles of royalty, and a watercolour contribute to moral
progress'—the contemporary version of this attitude is the
insistence that works of art must be judged from the point of
view of their contribution to progressive ideas, the exact nature
of which is assumed rather than stated. This is the left-wing
version of the attitude that works of art are allowed on suffer-
ance as long as they can be seen to reinforce acceptable opinions
and an assumed moral consensus. A letter to *The Times* of 5
October 1977 from a reader with a sure satirical touch attacks
this tiresomely sterile aesthetic as it was applied by a reviewer to
Osbert Sitwell's autobiography:

> *Sir*,
> Your newspaper is not yet subsidized by the Socialist
> Workers' Party, so why not employ reviewers who value
> books for themselves, and writers *as* writers, not as 'social
> documents' and 'products of their class'? Your review of
> Osbert Sitwell's autobiography by Kay Dick is not, I believe,
> your first to treat literature in this drab, disagreeable and
> uninformative way. Who would guess from it that the book is

in marvellous English, teeming with lyrical description, acute analyses of people and hilarious anecdote, or that its author often satirized his native milieu?

What would a Dick of previous generations, or Proto-Dick, have made of earlier masterpieces? A few conjectures:

'If music be the food of love, play on, give me excess of it.' *Proto-Dick* 'The Duke was of course used to excess of food, but too philistine to want excess of music except to serve his sexual appetites. Peacocks and drabs were his for the guzzling and fondling. Meanwhile in the Illyrian slave-galleys' etc., etc.

'I stood tiptoe on a little hill.' *Proto-Dick* 'He would have done better to stand flat-footed on a slag-heap. For while this consumptive young Cockney was a-twittering, in the industrial north the satanic mills were belching forth' etc.,etc.

Anyone can do their own Proto-Dick on Trollope and Thackeray, but what about the radical Dickens?—'The little room into which they were shown for dinner was delightful. Everything was delightful. The park was delightful, the dishes of fish were delightful, the wine was delightful' (*Our Mutual Friend*, ch. 8). *Proto-Dick* 'The successful writer, now basking in fame and fashionable dinner parties and battening on royalties five times the compositors' wages, omits to remind us—did he any longer care?—that the park gardener got two pence an hour, the fisherman six pence a stone, the vineyard workers one sou a day if they were lucky' etc., etc.

Dost think that because thou hast elephantiasis of the 'social conscience' there shall be no more cakes and ale?

I am Sir, etc.,
CHRISTOPHER GANDY

The pressures of ideology on a writer are only equalled by the pressures of commerce. Here is George Eliot in 1859 writing sharply to her publisher who had just sent her a batch of press cuttings, being the reviews of *Adam Bede*:

The folio of notices duly came, and are returned by today's post. The friend at my elbow ran through them for me, and read aloud some specimens to me, some of them ludicrous enough . . . I have not ventured to look into the folio myself;

but I learn that there are certain threatening marks in ink, by the side of such stock sentences as 'best novel of the season', or 'best novel we have read for a long time', from such authorities as the 'Sun' or 'Morning Star', or other orb of the newspaper firmament—as if these sentences were to be selected for reprint in the form of an advertisement. I shudder at the suggestion. Am I taking a liberty in entreating you to keep a sharp watch over advertisements, that no hackneyed puffing phrase of this kind may be tacked on to my book? One sees them garnishing every other advertisement of trash: surely no being 'above the rank of an idiot' can have his inclination coerced by them: and it would gall me, as much as any trifle could, to see my book recommended by an authority who doesn't know how to write decent English.

It is writing as a quest for perfection that is insisted on by most writers worth the name. Linked to this are the various motives for writing—to entertain, inform, stir consciences, and so forth. But doing the thing as well as it can be done is the hallmark of a craftsman. It's an attitude lucidly expressed by Raymond Chandler in a letter he wrote to Charles Morton of *Atlantic Monthly*. Chandler created the character of Philip Marlowe, a wise-cracking hard-bitten private eye, and his stories exploiting this character brought new possibilities and subtleties to the genre of thriller writing:

Dear Charles,
I do not write for you for money or for prestige, but for love, the strange lingering love of a world wherein men may think in cool subtleties and talk in the language of almost forgotten cultures. There is little of this world; there is a pale imitation of it created by people like Barzun. I like that world and I would on occasion sacrifice my sleep and my rest and quite a bit of money to enter it gracefully. That is not appreciated. It is something you cannot buy. It is something which, even when the gesture is imperfect, deserves respect. I can make $5000 in two days (sometimes), but I spend weeks trying to please the Atlantic for $250 or whatever it is. Do you think I want money? And as for prestige, what is it? What greater prestige can a man like me (not too greatly gifted but understanding) have than to have taken a cheap, shoddy, and utterly lost kind of writing and have made of it something that intellec-

tuals claw each other about? What more could I ask except the leisure and skill to write a couple of novels of the sort I want to write and to have waiting for them a public I have made myself?

All the best,
RAY

J. R. R. Tolkien was another writer who, when he embarked on his original tales of Hobbits and the Middle Earth, cannot have known or expected the financial rewards they would bring him. When he'd finished *The Lord of the Rings* he wrote diffidently to his publishers, apologizing for the lack of commercial potential in his latest production:

February 1950

. . . My work has escaped from my control, and I have produced a monster; an immensely long, complex, rather bitter, and rather terrifying romance, quite unfit for children (if fit for anybody); and it is not really a sequel to *The Hobbit*, but to *The Silmarillion*. Ridiculous and tiresome as you may think me, I want to publish them both—*The Silmarillion* and *The Lord of the Rings*. That is what I should like. Or I will let it all be. I cannot contemplate any drastic re-writing or compression. But I shall not have any just grievance (nor shall I be dreadfully surprised) if you decline so obviously unprofitable a proposition . . .

All this is not to say that writers as a breed are devoid of the desire to make money; merely that they cannot sit down at the typewriter solely with that aim in view and consequently deliver the goods. Marketing their wares is the publisher's responsibility, though publishers are notoriously erratic in the level of competence and dedication to the task. Being uncertain of your publisher and your public's reception of many years' hard labour is an occupational hazard for writers; but the loss of actual manuscripts ought not to be. It happened to Carlyle, however, and his letter to his brother relating the circumstances shows superhuman self-control considering how he must have been feeling:

Cheyne Row, Chelsea, London
23rd March, 1835

My Dear Brother,
  Your letter came in this morning (after sixteen days from

Rome); and, to-morrow being post-day, I have shoved my writing-table into the corner, and sit (with my back to the fire and Jane, who is busy sewing at my old dressing-gown) forthwith making answer. It was somewhat longed for; yet I felt, in other respects, that it was better you had not written sooner; for I had a thing to dilate upon, of a most ravelled character, that was better to be knit up a little first. You shall hear. But do not be alarmed; for it is 'neither death nor men's lives'; we are all well.

Mill had borrowed that first volume of my poor French Revolution (pieces of it more than once) that he might have it all before him, and write down some observations on it, which perhaps I might print as notes. I was busy meanwhile with Volume Second; toiling along like a Nigger, but with the heart of a free Roman: indeed, I know not how it was, I had not felt so clear and independent, sure of my self and of my task for many long years.

Well, one night about three weeks ago, we sat at tea, and Mill's short rap was heard at the door: Jane rose to welcome him; but he stood there unresponsive, pale, the very picture of despair; half articulately gasping. After some considerable additional gasping, I learned from Mill this fact: that my poor Manuscript, all except some four tattered leaves, was annihilated! he had left it out (too carelessly); it had been taken for waste-paper; and so five months of as tough labour as I could remember of, were as good as vanished, gone like a whiff of smoke. [A maid had used the paper to light a fire.]

There never in my life had come upon me any other accident of much moment; but this I could not but feel to be a sore one. The thing was lost, and perhaps worse; for I had not only forgotten all the structure of it, but the spirit it was written with was past; only the general impression seemed to remain, and the recollection that I was on the whole well satisfied with that, and could now hardly hope to equal it. Mill, whom I had to comfort and speak peace to, remained injudiciously enough till almost midnight, and my poor Dame and I had to sit talking of indifferent matters; and could not till then get our lament freely uttered.

Writing is a difficult and lonely enough profession without such additional and unnecessary burdens. But Carlyle's energy and dedication enabled him to rewrite the first volume and *The French Revolution* appeared in 1837, establishing his reputation as a literary heavyweight.

Energy and dedication are the sustaining qualities for any writer who may be amongst those who face years of neglect, but who must continue to believe in themselves. Two writers who had this self-confidence and unremitting application to their craft were Flaubert and Kafka. Although very different in character the two men share an almost neurotic obsession with the idea of writing—Flaubert, who finally succeeded in outraging and impressing his compatriots with the romantic realism of *Madame Bovary*, and Kafka, who unsettled his own and succeeding generations with his portraits of an inhuman, unresponsive society in which the individual is a lost wanderer with only his discredited rational faculties between him and the insanity of his environment. The extract from Flaubert's letter to Alfred Le Poittevin, dated 1843, is given first:

Two glasses of vinegar and one of wine are better than one of reddish water. As for me, I no longer feel the glowing enthusiasm of youth nor those dreadful old waves of bitterness. The two have merged, and the result is a single, universal tone, made up of everything, ground together and compounded. I notice that I seldom laugh any more, and no longer suffer from depressions. I am ripe. You speak of my serenity, dear friend, and are envious of it. It is true that it might seem surprising. Ill, agitated, prey a thousand times a day to moments of terrible anxiety, without women, without wine, without any of the tinsel the world offers, I continue my slow work like a good workman who rolls up his sleeves and sweats away at his anvil, indifferent to rain or wind, hail or thunder. Formerly I was not like that. The change came about naturally. My will too, played a certain role. It will take me further, I hope. My only fear is lest it give way, for there are days when my torpor is frightening. I think I have finally come to understand one thing, one great thing. That is, that for people like you and me happiness is in the *idea*, nowhere else. Seek out what is truly your nature, and be in harmony with it. '*Sibi constet*', says Horace. That is everything. I swear to you that I think neither about fame nor—very much— about art. I try to pass the time in the least boring way possible, and I have found it. Do as I do. *Break with the outside world*, live like a bear—a polar bear—let everything else go to hell—everything, yourself included, except your intelligence. There is now such a great gap between me and the rest of the world that I am sometimes surprised to hear people say the most natural and simple things. It's strange how the most banal utterance sometimes makes me marvel. There are gestures, sounds of people's voices, that I cannot get over, silly remarks that almost give me vertigo. Have you sometimes listened closely to people speaking a foreign language you didn't understand? That is my case. Precisely because I want to understand everything, anything at all sets me wondering. Still, it seems to me that this astonishment is not stupidity. The bourgeois, for example, is for me something unfathomable.

Everyone is quite well here. Adieu; answer quickly.

Franz Kafka to Felice Bauer, 1 November 1912:

. . . My life consists, and basically always has consisted, of attempts at writing, mostly unsuccessful. But when I didn't write, I was at once flat on the floor, fit for the dustbin. My energies have always been pitifully weak; even though I didn't quite realize it, it soon became evident that I had to spare myself on all sides, renounce a little everywhere, in order to retain just enough strength for what seemed to me my main purpose. When I didn't do so (oh God, even on a holiday such as this, when I am acting as duty officer, there is no peace, just visitor after visitor, like a little hell let loose) but tried to reach beyond my strength, I was automatically forced back, wounded, humbled, forever weakened; yet this very fact which made me temporarily unhappy is precisely what gave me confidence in the long run, and I began to think that somewhere, however difficult to find, there must be a lucky star under which it would be possible to go on living. I once drew up a detailed list of the things I have sacrificed to writing, as well as the things that were taken from me for the sake of writing, or rather whose loss was only made bearable by this explanation.

Just as I am thin, and I am the thinnest person I know (and that's saying something, for I am no stranger to sanatoria), there is also nothing to me which, in relation to writing, one could call superfluous, superfluous in the sense of overflowing. If there is a higher power that wishes to use me, or does use me, then I am at its mercy, if no more than as a well-prepared instrument. If not, I am nothing, and will suddenly be abandoned in a dreadful void.

MIND AND SPIRIT

1

Yours Faithfully and Unfaithfully

Pliny the Younger was born only sixty-two years after the death of Christ when Christianity was an outlawed religion, regarded by the Roman Emperors as a cult like any other, but for some reason more coherent, more subversive and more difficult to stamp out. In the following exchange between himself, acting in his capacity as Governor of Bithynia and Pontus, and the Emperor Trajan, we see him struggling to formulate a political strategy to deal with 'this wretched cult' as he calls it; in his reply, the Emperor warns against using methods which Christians themselves were later to employ against their fellow believers during the Counter-Reformation.

It is my custom to refer all my difficulties to you, Sir, for no one is better able to resolve my doubts and to inform my ignorance.

I have never been present at an examination of Christians. Consequently, I do not know the nature of the extent of the punishments usually meted out to them, nor the grounds for starting an investigation and how far it should be pressed. Nor am I at all sure whether any distinction should be made between them on the grounds of age, or if young people and adults should be treated alike; whether a pardon ought to be granted to anyone retracting his beliefs, or if he has once professed Christianity, he shall gain nothing by renouncing it; and whether it is the mere name of Christian which is punishable, even if innocent of crime, or rather the crimes associated with the name.

For the moment this is the line I have taken with all persons brought before me on the charge of being Christians. I have asked them in person if they are Christians, and if they admit it, I repeat the question a second and third time, with a warning of the punishment awaiting them. If they persist, I order them to be led away for execution; for, whatever the nature of their admission, I am convinced that their stubbornness and unshakeable obstinacy ought not to go unpunished. There have been others similarly fanatical who are Roman citizens. I have entered them on the list of persons to be sent to Rome for trial.

Now that I have begun to deal with this problem, as so often happens, the charges are becoming more widespread and increasing in variety. An anonymous pamphlet has been circulated which contains the names of a number of accused persons. Amongst these I considered that I should dismiss any who denied that they were or ever had been Christians when they had repeated after me a formula of invocation to the gods and had made offerings of wine and incense to your statue (which I had ordered to be brought into court for this purpose along with the images of the gods), and furthermore had reviled the name of Christ: none of which things, I understand, any genuine Christian can be induced to do.

Others, whose names were given to me by an informer, first admitted the charge and then denied it; they said that they had ceased to be Christians two or more years previously, and some of them even twenty years ago. They all did reverence to your statue and the images of the gods in the same way as the others, and reviled the name of Christ. They also declared that the sum total of their guilt or error amounted to no more than this: they had met regularly before dawn on a fixed day to chant verses alternately amongst themselves in honour of Christ as if to a god, and also to bind themselves by oath, not for any criminal purpose, but to abstain from theft, robbery, and adultery, to commit no breach of trust and not to deny a deposit when called upon to restore it. After this ceremony it had been their custom to disperse and reassemble later to take food of an ordinary, harmless kind—but they had in fact given up this practice since my edict, issued on your instructions, which banned all political societies. This made me decide it was all the more necessary to extract the truth by torture from two slave-women, whom they call deaconesses. I found nothing but a degenerate sort of cult carried to extravagant lengths.

I have therefore postponed any further examination and hastened to consult you. The question seems to me to be worthy of your consideration, especially in view of the number of persons endangered; for a great many individuals of every age and class, both men and women, are being brought to trial, and this is likely to continue. It is not only the towns, but villages and rural districts too which are infected through contact with this wretched cult. I think though that it is still possible for it to be checked and directed to better ends, for there is no doubt that people have begun to throng the temples which had been almost entirely deserted for a long time; the sacred rites which had been allowed to lapse are being performed again, and flesh of sacrificial victims is on sale everywhere, though up till recently scarcely anyone could be found to buy it. It is easy to infer from this that a great many people could be reformed if they were given an opportunity to repent.

Trajan to Pliny:

You have followed the right course of procedure, my dear Pliny, in your examination of the cases of persons charged with being Christians, for it is impossible to lay down a general rule to a fixed formula. These people must not be hunted out; if they are brought before you and the charge against them is proved, they must be punished, but in the case of anyone who denies that he is a Christian, and makes it clear that he is not by offering prayers to our gods, he is to be pardoned as a result of his repentance however suspect his past conduct may be. But pamphlets circulated anonymously must play no part in any accusation. They create the worst sort of precedent and are quite out of keeping with the spirit of our age.

Intolerance of heretical views is based on fear, especially the fear that the views might catch on amongst the orthodox. Of course, the orthodox themselves may begin their careers as rebels; as has frequently been pointed out, it is the fate of revolutionaries to found new orthodoxies. The defence of these is inclined to be every bit as violent and unscrupulous as was the behaviour of their former persecutors. A chilling example of this cast of mind is to be found in a letter from Cotton Mather announcing the arrival of Quakers in America in 1682, and suggesting that appropriate action be taken. Mather's father, who rejoiced in the christian name of 'Increase', had himself left England because of his non-conformist views, and was a good deal more moderate than this son. Cotton, intensely active in word as well as deed, produced no less than 382 books. In 1685 he published his *Memorable Providences relating to Witchcraft and Possessions*, an inflammatory work that encouraged inhuman bigotry amongst New Englanders. He was active with his pen during the Salem witch hunts and bears responsibility for much of the horrific and vindictive persecution that occurred at that time:

In the year of Our Lord 1682
To Ye Aged and Beloved, Mr John Higginson:
There be now at sea a ship called Welcome, which has on board 100 or more of the heretics and malignants called Quakers, with W Penn, who is the chief scamp, at the head of them. The General Court has accordingly given sacred orders to Master Malachi Huscott, of the brig Porpoise, to waylay the said Welcome slyly as near the Cape of Cod as may be, and make captive the said Penn and his ungodly crew, so that the Lord may be glorified and not mocked on the soil of this new country with the heathen worship of these people. Much spoil can be made of selling the whole lot to Barbados, where slaves fetch good prices in rum and sugar, and we shall not only do the Lord great good by punishing the wicked, but we shall make great good for His Minister and people.

Yours in the bowels of Christ,
COTTON MATHER

Intolerance amongst the faithful will doubtless continue to lurk just below the surface as long as religions are adhered to with conviction amongst large numbers of people; and challenges to fundamental beliefs will continue to be met with anger and threats as often as with argument. Bertrand Russell clearly enjoyed crossing swords with the representatives of conventional religion and his writings were often deliberately provocative. But he was not only hostile to the intolerance of official Christianity; in the second letter of the following exchange he gives short shrift to an irate Muslim who was furious about some of Russell's remarks concerning the prophet:

. . . In Wisdom of the West the picture of the Prophet of Islam has been cut from the copies of the book supplied to Pakistan . . . its publication is tabooed in Islam . . . I wonder where was the occasion for publishing the picture of the Holy

Prophet in a book, entitled, Wisdom of the West? In your book you have used the word 'Flight' for the migration of the Holy Prophet from Mecca to Medina . . . 'Hijrat' (migration) was a strategic withdrawal to a friendly place made according to plan, under Divine guidance. You will not like to use the word 'flight' when the British armies took to their heels at Dunkirk in World War II. How do you account for using the word 'flight' for an event that has a religious sanctity for the Muslim world? Sir, I wonder how you can undo the wrong that you have done to the Muslim world . . .

September 16, 1963

Dear Mr Irshad,

Thank you for your letter. 1. The British armies did flee from Dunkirk just as Mohammed fled from Mecca to Medina. 2. I do not believe that Mohammed or anyone else was impelled by 'divine inspiration'. 3. To call flight 'strategic withdrawal' is ludicrous. 4. The picture of the prophet should be displayed as a matter of interest to students and scholars. 5. Chauvinism is harmful and also accompanies the absence of any humour or humility.

Yours sincerely
BERTRAND RUSSELL

P.S. I am opposed to all superstition: Muslim, Christian, Jewish or Buddhist.

Russell's remarks implicitly accept the power of superstition, which he regards as harmful. Jack Butler Yeats, in a letter to his son, the poet W. B. Yeats, also analyses superstition and its roles in the history of Protestantism and Catholicism:

The value of Protestantism is that it enforced will power by the powers of superstition. It did not need much intelligence to learn by rote the ten commandments and understand them, but it needed a great deal of will power to do them. The Catholic religion cares very little about morality but enforces religion by the power of superstition, and you are saved by having a poetical mind; unfortunately with the intellect and the will power left out, Protestantism produces poetry which is mainly oratorical and didactic or hysterically rebellious. Catholicism produces poets in abundance, but being without intellectual strength, they have no desire to think or write.

Shakespeare and Milton, we must remember, began their lives under Catholic tuition and influences and then 'got' free thought and arrived too early to suffer from the deadening effects of Protestantism.

The English have become great through Protestantism; that is if we are content to call great what to me is mere bigness. If only we could get rid of the gospel of getting on and the deluded people who preach it and we could bring the right teachers to the peasants in the west of Ireland, the musicians and the free thinkers and the artists, and could touch those lips with the wand of the enchanter. If at the same time we could by some miracle free them from the fear of starvation and give them the kind of large and comfortable ease which every Englishman possessed when there were only about 5,000,000 in all England, population being then kept down by plague and pestilence and by the fact that then immigration was as impossible as armed invasion . . .

Yeats writes of religion largely as a political and historical phenomenon. It is against a similar background that the German theologian and fighter against Nazism Dietrich Bonhoeffer discusses the place of Christianity in the modern world. In his remarkable portrait of the 'world come of age' rather than as the forever backward child of Christian polemic, he tries to chart a course for the future of God in the lives of people of the twentieth century. His seminal ideas were discussed in his many letters and reflections composed in prison between 1943 and 1944. His idea of a 'religionless Christianity' has deeply influenced subsequent theologians and has perhaps indirectly affected many others. His style is wonderfully lucid, no matter how subtle the ideas he is unravelling:

. . . As in the scientific field, so in human affairs generally, 'God' is being pushed more and more out of life, losing more and more ground.

Roman Catholic and Protestant historians agree that it is in this development that the great defection from God, from Christ, is to be seen; and the more they claim and play off God and Christ against it, the more the development considers itself to be anti-Christian. The world that has become conscious of itself and the laws that govern its own existence has grown self-confident in what seems to us to be an uncanny way. False developments and failures do not make the world doubt the necessity of the course that it is taking, or of its development; they are accepted with fortitude and detachment as part of the bargain, and even an event like the present war is no exception. Christian apologetic has taken the most varied forms of opposition to this self-assurance. Efforts are made to prove to a world thus come of age that it cannot live without the tutelage of 'God'. Even though there has been surrender on all secular problems, there still remain the so-called 'ultimate questions'—death, guilt—to which only 'God' can give an answer, and because of which we need God and the church and the pastor. So we live, in some degree, on these so-called ultimate questions of humanity. But what if one day they no longer exist as such, if they too can be answered 'without God'? Of course, we now have the secularized offshoots of Christian theology, namely existentialist philosophy and the psychotherapists, who demonstrate to secure, contented, and happy mankind that it is really unhappy and desperate and simply unwilling to admit that it is in a predicament about which it knows nothing, and from which only they can rescue it. Wherever there is health, strength, security, simplicity, they scent luscious fruit to gnaw at or to lay their pernicious eggs in. They set themselves to drive people to inward despair, and then the game is in their hands. That is secularized methodism. And who does it touch? A small number of intellectuals, of degenerates, of people who regard themselves as the most important thing in the world, and who therefore like to busy themselves with themselves. The ordinary man, who spends his everyday life at work and with his family, and of course with all kinds of diversions, is not affected. He has neither the time nor the inclination to concern himself with his existential despair, or to regard his perhaps modest share of happiness as a trial, a trouble, or a calamity.

The attack by Christian apologetic on the adulthood of the world I consider to be in the first place pointless, in the second place ignoble, and in the third place unchristian. Pointless, because it seems to me like an attempt to put a grown-up man back into adolescence, i.e. to make him dependent on things on which he is, in fact, no longer dependent, and thrusting him into problems that are, in fact, no longer problems to him. Ignoble, because it amounts to an attempt to exploit man's weakness for purposes that are alien to him and to which he has not freely assented. Unchristian, because it confuses Christ with one particular stage in man's religiousness, i.e. with a human law.

One objection to Christianity raised by its opponents is the tendency to use the notion of 'God' to cover a multitude of virtues. The problem of pinning down the meaning of 'God'—as opposed to fixing it in ritual and dogma—is tackled by Shelley in a letter to Thomas Jefferson Hogg. His solution is to exclude the word God altogether, at least from philosophical parlance, because of its indefinability. All might have been well if Shelley had kept this radical notion as a matter for private discussion between himself and Hogg, but on 25 March 1811, two months after the following letter was written, he and Hogg published a tract entitled *The Necessity of Atheism*. The Oxford authorities, having regard to the reputation of the University as a Christian institution, could not tolerate this and expelled the two young men forthwith:

> *My dear Friend,*
> Before we doubt or believe the existence of anything it is necessary that we should have a tolerably clear idea of what it is. The word 'God' has been [and] will continue to be the source of numberless errors until it is erased from the nomenclature of Philosophy.—it does not imply 'the Soul of the Universe, the intelligent & *necessarily* beneficient actuating principle'—this I believe in; I may not be able to adduce proofs, but I think that the leaf of a tree, the meanest insect on which we trample are in themselves arguments more conclusive than any which can be adduced that some vast intellect animates Infinity—If we disbelieve *this*, the strongest argument in support of the existence of a future state instantly becomes annihilated. I confess that I think Pope's 'all are but parts of one tremendous whole' something more than poetry; it has ever been my favourite theory. For the immoral 'never to be able to die, never to escape from some shrine as chilling as the clay-formed dungeon which it now inhabits' is the future punishment which I believe in . . .

'God' may be a vague concept, but Jesus Christ is not. Mark Twain was asked in 1908 by one correspondent to suggest further candidates for an incomplete list of the world's 'One Hundred Greatest Men', i.e. those with the largest visible influence. Twain suggested Christ *and* Satan and gave succinct reasons for his choice:

> *Private.*
> Dear Sir,
>   By 'private', I mean don't print any remarks of mine.
>
>   I like your list.
>   The *'largest visible influence'*.
>   These terms *require* you to add Jesus. And they doubly and trebly require you to add Satan. From AD 350 to AD 1850 these gentlemen exercised a vaster influence over a fifth part of the human race than was exercised over that fraction of the race by all other influences combined. Ninety-nine hundredths of this influence proceeded from Satan, the remaining fraction of it from Jesus. During those 1500 years the fear of Satan and Hell made 99 Christians where love of God and Heaven landed *one*. During those 1500 years Satan's influence was worth very nearly a hundred times as much to the business as was the influence of all the rest of the Holy Family put together.
>   You have asked me a question and I have answered it seriously and sincerely. You have put in Buddha—a god with a following at one time greater than Jesus ever had, a god with perhaps a little better evidence of his godship than that which is offered for Jesus's. How then in fairness can you leave Jesus out? And if you put him in, how can you logically leave Satan out? Thunder is good, thunder is impressive, but it is the lightning that does the work.
>
> Very truly yours,
> S. L. CLEMENS

Without Satan it has to be admitted that a lot of the fire would go out of preachers. But if calamities occur, and if it is accepted that someone is responsible for them, it is not always convincing, and certainly not always convenient, to blame them on the Devil. Perhaps it is God punishing his children. Oblivious of Norman Douglas's observation that 'if God exists then he must be a monster', preachers have exploited the possibilities of a 'jealous God' for all it was worth. Horace Walpole records an instance of them in full cry in a letter to Sir Horace Mann in 1750:

You will not wonder so much at our earthquakes, as at the effects they have had. All the women in town have taken them up upon the foot of judgments:[1] and the clergy, who have had no windfalls of a long season, have driven horse and foot into this opinion. There has been a shower of sermons and exhortations: Secker, the Jesuitical Bishop of Oxford, began the mode; he heard the women were all going out of town to avoid the next shock; and so for fear of losing his Easter offerings, he set himself to advise them to await God's good pleasure in fear and trembling. But what is more astonishing, Sherlock, who has much better sense, and much less of the popish confessor, has been running a race with him for the old ladies, and has written a pastoral letter, of which ten thousand were sold in two days; and fifty thousand have been subscribed for, since the two first editions. You never read so impudent, so absurd a piece! This earthquake, which has done no hurt, in a country where no earthquake ever did any, is sent, according to the Bishop, to punish bawdy prints, bawdy books (in one of which a Mrs Pilkington drew his Lordship's picture) gaming, drinking—(no, I think, drinking and avarice, those orthodox vices are omitted) and all other sins, natural or not; particularly heretical books, which he makes a principal ingredient in the composition of an earthquake, because not having been able to answer a late piece, which Middleton has writ against him, he has turned the Doctor over to God for punishment, even in this world.

A few days later he returns to the subject:

I had not time to finish my letter on Monday—I return to the earthquake, which I had mistaken; it is to be today. This frantic terror prevails so much, that within these three days 730 coaches have been counted passing Hyde Park Corner, with whole parties removing into the country; here is a good advertisement which I cut out of the papers today:

On Monday next will be published (price 6d.) A true and exact list of all the nobility and gentry who have left or shall leave this place through fear of another earthquake.

---

[1] By *judgments* here is not meant anything that is the effect of *judiciousness*, but a kind of punishment, invented by divines, by which, on any great calamity, God is supposed to chastise a general people or posterity, for the crimes of particulars, or for the sins of their ancestors. (HW's note)

Several women have made earthquake gowns—that is, warm gowns to sit out of doors all tonight. These are of the more courageous. One woman still more heroic is come to town on purpose: she says, all her friends are in London, and she will not survive them. But what will you think of Lady Catherine Pelham, Lady Frances Arundel, and Lord and Lady Galway, who go this evening to an inn ten miles out of town, where they are to play at brag till five in the morning, and then come back—I suppose, to look for the bones of their husbands and families under the rubbish!

There were no casualties of the earthquake.

Some preachers are inclined to over-egg the pudding. John Wesley in a famous letter of July 1775 tried to damp down one of his American acolytes:

> *My dear Brother,*
> Always take advice or reproof as a favour: it is the surest mark of love.
> I advised you once, and you took it as an affront; nevertheless I will do it once more.
> Scream no more, at the peril of your soul. God now warns you by me, whom He has set over you.
> Speak as earnestly as you can, but do not scream. Speak with all your heart, but with a moderate voice. It is said of our Lord, 'He shall not *cry*'; the word properly means, He shall not *scream*. Herein, be a follower of me, as I am of Christ. I often speak loud, often vehemently, but I never scream, I never strain myself. I dare not, I know it would be a sin against God and my own soul. Perhaps one reason why that good man, Thomas Walsh, yea, and John Manners too, were in such grievous darkness before they died, was, because they shortened their own lives.
> O John, pray for an advisable and teachable temper! By nature you are very far from it; you are stubborn and headstrong. Your last letter was written in a very wrong spirit. If you cannot take advice from others, surely you might take it from your affectionate brother.

Wesley's letter indirectly raises the question of what is, or should be, the attitude of a sensible man to his religion. If they are as sensible about their faith as they are about every other aspect of their lives, an attitude of caution seems to be called for. Here is Benjamin Franklin's exceedingly canny reply to a correspondent who has asked him to write confidentially stating his exact religious beliefs:

> As to Jesus of Nazareth, my Opinion of whom you particularly desire, I think the System of Morals and his Religion, as he left them to us, the best the World ever saw or is likely to see; but I apprehend it has received various corrupting Changes, and I have, with most of the present Dissenters in England, some Doubts as to his Divinity; tho' it is a question I do not dogmatize upon, having never studied it, and think it needless to busy myself with it now, when I expect soon an Opportunity of knowing the Truth with less Trouble. I see no harm, however, in its being believed, if that Belief has the good Consequence, as probably it has, of making his Doctrines more respected and better observed; especially as I do not perceive, that the Supreme takes it amiss, by distinguishing the Unbelievers in his Government of the World with any peculiar Marks of his Displeasure.

The 'system of morals and religion' may have been, as Franklin claimed, the best the world is ever likely to see, but what exactly is it? Shaw, in a letter to the *Star* in 1888, suggested that this rather depended on your position in society. This letter was one of a number of provocative ones that he wrote in an assumed persona:

> *Sir*,
> I am a native of a country where Christianity is unknown. Having heard much of the English Protestant form of your religion in the course of my travels, I have devoted myself to its study—from men, not from books—since I entered England. My conclusion is that your question is hardly worth considering, as only a very small proportion of the population have any religious beliefs at all. Those who have are nearly all called Christians; but they have not all the same belief: there are at least as many creeds as there are classes. Among the poor, for instance, the Salvation Army spreads a vivid conceit (as your great poet Shakespeare would say) of the horrors of hell and the ecstasies of heaven, so that the uncertainty as to

whether the individual is 'saved'— or destined for heaven—or not, is intensely exciting. Here the hope of heaven makes the people content to bear their deep poverty.

Higher in the social scale there prevails the conception of a terrible divine wrath and vengeance, only to be propitiated by human sacrifice begun by the supreme immolation of Christ and continued daily in the mortified ascetic lives of his followers. Much of the gloom and aversion to fine art which characterizes the lower middle class is undoubtedly due to this terrible creed, which makes Sunday the especial scourge of childhood. Still higher up, in circles where the mind and artistic senses are highly cultivated, hell is disbelieved; only the more pleasing and amiable parts of the Bible are held to be valid; and the divine power is personified by the gentle and humane Jesus of Nazareth.

Besides these are also Christian Socialists, who look to the establishment of the Kingdom of heaven on earth by a Christ in whom may be discovered a general agreement with the doctrines of the American Mr Henry George. But among the most advanced classes, Christianity shades into an indefinite optimism without any belief in the supernatural. I am told by some that the beliefs in a personal God, and in an imperishable organ called the soul, which survives the body and is subject to reward or punishment according to the acts performed during the life of the body, are no vital part of Christianity and are rejected by many true Christians. But others of my acquaintance regard the slightest expression of doubt on these points as blasphemous in the highest degree, and will passionately declare that the sceptic is no Christian, but an atheist whose soul shall dwell in tormenting fire for ever.

This want of agreement among Christians is so striking that to a foreigner it does not seem possible to discuss whether Christianity is a failure whilst the word means so many different beliefs. Of the irreligious majority of the English people I notice that great numbers go to church because it is one of the duties which are included in what is called 'respectability'.

Shaw sardonically points out that Christianity is reinterpreted according to the class and inclination of the professed believer. But Tolstoy, writing to a young journalist involved in religious controversy, stresses the practicality of Christian teaching and

the necessity of using the teachings of Christ to combat the
evils of the world rather than as the pretext for withdrawal
from the world as happens in the orthodox monastic tradition:

> . . . It is said in Deuteronomy: love God and love your
> neighbour as yourself, but the application of this principle
> according to Deuteronomy consisted of circumcision, the
> sabbath and criminal law. The importance of Christianity is
> the indication of the possibility and the happiness of fulfill-
> ing the law of love. In the Sermon on the Mount Christ
> defined very clearly how, for one's own happiness and that
> of all people, it is necessary and possible to fulfil this law. In
> the Sermon on the Mount, but for which Christ's teaching
> would not exist— everyone agrees about this—in which
> Christ addressed himself not to wise men but to the illiterate
> and the uncouth, in a sermon which is furnished with an
> introduction that 'whosoever shall break one of these least
> commandments' (Matt. 5, 17–20) and a conclusion that one
> should not speak but fulfil (Matt. 7, 21–7)—everything is
> said in this sermon, and 5 commandments are given about
> how to fulfil the teaching. The Sermon on the Mount
> expounds the simplest, easiest, most understandable rules
> for loving God, one's neighbour, and life, without the recog-
> nition and fulfilment of which it is impossible to speak of
> Christianity. And no matter how strange it is to say this after
> 1800 years, it was my lot to discover these rules as if they
> were something new. Only when I understood these
> rules—only then did I understand the significance of Christ's
> teachings. These rules embrace the whole life of each man
> and of all mankind so amazingly that a man only need
> imagine fulfilling these rules on earth, and the Kingdom of
> Truth would come on earth. Then take each of these rules
> separately and apply them to yourself, and you will see that
> this inconceivably blissful and tremendous result follows
> from fulfilling the simplest, most natural easiest and most
> pleasant rules to fulfil. You may think: is it necessary to add
> anything to these rules to achieve the Kingdom of Truth?
> Nothing is needed. You may think: is it possible to reject one
> of these rules and not destroy the Kingdom of Truth? Impos-
> sible. If I knew nothing of Christ's teaching apart from these
> 5 rules, I would be just as much a Christian as I am now: (1)
> Do not be angry. (2) Do not fornicate. (3) Do not swear. (4)

Do not judge. (5) Do not make war. This is what the essence of Christ's teaching is for me.

Another writer, whose understanding of Christianity led her, like Tolstoy, to identify with the suffering of others, was the French philosopher Simone Weil. Her rich inner life, her mystical turn of mind, and her strong social conscience shine through all her letters to Father Perrin, and especially in this account (dated 15th May 1942) of how she came to understand the nature of what is inadequately translated as 'affliction', in French, *malheur*:

> . . . After my year in the factory, before going back to teaching, I had been taken by my parents to Portugal, and while there I left them to go alone to a little village. I was, as it were, in pieces, soul and body. That contact with affliction had killed my youth. Until then I had not had any experience of affliction, unless we count my own, which, as it was my own, seemed to me, to have little importance, and which moreover was only a partial affliction, being biological and not social. I knew quite well that there was a great deal of affliction in the world, I was obsessed with the idea, but I had not had prolonged and first-hand experience of it. As I worked in the factory, indistinguishable to all eyes, including my own, from the anonymous mass, the affliction of others entered into my flesh and my soul. Nothing separated me from it, for I had really forgotten my past and I looked forward to no future, finding it difficult to imagine the possibility of surviving all the fatigue. What I went through there marked me in so lasting a manner that still to-day when any human being, whoever he may be and in whatever circumstances, speaks to me without brutality, I cannot help having the impression that there must be a mistake and that unfortunately the mistake will in all probability disappear. There I received for ever the mark of a slave, like the branding of the red-hot iron which the Romans put on the foreheads of their most despised slaves. Since then I have always regarded myself as a slave.
>
> In this state of mind then, and in a wretched condition physically, I entered the little Portuguese village, which, alas, was very wretched too, on the very day of its patronal festival. I was alone. It was the evening and there was a full moon. It

was by the sea. The wives of the fishermen were going in procession to make a tour of all the ships, carrying candles and singing what must certainly be very ancient hymns of a heart-rending sadness. Nothing can give any idea of it. I have never heard anything so poignant unless it were the song of the boatmen on the Volga. There the conviction was suddenly borne in upon me that Christianity is pre-eminently the religion of slaves, that slaves cannot help belonging to it, and I among others.

In 1938 I spent ten days at Solesmes . . . There was a young English Catholic there from whom I gained my first idea of the supernatural power of the Sacraments because of the truly angelic radiance with which he seemed to be clothed after going to communion. Chance—for I always prefer saying chance rather than Providence—made of him a messenger to me. For he told me of the existence of those English poets of the seventeenth century who are named metaphysical. In reading them later on, I discovered the poem of which I read you what is unfortunately a very inadequate translation. It is called *Love* [by George Herbert]. I learnt it by heart. Often, at the culminating point of a violent headache, I make myself say it over, concentrating all my attention upon it and clinging with all my soul to the tenderness it enshrines. I used to think I was merely reciting it as a beautiful poem, but without my knowing it the recitation had the virtue of a prayer. It was during one of these recitations that, as I told you, Christ himself came down and took possession of me . . .

2

The Universal Soldier

At the outbreak of the First World War Henry James wrote the following portentous letter to Rhoda Broughton:

> . . . You and I, the ornaments of our generation, should have been spared this wreck of our belief that through the long years we had seen civilization grow and the worst become impossible. The tide that bore us along was then all the while moving to *this* as its grand Niagara—yet what a blessing we didn't know it. It seems to me to *undo* everything, everything that was ours, in the most horrible retroactive way—but I avert my face from the monstrous scene!—you can hate it and blush for it without my help; we can each do enough of that by ourselves. The country and the season here are of a beauty of peace, and loveliness of light, and summer grace, that make it inconceivable that just across the Channel, blue as *paint* today, the fields of France and Belgium are being, or about to be, given up to unthinkable massacre and misery. One is ashamed to admire, to enjoy, to take any of the normal pleasure, and the huge shining indifference of Nature strikes a chill to the heart and makes me wonder of what abysmal mystery or villainy indeed, such a cruel smile is the expression . . .

In contrast to Henry James, Dostoevsky wrote in praise of war in 1870, viewing it as a purgative for a society grown corrupt and stagnant:

> With your views on war I can't possibly agree. Without war, people grow torpid in riches and comfort, and lose the power of thinking and feeling nobly; they get brutal, and fall back into barbarism. I am not speaking of individuals, but of whole races. Without pain, one comprehends not joy. Ideals

are purified by suffering, as gold is by fire. Mankind must strive for his Heaven. France has of late become brutalized and degraded. A passing trial will do her no harm; France will be able to endure it, and then will awake to a new life, and new ideas. But hitherto France has been dominated on the one hand by old formulas, and on the other by craven-heartedness and pleasure-seeking.

The Napoleonic dynasty will be impossible henceforth. New life and reformation of the country are so important that even the bitterest trials are nothing by comparison. Do you not recognize God's hand in it?

Also our politics of the last seventy years—I mean Russian, European, and German politics—must inevitably alter. The Germans will at last show us their real faces. Everywhere in Europe great changes must inevitably come—and of their own accord.

What new life will be called forth everywhere by this mighty shock! For want of great conceptions, even science has sunk into arid materialism; what does a passing blow signify in face of that?

Tolstoy's view of war differs markedly from that of Dostoevsky. Instead of complacently regarding wars as part of the cleansing forces in history, he sees them as the inevitable end product of perverted Christianity and socio-economic pressures. He is writing to Prince Volkonsky about the Boer War:

. . . when people tell me that one side is solely to blame in any war that flares up, I can never agree. You may admit that one of the sides acts worse, but an analysis of which one it is that acts worse doesn't explain even the immediate cause of the origin of such a terrible, cruel and inhuman phenomenon as war. To any man who doesn't shut his eyes to them, these causes are perfectly obvious, as they are now with the Boer War and with all wars which have happened recently. These causes are three: first—the unequal distribution of property, i.e. the robbery of some people by others; second—the existence of a military class, i.e. people brought up and intended for murder; and third—false, and for the most part deliberately deceitful religious teaching, on which young generations are forcibly brought up. And so I think that it's not only useless but harmful to see the cause of wars in the

Chamberlains, the Wilhelms etc., and thereby conceal from
oneself the real causes which are far more immediate and to
which we ourselves are a party.

We can only be angry with the Chamberlains and the
Wilhelms and abuse them; but our anger and abuse will only
spoil our blood, not change the course of things: the Chamberlains and the Wilhelms are blind instruments of forces
which lie a long way behind them. They act as they have to
act, and can't act otherwise. All history is a series of just such
acts by all politicians as the Boer War, and so it's completely
useless, even impossible, to be angry with them and condemn
them, when you see the true causes of their activity and when
you feel that you yourself are to blame for this or that activity
of theirs according to your attitude to the three basic causes I
mentioned. As long as we go on enjoying exceptional wealth
while the masses of the people are ground down by hard
work there will always be wars for markets, goldmines etc.,
which we need in order to support our exceptional wealth.
Wars will be all the more inevitable as long as we are a party to
a military class, tolerate its existence, and don't fight against it
with all our powers. We ourselves either serve in the army, or
regard it as not only necessary but commendable, and then
when war breaks out we condemn some Chamberlain or
other for it. But the main thing is that there will be war as long
as we not only preach it but tolerate without anger and
indignation that perversion of Christianity which is called
ecclesiastical Christianity whereby it is possible to have a
Christ-loving army, the blessing of guns and the acceptance of
war as an act justified by Christianity. We teach *our children*
this religion, we profess it ourselves and then say—some of
us that Chamberlain and others that Kruger—is to blame for
the fact that people kill one another.

When the fervour of those who sent him has waned, the
fighting man is left all too often to extricate himself from the
mess that the politicians and public enthusiasm have got him
into. No wonder that a grim ardour for cracking skulls has
sustained many ordinary, and sometimes involuntary, soldiers
through the ages. In the following letter a press-ganged sailor
writes home at the outbreak of the War of Jenkins' Ear,
ostensibly caused by the maltreatment by the Spanish of a
British sea captain in 1739. The real issue was the British desire

to break the monopoly that the Spaniards had of trade with South America. The admiral referred to is Admiral Vernon.

> *My Dear Life,*—
> When I left you, hevens noes it was with an akin hart for i thout it very hard to be hault from you by a gang of rufins but hover i soon overcome that when I found that we were about to go in earnest to rite my natif contry and against a parcel of impadent Spaniards by whom I have often been ill treted and god nows my hearrt I have longed this four years past to cut of some of their ears and was in hopes i should haf sent you one for a sample now but our good Admiral God bless him was to merciful we have taken Port Belo with such coridge and bravery that I never saw before for my own part my heart was rased to the clouds and woud ha scaled the moon had a Spaniard been ther to come at him as we did the Batry. Jack Cox is my mesmate you know he was always a havy ased dog and sleepy headed but had you seen him clime the Wals of Batry you woud never forget him for a cat coud not xceed him in nimbleness and so in short it was with all of us i belefe i myself cod now overcum ten Spanards for i remember when I was in Spain that the Spanards called the English Galen den mare but we shall now make them kno that we are the Cox of the Seas for our Admiral is of true game breed had you se us english Salor now what altration what contnances what bravry can xceed us tha tell us we shall meet a french squadron by ann by but i wish it may be so And by G-d well jurch him.

An interesting recent example of an abrupt change from exuberant optimism to disillusionment and anger may be seen in the letters home of David Tinker RN written during the Falklands Campaign of 1982. Tinker was the son of a distinguished public servant Hugh Tinker, whose politics were considerably to the left of his son's; his father had misgivings about the expedition from the beginning for intellectual and moral reasons, but his son was initially enthusiastic and confident, as the following extract shows:

> . . . The news on the war front is more and more exciting. The Argentinian Fleet putting to sea, so we might get a chance to sink them (although I doubt that they'll venture outside

Argentinian coastal waters). Twenty RAF ground attack Harriers coming on the next container ship (as opposed to ours, which are interceptors). More troops coming in the *Uganda*. And tons of ships coming in a month's time, including *Illustrious* (our *third* aircraft carrier) which hasn't even done the Portland work-up yet. And the French are going to provide air-launched Exocet missiles (*the* missile we are scared of from the Argentinians: twenty miles range, sea-skimming, and almost invulnerable) for our helicopters to carry: in addition to 'Sea-Skuas' for our Lynx helicopters. This wasn't due to enter service until 1985, and is even better than Exocet. Ho ho ho: spend lots of government money, depress the pound, put up inflation: what fun! Man is the most extraordinary animal.

I cannot believe that the Argentinians will want to fight with all this lot coming against them. Already they look to be in danger of spending all their foreign currency reserves and losing all ability to obtain loans in the western world. Surely they must give in soon: hopefully, over the weekend, and then we can all go home.

A letter to his father written a month later off the Falkland Islands, illustrates the transformation of his attitude:

Your long marvellous letter of 6 May arrived today via HMS *Leeds Castle* (a most inappropriate name for a ship!) which is acting as postman between us and Ascension Island. It was like a breath of sanity coming into this totally mad world here. I am glad that you think that way about Mrs Thatcher and the war—as I have come to think since this business started. I sometimes wonder if I am totally odd in that I utterly oppose all this killing that is going on over a flag. Wilfred Owen wrote that 'There'll come a day when men make war on death for lives, not men for flags', but it has been the reverse here—'nations trek from progress' still.

It is quite easy to see how the war has come about; Mrs Thatcher imagined she was Churchill defying Hitler, and the Navy advised a quick war before the winter set in; the Navy chiefs also wanted maximum use made of the Navy for maximum publicity to reverse the Navy cuts: which has happened. For (utmost) worth, victory or defeat would have the same result; publicity and popular support, either congratulations or sympathy. The Navy thus overlooked the fact that we were fighting without all the necessary air cover which is provided by the USA in the Atlantic and by the RAF in the North Sea and Icelandic Sea. Although the Harrier is a marvellous little aircraft it is not a proper strike aircraft, and the best the Navy could get when carriers were 'abolished'. Consequently we have no proper carriers which can launch early-warning aircraft fitted with radar as strike aircraft. From the Fifties onwards these two were absolute essentials.

However, the Navy felt that we were British and they (the Argentinians) were wogs, and that would make all the difference. The Admiral said as much to us on [the task force] TV. Consequently, we have no way of spotting low level attacks beyond 20 miles, which is how *Sheffield* was sunk. In a grandiose statement after the *Sheffield* loss, Nott stated that the Nimrod aircraft (early warning) and more Seawolf Type 22 frigates (which can shoot down Exocet) would be sent to the Falklands to counter this situation. Total lies! There is only one more Type 22 frigate and Nimrods have not appeared— even if fitted with in-flight refuelling gear it would be a difficult job for them. The only way we can counter these missiles is to keep out of range, which is what we have had to do.

Apart from the military fiasco the political side is even more disgraceful. Even if Britain does reconquer the Falklands we still have to talk to the Argentinians and come to some arrangement, so why not settle before a war has devastated the Falklanders' Island?

In contrast to the questioning and sometimes firmly dissenting stance of a well-informed Naval Officer on active service in 1982, the next letter shows the soldier as dedicated victim. The writer was Ichizo Hayashi, a Japanese kamikaze pilot killed in an attack on the American fleet in the Pacific in 1945. He was twenty-four when he died. He wrote the letter to his mother just before his mission, and his chief preoccupation is that his mother should 'forgive' him—presumably for deserting her, but also for some implied resistance to an arranged marriage which she had been negotiating. It will be seen from the letter that Hayashi was a very devout Christian who takes courage from his religion in the performance of his duty. This fact should give pause to those belligerent clerics who are quick to enlist the Almighty's exclusive support for their side in the prosecution of wars.

Mother,

The time has come when I must give you sad news.

You love me more than I will ever be able to love you. What will you think of this letter? I am desperately sorry.

I have been really happy; perhaps I was too spoilt. But it is not my fault. I loved you, and it was so nice to be petted by you.

I am glad that I was selected as a pilot of a 'specialized attack' group, but I can hardly restrain my tears when I think of you.

You did all you could to educate me, to help me to face the future. I am very sad that I must die without having given you anything in exchange—neither happiness nor serenity. I can hardly ask you to make the sacrifice of my life as well, nor to take pride in my death, however glorious it may be. It is better that I should not speak of all that to you.

I never dared to refuse the young girl you intended me to marry. I did not want to lose your affection, and I was so happy to receive your letters.

I would have loved to see you once again and to go to sleep in your arms. But the only place where I could have met you is Moji. For the day after tomorrow I must leave, the day after tomorrow I must die.

It is possible that I shall fly over Hakata. I will bid you farewell in silence from above the clouds. Mother, you used to dream of a splendid future for me, and I am going to disappoint you. I shall never forget your anxiety when I had to pass the examination. I joined this group in spite of your disapproval, but I can see now that I would have done better to follow your advice.

Try to comfort yourself by remembering that I am a very good pilot, and that it is very rare that a member of the air force with so few hours in the air to his credit is chosen for such a mission.

When I am dead, you will still have Makio. You preferred me because I was the elder, but believe me, Makio is worth far more than I. He is very good at looking after all the family interests. You will also have my sisters Chiyoko and Hiroko, and your grandchildren.

Cheer up. My soul will always be near you. Your joys will be mine, but if you are sad, I shall be sorrowful too.

Sometimes I feel tempted to come back to you, but that would be a cowardly action.

When I was baptized the priest said these words over me: 'Renounce your own self.' I can remember that very well. I will commit my soul to our Saviour before I die, pierced by American bullets. For everything is in God's hands. There is neither life nor death for those who live in God. Jesus Himself has said: 'Thy will be done.'

I read the Bible every day. Then I feel very close to you. When I crash to my death, I shall have the Bible and the Book of Psalms in my aircraft. I will also take along the mission badge which the director of the college gave me, and your medal.

Perhaps I did not take that marriage business as seriously as I should have done. I would not like to give the impression that I lacked respect for my betrothed and her family. Could you make her understand that it is better to make an end. I would really have liked to marry her: I would gladly have given you that happiness. I did not have time. I ask only one thing of you: that you should forgive me. But I can go in peace, for I know that you always forgive me. Mother, how I admire you! You have always been so much braver than I. You are capable of forcing yourself to do painful things, and I find it impossible. Your only fault is that you spoilt me too much. But I myself wanted you to do so and I do not reproach you for that.

When I crash on to the enemy I will pray for you that all your prayers may be granted. I have asked Ueno to bring you this letter, but you must never show it to anybody. I am ashamed of it. I have the impression that it is not I whom death is waiting for. When I think that I shall never see you again, I am overcome with grief.

The loyalties which brought about Hayashi's act of blind self-destruction can sometimes be suspended. A memorable instance of this happening was during the First World War, when a Christmas truce produced a period of spontaneous fraternization between the two sides. Captain Sir Edward Hulse of the Scots Guards wrote to his mother on 28 December 1914 describing the extraordinary scenes he had just witnessed. He shows himself an open-minded sensitive man whose unwavering devotion to military duty is tempered by an understanding of the incomprehension of ordinary troops as to the purpose of the war. He also availed himself of the opportunity to gather as

much intelligence concerning the enemy's capability as he
could:

Just returned to billets again, after the most extraordinary
Christmas in the trenches you could possibly imagine. Words
fail me completely in trying to describe it, but here goes!
On the 23rd we took over the trenches in the ordinary
manner, relieving the Grenadiers, and during the 24th the
usual firing took place, and sniping was pretty brisk. We
stood to arms as usual at 6.30 A.M. on the 25th and I noted that
there was not much shooting; this gradually died down, and
by 8 A.M. there was no shooting at all, except for a few shots
on our left (Border Regt.). At 8.30 A.M. I was looking out, and
saw four Germans leave their trenches and come towards us; I
told two of my men to go and meet them, unarmed (as the
Germans were unarmed), and to see that they did not pass
the half-way line. We were 350–400 yards apart, at this point.
My fellows were not very keen, not knowing what was up, so
I went out alone, and met Barry, one of our ensigns, also
coming out from another part of the line. By the time we got
to them, they were ¾ of the way over, and much too near our
barbed wire, so I moved them back. They were three private
soldiers and a stretcher-bearer, and their spokesman started
off by saying that he thought it only right to come over and
wish us a Happy Christmas, and trusted us implicitly to keep
the truce. He came from Suffolk where he had left his best girl
and a 3½ H.P. motor-bike! He told me that he could not get a
letter to the girl, and wanted to send one through me. I made
him write out a postcard in front of me, in English, and I sent
it off that night. I told him that she probably would not be a bit
keen to see him again. We then entered on a long discussion
on every sort of thing. I was dressed in an old stocking-cap
and a man's overcoat, and they took me for a corporal, a thing
which I did not discourage, as I had an eye to going as near
their lines as possible . . . I asked them what orders they had
from their officers as to coming over to us, and they said *none*;
they had just come over out of good will.
They protested that they had no feeling of enmity towards
us at all, but that everything lay with their authorities, and
that being soldiers they had to obey. I believe that they were
speaking the truth when they said this, and that they never
wished to fire a shot again. They said that unless directly

ordered, they were not going to shoot again until we did . . .
We talked about the ghastly wounds made by rifle bullets,
and we both agreed that neither of us used dum-dum bullets,
and that the wounds are solely inflicted by the high-velocity
bullet with the sharp nose, at short range. We both agreed
that it would be far better if we used the old South African
round-nosed bullet, which makes a clean hole . . .

They think that our Press is to blame in working up feeling
against them by publishing false 'atrocity reports'. I told them
of various sweet little cases which I have seen for myself, and
they told me of English prisoners whom they have seen with
soft-nosed bullets, and lead bullets with notches but in the
nose; we had a heated, and at the same time, good-natured
argument, and ended by hinting to each other that the other
was lying!

I kept it up for half an hour, and then escorted them back as
far as their barbed wire, having a jolly good look round all the
time, and picking up various little bits of information which I
had not had an opportunity of doing under fire! I left
instructions with them that if any of them came out later they
must not come over the half-way line, and appointed a ditch
as the meeting place. We parted after an exchange of Albany
cigarettes and German cigars, and I went straight to H.-qrs. to
report.

On my return at 10 AM I was surprised to hear a hell of a
din going on, and not a single man left in my trenches; they
were completely denuded (against my orders), and nothing
lived! I heard strains of 'Tipperary' floating down the
breeze, swiftly followed by a tremendous burst of 'Deutsch-
land über Alles', and as I got to my own Coy H.-qrs. dug-
out, I saw, to my amazement, not only a crowd of about 150
British and Germans at the half-way house which I had
appointed opposite my lines, but six or seven such crowds,
all the way down our lines, extending towards the 8th
Division on our right. I bustled out and asked if there were
any German officers in my crowd, and the noise died down
(as this time I was myself in my own cap and badges of
rank).

I found two, but had to talk to them through an interpreter,
as they could neither talk English nor French . . . I explained
to them that strict orders must be maintained as to meeting
half-way, and everyone unarmed; and we both agreed not to

fire until the other did, thereby creating a complete deadlock
and armistice (if strictly observed) . . .

. . . From foul rain and wet, the weather had cleared up the
night before to a sharp frost, and it was a perfect day,
everything white, and the silence seemed extraordinary, after
the usual din. From all sides birds seemed to arrive, and we
hardly ever see a bird generally. Later in the day I fed about 50
sparrows outside my dug-out, which shows how complete
the silence and quiet was.

The First World War, and particularly the disillusionment so
powerfully expressed by the brilliant generation of poets who
emerged at that time, radically changed people's attitudes to
war in general. The utter wastage of human life for objectives
which were dimly perceived and doubtfully attainable outraged
and disgusted some of the most heroic and loyal of the participants. Siegfried Sassoon threw his Military Cross into the
mouth of the river Mersey in a gesture that summed up what
many felt who could not express their feelings for themselves.
While Sassoon concentrated his verse in fiercely satirical attacks
on the complacency and incompetence of staff officers and the
attitudes of those who attempted to dignify the war with
religious sanction and simplistic patriotism, Wilfred Owen
deepened the perspective by evoking the horror of war as a
means of trying to solve the problems of humanity or advance
political aims. Both Sassoon and Owen were homosexual and
the latter was particularly under the influence of his mother to
whom so many of his letters from the front were written. The
letter, dated May 1917, quoted below is to her:

41st Stationary Hospital
Already I have comprehended a light which will never filter
into the dogma of any national church; namely that one of
Christ's essential commands was: Passivity at any price!
Suffer dishonour and disgrace; but never resort to arms. Be
bullied, be outraged, be killed; but do not kill. It may be a
chimerical and an ignominious principle, but there it is. It can
only be ignored: and I think pulpit professionals are ignoring
it very skilfully and successfully indeed.
Have you seen what ridiculous figures Frederick and
Arthur Wood [two contemporary evangelists] are cutting? If

they made the Great Objection, I should admire them. They have not the courage.

. . . But I must not malign these Brethren because I do not know their exact Apologia.

And am I not myself a conscientious objector with a very seared conscience?

. . . Christ is literally in no man's land. There men often hear His voice: Greater love hath no man than this, that a man lay down his life—for a friend.

Is it spoken in English only and French?

I do not believe so.

Thus you see how pure Christianity will not fit in with pure patriotism.

One of the official artists appointed to record the war was Paul Nash. In the following letter to his wife he conveys his helplessness in the face of such carnage and devastation as defied pen or brush to describe:

> . . . I have just returned, last night, from a visit to Brigade Headquarters up the line, and I shall not forget it as long as I live. I have seen the most frightful nightmare of a country more conceived by Dante or Poe than by nature, unspeakable, utterly indescribable. In the fifteen drawings I have made I may give you some vague idea of its horror, but only being in it and of it can ever make you sensible of its dreadful nature and of what our men in France have to face. We all have a vague notion of the terrors of a battle, and can conjure up with the aid of some of the more inspired war correspondents and the pictures in the *Daily Mirror* some vision of a battlefield; but no pen or drawing can convey this country—the normal setting of the battles taking place day and night, month after month. Evil and the incarnate fiend alone can be master of this war, and no glimmer of God's hand is seen anywhere. Sunset and sunrise are blasphemous, they are mockeries to man, only the black rain out of the bruised and swollen clouds all through the bitter black of night is fit atmosphere in such a land. The rain drives on, the stinking mud becomes more evilly yellow, the shell holes fill up with green-white water, the roads and tracks are covered in inches of slime, the black dying trees ooze and sweat and the shells never cease. They alone plunge overhead, tearing away the

rotting-tree stumps, breaking the plank roads, striking down horses and mules, annihilating, maiming, maddening, they plunge into the grave which is this land; one huge grave, and cast up on it the poor dead. It is unspeakable, godless, hopeless. I am no longer an artist interested and curious, I am a messenger who will bring back word from the men who are fighting to those who want the war to go on for ever. Feeble, inarticulate, will be my message, but it will have a bitter truth, and may it burn their lousy souls.

The associations of glory and honour that are traditionally attached to war were easier to sustain when wars could be won in a convincing manner, and when not all victories were pyrrhic ones. Britain's most celebrated general who gave it its most celebrated and decisive victory on land was the Duke of Wellington. A brilliant soldier and a man of humour and humanity, Wellington expresses himself forcibly and pithily in his letters. Like most commanders in the field he suffered from the indecisiveness and penny-pinching shortsightedness of governments at home. In a letter to Sir W. W. Pole, written when Wellington was commanding during the Peninsular Campaign in Portugal and Spain of 1808 to 1813, he complains with grim sarcasm of the Government's apparent belief that he could get on perfectly well without money for the troops, let alone adequate equipment. However, Wellington deployed his limited forces so cunningly during the course of the war that in the end some 300,000 of Napoleon's troops were tied down in the Iberian peninsula. One of his strategies was to employ small groups of Spanish and Portuguese troops to fight widely dispersed campaigns. These gave rise to the term *guerrilla*, Spanish for 'little war', a concept with which we are now all too familiar:

> . . . I think you are mistaken respecting the facility with which an army could get on without money. Your reasoning is applicable only to the pay of the troops, which is but a small part of the expense which must be defrayed in money. But the necessity of paying in money the officers and soldiers of an army cannot be measured by the necessity of paying in money the officers and seamen of a fleet. First, the rations of the soldier are not sufficient for his subsistence for any great length of time. Secondly, all his necessaries are bought and paid for out of his daily subsistence, and there is the greatest

distress, as well for some descriptions of food not issued by
the commissary, as for necessaries when the pay is not issued.
In the same manner the officers of the army cannot live upon
their rations alone, and they, as well as the soldiers, must be
paid, or they must do as the French do, that is, plunder in
order to be able to get on at all.

I think, however, that measures might be adopted to
increase our supplies of specie in this country; but since
government have taken this subject into their own hands, and
have sent here a gentleman to make their own inquiries and
arrangements upon the subjects, I have given myself no
further trouble about it.

. . . I acknowledge that I doubt whether the government (I
mean the existing administration of England) have the power,
or the inclination, or the nerves to do all that ought to be done
to carry the contest on as it might be. I am the commander of
the British army without any of the patronage or power that
an officer in that situation has always had. I have remons-
trated against this system, but in vain. Then I am the
mainspring of all the other operations, but it is because I am
Lord Wellington; for I have neither influence nor support, nor
means of acquiring influence, given to me by the government.
I have not authority to give a shilling, or a stand of arms, or a
round of musket ammunition to anybody. I do give all, it is
true; but it is contrary to my instructions, and at my peril . . .

Wellington's subsequent victory at Waterloo crowned his
achievements in the struggle against Napoleon. Thomas
Creevey was at the famous ball three nights before the battle
where the Iron Duke displayed his sang-froid, imperturbably
participating in the festivities. Creevey also managed to interview Wellington immediately after the victory, a journalistic
coup which he hastened to record in a letter home:

About eleven o'clock, upon going out again, I heard a
report that the Duke was in Bruxelles; and I went from
curiosity to see whether there was any appearance of him or
any of his staff at his residence in the Park. As I approached, I
saw people collected in the street about the house; and when I
got amongst them, the first thing I saw was the Duke upstairs
alone at his window. Upon his recognising me, he immediately beckoned to me with his finger to come up.

I met Lord Arthur Hill in the ante-room below, who, after shaking hands and congratulation, told me I could not go up to the Duke, as he was then occupied in writing his dispatch; but as I had been invited, I of course proceeded. The first thing I did, of course, was to put out my hand and congratulate him (the Duke) upon his victory. He made a variety of observations in his short, natural, blunt way, but with the greatest gravity all the time, and without the least approach to anything like triumph or joy.—'It has been a damned serious business,' he said. 'Blücher and I have lost 30,000 men. It has been a damned nice thing—the nearest run thing you ever saw in your life.'

'Nothing,' adds Creevey in the same letter, 'could do a conqueror more honour than his gravity and seriousness at the loss of lives he had sustained, his admission of his great danger, and the justice he did his enemy.'

Also fortunate in winning battles, though it cost him his life, was Admiral Nelson. Like Wellington he coupled strategic ability with concern for the men who served under him. The affection in which he was held is well illustrated in a contemporary letter home from an English seaman after the Battle of Trafalgar:

Honoured Father,
    This comes to tell you I am alive and hearty except three fingers; but that's not much, it might have been my head. I told brother Tom I should like to see a deadly battle, and I have seen one, and we have peppered the Combined rarely: and for the matter of that, they fought us pretty tightish for French and Spanish. Three of our mess are killed, and four more of us winged. But to tell you the truth of it, when the game began, I wished myself at Warnborough with my plough again; but when they had given us one duster, and I found myself snug and tight, I set to in good earnest, and thought no more about being killed than if I were at Murrell Green Fair, and I was presently as busy and as black as a collier. How my fingers got knocked overboard I don't know, but off they are, and I never missed them till I wanted them. You see, by my writing, it was my left hand, so I can write to you and fight for my King yet. We have taken a rare parcel of

ships, but the wind is so rough we cannot bring them home,
else I should roll in money, so we are busy smashing 'em, and
blowing 'em up wholesale.

Our dear Admiral Nelson is killed! so we have paid pretty
sharply for licking 'em. I never set eyes on him for which I am
both sorry and glad; for, to be sure, I should like to have seen
him—but then, all the men in our ship who have seen him are
such soft toads, they have done nothing but blast their eyes,
and cry, ever since he was killed. God bless you! chaps that
fought like the devil, sit down and cry like a wench . . .

SAM

The affection that the greatest commanders have inspired in
their men is also illustrated in a letter from Pietro Aretino from
Mantua to Francesco degli Albizi in Florence. He is describing
the heroic death in December 1526 of Giovanni delle Bande Nere
(Giovanni de Medici). Giovanni was a relation of the Florentine
Medicis and a noted *condottiere*, a mercenery soldier of the type
much in evidence in Renaissance Italy. He was fatally wounded
on the River Po defending Italian territory against the advancing
imperial forces. His sacrifice was in vain, for a year later the
same forces reached Rome and sacked the city, killing 4,000
inhabitants, looting art treasures, and imprisoning Pope Cle-
ment VII in Castel Sant'Angelo. The 'end of the Renaissance' is
often said to be marked by this disaster:

At the approach of the hour that the fates with the consent
of God had prescribed for the end of our prince, his Highness
moved with his habitual fury against Governolo on whose
circumference the enemy was entrenched; and as he moved to
the attack near some lime-kilns, suddenly , alas, he was shot
by a musket in the leg which had previously been wounded
by an arquebus. And no sooner had he felt the blow, than the
army was seized by fear and melancholy, and in every heart
all ardour and joy were extinguished. Everyone, forgetful of
himself, wept over what had happened, and railed against
Chance for senselessly killing such an excellent and noble
general, incomparable in any century of remembrance, on the
threshold of such tremendous events and at the time of Italy's
greatest need.

. . . and as they talked about his far-sighted genius and
shrewdness of mind, they warmed with the heat of their

discussion the unwontedly heavy snow which fell as he was borne in a litter to the house of Signor Luigi Gonzaga in Mantua.

That very evening he was visited there by the Duke of Urbino, who loved him as much as he was loved himself, and respected him so highly for his great merits that he feared even to speak in his presence. As soon as he saw him he was visibly comforted; and the Duke, seizing his opportunity, said with great sincerity:

'It is not enough for you to be famous and glorious in the profession of arms. You must enhance this reputation of yours by practising the religion under whose rules we live.' Knowing that the Duke spoke these words because he wanted him to make his confession, he replied:

'As I have in all things always done my duty, if needs be I shall do it in this as well.' And then, after the Duke left, he started to talk with me, and he called for Lucantonio with great affection; but when I said 'We will send for him;' he added: 'Would you wish a man like him to desert the war to gaze on the sick?'

Then he recalled the Count of San Secondo, saying: 'If only he were here to take my place.'

At times he scratched his head with his fingers; then he put them to his mouth, saying: 'What will happen?' and he kept repeating: 'I have never done anything ignoble.'

Giovanni the mercenary was a not untypical victim of the dynastic wars of his time. Only twelve years previously Erasmus had written with cool perspicacity to his friend Anthony Bergen demythologizing the whole sordid business of killing in the name of patriotism, when the real issue was territorial greed.

. . . But suppose, you will say, the other side refuses to yield to the decision of good men; in that case what would you have me do? In the first place, if you are a true Christian, I would have you bear and forbear, disregarding that right of yours, whatever it may be. And in the next place, if you are only a wise man, pray calculate what the vindication of your right will cost you. If the cost is excessive, and it will surely be so, when you assert it by arms, do not then insist upon your title, perhaps, unfounded, after all, at the cost of so much misery to mankind, of so many killed, so many orphans, so many tears. What do you suppose the Turks think when they hear that Christian princes are raging with so much fury against each other, and that only for the title of sovereignty? Italy is now delivered from the French, and what has been the effect of so much bloodshed, but that where a Frenchman was in office before, somone else is in office now? And the country flourished better before than it does now!

If there are any rights which admit of being defended by war, they are rights of a grosser kind, which savour of a Christianity already becoming degenerate and burdened with the wealth of this world; and I know not whether I should sanction such wars; though I see that war is sometimes not disapproved by pious authors, when for the maintenance of the faith, the peace of Christendom is defended against the invasion of barbarians. But why should we dwell on these few human authorities, rather than on those many sayings of Christ, of the apostles, and of the orthodox and most approved Fathers on the subject of peace and the tolerance of evils? What policy is there that may not in some way be defended, especially when the persons who have the conduct of affairs are those whose very crimes are praised by many for the sake of flattery, while no one dares to find fault with their errors? But in the meantime it is not unknown what are the sighs and longings and prayers of reasonable men. But if you look a little closely, you will find that it is generally the private interests of princes that give occasion to war.

RULERS AND VICTIMS

1

A Few Royal Occasions

The problem of how to behave in the presence of royalty is not one that affects very many of us, but for those who need to know such things, Fanny Burney set out the following guidelines in a letter to her mother dated 17 December 1785. Fanny Burney, the author of *Evelina* and a famous diary, was appointed Second Keeper of the Robes to Queen Charlotte in 1786 and was initially unnerved by being pursued around the Royal gardens by the alarming figure of George III. However, he only wanted to converse with her.

. . . Now then to the etiquette. I inquired into every particular, that no error might be committed. And as there is no saying what may happen in this mortal life, I shall give you those instructions I have received myself, that should you find yourself in the royal presence, you may know how to comport yourself.
Directions for Coughing, Sneezing, or Moving, before the King and Queen.

In the first place, you must not cough. If you find a cough tickling in your throat, you must arrest it from making any sound; if you find yourself choking with the forbearance, you must choke—but not cough.

In the second place, you must not sneeze. If you have a vehement cold, you must take no notice of it; if your nose-membranes feel a great irritation, you must hold your breath; if a sneeze still insists upon making its way, you must oppose it, by keeping your teeth grinding together; if the violence of the repulse breaks some blood-vessel, you must break a blood-vessel,—but not sneeze.

In the third place, you must not, upon any account, stir either hand or foot. If, by chance, a black pin runs into your head, you must not take it out. If the pain is very great, you must be sure to bear it without wincing; if it brings the tears into your eyes, you must not wipe them off; if they give you a tingling by running down your cheeks, you must look as if nothing was the matter. If the blood should gush from your head, by means of the black pin, you must let it gush; if you are uneasy, to think of making such a blurred appearance, you must be uneasy, but you must say nothing about it. If, however, the agony is very great you may, privately, bite the inside of your cheek, or of your lips, for a little relief, taking care, meanwhile, to do it so cautiously as to make no apparent dent outwardly. And with that precaution, if you even gnaw a piece out, it will not be minded, only be sure either to swallow it, or commit it to a corner of the inside of your mouth till they are gone—for you must not spit.

I have many other directions, but no more paper; I will endeavour, however, to have them ready for you in time . . .

A more relaxed approach to a royal interview was taken by Stevie Smith when she went to collect the Queen's Gold Medal for Poetry in 1969. The 'Patricia' addressed is fellow poetess Patricia Beer:

> *Dear Patricia,*
> Thank you so much for your letter & congratulations. I *am* very pleased & surprised too! I went & collected it on Friday & enjoyed that very much too. One walks miles over pink carpets & H.M. is very gracious—& pretty. I rather liked the slightly giggly time I had first with the lady-in-waiting & a very decorative young man. Everything had got a bit late so it was rather longer than meant before I finally took my turn & then I had about 20 minutes alone with the Queen. The questions she asked rather kept us on the subject of poetry & I could not help feeling it wasn't *absolutely* her *very* favourite subject . . .
>
> Yours ever,
> STEVIE

Thomas Carlyle, in his amusing account in 1869 of meeting Queen Victoria, combines affection with some irreverence in describing his distinguished fellow author, whose modest demeanour he applauds:

. . . 'Interview' took place this day gone a week; nearly a week before that, the Dean and Dean*ess* (who is called Lady Augusta Stanley, once Bruce, an active hand and busy little woman) drove up here in a solemnly mysterious, though half quizzical manner, invited me for Thursday, 4th, 5 P.M.:—must come, a very 'high or indeed highest person has long been desirous', etc. etc. I saw well enough it was the Queen incognita; and briefly agreed to come. 'Half-past 4 COME *you*!' and then went their ways.

Walking up at the set time, I was then ushered into a long drawing-room in their monastic edifice. I found no Stanley there; only at the farther end, a tall old Gearpole[1] of a Mrs Grote,—the most wooden woman I know in London or the world, who thinks herself very clever, etc.,—the sight of whom taught me to expect others; as accordingly, in a few minutes, fell out. Grote and wife, Sir Charles Lyell and ditto, Browning and myself, were I saw to be our party. 'Better than bargain! These will take the edge off the thing, if edge it have!' which it hadn't, nor threatened to have.

The Stanleys and we were all in a flow of talk, and some flunkies had done setting coffee-pots, tea-cups of sublime patterns, when Her Majesty punctual to a minute, glided softly in, escorted by her Dame in Waiting (a Dowager Duchess of Athol) and by the Princess Louise, decidedly a very pretty young lady, and *clever* too, as I found in speaking to her afterwards.

The Queen came softly forward, a kindly little smile on her face; gently acknowledged with a nod the silent deep bow of us male monsters; and directly in her presence everybody was as if at ease again. She is a comely little lady with a pair of kind, clear, and intelligent grey eyes; still looks plump and almost young (in spite of one broad wrinkle that shows in each cheek *occasionally*); has a fine low voice; soft indeed her whole manner is and melodious perfect; it is impossible to image a *politer* little woman—nothing the least imperious; all gentle, all *sincere*-looking; unembarrassing, rather attractive even;—*makes* you feel too (if you have sense in you) that she is Queen . . .

. . . coffee (very black and muddy) was handed round; Queen and three women taking seats in opposite corners, Mrs

---

[1] An Irish weaver's implement.

Grote in a chair *intrusively close* to Majesty, Lady Lyell modestly at the *diagonal* corner; we others obliged to stand, and
hover within call. Coffee fairly done, Lady Augusta called me
gently to 'Come and speak with Her Majesty'. I obeyed, first
asking, as an old and infirmish man, Majesty's permission to
sit, which was graciously conceded. Nothing of the least
significance was said, nor *needed*: however, my bit of dialogue
went very well. 'What part of Scotland I came from?' 'Dum-
fries-shire (where Majesty might as well go some time);
Carlisle, *i.e. Caer-Lewal*, a place about the antiquity of King
Solomon (according to Milton, whereat Majesty smiled); Bor-
der-Ballads (and even old Jamie Pool slightly alluded to,—not
by name!) Glasgow, and even Grandfather's ride thither,—
ending in mere *psalms*, and street *vacant* at half-past nine
P.M.;—hard sound and genuine Presbyterian *root* of what has
now shot up to be such a monstrous ugly cabbage-tree and
Hemlock-tree!' all which Her Majesty seemed to take rather
well.

Whereupon Mrs Grote rose, and good naturedly brought
forward her Husband to her own chair, *cheek by jowl* with Her
Majesty, who evidently did not care a straw for him, but
kindly asked. 'Writing anything?' and one heard 'Aristotle,
now that I have done with Plato,' etc. etc.—but only for a
minimum of time. Majesty herself (I think apropos of some
question of my *shaking hand*) said something about her own
difficulty in writing by dictation, which brought forward Lady
Lyell and husband, naturally used to the operation—after
which, talk becoming trivial, Majesty gracefully retired,—
Lady Augusta with her,—and in ten minutes more, returned
to receive our farewell bows; which, too, she did very prettily;
and sailed out as if moving on skates, and bending her head
towards us with a smile.

Equally delightful is Felix Mendelssohn's letter to his mother
dated 19 July 1842 in which he describes a musical soirée with
the Queen and her consort:

    . . . the details of my last visit to Buckingham Palace I must
write you at once because they will amuse you so much, and
me, too. As Grahl says—and it is true—the only friendly
English house, one that is really comfortable and where one
feels at ease, is Buckingham Palace—as a matter of fact, I

know several others, but on the whole, I agree with him. Joking apart, Prince Albert had asked me to go to him on Saturday at two o'clock, so that I might try his organ before I left England. I found him all alone; and as we were talking away, the Queen came in, also quite alone, in a house dress. She said she was obliged to leave for Claremont in an hour; 'But, goodness! how it looks here,' she added, when she saw that the wind had littered the whole room, and even the pedals of the organ (which, by the way, made a very pretty feature in the room), with leaves of music from a large portfolio that lay open. As she spoke, she knelt down and began picking up the music; Prince Albert helped, and I too was not idle. Then Prince Albert proceeded to explain the stops to me, and while he was doing it, she said that she would put things straight alone.

. . . Then the Crown Prince of Gotha came in, and there was more conversation, and among other things the Queen asked if I had composed any new songs, and said that she was very fond of singing the published ones. 'You should sing one to him', said Prince Albert; and after a little begging she said she would try the 'Frühlingslied' in B-flat. 'Yes, if it were still here, for all my music is packed up for Claremont.' Prince Albert went to look for it, but came back saying it was already packed. 'Oh, perhaps it could be unpacked', said I. 'We must send for Lady N.N.', she said. (I did not catch the name.) So the bell was rung, and the servants were sent after it, but came back embarrassed; and then the Queen went herself, and whilst she was gone Prince Albert said to me: 'She begs you will accept this present as a remembrance'—and gave me a case with a beautiful ring, on which is engraved 'V.R. 1842'.

. . . Then the Queen came back and said, 'Lady N.N. has left and has taken all my things with her. It really is most unseemly.' (You can't think how that amused me.) I then begged that I might not be made to suffer for the accident, and hoped she would sing another song . . . to which she very kindly consented; and which did she choose? 'Schöner and schöner'; sang it beautifully in tune, in strict time, and with very nice expression. Only where, following 'Der Prosa Last und Müh', where it goes down to D and then comes up again by semitones, she sang D-sharp each time; and because the first two times I gave her the note, the last time, sure enough, she sang D—where it ought to have been D-sharp. But except for this little mistake it was really charming, and the last long G I have never heard better or purer or more natural from any amateur. Then I was obliged to confess that Fanny had written the song (which I found very hard, but pride must have a fall), and to beg her to sing one of my own, too. 'If I would give her plenty of help she would gladly try,' she said, and sang 'Lass dich nur nichts dauern' really without a mistake, and with charming feeling and expression. I thought to myself that one must not pay too many compliments on such an occasion, so I merely thanked her very much; but she said, 'Oh, if only I had not been so nervous; otherwise I really have a long breath.' Then I praised her heartily, and with the best conscience in the world; for just that part with the long C at the close she had done so well, taking it and the three notes next to it all in the same breath, as one seldom hears it done, and therefore it amused me doubly that she herself should have begun about it.

. . . Well, and then she said, 'I hope you will come and visit us soon again in England', and then I took my leave; and down below I saw the beautiful carriages waiting, with their scarlet outriders, and in a quarter of an hour the flag was lowered, and the papers said: 'Her Majesty left the Palace at 30 minutes past 3' . . .

Queen Victoria herself was an ardent letter writer, though her letters can be heavy-going. Henry James's comment on reading them was: 'She's more of a man than I expected.'

It has been aptly observed that Victoria was not a great woman like Elizabeth I or Catherine of Russia, but a very ordinary woman with an abundance of ordinary qualities which all could appreciate and imitate. In the following letter her undramatic courage in the face of an assassination attempt is evident. She is writing in May 1842 to her uncle King Leopold of the Belgians:

My Dearest Uncle, I wish to be the first to inform you of what happened yesterday evening, and to tell you that we are *saines et sauves*. On returning from the chapel on Sunday, Albert was observing how civil the people were, and then suddenly turned to me and said it appeared to him as though a man had held out a pistol to the carriage, and that it had hung fire; accordingly, when we came home he mentioned it to Colonel

Arbuthnot, who was only to tell it to Sir J. Graham and Sir Robert Peel, and have the police instructed, and *nobody else.* No one, however, who was with us, such as footmen, etc., had seen anything at all. Albert began to doubt what he believed he had seen. Well, yesterday morning (Monday) a lad came to Murray (who of course knew nothing) and said that he saw a man in the crowd as we came home from church, present a pistol to the carriage, which, however, did not go off, and heard the man say, 'Fool that I was not to fire!' The man then vanished, and this boy followed another man (an old man) up St James's Street who repeated twice, 'How very extraordinary!' but instead of saying anything to the police, asked the boy for his direction and disappeared. The boy accordingly was sent to Sir Robert Peel, and (doubtful as it still was) every precaution was taken, still keeping the thing completely secret, not a soul in the house knowing a word, and accordingly after some consultation, as *nothing* could be done, we drove out—many police then in plain clothes being distributed in and about the parks, and the two Equerries riding so close on each side that they must have been hit, if anybody had; still the feeling of looking out for such a man was not *des plus agréables*; however, we drove through the parks, up to Hampstead, and back again. All was so quiet that we almost thought of nothing—when, as we drove down Constitution Hill, very fast, we heard the report of a pistol, but not at all loud, so that had we not been on the alert we should hardly have taken notice of it. We saw the man seized by a policeman *next to whom he was standing when he* fired, but we did not stop. Colonel Arbuthnot and two others saw him take aim, but we only *heard* the report (looking both the other way). We felt both very glad that our drive had had the effect of having the man seized. Whether it was loaded or not we cannot yet tell, but we are again full of gratitude to Providence for invariably *protecting* us! The feeling of horror is very great in the public, and great affection is shown us. The man was yesterday examined at the Home Office, is called John Francis, is a cabinet-maker, and son of a machine-maker of Covent Garden Theatre, is good-looking (they say). I have never seen him at all close, but Arbuthnot gave the description of him from what he saw on Sunday, which exactly answered. Only twenty or twenty-one years old, and *not* the *least* mad—but very cunning. The boy identified him this morning, amongst many others. Everything is to be kept secret *this* time, which is very right, and altogether I think it is being well done. Every further particular you shall hear. I was really not at all frightened, and feel very proud at dear Uncle Mensdorff calling me *'sehr mutig'*, which I shall ever remember with peculiar pride, coming from so distinguished an officer as he is! Thank God, my Angel is also well! but he says that had the man fired on Sunday, he must have been hit in the head! God is merciful; that indeed we must feel daily more! Uncle and cousins were quite horrified . . . Ever your devoted Niece,

VICTORIA R.

You will tell Louise *all*, of course.

Queen Victoria's predecessor but one hardly inspired the feelings of affection that she did, and was the most unpopular monarch of modern times, not least for his behaviour to his wife, Caroline of Brunswick, and for the fact that a reluctant nation had to pay off £650,000 worth of his debts when he married her. As Prince Regent he presided over a circle of cronies in his own oriental folly at Brighton, and gained a reputation as a patron of the arts; also another reputation as a dissipated oaf. 'A corpulent Adonis of fifty', to paraphrase Leigh Hunt, he is reported by Disraeli as having 'believed that he was at the Battle of Waterloo and indeed commanded there. His friends were a little alarmed; but Knighton (his physician), who was a sensible man, said: "His Majesty has only to leave off curaçao, and rest assured he will gain no more victories."' Such a character was meat and drink to the politician and man about town Thomas Creevey. Writing to Mrs Creevey in 1805 he described one of the evening sessions at the Pavilion. It appeared that the Prince was well lubricated by the time he presented himself at the gathering:

> . . . Afterwards the Prince led all the party to the table where the maps lie, to see him shoot with an air-gun at a target placed at the end of the room. He did it very skilfully, and wanted all the ladies to attempt it. The girls and I excused ourselves on account of our short sight; but Lady Downshire hit a fiddler in the dining-room, Miss Johnstone a door and Bloomfield the ceiling . . . I soon had enough of this, and retired to the fire with Mac . . . At last a waltz was played by the band, and the Prince offered to waltz with Miss John-

stone, but very quietly, and once round the table made him giddy, so of course it was proper for his partner to be giddy too; but he cruelly only thought of supporting himself, so she reclined on the Baron.

In 1822 King George IV as he now was, made a visit to Scotland where he was lavishly entertained. However the levée didn't impress Mr Stuart of Edinburgh much, as he complained to his friend Mr Ferguson of Raith:

> . . . There was nothing interesting or imposing about it. A vast crowd, with barely standing room for two hours: afterwards moved to the Presence Chamber, where no one was for a minute . . . The King did not seem to move a muscle, and we all asked each other, when we came away, what had made us take so much trouble. He was dressed in tartan. Sir Walter Scott has ridiculously made us appear to be a nation of Highlanders, and the bagpipe and the tartan are the order of the day.

Walter Scott seems to have enjoyed the pageantry of monarchy; but he missed a previous royal visit, having to content himself with a very amusing description of it in a letter from his father. The occasion was the visit of Prince Leopold of Saxe-Coburg to Abbotsford in 1819.

> *My Dear Lord,*—I am honoured with your Buxton letter . . . *Anent* Prince Leopold, I only heard of his approach at eight o'clock in the morning, and he was to be at Selkirk by eleven. The Magistrates sent to ask me to help them to receive him. It occurred to me he might be coming to Melrose to see the abbey, in which case I could not avoid asking him to Abbotsford, as he must pass my very door. I mentioned this to Mrs Scott who was lying quietly in bed, and I wish you had heard the scream she gave on this occasion. 'What have we to offer him?' 'Wine and cake,' said I, thinking to make all things easy; but she ejaculated, in a tone of utter despair, 'Cake! where am I to get cake?' However, being partly consoled with the recollection that his visit was a very improbable incident, and curiosity, as usual proving too strong for alarm, she set out with me in order not to miss a peep at the great man. James Skene and his lady were with us, and we gave our carriages

such additional dignity as a pair of leaders could add, and
went off to meet him in full puff. The Prince very civilly told
me, that, though he could not see Melrose on this occasion,
he wished to come to Abbotsford for an hour. New despair on
the part of Mrs Scott, who began to institute a domiciliary
search for cold meat through the whole city of Selkirk, which
produced *one shoulder of cold lamb*. In the meanwhile, his Royal
Highness received the civic honours of the BIRSE very graciously. I had hinted to Bailie Lang that it ought only to be
licked *symbolically* on the present occasion; so he flourished it
three times before his mouth, but without touching it with his
lips, and the Prince followed his example as directed. Lang
made an excellent speech, sensible, and feeling, and well
delivered. The Prince seemed much surprised at this great
propriety of expression and behaviour in a magistrate, whose
people seemed such a rabble, and whose whole band of music
consisted in a drum and fife. He noticed to Bailie Anderson
that Selkirk seemed very populous in proportion to its extent.
'On an occasion like this it seems so,' answered the bailie,
neatly enough I thought. I question if any magistrates in the
kingdom, lord mayors and aldermen not excepted, could
have behaved with more decent and quiet good-breeding.
Prince Leopold repeatedly alluded to this during the time he
was at Abbotsford. I do not know how Mrs Scott ultimately
managed; but with broiled salmon, and blackcock, and par-
tridges, she gave him a very decent lunch; and I chanced to
have some very fine old hock, which was mighty germain to
the matter.

The Prince seems melancholy, whether naturally or from
habit I do not pretend to say; but I do not remember thinking
him so at Paris, where I saw him frequently, then a much
poorer man than myself; yet he showed some humour, for,
alluding to the crowds that followed him everywhere, he
mentioned some place where he had gone out to shoot, but
was afraid to proceed for fear of 'bagging a boy'. He said he
really thought of getting some shooting-place in Scotland, and
promised me a longer visit on his return. . . . I think I have
now given your lordship a very full, true, and particular
account of our royal visit, unmatched even by that of King
Charles at the Castle of Tillietudlem. That we did not speak of
it for more than a week after it happened, and that that
emphatic monosyllable, The Prince, is not heard amongst us

more than ten times a day, is on the whole, to the credit of my family's understanding. The piper is the only one whose brain he seems to have endangered; for, as the Prince said he preferred him to any he had heard in the Highlands (which, by the way, shows his Royal Highness knows nothing of the matter), the fellow seems to have become incapable of his ordinary occupation as a forester, and has cut stick and stem without remorse to the tune of *Phail Phranse, i.e.* the Prince's welcome.

How to entertain royal personages is a problem that has exercised the diplomatic skills of loyal subjects from time immemorial. One of the saddest stories concerning hospitality for a monarch that failed to come up to the mark is told by Madame de Sévigné in a letter to her daughter, Madame de Grignan in April 1671. Louis XIV was being entertained at Chantilly by the Prince de Condé, whose steward was an unfortunate gentleman named Vatel. Vatel had formerly been steward to Nicolas Foucquet, the superintendent of finance who had fallen foul of the King and been sentenced to life imprisonment; so he was obviously born under an unlucky star. The dinner at Chantilly turned out to be a disaster, as Madame de Sévigné relates:

The King arrived on Thursday evening. Hunting, lanterns, moonlight, a gentle walk, supper served in a spot carpeted with daffodils—everything was perfect. They had supper. There was no roast at one or two tables because of several unexpected guests. That upset Vatel, and he said more than once, 'I am dishonoured; this is a humiliation I will not bear.' He said to Gourville, 'I don't know where I am, I haven't slept for twelve nights. Help me give orders.' Gourville comforted him as far as he could, but this roast missing, not from the King's table but from the twenty-fifth down, constantly came back to his mind. Gourville told all this to Monsieur le Prince. Monsieur le Prince went to Vatel's room and said to him, 'Vatel, everything is all right, nothing was so perfect as the King's supper.' But he answered, 'Monseigneur, your kindness is overwhelming, but I know that there was no roast at two tables.' 'Not at all,' said Monsieur le Prince, 'don't upset yourself, everything is going splendidly.' Night falls. The fireworks are a failure owing to fog, and they cost 16,000 francs. By four in the morning Vatel was rushing round everywhere and finding everything wrapped in slumber. He found a small supplier who only had two loads of fish. 'Is that all?' he asked. 'Yes, Sir.' He did not know that Vatel had sent round to all the seaports. Vatel waited a short time, the other suppliers did not turn up, he lost his head and thought there would be no more fish. He went and found Gourville and said, 'Sir, I shall never survive this disgrace, my honour and my reputation are at stake.' Gourville laughed at him. Vatel went to his room, put his sword up against the door and ran it through his heart. But that was only at the third attempt, for the first two were not mortal. Then he fell dead. Meanwhile the fish was coming in from all quarters. They looked for Vatel to allocate it, went to his room, broke in the door and found him lying in his own blood. They rushed to Monsieur le Prince, who was terribly upset. Monsieur le Duc wept, for the whole of his trip to Burgundy depended on Vatel. Monsieur le Prince told the King very sadly, explaining that it was a matter of honour as he saw it; he was greatly praised. His courage was both praised and blamed. The King said that he had been putting off his visit to Chantilly for five years because he realized what an extreme embarrassment it would be.

Being at the court of the Sun King sounds as if it could be distinctly unnerving, even if you didn't have responsibility for all the food and drink. In the following letter, Madame de Sévigné is this time writing to her friend the Marquis de Pomponne, who was for a while Louis XIV's foreign minister. As a diplomatist he would have appreciated this tragi-comical anecdote, though it does not reflect well on the character of the King:

I must tell you a nice little story which is quite true and will amuse you. The King has taken lately to writing verse. Messieurs de Saint-Aignan and Dangeau are teaching him how to set about it. The other day he wrote a little madrigal, which he himself did not think much of. One morning he said to Maréchal de Gramont, 'Monsieur le Maréchal, will you kindly read this little madrigal and see whether you have ever seen anything so pointless. Just because it is known that I have recently taken to liking verses, people bring me all kinds.' Having read it the Marshal said, 'Sire, your Majesty is an inspired judge of everything, and it is true that this is the silliest and most ridiculous madrigal I have ever read.' The King burst out laughing and said, 'Isn't it true that whoever wrote this is a conceited puppy?' 'Sire, he cannot be called anything else.' 'That's excellent,' said the King. 'I am delighted that you have spoken so candidly; I wrote it myself.' 'Oh, Sire, what treachery! Will your Majesty please give it back to me, I only glanced through it rapidly.' 'No, Monsieur le Maréchal, first impressions are always the most natural.' The King laughed very much at this trick, but everyone thinks that is is the most cruel thing one can do to an old courtier. Personally I always like reflecting about things, and I wish the King would think about this example and conclude how far he is from ever learning the truth.

A capricious king whose loyalty to his servants cannot be relied on makes his service perilous as well as taxing. To be the object of his love, if he was Henry VIII was a dubious distinction, though one that Anne Boleyn eventually accepted and to her cost. While Henry's desires waxed hot, however, she was the recipient of glowing letters such as the following:

> Mine own Sweetheart, this shall be to advertise you of the great melancholy that I find here since your departing; for, I ensure you, methinketh the time longer since your departing now last than I was wont to do a whole fortnight. I think your kindness and my fervency of love causeth it; for, otherwise I would not have thought it possible that for so little a while it should have grieved me. But now I am coming towards you, methinketh my pains by half removed; and also I am right well comforted insomuch that my book maketh substantially for my matter; in looking whereof I have spent above four hours this day, which causeth me now to write the shorter letter to you at this time, because of some pain in my head. Wishing myself (especially an evening) in my sweetheart's arms whose pretty duckies I trust shortly to kiss. Written by the hand of him that was, is, and shall be yours by his own will,

> H. R.

After the King's ardour cooled, and it only took three months to do so, Anne Boleyn was clapped in the Tower accused of

adultery with, amongst others, her own brother. Her uncle, the
Duke of Norfolk, presided over the judges who sentenced her to
death in 1536.

An equally unfortunate queen was Lady Jane Grey, who came
to the throne as a result of the scheming of the Duke of
Northumberland. He hoped to exclude the Catholic Mary from
succeeding Edward VI, and forcibly married his fourth son,
Lord Guildford Dudley, to Jane Grey; she was not quite sixteen
at the time, but a highly educated and intelligent girl. The ruling
council made her Queen on 9 July 1553, but ten days later her
usurpation ended and she was placed in the Tower. In this letter
to Queen Mary she explains how it all happened. Mary, though
she may have been passively sympathetic, could not afford to
have a possible rallying point for Protestant disaffection in her
realm, and had Lady Jane Grey executed on 12 February 1554.

. . . On the day following (as is known to every one) I was
conducted to the Tower, and shortly afterwards were presented to me by the marquis of Winchester, lord high treasurer,
the jewels, with which he also brought me the crown,
although it had never been demanded from him by me or by
anyone in my name; and he further wished me to put it on my
head, to try whether it really became me well or no. The
which, although with many excuses, I refused to do, he
nevertheless added that I might take it without fear, and that
another also should be made to crown my husband and me.
Which thing I, for my part, heard truly with a troubled mind,
and with ill will, even with infinite grief and displeasure of the
heart. And, after the said lord was gone, and I was reasoning
of many things with my husband, he assented that if he were
to be made king, he would be made so by me, by act of
parliament. But afterwards I sent for the earls of Arundel and
Pembroke, and said to them that, if the crown belonged to
me, I should be content to make my husband a duke, but
would never consent to make him a king. Which resolution of
mine gave his mother (this my opinion being related to her)
great cause for anger and disdain, so that she, being very
angry with me and greatly displeased, persuaded her son not
to sleep with me any longer as he was wont to do, affirming to
me moreover that he did not wish in any wise to be a duke but
a king. So that I was constrained to send to him the earls of
Arundel and Pembroke, who had negotiated with him to

come, from me, otherwise I knew that the next morning he would have gone to Sion.

And thus in truth was I deceived by the duke and the council, and ill-treated by my husband and his mother. Moreover (as Sir John Gates has confessed) he (the duke) was the first to persuade King Edward to make me his heir. As to the rest, for my part, I know not what the council may have determined to do, but I know for certain that, twice during this time, poison was given to me, first in the house of the duchess of Northumberland, and afterwards here in the Tower, as I have the best and most certain testimony, besides that since that time all my hair has fallen off. And all these things I have wished to say for the witness of my innocence and the disburdening of my conscience.

Lady Jane Grey died a victim of political intrigue, one of the unlucky casualties of history. George II died naturally, as by that time England had ceased to execute monarchs who were unsuitable or unfortunate. Although he was not conspicuously virtuous, or vicious, his reign saw a period of great prosperity and at his funeral in Westminster Abbey he was given a fine send-off, an occasion described by Horace Walpole to George Montague with the maximum amount of malicious glee:

When we came to the chapel of Henry VII all solemnity and decorum ceased—no order was observed, people sat or stood where they could or would, the yeomen of the guard were crying out for help, oppressed by the immense weight of the coffin, the Bishop read sadly, and blundered in the prayers, the fine chapter, *Man that is born of a woman*, was chanted not read, and the anthem, besides being unmeasurably tedious, would have served as well for a nuptial. The real serious part was the figure of the Duke of Cumberland, heightened by a thousand melancholy circumstances. He had a dark brown adonis, and a cloak of black cloth with a train of five yards. Attending the funeral of a father, how little reason soever he had to love him, could not be pleasant. His leg extremely bad, yet forced to stand upon it near two hours, his face bloated and distorted with his late paralytic stroke, which has affected too one of his eyes, and placed over the mouth of the vault, into which in all probability he must himself so soon descend—think how unpleasant a situation! He bore it all with a firm and unaffected countenance. This grave scene was fully contrasted by the burlesque Duke of Newcastle—he fell into a fit of crying the moment he came into the chapel and flung himself back in a stall, the Archbishop hovering over him with a smelling bottle—but in two minutes his curiosity got the better of his hypocrisy and he ran about the chapel with his glass to spy who was or who was not there, spying with one hand and mopping his eyes with t'other. Then returned the fear of catching cold, and the Duke of Cumberland, who was sinking with heat, felt himself weighed down, and turning round, found it was the Duke of Newcastle standing upon his train to avoid the chill of the marble. It was very theatric to look down into the vault, where the coffin lay, attended by mourners with lights. Clavering, the Groom of the Bedchamber, refused to sit up with the body, and was dismissed by the King's order.

I have nothing more to tell you but a trifle, a very trifle—the King of Prussia has totally defeated Marshal Daun. This which would have been prodigious news a month ago, is nothing today; it only takes its turn among the questions, 'Who is to be Groom of the Bedchamber?' 'What is Sir T. Robinson to have?' I have been at Leicester Fields today; the crowd was immoderate; I don't believe it will continue so. Good night.

From a royal funeral we turn to a royal marriage, charmingly described by Joseph Mead in one of his many letters describing London life in the seventeenth century. In June 1625 Queen Henrietta Maria arrived at Dover, and the day after her arrival King Charles I went to greet her, the couple having already been married by proxy:

He came thither after 10 o'clock and she then being at meat, he stayed in the presence till she had done; which she, advertised of, made short work, rose, went unto him, kneeled down at his feet, took, and kissed his hand. The King took her up in his arms, kissed her, and talking with her, cast down his eyes towards her feet (she seeming higher than report was, reaching to his shoulders). Which she soon perceiving discovered [uncovered] and showed him her shoes, saying to this effect 'Sir, I stand upon mine own feet. I have no helps by art. Thus I am, and am neither higher nor lower.' She is nimble and quiet, black-eyed, brown-haired, and in a word a brave Lady, though perhaps a little touched with a green sickness.

One ship whereupon stood above an hundred people, not being balanced nor well tied to the shore, and they standing all upon one side, was overturned and sunk, all that were upon her tumbling into the Thames; and yet was not anyone lost that I can hear of, but all saved by the help of boats. The bells rang till midnight and all the streets were full of bonfires, and in this one street were above thirty.

At dinner (at Dover) being carved pheasant and venison by his Majesty (who had dined before) she ate heartily of both, notwithstanding that her confessor (who all this while stood by her) had forewarned her that it was the eve of St John Baptist, and was to be fasted, and that she should take heed how she gave ill example or a scandal at her first arrival.

The same night, having supped at Canterbury, her Majesty went to bed; and, some space of time after, his Majesty followed her. And having entered his bedchamber, the first thing he did, he bolted all the doors round about (being seven), with his own hand, letting in but two of the bedchamber to undress him, which being done, he bolted them out also. The next morning he lay till seven of the clock, and was pleasant with the lords that he had beguiled them; and hath ever since been very jocund.

In contrast to this joyous scene a tragic note from Charles himself to his physician Sir Theodore Mayne in 1644, asks him to attend to the Queen who was about to be delivered. The Civil War was already in progress and after the Queen set off for Exeter, he never saw her again. Henrietta, Duchess of Orleans was born ten weeks after the last time they were together:

MAYERNE,
    Pour l'amour de Moy, alle trouver ma femme.

                                        C. R.

Charles I paid with his life for his political ineptitude and stubbornness. So did Tsar Nicholas II. In a long and courageous letter to him in 1902, Leo Tolstoy warned him that his autocratic rule could not last. It must be one of the most outspoken letters ever sent to a ruling monarch. Here is an extract:

. . . If you could, as I can, walk along the lines of peasants strung out behind the soldiers or along an entire railway line while the tsar passes by, and hear what these peasants were saying: village elders and peasant policemen rounded up from neighbouring villages and waiting for several days in the cold and slush, without reward and with (only) their bread, for the tsar to pass, you would hear all along the line words totally incompatible with love for autocracy and its representative from the most genuine representatives of the people, the simple peasants. If some 50 years ago in the reign of Nicholas I the prestige of the tsar's authority was still high, during the past 30 years it has continually declined and has recently fallen so low that no one from any class constrains himself any longer from boldly condemning not only the decrees of the government but also the tsar himself, and even swearing at him and laughing at him.

Autocracy is an obsolete form of government which may suit the needs of a people somewhere in Central Africa, cut off from the whole world, but not the needs of the Russian people who are becoming more and more enlightened by the enlightenment common to the whole world. And therefore maintaining this form of government and the Orthodoxy linked with it can only be done as it is now, by means of every kind of violence: a state of emergency, administrative exile, executions, religious persecutions, the banning of books and newspapers, the perversion of education, and, in general, by bad and cruel actions of every type.

Such have been the actions of your reign up to now . . .

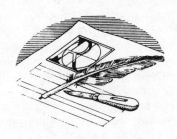

2

The Greasy Pole

'How envious are Statesmen!' wrote John Gay to Mrs Howard in 1723, 'and how jealous are they of rivals! A Highway-man never picks up an honest man for a companion, but if such a one accidentally falls in his way; if he cannot turn his heart he like a wise statesman discards him.'

John Gay's low view of public life, given graphic expression in *The Beggar's Opera*, has found many adherents since. Yet often politicians are forced into rather elastic notions of honour and propriety by the fickleness and hypocrisy of the people. One victim of such sudden changes in the political climate was Sir Francis Bacon who rose to be Lord Chancellor, but was impeached on charges of judicial bribery. In a letter of mitigation to King James I in 1621 he pleads not so much that he is entirely innocent, but that his conduct is no worse than that of the average politician in his position. As Edmund Clerihew Bentley put it:

> When their lordships asked Bacon
> How many bribes he had taken
> He had at least the grace
> To get very red in the face.

He escaped with his life, however, though not his reputation. After a few days in the Tower he was released and later received a Royal pardon, but was not allowed to return to politics. His demise was less ignominious, but also less dignified, than execution in the Tower. He died after catching a chill while stuffing a fowl with snow near Highgate in order to observe the effect of cold on the preservation of flesh:

> . . . And for the briberies and gifts wherewith I am charged, when the book of hearts shall be opened, I hope I shall not be

found to have the troubled fountain of a corrupt heart, in a depraved habit of taking rewards to pervert justice; howsoever I may be frail, and partake of the abuses of the times.

And therefore I am resolved, when I come to my answer, not to trick up my innocency, as I writ to the lords, by cavillations or voidances; but to speak to them the language that my heart speaketh to me, in excusing, extenuation, or ingenuously confessing; praying to God to give me the grace to see the bottom of my faults, and that no hardness of heart do steal upon me, under shew of more neatness of conscience, than is cause. But not to trouble your majesty any longer, craving pardon for this long mourning letter; that which I thirst after, *as the hart after the streams*, is, that I may know, by my matchless friend that presenteth to you this letter, your majesty's heart (which is an *abyssus* of goodness, as I am an *abyssus* of misery) towards me. I have been ever your man, and counted myself but an usufructuary of myself, the property being yours. And now making myself an oblation to do with me as may best conduce to the honour of your justice, the honour of your mercy, and the use of your service, resting as clay in your majesty's gracious hands,

&c., &c.

This kind of grovelling is sometimes necessary for survival in politics. Parliamentary candidates have also to please what Shakespeare rudely described as 'the mutable rank-scented many'. Pressing the flesh and kissing babies was already well-established practice in the eighteenth century as we learn from a letter from the poet William Cowper to his extremely gloomy friend the Reverend John Newton in 1784:

. . . We were sitting yesterday after dinner, the two ladies and myself, very composedly, and without the least apprehension of any such intrusion in our snug parlour, one lady knitting, the other netting, and the gentleman winding worsted, when to our unspeakable surprise a mob appeared before the window; a smart rap was heard at the door, the boys halloo'd, and the maid announced 'Mr Grenville'. Puss [Cowper's pet hare] was unfortunately let out of her box, so that the candidate, with all his good friends at his heels, was refused admittance at the grand entry, and referred to the back door, as the only possible way of approach.

Candidates are creatures not very susceptible of affronts, and would rather, I suppose, climb in at a window, than be absolutely excluded. In a minute, the yard, the kitchen, and the parlour, were filled. Mr Grenville, advancing toward me, shook me by the hand with a degree of cordiality that was extremely seducing. As soon as he and as many more as could find chairs were seated, he began to open the intent of his visit. I told him I had no vote, for which he readily gave me credit. I assured him I had no influence, which he was not equally inclined to believe, and the less, no doubt, because Mr Ashburner, the draper, addressing himself to me at this moment, informed me that I had a great deal. Supposing that I could not be possessed of such a treasure without knowing it, I ventured to confirm my first assertion, by saying, that if I had any I was utterly at a loss to imagine where it could be, or wherein it consisted. Thus ended the conference. Mr Grenville squeezed me by the hand again, kissed the ladies, and withdrew. He kissed likewise the maid in the kitchen, and seemed upon the whole a most loving, kissing, kind-hearted gentleman. He is very young, genteel, and handsome. He has a pair of very good eyes in his head, which not being sufficient as it should seem for the many nice and difficult purposes of a senator, he has a third also, which he wore suspended by a riband from his buttonhole. The boys halloo'd, the dogs barked, Puss scampered, the hero, with his long train of obsequious followers, withdrew . . .

Having got elected, the candidates have to keep up a show of interest in the welfare of their constituents. Nowadays they even have to purchase a second home, if not a first, in the area they represent. Sir George Leveson-Gower expressed his true feelings about the constituency grind in a letter from Stoke-on-Trent to Lady Wenlock of 1892:

I think that you once said that you regretted your disposition to allow the atmosphere to influence your frame of mind and were apt to envy mine as being less impressionable. To-day I feel no longer an object of envy, but rather of pity. It is just about sunset, only there is no sun to set, and the sky is overspread with one grey pall. In front of me is the station, built in sham Elizabethan style, with the gas-light from its windows glaring sullenly out into the gathering dusk and reflected in the puddles of the Square in front. In the middle of the Square is a statue of Wedgwood, the Father of the trade of the Potteries and Wilberforce's friend, meditatively contemplating a vase of his own manufacture, with the rain falling on his bare head and dripping unheeded from his coat-tails. The engines are shrieking and whistling as though in scorn at me, as I know from sad experience they will go on shrieking and screaming till an early hour tomorrow morning. The place itself is inseparably steeped in disagreeable associations of electioneering, agents, constituents, cold suppers after hot meetings, and of stale soles at breakfast, which are always stale owing to some unprecedented and never to be repeated mishap, and yet which are never any fresher the next time; of German waiters and bawling bagmen and of other horrors, numberless and unspeakable . . .

The fumes of a substantial banquet, to which the feast of Thyestes[1] would, in my present frame of mind, be almost preferable, ascend to my room, where they contend for mastery with the smoke which comes down instead of going up the chimney; a fact which an unnecessarily vivacious chambermaid attributes to 'chimney damp'.

The said banquet will drag along through four mortal hours, from 6 to 10, through endless courses and still more endless speeches, to which last I have to contribute one on the same invariable toast, to which I always have to respond every year. The feast is a complimentary dinner given by the Alderman and Councillors of the borough to the out-going Mayor.

. . . The dinner will begin in an hour and I have no joke, and don't think I shall have one, for my speech. This in itself is a hideous calamity, the full force of which you are happily unable to appreciate; but I assure you, punning apart, that this is no laughing matter! . . .

But the attractions of political life for its adherents clearly outweigh its very many inconveniences. Not least of these is the opportunity of participating in the great events of the day and helping, or hindering, the cause of progress (as it is always called). Here is Lord Macaulay on the passing of the Reform Bill

[1] *Thyestes* served his brother Atreus with a dish of his own sons' flesh, according to the myth of the ill-fated house of Pelops.

in March 1831. Macaulay himself sat for a pocket borough, i.e. one said to be in the pocket of the local magnate because of the tiny electorate, most of whom were bribed by him; but he used his considerable powers of oratory in favour of the Bill:

> . . . When the strangers were cleared out, and the doors locked, we had six hundred and eight members present— more by fifty-five than ever were in a division before. The ayes and noes were like two volleys of cannon from opposite sides of a field of battle. When the Opposition went out into the lobby, an operation which took up twenty minutes or more, we spread ourselves over the benches on both sides of the House, for there were many of us who had not been able to find a seat during the evening. When the doors were shut we began to speculate on our numbers. Everybody was desponding. 'We have lost it. We are only two hundred and eighty at most . . .' We were all breathless with anxiety, when Charles Wood, who stood near the door, jumped up on a bench and cried out, 'They are only three hundred and one.' We set up a shout that you might have heard to Charing Cross, waving our hats, stamping against the floor, and clapping our hands. The tellers scarcely got through the crowd: for the House was thronged up to the table, and all the floor was fluctuating with heads like the pit of a theatre. But you might have heard a pin drop as Duncannon read the numbers. Then again the shouts broke out, and many of us shed tears. I could scarcely refrain. And the jaw of Peel fell; and the face of Twiss was as the face of a damned soul; and Herries looked like Judas taking his necktie off for the last operation. We shook hands, and clapped each other on the back, and went out laughing, crying, and huzzaing into the lobby. And no sooner were the outer doors opened than another shout answered that within the House. All the passages and the stairs into the waiting-rooms were thronged by people who had waited till four in the morning to know the issue. We passed through a narrow lane between two thick masses of them; and all the way down they were shouting and waving their hats, till we got into the open air. I called a cabriolet, and the first thing the driver asked was, 'Is the bill carried?' 'Yes, by one.' 'Thank God for it, sir.' And away I rode to Gray's Inn,—and so ended a scene which will probably never be equalled till the reformed Parliament wants

reforming; and that I hope will not be till the days of our grandchildren . . .

In controversy over reform some of those who have been on the receiving end of political satire are more remembered for the attack they provoked than for themselves—a backhanded way of being honoured with a mention in the history books. Bishop Blomfield, an industrious bishop of London during whose episcopate some two hundred new churches were consecrated, is probably better known for Sydney Smith's witty attack on him for his enthusiasm for the work of the Ecclesiastical Commission of 1836. It was published in a letter to *The Times* on 5 September 1840 and must rank as one of the funniest pieces of invective on record. This almost succeeds in obscuring the dubious nature of Smith's case which appears to be that since the Bishop is a hypocrite about the emoluments of the hierarchy, his views on pluralism and other abuses are necessarily invalid:

> . . . A few words more, my dear Lord, before we part, after a controversy of four years:-
>
> In reading your speech, I was a good deal amused by your characteristic indignation at the idea of any man, or any body of men, being competent to offer you advice; at the same time I have a sort of indistinct recollection of your name, as defendant in courts of justice, where it appeared, not only to the judges who decided against you, but to your best friends also, that you would have made rather a better figure if you had begged a few contributions of wisdom and temper from those who had any to share . . .
>
> . . . You say that you always consult your archdeacon and rural dean; this I believe to be quite true—but then you generally consult them after the error, and not before. Immediately after this aspernation of all human counsel, I came to the following sentence,—such a sentence as I believe mortal and mitred man never spoke before, and the author of which, as it seems to me, should be loaded with four atmospheres of advice instead of one, and controlled regularly by that number of cathedral councils. In speaking of the 3,000 clergymen who have petitioned against the destruction of the church, you say—
>
> 'I could easily get as many to petition upon any subject

connected with the church. The mode by which in the present case a great proportion of these signatures have been obtained is as follows:- the Archdeacon, who has always great influence with the parochial clergy, and justly so, as visiting them every year, and as being in habits of more familiar intercourse with them than their Bishop, and who is morever considered by them as acting, in some degree, with the sanction of the Bishop, circulated printed forms of petition against the bill amongst the Rural Deans; the Rural Dean goes with them to the parochial clergy; and he must be a bold or a very well-informed man who refuses to sign a petition so recommended by his immediate ecclesiastical superiors.'

Now I am afraid you will be very angry with me, but for the life of me I cannot discover in this part of your speech any of those marks of unerring and unassistable wisdom—that perfect uselessness of counsellors to the Bishop of London of which you seem to be so intimately convinced; and this, remember, is not a lapse to be forgiven in the fervour of speaking, but a cold printed insult or what is the plain English of the passage? 'Archdeacons and rural deans are a set of base and time-serving instruments, whom their superiors can set on for any purpose to abuse their power and influence over the lower clergy, and the lower clergy themselves are either in such a state of intellectual destitution that they cannot comprehend what they sign, or they are so miserably enthralled by their ecclesiastical superiors that they dare not dissent. I could put this depraved machinery in action for any church purpose I wished to carry.' . . .

. . . In the eighth page of your speech you say—'I am continually brought into contact, in the discharge of my official duties, with vast masses of my fellow-creatures living without God in the world. I traverse the streets of this crowded city with deep and solemn thoughts of the spiritual condition of its inhabitants. I pass the magnificent church which crowns the metropolis, and is consecrated to the noblest of objects, the glory of God, and I ask of myself, in what degree it answers that object. I see there a dean and three residentiaries, with incomes amounting in the aggregate to between 10,000 l. and 12,000 l. a year. I see, too, connected with the cathedral 29 clergymen, whose offices are all but sinecures, with an annual income of about 12,000 l. at the present moment, and likely to be very much larger after the lapse of a few years. I proceed a mile or two to the E. and N.E., and find myself in the midst of an immense population in the most wretched state of destitution and neglect, artisans, mechanics, labourers, beggars, thieves, to the number of at least 300,000.'

This stroll in the metropolis is extremely well contrived for your Lordship's speech; but suppose, my dear Lord, that instead of going E. and N.E., you had turned about, crossed London-bridge, and, resolving to make your walk as impartial as possible, had proceeded in a S.W. direction, you would soon in that case have perceived a vast palace, containing, not a dean, three residentiaries, and 29 clergymen, but one attenuated prelate with an income enjoyed by himself alone, amounting to 30,000 l. per annum, twice as great as that of it given up by act of Parliament during his life to that spiritual destitution which he so deeply deplores, and 15,000 l. per annum secured to his successor: though all the duties of the office might be most effectually performed for one third of the salary . . .

. . . But these feelings upon spiritual destitution, my Lord, are of the most singular description; they seem to be under the most perfect control when bishops are to be provided for, and of irresistible plenitude and power when prebends are to be destroyed; such charity is the charity of my poor dear friend, old Lady C——, who was so powerfully affected (she said) by my sermon, that she borrowed a sovereign of some gentleman in the pew and put it in the plate.

. . . It is very easy, my Lord, to swing about in the House of Lords, and to be brave five years after the time, and to point out to their Lordships the clear difference between moral and physical fear, and to be nodded to by the Duke of Wellington, but I am not to be paid by such coin. I believe that old-fashioned, orthodox, hand-shaking, bowel-disturbing passion of fear had a good deal to do with the whole reform . . .

Letters to *The Times* can be good vehicles for political satire in the hands of a Sydney Smith. Another master of the form was A. P. Herbert who outlined the vocabulary of universal brotherhood as enshrined in socialist jargon in a letter of 12 January 1927. Oswald Mosley was at that time a Socialist MP for Smethwick, a constituency that hardly seems to have been very fortunate in its representatives.

. . . I have been studying a 'proletarian' song-book, which contains, in lyrical form, many of these 'intellectual convictions' recently expressed by Mr Mosley in less effective prose. The proletarian outlook is, of course, nothing if not brotherly, and I have made a list of the fraternal epithets devoted to those who do not believe that the nationalization of the means of production, distribution and exchange is the only cure for poverty, and are therefore enemies of the poor. They are called parasites, capitalists, idlers, drones, loafers, shirkers, tyrants, bullies, bosses, sweaters, exploiters, traitors, liars, despots, barons, spoilers, grafters, robbers, swindlers plunderers, thieves and sneaks. Nor do the poor come off much better. The poor are addressed as slaves, serfs, serf-men, bond-men, cringers, crouchers, bone-heads, boobs, dolts, dupes, duffers, fools, tools, prisoners, catspaws, thralls, cowards, cravens, dogs, and beasts of burden. And there is a song about parasites to the tune of 'Annie Laurie'. . . .

Another writer to make effective use of a letter to *The Times* was Evelyn Waugh, who wrote in 1955 with an innocent idea for the erection of a statue to Lloyd George:

> *Sir,*—Would not the House of Lords be the most appropriate place for a statue of the first Earl Lloyd George? He first made his mark by eloquent denunciations of that House. In his years of power he did more than any Prime Minister to embellish it with new names. In his wise old age he entered it himself.
> I am, Sir, your obedient servant,
>
> EVELYN WAUGH

Happily, not all politicians are mountebanks. In the following letter Giuseppe Verdi describes his life as a Deputy in which post he was regarded with universal affection. He is writing to Francesco Maria Piave, the librettist of *Rigoletto* and *La Traviata*:

> *8 February 1865*
> You ask me for news of my public life? I have no such thing as a public life. True, I am a Deputy, but that happened by mistake. However, I will tell you how it came about. In September 1860 I was at Turin. I had never seen Count Cavour and I was very eager to make his acquaintance. I

asked the then English Minister to present me. Since the Treaty of Villafranca [the peace treaty with Austria] the Count had withdrawn from public life and was living in retirement in his estate, which I think was on the Vercellese; and one fine morning we went to visit him. After that I had occasion to write to him and to receive from him several letters, in one of which he urged me to accept the nomination to parliament that my fellow-citizens were offering me and which I had refused. His letter was extremely amiable, and I did not feel I could answer no. I decided to go to Turin; I arrived in his presence one December day at 6 in the morning, when the thermometer stood at 12 or 14 degrees [centigrade] below freezing-point. I had prepared my speech, which I considered a masterpiece, and I poured it out at full length. He listened attentively, and when I described how unsuited I was to be a Deputy, and how impatient I would become with the long speeches one would sometimes have to swallow in the Chamber, I spoke so quaintly that he burst out laughing. Good, I said to myself, I have made my point. But then he began to demolish all my arguments, one after another, and he advanced some of his own that I found quite sensible. 'Well, *Signor Conte*,' I said at last, 'I accept; but on condition that I am allowed to resign after a few months.' . . . So there you are. If ever you want or are obliged to write my biography as Member of Parliament, you need only print in the middle of a blank page: 'The 450 are in reality only 449, because Verdi as a Deputy does not exist.' . . .

Another great composer, Béla Bartók, was also an eloquent letter writer. In contrast to Verdi, crowned with honours and enjoying the esteem of his fellow countrymen in his mellow middle-age, Bartók is writing to a Swiss friend in 1938 from a nation about to be overwhelmed by Nazism. The Horthy regime, in its quest to recover territories lost to Austria, Rumania, Czechoslovakia and Yugoslavia at the post-First World War Treaty of Trianon, was drawn into supporting Fascist Italy and Nazi Germany. The award of some lost territory in 1938 was merely the prelude to a full and disastrous engagement in the Second World War on the side of the Axis. Bartók describes the bitterness that many Hungarians felt at the time and the ominous moves of the homegrown Nazis as they increased their grip on the country:

. . . What I have been writing now has to do with Hungary where, unfortunately, 'cultured' people, Christians, are almost all submitting themselves to the Nazi regime. Really, I am ashamed to have been born into such a class!

. . . As for my personal situation, at the moment it is rather distressing, for not only has my publisher—Universal Edition—become a Nazi enterprise (the proprietor and the directors have simply been shown the door) but also the A.K.M. (the society which deals with authors' rights—to which both I and Kodaly belong) is a Viennese society that has just been nazified. In fact I have just received a scandalous questionnaire about grandparents and other topics, in a word: 'Are you of Germanic race, of similar race, or Non-Aryan?' Naturally, neither Kodaly nor I have filled in this questionnaire . . . but really it is a pity that we haven't, because we could have made fun of them, for we should have been able to reply that we are not Aryans—for in fact (as I have learnt from the dictionary) 'Aryan' means 'Indo-European': we Hungarians are Finno-Ugrians, and even perhaps northern Turks, and therefore definitely not Indo-Europeans, therefore not Aryans. Another question is: 'Where and when have you been wounded?' Answer: 'Vienna, the 11th, 12th and 13th of March, 1938!' [The date of the Nazi invasion.]

Unhappily, we cannot permit ourselves these jokes . . .

Many people had been slow to realize how evil and dangerous the Nazis were; even after the new barbarism was well advanced in its plans to conquer the world, there were some who preferred to bury their heads in the sand. To one of these Thomas Mann wrote bluntly in 1940 from his exile in Princeton:

I feel that it is my duty to write and tell you that I believe you grossly underestimate the terrible danger of Nazism. When you tell me that our enemy is not Hitler but war hysteria, and that the Allies incite alarm to encourage intervention, then I—as a German who truly knows what this vile thing, Hitlerism, is—must in all sincerity protest against such views.

You say that wars and depressions are but dream manifestations of alarm and that remedy lies in more optimistic and less pessimistic views. Today there is room neither for optimism nor pessimism but only for courage and action.

Where there is Nazism, there is to be found the denial of every decent human attribute and a reversion to the pagan and barbaric state of life in which murder, corruption, and intrigue are not merely condoned but advocated. Truth, justice, dignity have been ideals cherished by free men through the ages, but under Hitlerism they are simply empty words. Hitler means to destroy every liberty and to keep the masses in peonage and docility so as to permit him and his friends to enjoy the fruits of power and conquest. Hitler *is* the enemy, the enemy of mankind, and he must be destroyed at all costs before it is too late if anyone anywhere is to have the security to enjoy life, liberty, and the pursuit of happiness.

One of the most courageous letters of the Nazi era is that written by the Jewish author, Leon Feuchtwanger, whose picture of the sufferings of Central European Jewry under the title *Jud Süss* was a bestseller in 1925. His satire on Hitler's Munich putsch entitled *Erfolg* had earned him the hatred of the Nazis. After they had broken into and looted his house he wrote them an open letter from exile, magnificent in its contempt and sarcasm:

. . . I wonder to what use you have put the two rooms that formerly contained my library? I have been told by Herr X that books are not very popular in the Reich in which you live, and whoever shows interest in them is liable to get into difficulties. I, for instance, read your Führer's book and guilelessly remarked that his 140,000 words were 140,000 offences against the spirit of the German language. The result of this remark is that you are now living in my house . . . Sometimes I wonder to what uses bookcases can be put in the Third Reich. In case you should decide to have them ripped out, be careful not to damage the wall . . .

The Nazi barbarism was based on a doctrine of power and cynical greed, concepts dignified with the word 'Realpolitik' by their upholders. Nevertheless politics has always involved an uneasy reconciliation of power with ethical behaviour. A reflection on these matters which puts the foregoing letters into some sort of perspective is provided by Simone Weil in one of her long thought-developing letters to Father Perrin. This too was written in the shadow of the holocaust, and just before her embarkation for America in 1942. She died in England in 1943, her illness aggravated by a refusal to eat anything more than was given to her compatriots in Occupied France:

> . . . The Athenians, who were at war with Sparta, wanted to force the inhabitants of the little island of Melos, allied to Sparta from all antiquity and so far remaining neutral, to join with them. It was in vain that the men of Melos, faced with the ultimatum of the Athenians, invoked justice, imploring pity for the antiquity of their town. As they would not give in, the Athenians razed their city to the ground, put all their men to death and sold all their women and children as slaves.
>
> Thucydides has put the lines in question into the mouth of these Athenians. They begin by saying that they will not try to prove that their ultimatum is just.
>
> 'Let us treat rather of what is possible . . . You know it as well as we do; the human spirit is so constituted that what is just is only examined if there is equal necessity on both sides. But if one is strong and the other weak, that which is possible is imposed by the first and accepted by the second.'
>
> The men of Melos said that in the case of a battle they would have the gods with them on account of the justice of their cause. The Athenians replied that they saw no reason to suppose so.
>
> 'As touching the gods we have the belief, and as touching men the certainty, that always by a necessity of nature, each one commands wherever he has the power. We did not establish this law, we are not the first to apply it; we found it already established, we abide by it as something likely to endure for ever; and that is why we apply it. We know quite well that you also, like all the others, once you reached the same degree of power, would act in the same way.'
>
> Such lucidity of mind in the conception of injustice is the light which comes immediately below that of charity. It is the clarity which sometimes remains where charity once existed but has become extinguished. Below comes the darkness in which the strong sincerely believe that their cause is more just than that of the weak. That was the case with the Romans and the Hebrews . . .

'The weak' themselves seldom have an opportunity to be heard, which is why they need a spokesman—a Simone Weil or a Danilo Dolci. But this does not mean that the underdog is not an eloquent one when he is permitted to speak. The following interesting letter somehow elbowed its way into the columns of *The Times* in September 1970, eleven weeks into Mr Heath's ill-fated administration. It is clearly in response to some all too familiar noises emanating from the young Turks in the newly elected government, which was still in its politically paleolithic phase, before Selsdon Man was discovered to be no more authentic a human being than his relative at Piltdown:

Sir,
You have had a lot of letters about people being bloody-minded. You have not had any that I have seen about why people like me are what you would call bloody-minded.

I read your paper in the public library—I can't afford to purchase it every day. It is the same for a lot of ordinary working people like me. So you don't get much of what we think.

I am 50 years of age. I started work at 15 years of age. I will work, if I am lucky, until I am 65 years of age. I might live to 70, but I will be lucky if I can work to 70 because, even if I am able, and willing, the bosses don't want us. So I shall have the old-age pension. I have not been able to save. In all my working life the money I have got will amount to about £60,000. That is the highest it could be.

I saw in your paper that the Chairman of Bowring's insurance gets £57,000 a year. And of course he gets a free car, free drinks, trips abroad with his wife, etc. He gets in a year as much as I get in all my working life. The differential is a bit wrong somewhere. Or what about your reports about wills. Often you see someone, a stockbroker, for example, leaving £500,000. That is his savings, not what he lived on. It would take me 500 years to earn that little lot. Something wrong with the differential there too.

The Tory Party goes on about competition. How much competition was there when Brooke Bond put up their prices and all the others did the same. They didn't want to, they said. But they did it. Beer, petrol, milk, it all goes up the same . . . what price competition?

Then we get a lot of talk about the law of supply and demand. Well, this affluent society produces a lot of effluent. So dustmen are in short supply. So they ask for more money. What a howl from the papers, TV, radio, the lot. No howls about Brooke Bond or the others. Why? If you ask 99 people out of a hundred they can manage all right without stock-brokers. But they don't like being without dustmen. The law of supply and demand is fine for some, but not for others. Why?

We get lectured about our duty to the country through exports. Well, more and more we work for international firms. What country are they loyal to? Dividends and profits is the answer. The people who lecture us spend a lot of time, with the help of newspapers like yours, finding out how to miss paying taxes. We help to earn the money they should be paying taxes on . . . but we can't dodge by insurances or going abroad to live.

You talk about equality of opportunity. What was the first thing Mrs Thatcher did but help those with money to stay at grammar schools? And what about BOAC having some of its routes taken away to give them to a private company, private shareholders and bankers. It was some of my money through the taxes that built up BOAC. Nice social justice this is.

I am not a communist or an anarchist. I believe there must be differentials. But the trouble is the differentials are all wrong, and there's too much fiddling at the top. Where I work there are lavatories for bosses . . . you can only get in with a key, hot and cold, air conditioning, nice soap, individual towels. Then there are lavatories for senior staff . . . hot and cold, not so good soap, a few individual towels, but good rollers. Then there is ours . . . no hot and cold, rough towels, cheesecake soap. And no splash plates in the urinals. How do you think we feel about things like that in the twentieth century? Waving Union Jacks doesn't help.

. . .It's no good economists and financial experts preaching. You can use the telly, radio, papers the lot to try to convince us that we have got to be the first to suffer. That's useless. We know the papers and the telly and radio give one side of the story. We know the other. You don't. Or you don't want to. So there will be a fight. We might lose a round or two. But we will win in the end. And if we have to fight to win instead of being sensible on both sides, the losers are going to suffer a lot.

You can call this bloody-minded. Try bringing up three kids on my pay and see how you like it. There's plenty for everybody if it's shared reasonably. And if, as my mate says, we want to try to have the bridge and beaujolais as well as beer and bingo, what's wrong with that?

Yours faithfully
JAMES THOMSON

Thomson, who explicitly says he is not a Communist nor an anarchist, is writing at a time when Communism as a panacea for social and political evils has been discredited by sixty-seven years of failure. In 1926 this was by no means the case, and many intellectuals looked to government to be the suitable instrument to create and sustain Utopia. H. L. Mencken, writing to Upton Sinclair, gives short shrift to the latter's naive faith in the beneficence of the state:

> Your questions are easy. The government brings my maga-zine to you only unwillingly. It tried to ruin my business, and failed only by an inch. It charges too much for postal orders, and loses too many of them. A corporation of idiot Chinamen could do the thing better. Its machine for putting out fires is intolerably expensive and inefficient. It seldom, in fact, actually puts out a fire: they burn out. In 1904 two square miles of Baltimore burnt down. I lost a suit of clothes, the works of Richard Harding Davis, and a gross of condoms. The Army had nothing to do with the discovery of the cause of yellow fever. Its bureaucrats persecuted the men who did the work. They could have done it much more quickly if they had been outside the Army. It took years of effort to induce the government to fight mosquitoes, and it does the work very badly today. There is malaria everywhere in the South. It is mainly responsible for the prevalence of religion down there.
> You shock me with your government worship. It is unmanly. Today I got word from a friend who lately had a session with a Department of Justice moron. The moron told him that I was on the official list of Bolshevik agents, and that the American Mercury was backed by Russian money. What do you make of that! I am tempted to confess.

In the end politicians mostly muddle through the crises as best they can, often leaving the condition of the nation much as they found it. Those carrying little ideological baggage often travel further than those who believe their own propaganda. Poor

Upton Sinclair soon realized that nothing is achieved in politics without compromise—but this made some of his earlier rhetoric look rather hollow. Mencken crisply pointed this out to him ten years after writing the previous letter. To climb the greasy pole you need a lot of grease:

> You evade the question of your political sword-swallowing. What is to be thought of a great lover of the down-trodden who ran for Congress as a Socialist in 1920, for the United States Senate as a Socialist in 1922, for the Governor of California as a Socialist in 1926, and then popped up in 1934 as a life-long Democrat, and entered upon negotiations with such professional politicians as Franklin D. Roosevelt and Jim Farley, and incidentally, was taken for a ride? What is to be thought of him save that he has learned, like any other chronic job-seeker, to rise above principle? What is to be thought of him save that the itch for office has got him down, and is burning him up?
>
> According to news items reaching the East, you were lately running for something or other again. The people of California, it appears, turned you down, along with your brother messiah, Dr Townsend. With the utmost friendliness, I can only say that I think they showed sound judgment. They have plenty of chance to estimate both you and Townsend, and they prefer anybody else, including even Hoover. They refused to follow you as a Socialist, they refused to follow you as a Prohibitionist, they refused to follow you as an electronic vibrator, they refused to follow you as a thought-transferer, they refused to follow you as a Democrat, and now refuse to follow you as anything whatsoever. The rule is that three strikes are out. To the bench, Comrad; to the bench!

3

The Price of Failure

'. . . History to the defeated
May say Alas but cannot help or pardon.'
W. H. Auden later disowned these lines from his poem 'Spain',
written in 1937; but they well express the bleak pity shown
towards the unluckier protagonists of history by posterity. Some
may have done everything possible to provoke their fates, but
others, like Admiral Byng, did not. Walpole, writing to Sir
Horace Mann in 1757, gives a typical description of the unfortunate Admiral, who had been court-martialled for failing to
engage the French successfully in the Mediterranean. Byng was
sacrificed, as Voltaire mordantly observed, *'pour encourager les
autres'*.

Admiral Byng's tragedy was completed on Monday—a
perfect tragedy, for there were variety of incidents, villainy,
murder, and a hero! His sufferings, persecutions, aspersions,
disturbances, nay, the revolutions of his fate, had not in the
least unhinged his mind; his whole behaviour was natural
and firm. A few days before, one of his friends, standing by
him, said, 'Which of us is tallest?' He replied, 'Why this
ceremony? I know what it means; let the man come and
measure me for my coffin.' He said, that being acquitted of
cowardice, and being persuaded on the coolest reflection that
he had acted for the best, and should act so again, he was not
unwilling to suffer. He desired to be shot on the quarter-deck,
not where common malefactors are; came out at twelve, sat
down in a chair, for he would not kneel, and refused to have
his face covered, that his countenance might show whether
he feared death; but being told that it might frighten his
executioners, he submitted, gave the signal at once, received
one shot through the head, another through the heart, and
fell. Do cowards live or die thus? Can that man want spirit

who only fears to terrify his executioners? Has the aspen
Duke of Newcastle lived thus? Would my Lord Hardwicke die
thus, even supposing he had nothing on his conscience?

Even more graphic is his account, again sent to Sir Horace
Mann, of the execution of the Jacobite rebels after the rebellion
of 1745. Walpole is not much impressed by the ritual nature of
the executions, but has some fun at the expense of foolish
society ladies who were fashionably in love with the rebels.

. . . The most now pretended, is, that it would have come
to Lord Kilmarnock's turn to have given the word for the
slaughter, as Lieutenant-General, with the patent for which
he was immediately drawn into the rebellion, after having
been staggered by his wife, her mother, his own poverty, and
the defeat of Cope. He remained an hour and half in the
house, and shed tears. At last he came to the scaffold,
certainly much terrified, but with a resolution that prevented
his behaving in the least meanly or unlike a gentleman. He
took no notice of the crowd, only to desire that the bays might
be lifted up from the rails, that the mob might see the
spectacle. He stood and prayed some time with Forster, who
wept over him, exhorted and encouraged him. He delivered a
long speech to the sheriff, and with a noble manliness stuck to
the recantation he had made at his trial; declaring he wished
that all who embarked in the same cause might meet the same
fate. He then took off his bag, coat and waistcoat with great
composure, and after some trouble put on a napkin cap, and
then several times tried the block, the executioner who was in
white with a white apron, out of tenderness concealing the
axe behind himself. At last the Earl knelt down, with a visible
unwillingness to depart, and after five minutes dropped his
handkerchief, the signal, and his head was cut off at once,
only hanging by a bit of skin, and was received in a scarlet
cloth by four of the undertaker's men kneeling, who wrapped
it up and put it into the coffin with the body; orders having
been given not to expose the heads, as used to be the custom.
The scaffold was immediately new strowed with sawdust, the
block new covered, the executioner new dressed, and a new
axe brought. Then came old Balmerino, treading with the air
of a general. As soon as he mounted the scaffold, he read the
inscription on his coffin, as he did again afterwards: he then

surveyed the spectators, who were in amazing numbers, even upon masts of ships in the river; and pulling out his spectacles read a treasonable speech which he delivered to the sheriff, and said, the young Pretender was so sweet a prince, that flesh and blood could not resist following him; and lying down to try the block, he said, 'If I had a thousand lives, I would lay them all down here in the same cause.' He said, if he had not taken the Sacrament the day before, he would have knocked down Williamson, the lieutenant of the Tower, for his ill usage of him. He took the axe and felt it, and asked the headsman, how many blows he had given Lord Kilmarnock; and gave him three guineas. Two clergymen, who attended him, coming up, he said, 'No, gentlemen, I believe you have already done me all the service you can.' Then he went to the corner of the scaffold, and called very loud for the warder, to give him his periwig, which he took off, and put on a nightcap of Scotch plaid, and then pulled off his coat and his waistcoat and laid down; but being told he was on the wrong side, vaulted round, and immediately gave the sign by tossing up his arm, as if he were giving the signal for battle. He received three blows, but the first certainly took away all sensation. He was not a quarter of an hour on the scaffold; Lord Kilmarnock above half an one. Balmerino certainly died with the intrepidity of a hero, but with the insensibility of one too. As he walked from his prison to execution, seeing every window and top of house filled with spectators, he cried out, 'Look, look! How they are all piled up like rotten oranges!' My Lady Townshend, who fell in love with Lord Kilmarnock at his trial, will go nowhere to dinner, for fear of meeting with a rebel pie; she says, everybody is so bloody minded, that they eat rebels!

The execution of another failed rebel is spiritedly described by Dr Lloyd, Bishop of St Asaph in a letter to Dr Fell, Bishop of Oxford. The Duke of Monmouth was the natural son of Charles II and Lucy Walter. He had landed with some eighty followers at Lyme Regis in 1685 in an attempt to seize the throne from James II. A weak libertine, Monmouth was not without some humorous bravado as this letter illustrates:

> . . . They [the seven bishops who examined Monmouth] got him to own the King's titles to the crown, and to declare in

writing that the last King told him he was never married to his mother, and by word of mouth to acknowledge his invasion was sin; but could never get him to confess it was a rebellion. They got him to own that he and Lady Harriot Wentworth had lived in all points like man and wife, but they could not make him confess it was adultery.

He acknowledged that he and his Duchess were married by the law of the land, and therefore his children might inherit, if the King pleased. But he did not consider what he did when he married her. He confessed that he had lived many years in all sorts of debauchery, but said he had repented of it, asked pardon, and doubted not that God had forgiven him. He said that since that time he had an affection for Lady Harriot, and prayed that if it were pleasing to God, it might continue, otherwise that it might cease; and God heard his prayer. The affection did continue, and therefore he doubted not it was pleasing to God; and that this was a marriage , their choice of one another being guided not by lust, but by judgment upon due consideration.

They endeavoured to shew him the falsehood and mischievousness of this enthusiastical principle. But he told them it was his opinion, and he was fully satisfied in it. After all, he desired them to give him the communion next morning. They told him they could not do it, while he was in that error and sin. He said he was sorry for it.

The next morning, he told them he had prayed that if he was in an error in that matter God would convince him of it, but God had not convinced him, and therefore he believed it was no error.

When he was upon the scaffold, he professed himself a Protestant of the Church of England. They told him he could not be so, if he did not own the doctrine of the church of England in the point of non-resistance, and if he persisted in that enthusiastic persuasion. He said he could not help it, but yet he approved the doctrine of the church in all other things. He then spoke to the people, in vindication of the lady Harriot, saying she was a woman of great honour and virtue, a religious godly lady (those were his words). They told him of his living in adultery with her. He said, no. For these two years last past he had not lived in any sin that he knew of; and that he had never wronged any person, and that he was sure when he died to go to God, and therefore he did not fear death, which (he said) they might see in his face. Then they prayed for him, and he knelt down and joined with them. After all they had a short prayer for the king, at which he paused, but at last said Amen.

Entirely characteristic in defeat also was Napoleon Bonaparte, proud, alert, and perhaps even after 1815 nursing hopes of a comeback. William Warden was a naval surgeon on the *Northumberland* which conveyed the defeated emperor to St Helena. He conversed as much as he could with the famous prisoner, and sent back accounts of their talks to his future wife:

> *My Dear Miss Hutt,*
> I renew my desultory occupation—*la tâche journalière, telle que vous la voulez*. On the first day of his [Napoleon's] arrival on board, our distinguished passenger displayed rather an eager appetite; I observed that he made a very hearty dinner, which he moistened with claret. He passed the evening on the quarter-deck, where he was amused by the band of the 53rd Regiment; when he personally required them to give the airs of 'God Save the King' and 'Rule Britannia'. At intervals he chatted in a way of easy pleasantry with the officers who were qualified to hold a conversation with him in the French language. I remarked, that on these occasions he always maintains what seems to be an invariable attitude which has somewhat of importance in it, and probably such as he had been accustomed to display at the Tuileries when giving audience to his marshals or officers of State. He never moves his hands from their habitual places in his dress, but to apply them to his snuff-box; and it struck me as a particular circumstance, to which I paid an observing attention, though it might have been connected with his former dignity—that he never offered a pinch to anyone with whom he was conversing.
> . . . Notwithstanding it blew fresh, and there was considerable motion, Bonaparte made his appearance upon deck between three and four P.M., when he amused himself with asking questions of the Lieutenant of the Watch; such as, how many leagues the ship went in an hour? whether the sea was likely to go down? what the strange vessel was on the bow of the *Northumberland*? In short, enough to prove that nothing escaped his notice. But I could not help smiling when I beheld

the man who had stalked so proudly, and with so firm a step over submissive countries, tottering on the deck of a ship, and catching at any arm to save himself from falling; for he has not yet found his sea-legs. Among other objects of his attention, he observed Mr Smith, who was taking the usual to-and-fro walk with his brother midshipmen, to be much older than the rest; and, on this account he appears to have asked him how long he had been in the service; and being answered nine years, he observed: 'That surely is a long time.' 'It is indeed,' said Mr Smith; 'but part of it was passed in a French prison: and I was, sir, at Verdun when you set out on your Russian campaign.' Napoleon immediately shrugged up his shoulders with a very significant smile, and closed the conversation.

Napoleon maintained his dignity to the end. His letter to the Prince Regent from Rochefort about a month after Waterloo is impressive, if a little disingenuous. The Prince didn't bother to reply.

> *Altesse Royale,*
> En butte aux factions qui divisent mon pays, et à l'inimitié des plus grandes puissances de l'Europe, j'ai consommé ma carrière politique. Je viens, comme Themistocle, m'assoir sur le foyer du peuple britannique; je me mets sous la protection de ses lois, que je reclame de Votre Altesse Royale, comme celle du plus puissant, du plus constant, du plus généreux d'ennemis.
>
> NAPOLEON

Less attractive in defeat, as they had been in power, were the Nazi leaders whom John Dos Passos described with a jaundiced eye in a letter to Katy Dos Passos from Nuremberg, 22 November 1945—a cold raw day, as he remarks:

> . . . Robert Jackson's opening for the prosecution yesterday I thought magnificent. A few more speeches like that and the poor old ship of state that's been wallowing rudderless in the trough of the sea will be back on its course. He really is making an effort to make some sense out of what without him would be an act of vengeance. His delivery was amazingly without pomp or self-importance—he might very well be a first rate man. There was a moment when the Nazis in the

prisoners dock seemed to see themselves for the first time as the world sees them. I'll never forget the look of horror and terror that came over their faces when Jackson read the orders for the massacre of the Jews. Either they had not known what documents were in our possession or something like remorse swept over them for a few minutes. Jackson represented the USA as I like to see it represented. He was reasonable, practical and full of a homey kind of dignity. The Nazis are a strange crew. Hess really looks like a man with some disease of the brain—Streicher and Funk are monstrosities but the rest of them look like men of considerable intellectual brilliance. I had a very good seat and was able to see them very well. Goering's a weird character. He still seems to think he can laugh it all off.

In contrast to the ugly conclusions of two horrific world wars, the end of the American War of Independence was marked by a refreshing absence of rancour between the leaders of the two nations, if this account by John Adams of his reception of George III is to be believed. Adams was presenting his credentials as the first Ambassador to the Court of St James from the newly independent ex-colonies:

. . . The door was shut, and I was left with his Majesty and the secretary of state alone. I made the three reverences,— one at the door, another about half way, and a third before the presence,—according to the usage established at this and all the northern Courts of Europe, and then addressed myself to his Majesty in the following words:-

'Sir,—The United States of America have appointed me their minister plenipotentiary to your Majesty, and have directed me to deliver to your Majesty this letter which contains the evidence of it. It is in obedience to their express commands, that I have the honor to assure your Majesty of their unanimous disposition and desire to cultivate the most friendly and liberal intercourse between your Majesty's subjects and their citizens, and of their best wishes for your Majesty's health and happiness, and for that of your royal family. The appointment of a minister from the United States to your Majesty's Court will form an epoch in the history of England and of America. I think myself more fortunate than all my fellow-citizens in having the distinguished honor to be the first to stand in your Majesty's royal presence in a diplomatic character; and I shall esteem myself the happiest of men, if I can be instrumental in recommending my country more and more to your Majesty's royal benevolence, and of restoring an entire esteem, confidence, and affection, or, in better words, the old good nature and the old good humor between people, who, though separated by an ocean, and under different governments, have the same language, a similar religion, and kindred blood.

'I beg your Majesty's permission to add, that, although I have some time before been intrusted by my country, it was never in my whole life in a manner so agreeable to myself.'

The King listened to every word I said, with dignity, but with an apparent emotion. Whether it was the nature of the interview, or whether it was my visible agitation, for I felt more than I did or could express, that touched him, I cannot say. But he was much affected, and answered me with more tremor than I had spoken with, and said:-

'Sir,—The circumstances of this audience are so extraordinary, the language you have now held is so extremely Proper, and the feelings you have discovered so justly adapted to the occasion, that I must say that I not only receive with pleasure the assurance of the friendly dispositions of the United States, but that I am very glad the choice has fallen upon you to be their minister. I wish you, sir, to believe, and that it may be understood in America, that I have done nothing in the late contest but what I thought myself indispensably bound to do, by the duty which I owed to my people. I will be very frank with you. I was the last to consent to the separation; but the separation having been made, and having become inevitable, I have always said, as I say now, that I would be the first to meet the friendship of the United States as an independent power. The moment I see such sentiments and language as yours prevail, and a disposition to give this country the preference, that moment I shall say, let the circumstances of language, religion, and blood have their natural and full effect.'

I dare not say that these were the King's precise words, and it is even possible, that I may have in some particular mistaken his meaning; for, although his pronunciation is as distinct as I ever heard, he hesitated some time between his periods, and between the members of the same period. He was indeed much affected, and I confess I was not less so . . .

George III may have lost the American colonies, but he did not pay for his political mistakes with his head. This, however, was the fate reserved for his counterpart across the Channel. Mary Wollstonecraft, the feminist wife of William Godwin and mother of Shelley's wife, wrote from Paris in December 1792, after Louis XVI had passed by her window on his way to be tried for treason. She writes as if he were on his way to the guillotine, although he was not in fact executed until 21 January of the following year; but it was already clear that he was doomed:

> I should immediately on the receipt of your letter, my dear friend, have thanked you for your punctuality, for it highly gratified me, had I not wished to wait till I could tell you that this day was not stained with blood. Indeed the prudent precautions taken by the National Convention to prevent a tumult, made me suppose that the dogs of faction would not dare to bark, much less to bite, however true to their scent; and I was not mistaken; for the citizens, who were called out, are returning home with composed countenances, shouldering their arms. About nine o'clock this morning, the king passed by my window, moving silently along (excepting now and then a few strokes on the drum, which rendered the stillness more awful) through empty streets, surrounded by the national guards, who, clustering round the carriage, seemed to deserve their name. The inhabitants flocked to their windows, but the casements were all shut, not a voice was heard, nor did I see anything like an insulting gesture. For the first time since I entered France, I bowed to the majesty of the people, and respected the propriety of behaviour so perfectly in unison with my own feelings. I can scarcely tell you why, but an association of ideas made the tears flow insensibly from my eyes, when I saw Louis sitting, with more dignity than I expected from his character, in a hackney coach, going to meet death, where so many of his race have triumphed. My fancy instantly brought Louis XIV before me, entering the capital with all his pomp, after one of the victories most flattering to his pride, only to see the sunshine of prosperity overshadowed by the sublime gloom of misery. I have been alone ever since; and, though my mind is calm, I cannot dismiss the lively images that have filled my imagination all the day. Nay, do not smile, but pity me; for, once or twice, lifting my eyes from the paper, I have seen eyes

glaring through a glass-door opposite my chair, and bloody hands shook at me. Not the distant sound of a footstep can I hear. My apartments are remote from those of the servants, the only persons who sleep with me in an immense hotel, one folding door opening after another. I wish I had even kept the cat with me! I want to see something alive; death in so many frightful shapes has taken hold of my fancy. I am going to bed—and, for the first time in my life, I cannot put out the candle.

M. W.

THE AIR WE
BREATHE

1

Travellers' Tales

Dr Johnson, in exploding the idea that travel necessarily broadens the mind, quotes a Spanish proverb to the effect that he who wishes to bring back wealth from the Indies must take the wealth of the Indies with him. But he does concede that travelling should enable us to learn how things really are, as opposed to how they ought to be. He was not always himself a beneficiary of this latter process, as when he promoted the ridiculous notion that there are no trees in Scotland; this observation led Cobbett to remark unkindly that he must have been led around that country blindfold.

Travel can certainly have a debilitating effect on those with the wrong temperament for it. James Joyce for instance, a permanent exile but a reluctant traveller, is given to morose remarks about the places he visits. Rome reminded him of 'a man who lives by exhibiting to travellers his grandmother's corpse', and he is even ruder about the inhabitants of Ancona, who he thought had robbed him. To the really bilious traveller such misfortunes as poverty and starvation become yet another stick to beat their victims with, as if the absence of a hot bath for a travelling gentleman were more important than the absence of any hot water at all for the resident population. Whole nationalities are dismissed with a few slighting remarks in this way: 'The ordinary women of Wales,' says David Mallet in a letter to Alexander Pope in 1734 'are generally short and squat, ill-favoured and nasty. Their headdress is a remnant of coarse blanket and for their linen—they wear none, and they are all barefooted. But then,' he adds patronizingly, 'they are wonderfully good-natured.'

The reluctance of travel writers to travel may seem odd but is is not unusual. Henry Miller, the author of a classic, if overblown, book about Greece and of a book about travelling around America, actually hated leaving his Parisian base, as he explained in a letter to his friend Anais Nin:

I think that the moment one begins to travel one is really wretched. One becomes stupefied by the succession of petty, annoying, perplexing trivialities encountered. 'Abruti'? Is that the word? A word I like, whether it means stupefied, or not. One travels to form associations, comparisons, to live back. I hate that. One is always detached, uprooted. One doesn't think consecutively. One thinks fragmentarily. Or I do at least. When I return to the hotel at night I feel like a prisoner returning to his cell. A place to pass the night. Not a place to live in, think, or plan. What tip will I leave the chambermaid? Is the toothbrush packed away? Do you change trains? And most of all I wonder if at the last moment there is going to be some unexpected and staggering sum added to my bill which I shan't be able to pay. It is a torture to go to the desk and ask for the bill. I am almost afraid to look at it. I always think—if you only knew how little money I have in my pocket you would not be so polite to me. You would treat me like a criminal.

That's travelling for me. I'm cured. Never again, until I can do it with a free conscience. I am so afraid of being cut off from my base, Paris. Of getting to some distant point and being told 'you can't go back . . . vamoose!' Why? Because, when I look back on it, all my travelling has been done under great anxiety. I shall never forget my terrible mortification one day in North Carolina, when we were hitch-hiking. We started out, as we always did, without a cent in our pockets, intending to get a hitch for a couple of hundred miles and return to Asheville, where we were living, by nightfall. Everything goes well. We go a tremendous distance, in fine cars. Always hailed only the fast cars. On the return, we somehow are picked up by a Ford car. The man is a convalescent. Had been working on the telephone poles and was permanently injured by an electric shock which threw him off the pole some forty feet away. He tells us all the way back about his life in the hospital. Finally he deposits us on the road near our joint. I get out and shake hands with him thanking him for his courtesy. Suddenly he sits bolt upright and stares at me uncomprehendingly. What! Aren't you going to pay me? I explain that I never paid for a lift before, that we've been doing that all the time. . . . 'But I'm a poor man,' he says. 'You could at least pay me something for the gas it cost me.' I tell him I haven't a cent in my pocket. He swears.

He thinks we have a hell of a nerve. I feel so conscience-stricken that I could get down on my knees and apologize to him. But June is herself, and very impudent. She walks off courageously. I stand there and babble with the guy. I don't know whether you know what an ignorant Southerner is like, a mountaineer who lives that desolate life which only people in Tennessee and West Virginia and such places understand. Anyway, I walk off too, finally, leaving him to curse and shout after me. But that experience takes the heart out of me.

In contrast to the Miller approach Thomas Gray is a dry chronicler of people and events, always happy in his phrasing and always entertaining. His letters from Italy to his friend West, from one of which the following extract is taken, are full of delightful insights and humorously observed scenes.

This day being in the palace of his Highness the Duke of Modena, he laid his most serene commands upon me to write to Mr West, and said he thought it for his glory, that I should draw up an inventory of all his most serene possessions for the said West's perusal. —Imprimis, a house being in circumference a quarter of a mile, two feet and an inch; the said house containing the following particulars, to wit, a great room. Item, another great room; item, a bigger room; item, another room; item, a vast room; item, a sixth of the same; a seventh ditto; an eighth as before; a ninth as abovesaid; a tenth (see No. 1); item, ten more such, besides twenty besides, which, not to be too particular, we shall pass over. The said rooms contain nine chairs, two tables, five stools, and a cricket. From whence we shall proceed to the garden, containing two millions of superfine laurel hedges, a clump of cypress tress, and half the river Teverone, that pisses into two thousand several chamberpots. Finis. —Dame Nature desired me to put in a list of her little goods and chattels, and, as they were small, to be very minute about them. She has built here three or four little mountains, and laid them out in an irregular semi-circle; from certain others behind, at a greater distance, she has drawn a canal, into which she has put a little river of hers, called Anio; she has cut a huge cleft between the two innermost of her four hills, and there she has left it to its own disposal; which she has no sooner done, but, like a heedless chit, it tumbles headlong down a declivity fifty feet perpendicular, breaks itself all to shatters, and is converted into a shower of rain, where the sun forms many a bow, red, green, blue and yellow.

Another suave chronicler of his surroundings was Anton Chekhov. As one would expect he has an eye for detail and a dispassionate view of the often alarming vagaries of human nature that he encounters:

Travelling is a cold business. I have my sheepskin on. My body is comfortable, but my feet and legs are freezing. I wrap them in my leather overcoat, but it doesn't help. I am wearing two pairs of trousers. Well, you ride and ride. Mileposts flash by, puddles, birch groves. We pass tramping settlers, a file of convicts under guard. We have met vagabonds with pots on their backs; these gents roam the Siberian highway freely. On occasion they will do in an old woman in order to use her skirt for puttees, or they'll remove from a milepost a metal sign with a number on it, just on the chance that it may come in handy. Again, they will bash in the head of a beggar they meet or gouge out the eyes of their fellow deportee, but they won't touch a traveller. As far as robbery is concerned, travel hereabouts is entirely safe. From Tyumen to Tomsk neither the coachmen on the post vehicles nor the self-employed drivers can recall that anything has been stolen from a traveller. When you enter a station you leave your things in the courtyard; when you ask if they won't be stolen, the reply is a smile. It is even bad form to mention burglaries and murders on the highway. It seems to me that were I to lose my money at a station or in a vehicle, if the coachman found it, he would return it to me without fail, and wouldn't brag about the matter.

Generally speaking, people here are good, kindly, and with pleasing folkways. The rooms are tidy and the furniture simple, with some pretensions to luxury; the sleeping accommodations are soft, with feather-beds and big pillows; the floors are painted or covered with home-made linen rugs. All this is due to the general prosperity, to the fact that a family has an allowance of 43 acres of excellent black earth which produces rich crops of wheat (30 copecks is the price of 36 pounds of wheat flour). However, not everything is explained by material welfare, the people's way of life must not be

overlooked. On entering a Siberian bedroom at night you are
not assailed by the peculiar Russian stench. True, handing me
a teaspoon, an old woman wiped it on her behind, but then
they will not serve you tea without a tablecloth, people don't
belch in your presence, don't search for insects in their hair;
when they hand you water or milk, they don't put their
fingers in the glass; the plates and dishes are clean, kvass is as
transparent as beer. In sum, such cleanliness as there is here
can only be dreamed of by the Khokhols, who are cleaner
than Katzaps. The bread they bake here is delicious; the first
days I could not get my fill of it. Equally tasty are the pies,
tarts, and turnovers; family bread resembles Ukrainian
spongy rolls. Pancakes are thin. The rest of Siberian cookery is
not for the European stomach.

If Chekhov took the habits of the Asiatic tribes in his stride, Sir
Stamford Raffles was quite unperturbed by the Sumatrans'
long-established custom of eating each other. He describes it all
with admirable sang-froid in a letter dated 12 February 1820 and
written 'somewhere off Sumatra'. Apart from establishing a
settlement at Singapore (without Government authorization),
Raffles was also the founder of the London Zoo, and its first
president. A man of wide sympathies and scientific curiosity, he
saw no reason to hold the Sumatrans' eating habits against
them:

. . . I have said the Battas are not a bad people, and I still
think so, notwithstanding they eat one another, and relish the
flesh of a man better than that of an ox or a pig. You must
merely consider that I am giving you an account of a novel
state of society. The Battas are not savages, for they read and
write, and think full as much, and more, than those who are
brought up at our Lancastrian and National Schools. They
have also codes of laws of great antiquity; and it is from a
regard for these laws and a veneration for the institutions of
their ancestors, that they eat each other. The Law declares
that, for certain crimes, four in number, the criminals shall be
eaten ALIVE. The same law declares, also, that in great wars,
that is to say, one district with another, it shall be lawful to eat
the prisoners, whether taken alive, dead, or in their graves. In
the four great cases of crimes, the criminal is also duly tried
and condemned by a competent tribunal. When the evidence

is heard, sentence is pronounced, when the chiefs drink a dram each, which last ceremony is equivalent to signing and sealing with us. Two or three days then elapse, to give time for assembling the people; and in cases of adultery it is not allowed to carry the sentence into effect unless the relations of the wife appear and partake of the feast. The prisoner is then brought forward on the day appointed, and fixed to a stake, with his hands extended. The husband, or party injured, comes up, and takes the first choice pieces, each helping himself according to his liking. After all have partaken, the chief person goes up and cuts off the head, which he carries home as a trophy. The head is hung up in front of the house, and the brains are carefully preserved in a bottle, for the purposes of witchcraft, etc. In devouring the flesh, it is sometimes eaten raw, and sometimes grilled; but it must be eaten upon the spot. Limes, salt and pepper are always in readiness, and they sometimes eat rice with the flesh; but they never drink toddy or spirits. Many carry bamboos with them, and, filling them with blood, drink it off. The assembly consists of men alone, as the flesh of man is prohibited to the females; it is said, however, that they get a bit by stealth now and then. I am assured, and *really* do believe, that many of the people do prefer human flesh to any other; but notwithstanding this *penchant* they never indulge the appetite except on lawful occasions. The palms of the hands, and the soles of the feet, are the delicacies of epicures

On expressing my surprise at the continuance of such extraordinary practices, I was informed, that formerly it was usual for people to eat their parents when too old for work. The old people selected the horizontal branch of a tree, and quietly suspended themselves by their hands, while their children and neighbours, forming a circle, danced round them, crying out, 'When the fruit is ripe, then it will fall.' This practice took place during the season of limes, when salt and pepper were plenty, and as soon as the victims became fatigued, and could hold on no longer, they fell down when all hands cut them up, and made a hearty meal of them. The practice, however, of eating the old people has been abandoned, and thus a step in civilisation has been attained, and, therefore, there are hopes of future improvement. This state of society you will admit to be very peculiar, and it is calculated that certainly not less than from sixty to one hundred Battas are thus eaten in a year in times of peace. I was going to tell your grace much about the treatment of the females and children, but I find that I have already filled several sheets, and that I am called away from the cabin; I will therefore conclude with entreating you not to think the worse of me for this horrible relation. You know that I am far from wishing to paint any of the Malay race in the worst colours, but yet I must tell the truth. Notwithstanding the practices I have related, it is my determination to take Lady Raffles into the interior, and to spend a month or two in the midst of these Battas. Should any accident occur to us, or should we never be heard of more, you may conclude we have been eaten.

A different perspective on travelling is offered by Gustave Flaubert. The letters he wrote while in Arab lands are full of often scurrilous anecdote, and of a frankness that is frequently brutal but which makes for compulsive reading. Running through them all is what his translator Francis Steegmuller aptly calls a 'romantic realistic dichotomy.' The novelist cannot resist highly coloured scenes, especially sensual ones, but always insists that he is describing them with the utmost realism. 'Do not imagine,' he writes on one occasion, that 'you can exorcise what oppresses you in life by giving vent to it in art: No, the heart's dross does not find its way on to paper: all you pour out there is ink.' But Flaubert's letters are often full of the heart's dross, presented in such a way that the writer seems to distance himself from the events he describes while at the same time being their principal protagonist. A story he tells of going to a very young whore, the daughter of the house, being challenged by her as to whether he was carrying VD and, since he was, castigating her for the indelicacy of her question to a gentleman of standing, is not untypical in its mixture of comedy and callousness. These ingredients are visible on the following description of the Coptic monks on the Nile:

> . . . At a place called Begel-el-Teir we had an amusing sight. On the top of a hill overlooking the Nile there is a Coptic monastery, whose monks have the custom, as soon as they see a boatload of tourists, of running down, throwing themselves in the water, and swimming out to ask for alms. Everyone who passes is assailed by them. You see these fellows, totally naked, rushing down their perpendicular cliffs

and swimming towards you as fast as they can, shouting: 'Baksheesh, baksheesh, cawadja christiani!' And since there are many caves in the cliff at this particular spot, echo repeats 'Cawadja, cawadja!' loud as a cannon. Vultures and eagles were flying overhead, the boat was flashing through the water, its two great sails very full. At that moment one of our sailors, the clown of the crew, began to dance a naked, lascivious dance that consisted of an attempt to bugger himself. To drive off the Christians he showed them his prick and his arse pretending to piss and shit on their heads (they were clinging to the sides of the *cange*). The other sailors shouted insults at them repeating the names of Allah and Mohammed. Some hit them with sticks, other with ropes; Joseph rapped their knuckles with his kitchen tongs. It was a *tutti* of cudgelings, pricks, bare arses, yells and laughter. As soon as they were given money they put it in their mouths and returned home the way they had come. If they weren't greeted with a good beating, the boats would be assailed by such hordes of them that there would be danger of capsizing.

In another place it's not men who call on you, but birds. At Sheik Sa'id there is a tomb-chapel built in honour of a Moslem saint where birds go of their own accord and drop food that is given to them—this food is then offered to poor travellers—You and I, 'who have read Voltaire', don't believe this. But everyone is so backward here! You so seldom hear anyone singing Béranger's songs!

'What, sir, the benefits of civilization are not being introduced into this country? Where are your railway networks? What is the state of elementary education? Etc.' [mimicking the remarks of a conservative and rather ignorant French gentleman satirized by Flaubert]—so that as you sail past this chapel all the birds flock around the boat and land on the rigging—you throw them bits of bread, they wheel about, pick it up from the water, and fly off . . .

Monks in the East have fascinated and repelled travellers from Britain ever since the seventeenth-century English chaplain at Constantinople visited Mount Athos. He reported somewhat unfavourably on what he termed 'monkery', but praised the lampreys. Edward Lear painted all of the monasteries when he visited Athos two centuries later but was made to feel distinctly queasy by the life-style of the inhabitants:

. . . But however wondrous and picturesque the exterior &
interior of the monasteries, & however abundantly &
exquisitely glorious & stupendous the scenery of the mountain, I would not go again to the '*Ayios Opos*' for any money,
so gloomy, so shockingly unnatural, so lonely, so lying, so
unatonably odious seems to me all the atmosphere of such
monkery. That half of our species[1] which it is natural to every
man to cherish & love best, ignored, prohibited and
abhorred— all life spent in everlasting repetition of monoto-
nous prayers, no sympathy with ones fellow-beans of any
nation, class or age. The name of Christ on every garment and
at every tongue's end, but his maxims trodden under foot.
God's world and will turned upside down, maimed, &
caricatured:—if this I say be Xtianity let Xtianity be rooted out
as soon as possible. More pleasing in the sight of the
Almighty I really believe & more like what Jesus Christ
intended man to become, is an honest Turk with 6 wives, or a
Jew working hard to feed his little old clo' babbies, than these
muttering, miserable, mutton-hating, man-avoiding, misogy-
nic, morose, & merriment-marring, monotoning, many-mule-
taking, mocking, mournful, minced-fish & marmalade masti-
cating Monx . . .

Since the British have such very odd notions about other nations
it is perhaps appropriate to record an opinion of the British
themselves as foreign travellers are, or were, likely to encounter
them. Mark Twain writing to J. A. Y. MacAlister in 1900 showed
that he was making himself a master of peculiarly British
notions of what a hotel should be like:

We do really start next Saturday. I meant to sail earlier but
waited to finish some studies of what are called Family
Hotels. They are a London specialty. God has not permitted
them to exist elsewhere. They are ramshackle clubs which
were dwelling at the time of the Heptarchy. Dover and
Albemarle Streets are filled with them. The once spacious
rooms are split up into coops which afford as much discomfort as can be had anywhere out of jail for any money. All the
modern inconveniences are furnished, and some that have
been obsolete for a century. The prices are astonishingly high

---

[1] Females are not allowed to visit Mt Athos.

for what you get. The bedrooms are hospitals for incurable furniture. I find it so in this one. They exist upon a tradition. They represent the vanishing home-like inn of fifty years ago, and are mistaken by foreigners for it. Some quite respectable Englishmen still frequent them through inherited habit and arrested development; many Americans also, through ignorance and superstition. The rooms are as interesting as the Tower of London, but older I think. Older and dearer. The lift was a gift of William the Conqueror. Some of the beds are prehistoric. They represent geological periods.

Mine is the oldest. It is formed in strata of Old Red Sandstone, volcanic tufa, ignis fatuus, and bicarbonate of hornblende, superimposed upon argillaceous shale, and contains the prints of prehistoric man. It is in No. 149. Thousands of scientists come to see it. They consider it holy. They want to blast out the prints but cannot. Dynamite rebounds from it.

Perhaps it is fortunate that Twain never sampled British Rail, the all-purpose Aunt Sally for correspondents of *The Times*. A Mr Richard Harvey, writing in 1968, gives us the unforgettable flavour of a railway journey of the sort that people dine out on for years:

Sir,
This afternoon I caught the 15:05 train from the recently modernized Euston Station.

According to the new electronic departure indicator, its destination was Rugby; according to the ticket collector and a notice on the platform it was Coventry; according to the destination blind on the train it was Wolverhampton. I got off at Watford to hear the station announcer declare it was Wolverhampton and walked home to look it up in my copy of the timetable and discover it was Birmingham.

Perhaps now that their modernization scheme is complete British Rail's executives will have enough time to decide where their trains are going to?

Yours faithfully,
RICHARD HARVEY

2

Town and Country

The fascination exercised by London was already evident before
Dr Johnson laid it down that to be tired of London was to be
tired of life. Indeed, London's influence is such that it can turn
men into quite different sorts of people from the kind they are in
the country.

The writer of the following letter, an anonymous correspondent of the early eighteenth century, has come up to the city
from Devon and is evidently half entranced and half horrified by
the glitter, corruption and rough behaviour he encounters. He is
also extremely put out to find himself cut by two judges and an
MP of his acquaintance, whose former conviviality is thereby
revealed as insulting condescension:

> . . . London is certainly the greatest city upon earth, at least
> there is nothing like it in Devonshire; but our beer is infinitely
> better than theirs, which is as black as bull's blood, and as
> thick as mustard. Everything is shamefully dear here; you pay
> half-a-crown or three shillings for a chicken, which with us
> would not yield above a groat or fivepence; but they have so
> many customers, that they ask and have just what they
> please. You see a great many coaches standing in the street
> ready to be hired, and they will carry a beggar for his money
> as soon as a lord, and sooner; for they say that persons of
> quality, instead of paying the coachman, do often run him
> through the body; and it seems there is no law against lords,
> which is the reason that persons of quality are greater than
> any sort of men whatsoever. These coaches are very conve-
> nient, if they were not so confounded dear; but if one of them
> carries you but three doors, he will have a shilling; whereas in
> our country, you may have a couple of horses a dozen miles
> for half-a-crown . . .

There are here houses called chocolate-houses, covered all

over with sconces and looking-glasses. Hither gentlemen who have nothing to do but to dress themselves, repair to show their fine clothes; it is worth while to see a whole row of those beaus sit looking at one another, or at themselves; or if they do anything else, it is only to swear and take snuff, or to play at dice, and then all the while they play they are constantly damning themselves. It is almost become a proverb here, in London, that all your fine fellows are prodigiously ignorant and prodigiously wicked; insomuch that they are the jest of men of wit, and pitied by men of virtue, and shunned by both.

There is a fine river running by London full of ships and boats; one of these boats will carry you for sixpence, and some of them for threepence, a great way; and it would be very pleasant, if it were not for the abuse and ugly language you meet with; for the people upon the water will affront you to your teeth, and call you a hundred names, though you do not say a word to them; it is to no purpose to be angry, or to threaten them: they laugh at all that. I offered to get out of the boat and to box with several of those saucy fellows, but not one of them would accept of my challenge; nay, the women are as bad as the men. The more shame is theirs!

. . . Westminster Hall is a vast great room, where law and justice have been bought so dear, that one had oftener better go without them. The lawyers stroll about here, and look—sharp and greedy for fees. There are in the hall other toymen besides lawyers, and they will sell you their baubles at treble prices, so there is nothing but biting on all hands.

Not far from hence is the House of Commons. I went to see it, and to see the manner of their proceedings, and came away very much dissatisfied; for a dozen members talked at a time, and I could not understand a word of the debate. I also visited the House of Lords; there indeed I perceived more order, but neither heard nor saw anything remarkable, but some grave folks in odd habits.

In this great city they are quite another thing than what they are out of it; insomuch, that he who will be great with you in the country will scarce pull off his hat to you in London. I once dined at Exeter with a couple of judges, and they talked to me there, and drank my health, and we were very familiar together; so when I saw them again, passing through Westminster Hall, I was glad of it, with all my heart, and ran to meet them with a broad smile, and asked them how they did, and to shake hands with them; but they looked at me so coldly, and so proudly, as you cannot imagine, and did not seem to know me; at which I was confounded angry and mad; but I kept my mind to myself. At another time I was at the play-house (which is a rare place for mirth, and music, and dancing), and being in the pit, saw in one of the boxes a member of Parliament of our country, with whom I have been as great as hand and glove; so being overjoyed to see him, I called to him aloud by his name, and asked him how he did; but instead of saluting me again, or making any manner of answer, he looked plaguey sour, and never opened his mouth; though when he is in the country, he is as merry a grig as any in fifty miles, and we have cracked many a bottle together.

The literary and satirical tone of the foregoing letter suggests that it was written with publication in mind. Some of the writer's more jaundiced comments still strike a chord, though we are nowadays spared the abuse of the Thames boatmen. One can see why Dr Johnson, after nearly being tipped into the Thames, told one of them: 'Sir, your wife, under pretence of keeping a bawdy house, is a receiver of stolen goods.'

About a century later Thomas Carlyle was adjusting to London life; he also was attracted and repelled at the same time, as he describes in his letter to a Scots friend written in 1824:

. . . There is an excitement in all this, which is pleasant as a transitory feeling, but much against my taste as a permanent one. I had much rather visit London from time to time, than live in it. There is in fact no *right* life in it that I can find: the people are situated here like plants in a hot-house, to which the quiet influences of sky and earth are never in their unadulterated state admitted. It is the case with all ranks; the carman with his huge slouch-hat hanging half-way down his back, consumes his breakfast of bread and tallow or hog's lard, sometimes as he swags along the streets, always in a hurried and precarious fashion, and supplies the deficit by continual pipes, and pots of beer. The fashionable lady rises at three in the afternoon, and begins to live towards midnight. Between these two extremes, the same false and tumultuous manner of existence more or less infests all ranks. It seems as

if you were for ever in 'an inn', the feeling of *home* in our
acceptation of the term is not known to one of a thousand.
You are packed into paltry shells of brick-houses (calculated to
endure for forty years, and then fall); every door that slams to
in the street is audible in your most secret chamber; the
necessaries of life are hawked about through multitudes of
hands, and reach you, frequently adulterated, always at
rather more than *twice* their cost elsewhere; people's friends
must visit them by rule and measure; and when you issue
from your door, you are assailed by vast shoals of quacks, and
showmen, and street-sweepers, and pickpockets, and mendi-
cants of every degree and shape, all plying in noise or silent
craft their several vocations, all in their hearts like 'lions
ravening for their prey'. The blackguard population of the
place is the most consummately blackguard of anything I ever
saw . . .

For some, however, London is a drug. Withdraw them from its
racy and stimulating atmosphere and they begin to wilt like
flowers out of water. The noise, the garishness, even the squalor
itself are for them aphrodisiacs of the soul conducive to a state of
heightened and sensual enjoyment of life. Charles Lamb was
one of these as can be seen from his letter to William Wordsworth turning down an invitation to the Lake District:

I ought before this to have reply'd to your very kind
invitation into Cumberland. With you and your Sister I could
gang anywhere. But I am afraid whether I shall ever be able to
afford so desperate a Journey. Separate from the pleasure of
your company, I don't much care if I never see a mountain in
my life. I have passed all my days in London, until I have
formed as many and intense local attachments, as any of you
mountaineers can have done with dead nature. The Lighted
shops of the Strand and Fleet Street, the innumerable trades,
tradesmen and customers, coaches, waggons, playhouses, all
the bustle and wickedness round about Covent Garden, the
very women of the Town, the Watchmen, drunken scenes,
rattles,—life awake, if you awake, at all hours of the night,
the impossibility of being dull in Fleet Street, the crowds, the
very dirt & mud, the Sun shining upon houses and pavements,
the print shops, the old book stalls, parsons cheap'ning books,
coffee houses, steams of soups from kitchens, the panto-

mimes, London itself a pantomime and a masquerade,—all these things work themselves into my mind and feed me, without a power of satiating me . . .

But if living in the country is a penance for some, it is the ultimate in a satisfying existence for others, notwithstanding the characters in the plays of Chekhov who complain endlessly of the tedium of the rural scene, and spend their time analysing their failure or getting drunk in between bouts of masochistic courtship. In England the principal complaints against the country are the discomfort and the philistinism of some of the inhabitants. The hazards of keeping up an English country estate are related in a hilarious satirical letter of 1772 written by Sir John Dalrymple. They include crumbling buildings, recalcitrant servants, ghosts and unpleasant neighbours:

You ask me, what I have been doing? To the best of my memory, what has passed since I came home is as follows:

Finding the roof bad, I sent slaters, at the peril of their necks, to repair it. They mended three holes, and made thirty themselves.

I pulled down as many walls round the house as would have fortified a town. This was in summer: but now, that winter is come, I would give all the money to put them up again, that it cost me to take them down.

I thought it would give a magnificent air to the hall, to throw the passage into it. After it was done, I went out of town to see how it looked. It was night when I went into it; the wind blew out the candle from the over-size of the room; upon which I ordered the partition to be built up again, that I might not die of cold in the midst of summer.

I ordered the old timber to be thinned; to which, perhaps, the love of lucre a little contributed. The workmen, for every tree they cut, destroyed three, by letting them fall on each other. I received a momentary satisfaction from hearing that the carpenter I employed had cut his thumb in felling a tree. But this pleasure was soon allayed, when, upon examining his measure, I found that he had measured false, and cheated me of 20 per cent.

Instead of saddle-horses I bought mares, and had them covered with an Arabian. When I went, some months after, to mount them, the groom told me I should kill the foals; and, now I walk on foot, with the stable full of horses, unless when, with much humility, I ask to be admitted into the chaise, which is generally refused me.

. . . I made a fine hay-stack; but quarrelled with my wife as to the manner of drying the hay, and building the stack. The hay-stack took fire; by which I had the double mortification of losing my hay, and finding my wife had more sense than myself.

I kept no plough; for which I thank my Maker; because then I must have wrote this letter from a gaol.

I paid twenty pounds for a dung-hill, because I was told it was a good thing; and, now, I would give anybody twenty shillings to tell me what to do with it.

I built, and stocked a pigeon-house; but the cats watched below, the hawks hovered above; and pigeon-soup, roasted pigeon, or cold pigeon-pie, have I never seen since.

. . . I brewed much beer; but the small turned sour, and the servants drank all the strong.

I found a ghost in the house, whose name was McAlister, a pedlar, that had killed in one of the rooms at the top of the house two centuries ago. No servant would go on an errand after the sun set, for fear of McAlister, which obliged me to set off one set of my servants. Soon after, the housekeeper, your old friend Mrs Brown, died, aged 90; and then the belief ran, that another ghost was in the house, upon which many of the new set of servants begged leave to quit the house, and got it.

In one thing only have I succeeded. I have quarrelled with all my neighbours; so that, with a dozen gentleman's seats in my view, I stalk alone like a lion in a desert.

I thought I could be happy with my tenants, because I could be insolent to them without their being insolent to me. But they paid me no rent; and in a few days I shall have above one half of the very few friends I have in the country in a prison.

Such being the pleasures of a country life, I intend to quit them all in about a month, to submit to the mortification of spending the spring in London.

If the owners of country houses have an uncomfortable time, so do some of their guests, as we see from an ill-tempered note sent by the Earl of Carlisle to George Selwyn in 1776:

I came this morning with Lady Carlisle from Cashiobury. What a house! What people! What manners! I lost my money and my temper; lay in damp and dirty sheets; and what with the moisture, the gnats, and the dirt, we might as well have slept in a fen.

The complaint of discomfort in the countryside—only relative discomfort, it must be admitted—is taken up by Josef Haydn in a letter to Frau von Genzinger from Esterhaz written in February 1790. February is a miserable month almost anywhere in Europe, so doubtless he was feeling the cold a bit in the draughty Esterhaz palace. He was already fifty-eight, and successful, and retired from his patron's service the same year. He is obviously missing the Viennese culinary delicacies:

. . . At home I found everything in confusion and for 3 days I did not know whether I was Kapell-master or Kapell-servant, nothing could comfort me, my whole apartment was in disorder, my Forte-piano, which I used to love, was out of order, disobedient, it rather vexed than soothed me, I got little sleep, even my dreams were a persecution, for when I dreamt that I was hearing an excellent performance of *Le Nozze di Figaro* that odious North wind woke me and almost blew my nightcap off my head. In 3 days I lost 20 pounds in weight, for the good Viennese titbits had already disappeared during the journey. Yes, yes, thought I to myself as I sat in my boarding-house, obliged to eat a piece off a 50-year-old cow instead of that delicious beef, an ancient mutton-stew with yellow turnips instead of the ragout with little dumplings, a slice of roast leather instead of the Bohemian pheasant, a so-called Dschabl or Gros-Salat instead of those delicious, delicate oranges, tough apple-rings and hazelnuts instead of those pastries— and so forth. Yes, yes, thought I to myself, if only I had here all those titbits I could not manage to eat at Vienna!—Here at Esterhaz nobody asks me—do you take chocolate with milk or without, would you like coffee, black or with cream, what can I get you, my dear Haydn, would you like vanilla ice or a pineapple one? If only I had here a piece of good Parmesan cheese, especially on fast days to help the black dumplings and noodles down more easily,—this very day I ordered our porter to send me down a few pounds of it.

Haydn's sojourn in the country was an enforced one, in so far as he had to do his patron's bidding. Another enforced exile from the city was endured by Niccolo Machiavelli in 1513. He had been associated with the losing side in one of the endless struggles for power in sixteenth-century Florence. When the Medici returned, the power of Machiavelli's patron, the Gonfaloniere Soderini, was eclipsed. Machiavelli was arrested on a conspiracy charge and tortured; he refused to admit any wrongdoing and was subsequently pardoned, but had to withdraw from public life. In a letter from his country house at S. Andrea in Percussina, addressed to Francesco Vettori and dated 10 December 1513, he describes how he spends his day. The 'little book' he mentions was *De Principatibus*, better known to us as *The Prince*, a work that was to prove the foundation of the study of political science. The clergy of the time condemned Machiavelli's works, which included licentious satirical comedies, and the first major edition of them did not appear until more than two hundred and fifty years after his death in 1527.

. . . Having left the wood, I make my way to a spring, and thence to a fowling-hut of mine, taking with me a book, either Dante or Petrarch or one of the minor poets such as Tibullus, Ovid and their like. I read about their amorous passions and loves and remember my own; and find delight for a while in these thoughts. Then I turn up the road, to the inn, and talk to the passers-by, asking them for news of their homes; I learn many things, and observe the various tastes and fancies of mankind. Meanwhile the dinner hour has come, at which my company and I eat the food which my poor farm and meagre fortune provide. Having eaten, I go back to the inn, where the host generally is, and a butcher, a miller and two workmen from the kiln. With them I become a lazy lout all day, playing cards or backgammon, during which a thousand arguments arise and an exchange of insulting words; most often we are fighting over a farthing, and our shouts are heard as far as San Casciano . . .

When evening comes, I go home again and enter my study, and on entering I cast off my every-day clothing, full of mud and clay, and put on a courtier's or a lawyer's gown; and thus decently clad, I enter the ancient courts of great men of the past, where, lovingly welcomed by them, I draw my sustenance from the food which is mine alone, and for which I was born. There I am not ashamed to speak with them and to ask them the reasons for their actions, and they, out of their courtesy, reply to me; and for four hours I know no tedium, remember no anxiety, fear no poverty, am not dismayed by death: I am wholly caught up in them. And since Dante says that there is no knowledge unless one holds fast to what one has understood, I have set down the essence of what I have drawn from their conversation, and have composed a little book, *De Principatibus*.

Machiavelli's use of his fowling hut for perusing the works of Dante and Petrarch is in sharp contrast with the mania for killing things that is typical of so much country life. 'The unspeakable in full pursuit of the uneatable', as Oscar Wilde called the foxhunting fraternity, have always featured prominently in English rural life. In the following letter to his patron, Lady Hesketh, the poet William Cowper gives a puzzled and somewhat chilling account of the scenes he witnessed at the death of a fox:

One day last week, Mrs Unwin and I, having taken our morning walk and returning homeward through the wilderness, met the Throckmortons. A minute after we had met them, we heard the cry of hounds at no great distance, and mounting the broad stump of an elm which had been felled, and by the aid of which we were enabled to look over the wall, we saw them . . . Before we could reach the other end of the wilderness, the hounds entered also; and when we arrived at the gate which opens into the grove there we found the whole weary cavalcade assembled. The huntsman dismounting, begged leave to follow his hounds on foot, for he was sure, he said, that they had killed him: a conclusion which I suppose he drew from their profound silence. He was accordingly admitted, and with a sagacity that would not have dishonoured the best hound in the world, pursuing precisely the same track which the fox and the dogs had taken, though he had never had a glimpse of either after their first entrance through the rails, arrived where he found the slaughtered prey. He soon produced dead reynard, and rejoined us in the grove with all his dogs about him . . . The huntsman remounted: cut off a foot, and threw it to the hounds:- one of them swallowed it whole like a bolus. He then once more alighted, and drawing down the fox by the hinder legs, desired the people, who were by this time rather numerous, to open a lane for him to the right and left. He was instantly obeyed, when throwing the fox to the distance of some yards, and screaming like a fiend, 'tear him to pieces'—and at least six times repeatedly, he consigned him over absolutely to the pack, who in a few minutes devoured him completely. Thus, my dear, as Virgil says, what none of the gods could have ventured to promise me, time itself, pursuing its accustomed course, has of its own accord presented me with. I have been in at the death of a fox, and you now know as much of the matter as I, who am as well informed as any sportsman in England.

A more bizarre form of the chase is related in December 1775 by Gilbert White in one of his letters that are so full of colourful detail about the fauna and flora of his beloved Selborne. Quite a lot of his observations have subsequently been found to be inaccurate, but he is always a delight to read. His account of the bee boy takes a bit of swallowing, but even if White exaggerates the idea of him is agreeable:

Dear Sir,—We had in this village more than twenty years ago an idiot boy, whom I well remember, who from a child, showed a strong propensity to bees; they were his food, his amusement, his sole object. And as people of this caste have seldom more than one point of view, so this lad exerted all his few faculties on this one pursuit. In the winter he dozed away his time, within his father's house, by the fireside, in a kind of torpid state, seldom departing from the chimney-corner; but in the summer he was all alert, and in quest of his game in the field, and on sunny banks. Honey-bees, bumble-bees, and wasps, were his prey wherever he found them; he had no apprehensions from their stings, but would seize them *nudis manibus*, and at once disarm them of their weapons, and suck their bodies for the sake of their honey-bags. Sometimes he would fill his bosom between his shirt and his skin with a number of these captives, and sometimes would confine them in bottles. He was a very *merops apiaster*, or bee-bird, and very injurious to men that kept bees; for he would slide into their bee-gardens, and, sitting down before the stools, would rap with his finger on the hives, and so take the bees as they came out. He has been known to overturn hives for the sake of honey, of which he was passionately fond. Where metheglin was making he would linger round the tubs and vessels, begging a draught of what he called bee-wine. As he ran about he used to make a humming noise with his lips, resembling the buzzing of bees. This lad was lean and sallow, and of a cadaverous complexion; and, except in his favourite pursuit, in which he was wonderfully adroit, discovered no manner of understanding. Had his capacity been better, and directed to the same object, he had perhaps abated much of our wonder at the feats of a more modern exhibitor of bees; and we may justly say of him now—

> . . . Thou,
> Had thy presiding star propitious shone,
> Shouldst Wildman be . . .

When a tall youth he was removed from hence to a distant village, where he died, as I understand, before he arrived at manhood.

The pursuit of bees may attract a few fanatics, but it is not a widespread activity. Fishing, however, is often an obsession among its enthusiasts. Here is a somewhat breathless letter written from Inverary in the nineteenth century, recording an English lady's first experience of a Highland fishing expedition. She is still having a little trouble with the local argot:

Of all our pranks the most delightful was the other night going to the herring fishing. We did not go to bed, & sett off at two o'Clock with the piper in the boat, & saw some nets drawn. It was really a night fit to send any one to the house on the hill at Glasgow—from very craziness with its beauty, and we had pibrochs and all sorts of music. There were about 200 boats out. Did you ever see the nets drawn? It is so beautiful in the dark or dim light: the silvery glittering of the fish, and the calls of the men from one boat to another. We went up the Loch that we might see the morning break over the Loch Awe hills, or, as Miss Helen would say, 'See the Sin rise over the hills from the muddle of the Loch.' It was so lovely as the light got up, one by one the boatmen hoisting their sails and retiring into all the creeks round. We came home about half-past 4, and had a very jolly supper or whatever you call it on our spoils.

This is a charming description, but it steers the countryside and its life back towards the picturesque. That was what the eighteenth century, too, preferred. Alexander Pope is extremely acid about attempts to romanticize the country by those who merely own bits of it. In an aside in one of his letters to Dean Swift written from Lord Bolingbroke's estate where he was staying, he remarks unkindly of his host:

> Now his Lordship is run after his Cart, I have a moment left to myself to tell you, that I overheard him yesterday agree with a Painter for 200 l. to paint his Country-Hall with Trophies of Rakes, Spades, Prongs, etc., and other Ornaments, merely to countenance his calling this Place a Farm.

By the same token ruins were more picturesque than intact buildings. William Cowper writing to William Unwin in 1779 sums up the attitude with dry humour:

> There was not, at that time, much to be seen in the Isle of Thanet, besides the beauty of the country, and the fine prospects of the sea, which are nowhere surpassed except in the Isle of Wight, or upon some parts of the coast of Hampshire. One sight, however, I remember, engaged my curiosity, and I went to see it: —a fine piece of ruins, built by the late Lord Holland, at a great expense, which, the day after I saw it, tumbled down for nothing. Perhaps, therefore, it is still a ruin; and if it is, I would advise you by all means to visit it, as it must have been much improved by this fortunate incident. It is hardly possible to put stones together with that air of wild and magnificent disorder which they are sure to acquire by falling of their own accord.

But the laurels for elegant and controlled experience of nature must surely go to Anna Seward, the 'Swan of Lichfield', whose *Elegy on Captain Cook* was commended by Dr Johnson. Writing to Mr Saville from Scarborough in 1793 she explains how, with great personal courage (though accompanied by a muscular servant) she braved the waves of the 'sublimely agitated sea':

> Whenever the wind blows from the east at this port, however calmly it may breathe on shore, the sea runs high. All yesterday it had a large portion of the sublimity I had

invoked. About a quarter of a mile down the right-hand sands, a small promontory juts out; upon its topmost bank, about twenty yards high, the chalybeate springs arise; and there also a fort is constructed with parapet walls, to which we ascend by steps. At high-water, the sea encircles this promontory, and lashes its rocks.

Last night, at eight o'clock, as we walked upon the cliff, we saw the waves of a sublimely agitated sea dashing and bounding up the sides of the fort, their spray flying over its parapets. The tide was then on the turn, and we were told that, in about an hour, we might walk to the promontory, by keeping close to the base of the rocks, and attain the elevation before the waves had ceased to lash and clamber up its walls. Nobody but myself being inclined to venture, I went home to undress, resolved to taste, amidst the incumbent gloom of a very lowering night, a scene congenial to my taste for the terrible graces. Requesting the stout arm of Mr Dewe's servant, I began with him my sombre expedition. As I passed along the sands, the tide twice left its white surf upon my feet; and the vast curve of those fierce waves, that burst down with deafening roar, scarce three yards from me, sufficiently gratified my rage for the terrific.

We found the lower steps of the fort inaccessible, from the waters not having yet receded from them; but, with some difficulty, climbing behind the rocks, I got upon a level with the sixth step, and was thus enabled to ascend the eminence. By this time, the last gloom of the night had fallen, and the white foam of the thundering waters made their 'darkness visible'. It seemed scarce possible that an unconscious element could wear such horrid appearances of living rage. Each billow seemed a voraginous monster, as it came roaring on, and dashed itself against the repelling walls. The spray of each flashing wave flew over my head, and wet me on its descent. The pealing waters, louder than thunder, made it impossible for me or the servant to hear each other speak. My own maid would not venture to accompany me on an expedition of such seeming peril. I stood at least half an hour on the wild promontory's top, almost totally encircled by the dark and furious main. It was half past ten when I returned to Lord Lifford's, to take my leave of the party, and to acknowledge the infinitely kind attentions with which they had honoured me.

T·H·E ·E·N·D

Sources and Acknowledgements

Nicholas Parsons and Buchan & Enright are extremely grateful to the following for permission to reprint copyright material; while every effort has been made to trace the owners of copyright, in a few cases it has not been possible to locate them; the publishers will be pleased to hear from any such and to make the requisite acknowledgements in any subsequent edition of this work.

George Allen & Unwin for extracts from *The First Cuckoo* edited by Kenneth Gregory; for extracts from *The Autobiography of Bertrand Russell* and the collection *Dear Bertrand Russell* (copyright the Bertrand Russell Peace Foundation), and extracts from *The Letters of J. R. R. Tolkien* edited by Humphrey Carpenter and Christopher Tolkien; Edward Arnold (Publishers) Ltd for extracts from *Erasmus* edited by Richard L. De Molen in the documents of Modern History series; The Athlone Press Limited for extracts from *Collected Letters of Leo Tolstoy* edited by R. F. Christian; Richard Barber for an extract from his edition of *The Pastons: A Family in the Wars of the Roses* published by Penguin Books in the Life and Letters series; Jonathan Cape Ltd for extracts from *The Letters of Anton Chekhov* edited and translated by Avrahm Yarmolinsky, for extracts from *Selected Letters of Robert Frost* edited by Lawrence Thompson copyright the Estate of Robert Frost, for extracts from *Letters from Prison of Antonio Gramsci* translated by Lynne Lawner, and for extracts from *The Letters of T. E. Lawrence* edited by David Garnett; Jonathan Cape and Bernard Levin for extracts from *Taking Sides* by Bernard Levin; Chatto & Windus for an extract from *Dostoevsky's Letters to Family and Friends* translated by Ethel Coburn Mayne, copyright the Literary Estate of Ethel Coburn Mayne; Chatto & Windus and the Literary Estate of Marie Belloc Lowndes for an extract from *Letters and Diaries of Marie Belloc Lowndes* edited by Susan Lowndes; Chatto & Windus and Iris Origo for extracts from *The Vagabond Path* by Iris Origo; William Collins Sons Ltd, Publishers, for an extract from *Children's Letters to God* edited by E. Marshall and S. Hemple; Constable Publishers for an extract from *Letters of Vincent Van Gogh* edited by Mark Roskill; the Noël Coward Estate for a letter from Mrs Violet Coward to her husband; Curtis Brown Ltd, on behalf of Lawrence Durrell and Henry Miller for extracts from *Lawrence Durrell and Henry Miller: A Private Correspondence* edited by George Wickes and published by Faber, © 1962, 1963 by Lawrence Durrell and Henry Miller; Curtis Brown and Lady Antonia Fraser for an extract from *Love Letters* published by **Weidenfeld and Nicolson** © Antonia Fraser 1976; J. M. Dent & Sons Ltd for an extract from *Greek Social Life* by F. A. Wright; André Deutsch Limited for an extract from *The 14th Chronicle, Letters and Diaries of John Dos Passos* edited by Townsend Ludington (1974); The Board of Trinity College Dublin for letters by William Lecky published in *A Victorian Historian, Private Letters of William Lecky 1859–1878* edited by H. Montgomery Hyde; Duckworth and Company Limited for an extract from *The Letters of J. R. Ackerley* edited by Neville Braybrooke; Faber and Faber Ltd for two lines from 'Spain 1937' by W. H. Auden which appears in *The English Auden: Poems, Essays and Dramatic Writings 1927–1939* by W. H. Auden; and for a letter by Ezra Pound in *Pound/Joyce—Letters of Ezra Pound and James Joyce* edited by Forrest Read; Christopher Gandy for a letter to *The Times* reprinted in *The Second Cuckoo* published by Allen & Unwin; Professor Creighton E. Gilbert for extracts from his translations of letters by Michelangelo published as *Complete Poems and Selected Letters of Michelangelo* by Princeton University Press; Granada Publishing Ltd for extracts from *Selected Letters of Henry James* edited by Leon Edel; Hamish Hamilton Limited and Penguin Books for an extract from *Selected Letters of James Thurber*; The Hamlyn Publishing Group Limited for an extract from *My Early Life* by Winston Churchill (originally published by Odhams Press Limited); Harper and Row Publishers Inc. for extracts from *The Selected Letters of Mark Twain* edited by Charles Neider, copyright 1917 by the Mark Twain Company, renewed 1945 by Clara Clemens Samossoud, copyright © 1982 by Charles Neider; Harper and Row Publishers Inc. for extracts from *The Letters of E. B. White* edited by Dorothy Lobrano Guth, copyright © 1976 by E. B. White; Harrap Limited for extracts from *The Selective Ego* by James Agate edited by Timothy Beaumont; Harvard University Press for extracts from *Letters of Gustave Flaubert Volume 1 1830–1857* translated and edited by Francis Steegmuller and reprinted by permission of Harvard University Press; A. M. Heath & Company Ltd for an extract from *Selected Letters of Raymond Chandler* edited by Frank Macshane published by Jonathan Cape Ltd; David Higham Associates Limited for an extract from *A Free House* by Walter Sickert edited by Osbert Sitwell published by Macmillan; for extracts from *Fire of the Mind*, an anthology of Edith Sitwell's writing edited by Allanah Harper and Elizabeth Salter published by Michael Joseph; and for a letter by Dylan Thomas published in *Selected Letters of Dylan Thomas* edited by Constantine Fitzgibbon published by J. M. Dent; The Hogarth Press for an extract from Volume 2 of *Virginia Woolf, a Biography* by Quentin Bell, for a letter by Sigmund Freud published in *The Freud/Jung Letters* edited by William Mcguire and jointly published in the United Kingdom by Routledge Kegan Paul and The Hogarth Press, and for extracts from *The Flight of the Mind: Letters of*

Virginia Woolf, Volume 1 edited by Nigel Nicolson, copyright the Literary Estate of Virginia Woolf; Hutchinson Publishing Group for an extract from *The Love Letters of Great Men and Women* edited by D. Charles; Michael Joseph Ltd for extracts from *The Groucho Letters* by Groucho Marx; William Kimber & Co Ltd for an extract from *The Sun Goes Down* edited by Jean Lartéguy translated by Countess Nora Wydenbruck; Macmillan, London and Basingstoke, for extracts from *Letters of Beethoven* translated by Emily Anderson; and for an extract from *Stranger and Brother: A Portrait of C. P. Snow* by Philip Snow; John Murray (Publishers) Ltd for extracts from *Byron's Letters and Journals* edited by Leslie A. Marchand and from *The Lyttleton Hart-Davis Letters* edited by Rupert Hart-Davis; Peter Owen Ltd, London for an extract from *Letters to Anais Nin* by Henry Miller edited and with an introduction by Gunther Stuhlmann; Oxford University Press for an extract from *A Packet of Letters: Selections from the Correspondence of John Henry Newman* edited by Joyce Sugg © The Birmingham Oratory 1983; for an extract from *Wifred Owen: Collected Letters* edited by Harold Owen and John Bell © OUP 1967; and for an extract from *Selected Letters of Oscar Wilde* edited by Rupert Hart-Davis (1979) © Vyvyan Holland 1962; extracts from Newman, Owen and Wilde all reprinted by permission of Oxford University Press; Penguin Books Ltd for extracts from *Madame de Sévigné: Selected Letters* translated by Leonard Tancock (Penguin Classics 1982) copyright © Leonard Tancock, 1982; for extracts from *The Letters of the Younger Pliny* translated by Betty Radice (Penguin Classics, Revised Edition 1969) copyright © Betty Radice 1963, 1969; for extracts from *Aretino: Selected Letters* translated by George Bull (Penguin Classics 1976) Introduction, translation and notes copyright © George Bull, 1976; for extracts from *The Letters of Abélard and Héloïse* translated by Betty Radice (Penguin Classics 1974) copyright © Betty Radice, 1974; and for an extract from *Christmas Crackers* by John Julius Norwich (Penguin Books 1982) Collection and Introduction Copyright © John Julius Norwich, 1980; extracts from de Sévigné, Pliny, Aretino, Abélard and Héloïse and Norwich all reprinted by permission of Penguin Books Ltd; A. D. Peters & Co Ltd for extracts from *Letters to a Sister* by Rose Macaulay published by William Collins Sons & Co Ltd for extracts from *The Stanleys of Alderley* edited by Nancy Mitford published by Chapman and Hall Ltd; Laurence Pollinger Ltd and The Estate of Mrs Frieda Lawrence Ravagli for an extract from *The Collected Letters of D. H. Lawrence* edited by Harry T. Moore published by William Heinemann; Random House Inc (Alfred A. Knopf) for an extract from *Letters of Thomas Mann, 1889–1955* translated by Richard and Clara Winston; and Random House Inc (Alfred A. Knopf) for extracts from *Letters of H. L. Mencken* edited by Guy J. Forgue; Mrs Eva Reichmann for an extract from *And Even Now* by Max Beerbohm published by William Heinemann; Routledge Kegan Paul PLC for a letter of Carl Gustav Jung published in *The Freud/Jung Letters* edited by William McGuire and jointly published by Routledge Kegan Paul and the Hogarth Press; and for extracts from *Waiting On God* by Simone Weil translated by Emma Cranfurd and published by Routledge Kegan Paul PLC in 1951 in London; SCM Press Ltd for extracts from *Dietrich Bonhoeffer: Letters and Papers from Prison* edited by Eberhard Bethge and translated by Reginald Fuller, Frank Clarke and others; Martin Secker & Warburg Limited for extracts from *The Correspondence between André Gide and Paul Claudel 1889–1926* edited by J. Russell; for extracts from *Letters to Felice* by Frank Kafka translated by James Stern and Elisabeth Duckworth; and for an extract from *Letters to Georgian Friends* by Boris Pasternak translated by D. Magarshack; Sheed and Ward Limited for a letter by G. K. Chesterton published in *Gilbert Keith Chesterton* by Maisie Ward; Anthony Sheil Associates Ltd for extracts from *A Message from the Falklands* by David Tinker published by Junction Books and Penguin Books Copyright © Hugh Tinker 1982; and for extracts from *J. B. Yeats: Letters to his Son and Others* published by Faber and Faber; Shepheard Walwyn (Publishers) Ltd for an extract from *The Letters of Marsilio Ficino Volume 1* edited and translated by the Language Department of The London School of Economics; Sidgwick and Jackson Ltd for an extract from *Letters To A Young Poet* by Rainer Maria Rilke translated by R. Snell; The Society of Authors as the Literary Representative of the Estate of James Joyce for extracts from *Selected Letters of James Joyce* edited by Richard Ellmann published by the Viking Press, New York; The Society of Authors on behalf of the Bernard Shaw Estate for extracts from *Collected Letters of Bernard Shaw Volumes 1 and 2* edited by Dan H. Laurence published by The Bodley Head; Thames & Hudson Ltd for extracts from *Letters of the Great Artists* edited by R. Friedenthal and translated by Daphne Woodward; and for extracts from *The Musician's World* edited by Hans Gel and translated by Daphne Woodward; *Time* Magazine for letters from Billy Rose and Humphrey Bogart copyright 1983 Time Inc.; The Viking Press for extracts from *The Literary Life and Other Curiosities* by Robert Hendrickson; Virago Press Ltd for an extract from *Me Again: The Uncollected Writings of Stevie Smith* edited by Jack Barbera and William McBrien published by Virago Press Ltd 1981; A. P. Watt Ltd and Robert Graves for a letter to *The Times* by Robert Graves; Weidenfeld and Nicolson Ltd for extracts from *Letters of Evelyn Waugh* edited by Mark Amory.

Index of Names